WINGS
OF FAME

Aerospace Publishing Ltd
AIRtime Publishing Inc.

Published quarterly by
Aerospace Publishing Ltd
179 Dalling Road
London W6 0ES
UK

Copyright © Aerospace Publishing Ltd
1996

ISSN 1361-2034

Aerospace ISBN 1 874023 70 0
                 (softback)
                 1 874023 76 X
                 (hardback)
AIRtime ISBN 1-880588-23-4

Published under licence in USA and
Canada by AIRtime Publishing Inc.,
10 Bay Street, Westport,
CT 06880, USA

Editorial Offices:
WINGS OF FAME
Aerospace Publishing Ltd
3A Brackenbury Road
London W6 0WE UK

Publisher: Stan Morse
Managing Editor: David Donald
Assistant Editor: Jim Winchester
Sub Editor: Karen Leverington
Editorial Assistant: Tim Senior
US Correspondent: Robert F. Dorr

Artists: Chris Davey
         Keith Fretwell
         Tim Maunder
         Mark Rolfe
         John Weal

Origination by
  Chroma Graphics, Singapore
Printed by
  Officine Grafiche DeAgostini,
  Novara, Italy

The editors of WINGS OF FAME
welcome photographs for possible
publication, but cannot accept any
responsibility for loss or damage to
unsolicited material.

The publishers gratefully acknowledge
the assistance given by the following
people:

Thanks to these F-100 pilots: Tom
Barnes, Mark Berent, Tom Birge, Louis
A. Bowerman, Gene Buttyan, Michael
P. Curphey, Dan Druen, Forrest Fenn,
Mike Filliman, Ronald R. Fogleman,
John France, Maurice D. Fricke, Don
Kilgus, Howard M. 'Mac' Lane,
Robert C. Mikesh, Andy Olman, Hank
Rettinger, Foster L. Smith, and Jack
Smith. Also to TSgt Jon Sams in the
office of Gen. Ronald R. Fogleman,
US Air Force Chief of Staff, North
American Aviation (NAA)
aerodynamicist Edward Horkey, NAA
technical representatives John
Henderson and Oscar Niederman, and
to David A. Anderton, Rhodes Arnold,
Bill Crimmins, Larry Davis, David
Mclaren, David W. Menard, David
Ostrowski, Norman Taylor for their
considerable efforts in producing the
Super Sabre feature, and assistance
provided for the B-25 variant briefing

Joshua Stoff (Curator, Cradle of
Aviation Museum) for his assistance
with the XF-12 article

David Walton, of C. Walton Ltd.,
owner of XH558, and Bill Hunt of
CS(Photo) for their help with the
Vulcan article

WINGS OF FAME is published
quarterly and is available by
subscription and from many fine
book and hobby stores.

**SUBSCRIPTION AND BACK
NUMBERS:**

**UK and World (except USA and
Canada) write to:**
Aerospace Publishing Ltd
FREEPOST
PO Box 2822
London
W6 0BR
UK
**(No stamp required if posted in
the UK)**

USA and Canada, write to:
AIRtime Publishing Inc.
Subscription Dept
10 Bay Street
Westport
CT 06880, USA
(203) 838-7979
Toll-free order number in USA:
1 800 359-3003

**Prevailing US subscription rates
are as follows:**
**Softbound edition for 1 year:
$58.00**
**Softbound edition for 2 years:
$108.00**

**Softbound back numbers
(subject to availability) are
$19.00 each. All rates are for
delivery within mainland USA,
Alaska and Hawaii. Canadian
and overseas prices available
upon request. American Express,
Discover Card, MasterCard and
Visa accepted. When ordering
please include your card
number, expiration date and
signature.**

**Publisher, North America:
  Mel Williams**
**Subscription Director:
  Linda DeAngelis**
**Retail Sales Director:
  Jill Brooks**
**Charter Member Services
Manager:
  Janie Munroe**
**Shipping Manager:
  E. Rex Anku**

WINGS
OF FAME

CONTENTS

Volume 3

Carrying cluster bombs, an F-100D of the 615th TFS launches from Phan Rang for a close support mission. A total of 490 Super Sabres in the combat zone flew 360,000 combat sorties – more than all the 15,684 P-51s managed during World War II.

While F-4s and F-105s stole the thunder in forays 'up North', the F-100 Super Sabre became the stalwart of the dirty war against the Viet Cong in South Vietnam. Serving in-theatre in large numbers, it flew far more combat missions than any other type.

The North American F-100 Super Sabre was introduced to combat by Americans not in Vietnam but in Laos. There, the United States flirted briefly during 1962-64 with a conflict that was soon to become all too familiar next door in Vietnam.

In Vietnam, as in that first tentative effort in Laos, pilots, maintainers and armourers of the United States Air Force – later augmented by the Air National Guard – were hurled into the breech to achieve goals that were never clear, against an enemy they never knew, while the tactics of aerial combat were micro-managed from as far away as the White House. Preparations for World War II combat veteran Colonel George Laven's first combat mission into Laos on 9 June 1964 took on a life of their own, a process which was to be repeated again and again as Americans sank into a Southeast Asian quagmire of their own making. After Laven chose ordnance – two pods totalling 38 2.75-in rockets and four 500-lb (227-kg) bombs – the F-100 weapons load was changed by an officer on the scene, then changed again on orders from Washington. Laven later told author David A. Anderton that, "It looked as if I wasn't going to be able to fart without getting it cleared by Washington." Laven "was beginning to feel that my squadron

On 4 April 1965, Captain Don Kilgus of the 416th TFS almost certainly shot down a MiG-17 while flying this F-100D during the 'Hun's' brief tenure escorting warplanes attacking North Vietnam. The MiG was officially listed as a 'probable'. As soon as F-4s arrived in-theatre the F-100 returned to its ground attack role, and never again tangled with MiGs.

commander was LBJ [President Lyndon B. Johnson] and my operations officer was McNamara [Secretary of Defence Robert S. McNamara]."

The feeling was to persist as brass hats from PACAF to the Pentagon made decisions on issues as arcane as what size bomb to hang from a pylon. Pacific Air Forces was the US Air Force's major command for the region; it was located in Hawaii, but to a hard-pressed fighter commander in South Vietnam, PACAF – like the Pentagon – might have been on another planet.

Not that those on the scene were without fault. One participant of the first F-100 combat mission remembers Laven – a respected figure elsewhere – as "some prima donna diddling around trying to pretend he was a fighter pilot." This was one last chance for the World War II generation, and some may have been over-eager to leap into a situation for which there had been little preparation. The critic is not alone in characterising that first combat mission as a fiasco.

From 1962 to 1965, in fits and starts, the US shaped its role in Vietnam and with it, the warplanes, weapons and

'Huns' over Vietnam
The F-100 Super Sabre in Southeast Asia

tactics to be employed. The men who flew the F-100 Super Sabre were typical American fighter pilots. They were able, experienced, dedicated, at times arrogant; they saw the Air Force not as a job but as a way of life. Although none would ever admit it, they saw as sacred the three themes of General Douglas MacArthur's landmark 1962 speech at West Point – duty, honour, country. Given an enemy they could understand and a mission with clear goals, these F-100 pilots would fight their way to hell and back.

During 1962-65, as always, a considerable amount of soldiering consisted of hurrying, waiting, listening to rumours and seeing very little action. F-100 Super Sabre squadrons were rotated through Southeast Asia on temporary duty ('TDY') stints that typically lasted only three or four months, during which time a pilot might 'show the flag' at Don Muang, Thailand or Da Nang, South Vietnam for a few weeks, stand nuclear alert at Tainan, Formosa with a tactical atomic bomb aimed at the Chinese mainland for a few weeks (China, it will be remembered, exploded its first nuclear device in 1964), fill in for a few weeks at Clark

Above: An F-100F from the 481st TFS, 27th TFW, is guarded between missions at Tan Son Nhut in October 1965. The two-seat F model was used for forward air control and bomb damage assessment work for much of the war, this task later being assigned to the specialist Misty unit (Det 1, 612th TFS).

Left: An effective weapon which gained much notoriety was napalm, essentially jellied gasoline packaged in a casing. When dropped at low level the results were devastating against personnel and soft targets.

An F-100D from the 416th TFS cruises high over the jungle. Such colourful markings soon gave way to drab camouflage as the war 'got serious' in 1965, although many aircraft gained nicknames and nose art.

Most forms of unguided ordnance were expended by the F-100 during its sojourn in Southeast Asia, but the M117 750-lb (340-kg) bomb was the most common.

bombed North Vietnam for the first time – was followed by the sustained campaign against the North beginning in early 1965 and dubbed Operation Rolling Thunder. At the same time, the massive build-up of forces in Vietnam was under way. By then in Vietnam in larger numbers but still there temporarily, Super Sabres began escorting bombing missions that went north.

Along the way, every last man wanted his shot at that highest of goals: to bag a MiG. The F-100 had long ago lost its gloss as a high-glamour, air-to-air 'Top Gun', and was soon to settle into its niche as an air-to-ground tactical bomber. When the first raids into North Vietnam were launched in 1965 – airfields at Da Nang and Tan Son Nhut being the temporary location of the Super Sabre – the 'Hun' enjoyed a brief final gasp in the air-to-air realm, flying MiGCAP (fighter escort) until it could be replaced in this duty by the F-4 Phantom.

MiG kill

Every man in the air on 4 April 1965 knows that when Captain Don Kilgus of the 416th Tactical Fighter Squadron poured burst after burst of 20-mm cannon fire into a fleeing MiG-17, Kilgus inflicted mortal damage which caused the MiG to fall from the sky. The captain was credited only with a 'probable' kill. No American F-100 pilot ever toted up an aerial victory. Once Phantoms arrived the Super Sabre reverted to its mud-moving mandate. Da Nang reverted to other purposes and was not one of the four principal bases where the 'Hun' settled for the long slog from 1965 to 1973.

Field, Philippines which became the nexus of these operations, and then head home. More than three decades later, even with the help of official records and personal memories, it is difficult to trace an exact picture of Super Sabre movements during that era of prelude before the real war began. Men often went home and left their aircraft for others to fly. At the time, they were ready for action that never came. Today, their memories are inconsistent.

The 1964 Gulf of Tonkin incident – when the US

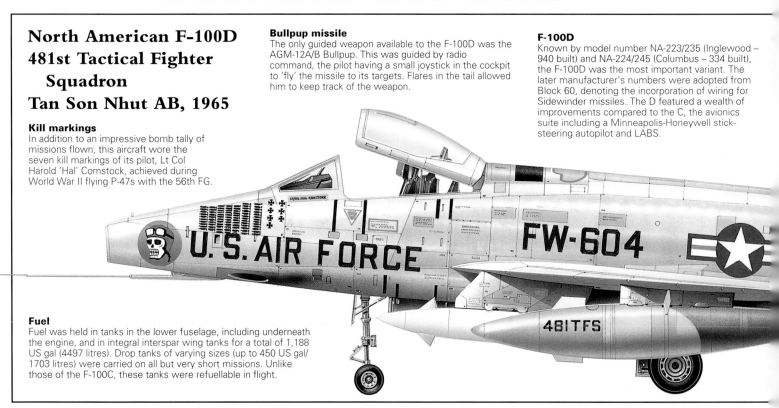

North American F-100D 481st Tactical Fighter Squadron Tan Son Nhut AB, 1965

Kill markings
In addition to an impressive bomb tally of missions flown, this aircraft wore the seven kill markings of its pilot, Lt Col Harold 'Hal' Comstock, achieved during World War II flying P-47s with the 56th FG.

Bullpup missile
The only guided weapon available to the F-100D was the AGM-12A/B Bullpup. This was guided by radio command, the pilot having a small joystick in the cockpit to 'fly' the missile to its targets. Flares in the tail allowed him to keep track of the weapon.

F-100D
Known by model number NA-223/235 (Inglewood – 940 built) and NA-224/245 (Columbus – 334 built), the F-100D was the most important variant. The later manufacturer's numbers were adopted from Block 60, denoting the incorporation of wiring for Sidewinder missiles. The D featured a wealth of improvements compared to the C, the avionics suite including a Minneapolis-Honeywell stick-steering autopilot and LABS.

Fuel
Fuel was held in tanks in the lower fuselage, including underneath the engine, and in integral interspar wing tanks for a total of 1,188 US gal (4497 litres). Drop tanks of varying sizes (up to 450 US gal/1703 litres) were carried on all but very short missions. Unlike those of the F-100C, these tanks were refuellable in flight.

The situation stabilised while the war grew. The US went from 15,000 troops in Vietnam in 1964 to 535,000 in 1969. When the US began its massive build-up of forces, there was not enough infrastructure to support the number of tactical fighters needed. Air bases in South Vietnam were rapidly expanded for this build-up while other bases were constructed from scratch on open terrain. It was impossible for this tiny country to contain all the wings of tactical aircraft that were felt needed, so a programme was devised that would send a squadron at a time from tactical wings to air bases in Vietnam for 90 to 120 days in TDY status before being replaced by companion units, usually from the same wing. In late 1965, the situation of TDY for combat units changed to that of PCS (permanent change of station).

Four bases in South Vietnam became home to the F-100. Bien Hoa, Phan Rang, Phu Cat and Tuy Hoa were the fields from which the Super Sabre flew air-to-ground missions, not against North Vietnam but in support of friendly troops in South Vietnam. F-100D and F-100F were operated by active-duty Air Force personnel, while F-100C and F-100F were the aircraft flown by activated Air National Guardsmen. Later in the conflict, the two-seat F-100F evolved into new roles as a forward air control (Misty FAC) spotter and as a pioneer air defence radar site (Wild Weasel) nemesis.

The first flush of F-100 action against the Pathet Lao in 1964 was a false start, if anyone expected it to define the war that followed. The F-100 Super Sabre flew the bulk of its combat missions in South Vietnam in support of friendly troops. Around 1968, Super Sabres returned to Laos for a sustained serial campaign, with a purpose different from the original actions in that country – not to strike Laotian insurgents but to attack North Vietnamese forces.

The 'in-country war' was the slog in South Vietnam where Super Sabre pilots supported Allied troops, employing rockets, CBUs (cluster bomb units), napalm and HE (high-explosive) bombs against enemy forces pinpointed by

Photographed in September 1970, a pair of 612th TFS aircraft (including an F-100F) drops Mk 82 bombs from medium level. At this sort of altitude the F-100 was not an accurate bomber: it was far more effective in a low-level dive attack. The object in this case is obviously an area target, hence the 'daisy-cutter' fuse extenders to ensure an above-ground burst and maximum area blast coverage.

416th TFS aircraft line the apron at Da Nang in 1965. The taxiing aircraft is armed for a short-range mission with napalm and M117s.

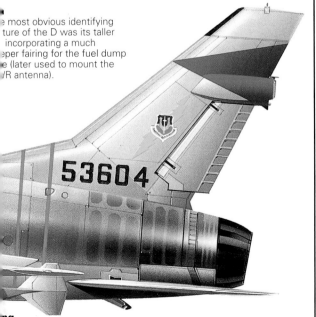

e most obvious identifying
ture of the D was its taller
incorporating a much
eper fairing for the fuel dump
e (later used to mount the
/R antenna).

53604

ng
ey feature of the F-100D was its redesigned wing. This was
racterised by a kinked trailing edge (with broad, slotted inboard flaps)
outboard fences which extended back over the ailerons. Extra
rnal tankage was provided, and the pylons were made jettisonable.

Another weapon which gave good area coverage against soft targets was the 2.75-in unguided rocket, usually fired from a 19-round launcher. However, the weapon needed to be fired from close range to achieve good results, putting the F-100 into the groundfire danger area. Graphically shown above is the dispersion of the unguided projectiles from one pod after launch, while the image at right is taken from a ventral strike camera showing two pods being fired at a suspected VC position.

Below right: Refuelling from a KC-135 is a Misty FAC F-100F two-seater, carrying seven-round rocket pods for target-marking.

Below: The 'Hun' was not noted for its range, so drop tanks were carried on most missions. Refuelling was often carried out, but required the use of KC-135s equipped with a drogue attachment to the boom, as demonstrated below by an F-100D from the Tuy Hoa-based 309th TFS.

a FAC (forward air control) aircraft. The 'out-country war' was a campaign of aerial interdiction of troops and supplies in North Vietnam and along the tributaries of the Ho Chi Minh Trail which snaked their way through Laos (two sectors of Laos were known in US jargon as Barrel Roll and Steel Tiger).

In 1969, when a high-ranking official of the Nixon administration asserted that no American had been killed in Laos, hundreds had, F-100 pilots among them. In 1970, a secret bombing campaign in Cambodia added another country to the roster of F-100 targets. Another astonishing fact was learned in the preparation of this history: at least one, two-aircraft night strike was flown by F-100 Super Sabres against a target in China, apparently with the purpose of killing a political figure whose identity is unknown. Like so much of the confusing geography and politics of the Vietnam War, the secret raid into China reveals more

about American purpose than enemy intent: from the beginning of the conflict to its end, Americans never recognised that Hanoi was a Soviet ally, and that the Chinese were grudgingly providing only token assistance to the North Vietnamese, whom they despised.

The 'Hun' described

The F-100D Super Sabre of the Vietnam era was a mature combat aircraft with a solid record of performance. A decade earlier, the F-100 had overcome teething troubles which often beset a new aircraft, including the initial short-fin design which caused a loss of stability and the death of test pilot George Welch. The F-100 had become the USAF's standard fighter. The older men in its cockpit had earned their spurs on the F-86 Sabre and were staunch advocates of North American Aviation, which could claim in 1959 to have manufactured more aircraft than any other US company. Twelve F-86 Sabre air aces from the Korean War flew the F-100 operationally and most commanded squadrons. The Air Force was rapidly skipping ahead to its next-generation fighter, the McDonnell F-110 Phantom (redesignated F-4 on 1 October 1962), but the Phantom had yet to prove itself and the F-100 had nothing left to prove.

The F-100D was powered by a 10,200-lb (45.37-kN) static thrust Pratt & Whitney J57-P-21A turbojet which had a thrust rating of 16,000 lb (71.17 kN) when afterburning was applied. In its heyday, it had been the world's first operational fighter capable of sustained supersonic speed in level flight and was routinely credited with a maximum speed of 835 mph (1343 km/h) at 35,000 ft (10836 m), although nothing approaching this velocity was ever

Armed with M117 bombs on its four pylons, a 120th TFS F-100C is ready for a mission. The four ANG units deployed in 1968/69 were the only operators of the C model in the warzone. Note the 120th's cougar badge on the nosewheel door.

Wing
The F-100C's wing had a straight trailing edge and no flaps. Automatic leading-edge slats provided extra lift across most of the span. The two-spar structure had a 7 per cent thickness-chord ratio, and was set at 45° sweepback at the quarter-chord.

Braking
The wheels were fitted with segmented rotor brakes with Hytrol anti-skid sensing units. A brake chute was located under the jetpipe. The F-100Ds were fitted with an emergency arrester hook.

North American F-100C
120th Tactical Fighter Squadron, Colorado ANG
35th Tactical Fighter Wing
Phan Rang AB, 1968

n 24 January 1968, the North Koreans seized e US spy-ship USS *Pueblo*, sparking a major isis. Two days later President Johnson lled eight Air National Guard F-100C quadrons to federal active duty. In May/June ur of these deployed to bases in South etnam to undertake combat operations. an Rang gained the 120th TFS/Colorado and u Cat the 174th TFS/Iowa, while Tuy Hoa ceived the 136th TFS/New York and 188th S/New Mexico. Two further units (127th S/Kansas and 166th TFS/Ohio) were ployed to the 354th TFW at Kunsan AB, uth Korea, while the remaining pair (119th S/New Jersey and 121st TFS/DC) went to yrtle Beach, South Carolina. Here they dertook conversion training work, but also spatched personnel to Phu Cat to provide per cent of the manning of the active-duty 5th TFS.

Markings
All ANG aircraft in Southeast Asia wore the standard T.O. 1-1-4 camouflage pattern. The 'VS' tailcode was worn only in-theatre (later assigned to the 35th TFW's 612th TFS). The 120th TFS retained its mountain lion badge, to be seen on the tail and nosewheel door of this aircraft.

Tail unit
All surfaces of the tail were set at 45° sweepback. The vertical fin had a small fuel dump fairing. The tailplanes were all-moving, set low on the fuselage so that they could be interconnected beneath the jetpipe.

F-100C
First flying on 17 January 1955, the F-100C was the first fighter-bomber version, featuring a strengthened wing with eight hardpoints. North American built 451 at Inglewood and 25 at Columbus. Turkey later received 260.

ake
e oval intake fed air below the kpit and up over the wing carry-ough to the compressor face. In upper lip of the intake was a small n-laying radar, while mounted ow was the long pitot probe, ich hinged upwards for stowage.

Powerplant
Power for the F-100C came from the Pratt & Whitney J57-P-21, rated at 16,950 lb (75.43 kN) thrust with full afterburner.

rmament
ternal armament consisted of four Pontiac M39E -mm cannon in the lower fuselage aimed with an 4 gunsight. The 200 rounds per gun were held in wnward-feeding chutes located in the fuselage les. The six underwing hardpoints could carry up to 000 lb (2722 kg) of stores, 1,500 lb (680 kg) less an the F-100D.

An underside view of a 614th TFS aircraft shows the four main weapons-carrying attachments, here loaded with Mk 82 'slicks'. TERs on the inboard pylons allowed the carriage of multiple weapons.

BLU-1 and BLU-27 napalm fire bombs had optional fin kits (fitted here) for greater accuracy.

Above: The Super Sabre was a sturdy bird, and it needed to be operating continuously in a constant groundfire environment.

Air Force depots with a tail hook identical to that used on US Navy carrier-based warplanes. The hook enabled a pilot to use a cable arresting system when making an emergency landing.

The F-100 was never the easiest aircraft to maintain and service, especially in the primitive conditions which first greeted Americans at Southeast Asian airfields. "It was a hydraulic engineer's nightmare," one pilot said of the Super Sabre. Once they were settled into a regular cycle of operations, F-100s performed remarkably well. The F-100 had the highest sortie-generation rate of any US warplane in Southeast Asia (a figure reflecting total sorties divided by daily average of possessed aircraft, divided by days of the month), a figure which reached 1.15 in 1968, as compared with a respectable 1.01 for the B-57 Canberra, and a rock-bottom 0.72 for the B-26K Invader. The F-100 also flew by far the largest number of combat sorties of any US aircraft in Southeast Asia. In 1969, for example, F-100s flew 52,699 combat sorties in South Vietnam while F-4 Phantoms flew 19,185 and A-37 Dragonflys 8,305. At the height of Super Sabre operations, 490 aircraft (of 2,294 manufactured) were committed to battle in four augmented fighter wings.

When it first began to appear in Southeast Asia in those early TDY deployments to Thailand, the Super Sabre was a glittering silvery machine with colourful markings, buzz numbers, and – often – individual nicknames and art work. When the Vietnam War grew, F-100s began to wear T. O. 1-1-4 camouflage, named after the technical order which prescribed colours. This camouflage included two greens

attained on a real-life combat mission with ordnance. The F-100D was armed with four 20-mm Pontiac M39E cannons with 1,200 rounds and had underwing pylons for up to 7,040 lb (3193 kg) of bombs, rockets or missiles. The Super Sabre carried some weapons that were utterly without redeeming merit – early versions of the AGM-12A/B Bullpup missile bounced harmlessly off any hard target they struck and failed to detonate – and some which were quite potent. But from beginning to end, its most important weapon was the ungainly, unglamorous and 'unsmart' 750-lb (340-kg) high-explosive iron bomb.

By the time of Vietnam, all F-100s had been modified at

Shrike missile
Developed by the Navy, the AG[M] had a radar-homing seeker and [a] 145-lb (65.8-kg) fragmentation warhead. The missile did not n[eed] specialist launch aircraft, but it [was] far more effective when used [by a] defence-suppression platform.

Individual differences
Apart from the main Mod 1778 equipment, one aircraft was fitted with a KA-60 strike camera to record results, while another (58-122[) was fitted with a different threat analysis system to IR-133.

(FS 34079, FS 34102) and a tan (FS 30219) painted in a specified pattern on the upper surfaces and sides of the aircraft. The lower surfaces of the aircraft were painted a very pale grey (FS 36622). At first, only a small black 'USAF' and tail number were applied to the fin, but white letters and larger numbers were also used. Large white tailcodes 18 in (0.46 m) in height began to appear soon after the camouflage, and the style of the tail number presentation was changed. A small black 'AF' had two digits of the serial number located under it in 5-in (0.15-m) black numerals, with the last three digits of the serial painted in larger, 12-in (0.31-m) numbers.

The last combat F-100 departed Vietnam in 1971, after nearly eight years of combat. According to official figures, Super Sabres flew 360,283 combat sorties. The USAF lost 186 F-100 Super Sabres to anti-aircraft fire, none to MiGs, seven during Viet Cong assaults on its air bases, and 45 to operational incidents.   **Robert F. Dorr**

Above: A 308th TFS F-100F from Tuy Hoa leads a 352nd TFS F-100D from Phan Rang. Super Sabre operations settled at these bases, plus Bien Hoa and Phu Cat, for most of the war, with large numbers of aircraft assigned to the theatre.

A pair of Wild Weasel F-100Fs from the 6234th TFW detachment cruises over Vietnam in 1966. The Weasels usually operated singly with three F-105s in support, the F-100F locating radars for the 'Thuds' to attack in a hunter/killer team.

North American F-100F 6234th Tactical Fighter Wing, Wild Weasel Detachment Korat RTAFB, 1966

Wild Weasel operations
Between 1 December 1965 and 11 July 1965, the F-100F flew Iron Hand defence suppression missions, accounting for nine SAM sites and many others which stayed 'off air' while strike packages went about their business. Initially, the F-100s carried rocket pods to attack SAM radars and to mark the target for accompanying F-105Ds. From 18 April 1966 the AGM-45 Shrike was carried.

Project Wild Weasel
Originally known as Project Ferret, Wild Weasel arose from successes using radar homing and warning systems in exercises in 1964. With obvious applications in Southeast Asia, a crash programme was started to provide the aircraft with RHAW equipment under North American modification 1778. Testing was hastily accomplished at Edwards and Eglin, while training started at the latter, using experienced F-100 pilots and EWOs from the B-52 force. The aircraft left Eglin for Korat on 21 November 1965. Arrival in-theatre was 84 days after the programme started.

Modification 1778
The main distinguishing feature of the Wild Weasel modification was the Vector IV RHAW system, with a pair of antennas – each of which faced outwards at 45° – mounted underneath the nose and a similar pair on the fin trailing edge. The IR-133 threat analysis system had three flush antennas, while the WR-300 Launch Warning Receiver was served by a small blade antenna forward of the nosewheel door. The Vector IV had a 3-in CRT display in both cockpits, while the LWR had a simple red 'launch' indicator.

11

F-100 Deployments

The following section handles each of the deployments made by Super Sabre squadrons to the war zone. These are arranged base-by-base, the locations being presented chronologically according to the first F-100 deployment to that airfield. In order, these were Don Muang, Takhli, Da Nang, Tan Son Nhut, Bien Hoa, Korat, Tuy Hoa, Phan Rang and Phu Cat. The final three, plus Bien Hoa, became the main centres of F-100 activity.

Don Muang International Airport, Bangkok, Thailand

Don Muang was, and is, Bangkok's International Airport, a celebrated hub of air commerce not merely in Asia but in the world. Here, in the early 1960s, the first commercial jet airliners appeared daily, opening a new age of air travel. Among them were the Boeing 707s of Pan American's celebrated Flight 1 'around the world' (San Francisco-New York) and the Convair 880 of Taiwan's Civil Air Transport, dubbed a 'Flying Oriental Palace'. With its 10,500-ft (3250-m) concrete runway, the airfield was always a little crowded, and the small American military detachments which began popping into the place added little to its existing bustle. Don Muang was not conveniently located to any obvious targets in Laos or Vietnam, but it was to become home for rotating batches of 'Huns' until the war next door grew too big for small stuff. Following the initial 510th TFS deployment (separate entry follows), other F-100 units apparently sent men and machines on TDY from Clark Field in the Philippines, which was the nexus of F-100 rotational excursions in 1962-65.

510th Tactical Fighter Squadron

TDY 16 April 1961 - ca. late 1961
On 16 April 1961, six F-100 Super Sabres of the 510th TFS 'Buzzards' (also known as the 'Screaming Falcons' and the 'Nickel Dime'), were deployed to the Thai capital, ostensibly for the air defence mission. They were the first American F-100s to enter a combat zone. The squadron was part of the 405th FW at Clark Field, Philippines, along with the F-102A-equipped 509th Fighter-Interceptor Squadron. Major Mike Filliman, who led that first detachment, recalls that "RTAF [Royal Thai Air Force] support was enthusiastic. The flying was mostly a 'show of the flag' type." The Thai deployment involved both F-100D and F-100F models. The presence in the Thai capital was just the beginning for the 510th, which later returned to the region (at Bien Hoa).

This 510th TFS aircraft is seen just prior to its Don Muang deployment.

Takhli Royal Thai Air Base, Thailand

Takhli was a military base, destined later to become one of two principal airfields for F-105 Thunderchief operations against North Vietnam. During 1962-65, Takhli was still growing as a factor in the gathering conflict. The base had a 9,800-ft (3034-m) concrete runway, hardly a luxury for fast-jet operations, and adequate buildings and facilities. Here, while Super Sabres were still performing only temporary rotational duties, several squadrons made brief appearances. For some, it was their only time in the war zone. For other squadrons, it was a prelude in a widening conflict.

428th Tactical Fighter Squadron

TDY 18 May 1962 - 3 September 1962
As part of Operation Saw Buck, a Tactical

This line-up of F-100Ds from a Tactical Air Command unit is seen in Southeast Asia during the period of early deployments to the theatre. In 1962/64 Takhli housed the majority of the deployments, the F-100s flying missions into Laos.

Air Command CASF (Composite Air Strike Force) began temporary deployments of F-100s from Cannon AFB, New Mexico and England AFB, Louisiana. Beginning on 18 May 1962, the 428th TFS 'Buccaneers' served temporarily at Takhli.

F-100s returned to Takhli in 1964 as the US began a slow, gradual build-up to fight, not in Laos but in Vietnam. Laotian action stayed at the top of the bill for a time, however. On 18 August 1964, fighters of the 428th TFS flew an unsuccessful ResCAP (Rescue Combat Air Patrol) mission intended to support an Air America helicopter that was attempting to rescue the crew of a downed T-28. The helicopter, too, was shot down. The F-100Ds, moving at jet speed in a prop war, were helpless to assist, and one became the first Super Sabre loss of the Southeast Asia conflict. The F-100Ds were strafing suspected gun

emplacements when Pathet Lao gunners zeroed in on them. The pilot of the aircraft (56-3085) wrestled his crippled craft up to safe altitude and turned south toward Udorn. He managed to nurse the aircraft to the Mekong River, then ejected and landed on the southern outskirts of the Thai river town of Nong Khai. An Air America helicopter plucked him to safety.

On 21 December 1964, a week into Barrel Roll operations against North Vietnamese targets in Laos, the 428th TFS despatched four F-100s on an armed reconnaissance strike along Route 8. They were lightly armed with cluster munitions and 2.75-in rockets; the enemy was heavily armed with flak. The F-100s briefly lost their way, could not find any secondary targets, and soon were low on fuel. The mission ended up being a total "foul-up," as one pilot acknowledged, and resulted in a "nasty-gram" from USAF chief of staff General Curtis E. LeMay telling 2nd Air Division commander Major General Joseph H. Moore that he (LeMay) expected a higher level of professionalism from USAF pilots.

430th Tactical Fighter Squadron

TDY 3 September 1962 - 13 December 1962
On 3 September 1962 in Operation Saw Buck II, the 430th TFS (from Cannon) replaced its sister squadron 428th TFS on temporary deployment to Takhli. The 430th was relieved after 90 days by the 522nd TFS.

522nd Tactical Fighter Squadron

TDY 13 December 1962 - 1 June 1963
TDY 16 March 1964 - 6 May 1964
On 13 December 1962, in Operation Saw Buck III, the 522nd TFS 'Fireballs' (also part of the 27th TFW at Cannon, with a red fin-cap colour), commanded by Lieutenant Colonel Hank Rettinger, relieved the 430th TFS on temporary deployment to Takhli. Pilots of the 522nd TFS flew from Cannon to Takhli on a C-135 Stratolifter of the Military Air Transport Service and arrived to find 18 Super Sabres (16 F-100Ds and two F-100Fs) waiting for them. In about February 1963, a decision was made to reduce the commitment at Takhli from 18 to six aircraft. Most 522nd members returned to Cannon. Pilots ferried 12 aircraft (11 F-100Ds and one F-100F) back to the US, leaving behind six (five F-100Ds and one F-100F). The squadron remained at Takhli until 15 February 1963. It appears that some 522nd members remained with the half a dozen Super Sabres left behind until about 1 June 1963, when the Takhli commitment was ended.

A second deployment of the 522nd TFS from its home base in New Mexico to Takhli took place from 16 March 1964 until 6 May 1964. (The squadron also went to Da Nang in 1964 and to the Philippines in 1965.)

524th Tactical Fighter Squadron

TDY 1963 - 64
The 524th TFS 'Hounds of Heaven' (part of the 27th Tactical Fighter Wing at Cannon AFB, New Mexico) made just one deployment to Southeast Asia – a stay at Takhli which ran from late 1963 to early 1964, preceding the Super Sabre's first actual combat by several months.

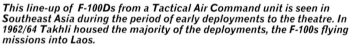

Da Nang Air Base, South Vietnam

Known as Tourane during the French era, Da Nang was the northernmost major air base in South Vietnam. It was situated in the northeast coastal area 85 miles (137 km) south of the Demilitarized Zone (where the 17th Parallel separated the two Vietnams) and 400 miles (644 km) north of Saigon. Located on flat, sandy ground south of the port of Da Nang, the airfield grew to a size of 2,350 acres (951 hectares) with two 10,000-ft (3048-m) asphalt runways with concrete touchdown pads, parallel taxiways, and a heliport. In addition to combat units, the base was a port for Military Airlift Command transports. Da Nang competed with Bien Hoa for the title of 'busiest' airdrome, with 55,000 fixed-wing aircraft movements per month by 1968, a figure which rose to 67,000 when helicopter take-offs and landings were added.

416th Tactical Fighter Squadron

March – June 1965
The 416th TFS 'Silver Knights', with its roots at England AFB, Louisiana, embarked on a zig-zag journey which was eventually to include Clark Field (from 18 March 1965), Da Nang (from late March 1965), Bien Hoa (mid-June to mid-July 1965), Tan Son Nhut (from November 1965), Phu Cat (from April 1967) and Tuy Hoa (from May 1969). The squadron had been in Asia before: the 416th had been stationed at Misawa in northern Japan until it moved to England AFB in spring 1964.

Commanded initially by Lieutenant Colonel Emmett L. Hayes and soon thereafter by Lieutenant Colonel Ralph Haven, the squadron arrived at Clark Field on 18 March 1965 as part of a CASF

This 416th TFS aircraft is flown by Captain Don Kilgus, who scored a probable MiG-17 kill while flying from Da Nang on 4 April 1965.

(Composite Air Strike Force) Sawbuck movement. The squadron moved to Da Nang a few days later, still in March 1965. The CASF deployment had occurred so rapidly, as F-100 pilot Captain Don Kilgus remembered, that, "We had guys down from England [AFB] with wives seven months pregnant." On 4 April 1965 over North Vietnam in his F-100D *Kay Lynn* (55-2894), Kilgus fought a prolonged duel with a MiG-17 and pumped 20-mm cannon rounds at it while descending vertically through "typical coffee-brown smaze [smoke and haze] with no horizon." Kilgus chased the MiG down from high altitude to 7,000 ft (2167 m) and thought he saw pieces of it falling off as his shells hit home. Both Kilgus and Haven believed that the captain had got the MiG, which would have been the only air-to-air victory by an F-100 in Southeast Asia. It would have been small comfort to US officials who had been humiliated when the same MiG flight ambushed and shot down two F-105 Thunderchiefs moments before Kilgus reached the scene – the only air-to-air losses for some months – but a kill for the 'Hun' would have made all who flew it happy.

On 6 June 1965 while still at Da Nang, the 'Silver Knights' lost an F-100D (55-3600) on a combat mission over South Vietnam.

Kilgus' notes show that the 416th moved from Da Nang to Bien Hoa in June 1965, and returned to England AFB in July 1965 (only to return to Tan Son Nhut in November 1965).

522nd Tactical Fighter Squadron

TDY 8 August 1964 – 15 November 1964
The 522nd TFS 'Fireballs' (part of the 27th TFW, Cannon AFB, New Mexico) followed up on two earlier deployments to Takhli, and made a temporary deployment to Da Nang between 8 August 1964 and 15 November

Below: A typical scene from the early days in Vietnam shows 416th TFS F-100Ds packing the ramp. The squadron moved in mid-1965.

1964. (The squadron also deployed to the Philippines the following year.)

613th Tactical Fighter Squadron

ca. November 1964 – July 1965
The 613th TFS made its only appearance in Southeast Asia (borrowed from the 401st TFW) operating temporarily at Da Nang in late 1964 and early 1965 – first in Laos, then in the initial sustained operations over North Vietnam. During a raid into Laos on 18 November 1964, the second F-100D to be lost in action (callsign BALL 03, its serial never recorded) was lost while attacking an anti-aircraft gun emplacement during escort of a reconnaissance mission against Pathet Lao positions in Laos; a massive search and rescue effort ended when an Air America helicopter crew found the pilot dead at the crash site.

When attention shifted toward North Vietnam, during early missions, Super Sabres flew escort deep into the north and pilots had hopes of prevailing over Hanoi's MiGs. Instead, on 19 February 1965, the 613th lost the third F-100D (55-3783) to go down in combat. The fourth (55-2857) followed on 2 March 1965. The 613th also lost an F-100D (55-2906) on 31 March 1965 and another on 3 April 1965.

The 613th withdrew in July 1965.

614th Tactical Fighter Squadron

August-November 1964
The 614th TFS 'Lucky Devils' (part of the 401st TFW, England AFB, Louisiana) deployed F-100s to Clark Field with a detachment at Da Nang from August to November 1964.

615th Tactical Fighter Squadron

June 1964
In June 1964, a decision was made to launch an air strike against Communist Pathet Lao forces in Laos' Plain of Jars. The job went to the 405th Fighter Wing at Clark AB, Philippines, commanded by World War II P-38 Lightning pilot Colonel George Laven. Laven took from Clark to Da Nang eight F-100Ds of the newly-arrived, temporary-duty 615th TFS (a squadron of the 401st TFW at England AFB, Louisiana that was 'attached' to Laven's wing for 90 to 120 days). The 615th had been in the Far East only for hours and the mere act of moving from Clark to Da Nang was unusual and unprecedented.

Laven encountered monstrous communications glitches over every aspect of the mission, from last-minute changes in the ordnance assigned to confusion over the rendezvous with KC-135 Stratotankers of the recently-arrived Young Tiger Task Force. The 9 June 1964 mission – the first combat mission by American Super Sabres, although the French had flown the F-100 in combat in Algeria in 1960 – resulted in what Laven called "visual bombing in lousy weather." Captain Michael P. Curphey recalled later that, "We had no idea what we were bombing or why." F-100Ds had to recover at Udorn, Thailand and returned to Da Nang only after refuelling on the ground. To this day there is confusion over whether Laven's 'Huns' inflicted 40 per cent damage to Pathet Lao buildings as claimed, or even whether they hit the right target. The Pathet Lao had downed two US Navy reconnaissance aircraft earlier in the month and this air strike was in retaliation. The F-100D Super Sabre performed as advertised, but the confusion over the American purpose and the mission's execution was a harbinger of the long war to come in next-door Vietnam.

Following the Gulf of Tonkin incident of 2 August 1964, in which North Vietnamese torpedo boats fired on US warships, the 615th TFS again deployed a small number of F-100Ds to Da Nang. Maury Fricke, who served in the 615th squadron, remembers arriving at Da Nang at early 1965. The 615th was back – now rotating among Clark Field (in effect, its temporary home overseas), Taiwan (where Super Sabre pilots stood on nuclear alert with tactical atomic bombs), and Da Nang (where the ministrations of the American war machine had shifted from Laos to North and South Vietnam).

In the first days of the 1965-68 campaign against North Vietnam known as Operation Rolling Thunder, the 615th suffered its first combat loss and its only loss of this segment of the war. An F-100D (55-3702) was shot down by Viet Cong gunfire over South Vietnam on 12 June 1965. Soon afterward, the deployment of the 615th to Da Nang ended – although the squadron was to return (to Phan Rang) later in the conflict.

531st Tactical Fighter Squadron

ca. February – July 1965
The 531st TFS (later to play a major role at Bien Hoa) was on temporary duty at Da Nang when the major US build-up gathered

steam at the beginning of 1965.

On 2 March 1965, Operation Rolling Thunder – the first sustained bombing campaign over North Vietnam – began with a strike against an ammunition depot at Xom Bong, 35 miles (56 km) inside North Vietnam. The mixed force included 44 F-100Ds from Da Nang (apparently the 531st TFS plus one other squadron), an equal number of F-105 Thunderchiefs from bases in Thailand, and 20 B-57 Canberras from Tan Son Nhut. The F-100s went in first, firing 2.75-in rockets and cannon rounds. One of the F-100s was hit and its pilot, First Lieutenant Hayden Lockhart, ejected and became the first USAF pilot captured by the North Vietnamese.

Replaced at Da Nang (by the 416th TFS) in 1965, the 531st TFS withdrew only days before the first F-4 Phantom squadron arrived in Vietnam: the US Marine Corps' VMFA-531 'Gray Ghosts'. Thus, by only a few days, the base at Da Nang missed being home for Air Force and Marine Corps squadrons with the same number.

Armed with SUU-7 cluster bomb dispensers, a 'Hun' of the 615th TFS, 401st TFW taxis out for a mission at Da Nang in early 1965. Apart from deployment for the 4 June mission (the first combat for the F-100), the 615th sent small detachments of aircraft to Da Nang on a regular basis during the year.

Tan Son Nhut Air Base, South Vietnam

Tan Son Nhut was located 3 miles (5 km) northwest of the capital, Saigon. Even before World War II, it had been the main airfield for French Indochina, and served domestic as well as international airline flights. By 1966, there were over 24,000 military personnel and 400 aircraft at Tan Son Nhut. Even when construction expanded its facilities and gave it two 10,000-ft (3048-m) runways, Tan Son Nhut remained essentially overtaxed.

481st Tactical Fighter Squadron

TDY 29 June 1965 – 1 January 1966
The 481st TFS 'Crusaders', part of the 27th TFW at Cannon AFB, New Mexico, was deployed to Clark AB, Philippines in 1965 and during this period made a June to November 1965 deployment to Tan Son Nhut. The stay at the latter airfield began on 29 June 1965. While in Vietnam, the squadron's F-100s wore green forward-facing triangles on their tail fins and had the squadron designation stencilled on wing tanks.

The 481st TFW lost five aircraft during its brief stay at Tan Son Nhut. The pilot of an F-100D (56-3334) shot down on 21 July 1965 was rescued intact, but on 31 July 1965 another F-100D (55-2837) was downed and First Lieutenant Donald D. Watson became the first pilot from Cannon to be lost in the Vietnam conflict. Another 481st Super Sabre (apparently 56-3316, although the record is unclear) was shot

down on 29 September 1965, but the pilot apparently survived. On 5 October 1965, enemy groundfire during a pre-strike mission claimed the life of First Lieutenant John C. Hauschilt, the second and last pilot from Cannon to die in Vietnam. Hauschilt's aircraft (56-3074) was followed on 13 November 1965 by the final loss for the 481st – yet another F-100D (55-2795).)

The Cannon-based F-100D wing became a replacement training unit on 1 January 1966.

416th Tactical Fighter Squadron

November 1965 – April 1967
In November 1965, the 416th TFS 'Silver Knights' deployed to Tan Son Nhut Air Base near Saigon (while its parent 3rd TFW moved with two other squadrons to Bien Hoa). The much-travelled 'Knights' suffered a loss on 29 December 1965 when an F-100D (55-3719) was downed in South Vietnam. Another (55-3780) was shot down in South Vietnam on 5 March 1966 and another (55-3534) on 30 March 1966.

The 'Silver Knights' lost an F-100D (56-3100) on 3 October 1966 in a shootdown over South Vietnam.

Below right: A 481st TFS F-100D rolls in with divebrake deployed. The centreline pod was a strike camera.

Left: Armourers handle a CBU-2 cluster bomb with a 416th TFS aircraft in the background. The CBU-2 was based on the SUU-7 dispenser and contained 409 BLU-3 fragmentation sub-munitions in 19 rearward-launching tubes.

Below: This 416th TFS was previously with the 481st, and still carried the nose art added by Hal Comstock while it was with the previous unit.

Above: During their stay at Tan Son Nhut, the aircraft of the 481st TFS began to adopt the T.O. 1-1-4 camouflage, as displayed in this mixed formation.

Below: An armed guard stands watch over 481st TFS aircraft at Tan Son Nhut. The revetments were a necessity following VC mortar attacks against the airfields.

Bien Hoa Air Base, South Vietnam

Bien Hoa was 15 miles (24 km) north of Saigon. Before the arrival of the 3rd TFW as permanent resident, the air base saw temporary deployments by the 307th TFS and 429th TFS in 1965.

In January 1967, Robert R. Rodwell of *Flight International*, reporting from Saigon, called Bien Hoa the world's busiest airport. It logged an average of 64,000 "runway actions" per month, or an average of one every 31 seconds. Bien Hoa's runway was lengthened to 10,000 ft (3048 m) early during the US build-up, and had a second runway of equal length added in 1969. Bien Hoa's facilities grew constantly and included ever-increasing numbers of taxiways and parking ramps with covered aircraft shelters ('wonder' shelters) and – more familiar to Super Sabre pilots – typical open revetments. With its proximity to the international airport at Saigon, Bien Hoa was the easiest tactical air base to be reached by throngs of visiting reporters, so it received constant attention.

Because of its proximity to Saigon, Bien Hoa was bordered on two corners by what the provost marshal called "a sea of humanity" and was thus deemed even more vulnerable to Viet Cong mortar, rocket and sapper attack than other bases in Vietnam. No fewer than five F-100Ds were destroyed by mortar and rocket attacks on different dates over 1967-69.

307th Tactical Fighter Squadron

July – November 1965

The 307th TFS (until then, part of the 31st TFW at Homestead AFB, Florida) was on TDY at Bien Hoa from July to November 1965. During this period, one of its aircraft was an F-100D (56-3440), which later became a display at the National Air and Space Museum in Washington. During its six-month tour, the squadron flew 3,502 combat sorties without a single combat loss.

In November 1965, the squadron turned its aircraft over to the arriving 531st TFS/3rd TFW so that the squadron's F-100s remained at Bien Hoa while its flag and

people moved, initially, back to Homestead. (Unlike other squadrons of the 31st TFW, the 307th did not accompany the Homestead wing thereafter to its new 'turnkey' base at Tuy Hoa: the 307th moved to Torrejon AB, Spain in April 1966.)

308th Tactical Fighter Squadron

ca. early 1966 – 15 November 1966

The 308th TFS 'Emerald Knights' served at Bien Hoa in 1966, arriving in Southeast Asia for the first time on temporary status to replace the outgoing 531st TFS. This was apparently the final temporary deployment of Super Sabres while the brass in Saigon sorted out plans for a more permanent presence. (Later, the squadron bedded down with its parent 31st TFW at Tuy Hoa.) The squadron's apparent first combat loss was an F-100D (56-3375) downed over

The 307th Tactical Fighter Squadron (from the 31st TFW) arrived at Bien Hoa in July 1965, and was immediately involved in action. This aircraft, wearing the squadron's double stripe fin markings, carries an impressive mission tally on the nose.

South Vietnam by Viet Cong gunfire on 3 August 1966. The squadron's second combat loss during its stay at Bien Hoa was another D model 'Hun' (55-3589) on 14 October 1966. A month later, on 15 November 1966, the squadron transferred to Tuy Hoa on permanent status; its story resumes with the Tuy Hoa entry.

429th Tactical Fighter Squadron

ca. July – November 1965

The 429th TFS (part of the 27th TFW at Cannon AFB, New Mexico) appeared briefly on TDY status in Vietnam, flying from Bien Hoa during the approximate period of July to November 1965. The squadron suffered at least two aircraft losses in combat, an F-100D (56-3185) on 9 August 1965 and another (55-3543) on 1 October 1965.

3rd Tactical Fighter Wing

The 3rd TFW at England AFB, Louisiana despatched all four of its flying squadrons (90th, 416th, 510th and 531st TFS) on temporary deployments to Southeast Asia during the busy F-100 activity of 1962-65. The 3rd TFW transferred PCS from England AFB to Bien Hoa in November 1965. The wing took over aircraft of the 307th TFS/31st TFW already located at that base (which remained for several weeks and was replaced by the 308th TFS).

The 3rd dates to 1919, and by 1965 it had uninterrupted service as a combat group/wing, possibly the longest in the US Air Force. From the outbreak of World War II, the well-established 3rd Attack Group moved to the Pacific as a light/medium bomber unit. The 3rd took up residence in Japan following the Pacific war, fought in

Above: The 308th TFS was also part of the 31st TFW, and followed the 307th in manning a deployment to Bien Hoa. The sharkmouth markings are notable on this aircraft.

Above right: The 429th TFS came to Bien Hoa from the 27th TFW at Cannon. This aircraft is seen armed with standard 750-lb M117 bombs.

Right: The 429th TFS was among the most colourful of F-100 units to see action in Southeast Asia thanks to the large unit markings and rudder stripes. This aircraft carries an SUU-7 dispenser on the outboard pylon, a commonly seen area denial weapon during the early years.

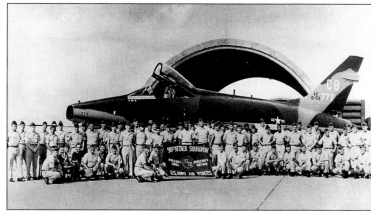

The 90th TFS was one of the component squadrons of the 3rd TFW for five years.

the Korean War, and returned to Japan. There it was equipped for many years with Martin B-57 Canberras. The 3rd was transferred to England AFB, Louisiana in January 1964.

The wing's move to Bien Hoa in November 1965 was initially made with the 510th TFS, while the 416th TFS moved to Tan Son Nhut air base near Saigon in late November 1965. Also to Bien Hoa came the wing's 531st TFS in December 1965 and 90th TFS in February 1966. The 3rd TFW was commanded in Vietnam by Colonels Robert A. Ackerly (1965-66), Richard C. Catledge (1966-67), George W. McLaughlin (1967-68), Homer K. Hansen (1968-69), Howard M. 'Mac' Lane (1969-70), and William E. Carson (1970-71).

During its first six months in combat while at Bien Hoa, the 3rd TFW logged more than 13,000 sorties. During this time, the 3rd grew from an initial strength of approximately 40 F-100Ds and Fs to approximately 100. The wing was averaging about one combat sortie per F-100 per day – an extraordinarily good figure for an aircraft difficult to maintain in a place of primitive

facilities.

During its stay in Vietnam, the 3rd TFW also participated in combat evaluations of F-5 Freedom Fighter and A-37 Dragonfly aircraft. The 3rd TFW shifted to 'unmanned and unequipped' status after its final Vietnam flight on 31 October 1970. The wing's designation was applied to an F-4 Phantom-equipped combat wing at Kunsan, Korea, on 15 March 1971.

90th Tactical Fighter Squadron

8 November 1965 – 31 October 1970
The 90th TFS 'Pair o' Dice' ('CB' tailcode; light blue) operated from Bien Hoa as a component of the 3rd TFW, apparently from 8 November 1965. The squadron suffered its first combat loss on 14 March 1966 when an F-100D (55-3793) was shot down over South Vietnam. Another (56-2925) went down on 22 June 1966 and the squadron lost an F-100F (58-1217) on 19 July 1966. A two-seater (56-3869) was downed in South Vietnam on 12 October 1966, plus a F-100D (55-3787) on 11 December 1966.

The 90th TFS apparently continued the fight without another loss until 6 August 1967, when an F-100D (55-3639) was shot

Above: Personnel of the 90th TFS 'Pair o' Dice' pose in front an F-100D at Bien Hoa.

Below: A 90th TFS pilot gets a hose down after completing his 100th combat mission.

down over South Vietnam. Following another long gap, an F-100D (56-3304) was shot down over the south on 14 February 1968 and another (55-3762) a fortnight later on 26 February 1968.

On 6 March 1969, a 90th TFS F-100D (56-3270) was shot down on a mission in South Vietnam. The war continued for the 90th TFS with the loss of an F-100D (55-3522) on 9 May 1969.

The official date for conclusion of 90th TFS operations in Southeast Asia is 31 October 1970 – just a few months before all Super Sabre missions ended.

510th Tactical Fighter Squadron

8 November 1965 – 15 March 1971
The 510th TFS 'Nickel Dime' or 'Buzzards' ('CE' tailcode; purple) began regular combat missions from Bien Hoa in November 1965.

The squadron had been on TDY in Bangkok at an earlier juncture.

No combat losses are recorded for this squadron for its first 10 months in the combat zone. Then, losses piled up as follows, all in South Vietnam: 14 September 1966 – F-100D (55-3640), 8 December 1966 – F-100D (56-3063), 12 February 1967 – F-100D (56-3925), 22 August 1967 – F-100D (56-3264), 15 September 1967 – F-100D (55-2904), 19 November 1967 – F-100D (56-3040). After a gap of several months, another 510th TFS F-100D (56-3269) was shot down in South Vietnam on 6 March 1968.

First Lieutenant Fredric Neumann, who served with the 510th, called it the "fightin'est" Super Sabre squadron of the war and acknowledges that the squadron paid a high price. Certainly, the 510th competed with the 416th for the title of most-blooded Super Sabre outfit. Combat losses continued with an F-100D (55-3707) on 1 April 1968 and another (55-2875) on 2 April 1968, both in South Vietnam.

When Captain Ronald R. Fogleman reached Phu Cat in June 1968, the squadron was commanded by Lieutenant Colonel Lloyd G. McBride. Fogleman flew an F-100 (56-3087) bearing the apt nickname *Buzzard of Bien Hoa*. Captain Jack Doub's ship (56-3053) was nicknamed *El Viejo Cazador* (the old warrior). Most 510th TFS nicknames appeared in small, stencilled white letters on the aircraft nose, with no artwork. It was a matter of perverse pride to 510th members that their squadron fin cap colour was a non-regulation purple.

The 510th took another hit on 25 July 1968 when an F-100D (55-3608) was shot down in South Vietnam on 25 July 1968. On 12 September 1968, Fogleman was shot down in the I Corps area 200 miles (320 km) north of Bien Hoa while flying F-100D 56-3245. The aircraft was assigned to squadron maintenance officer Captain Dave Osterhout. Fogleman became the first Air Force pilot to be rescued by riding out on a Cobra helicopter: the US Army AH-1G reached him and he came out clinging to a

Above and below: The 510th TFS was one of the mainstays of the F-100's efforts in Vietnam, although it lost at least 12 aircraft in combat.

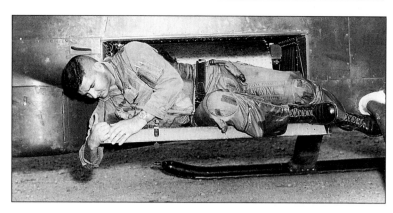

El Viejo Cazador *was the F-100 assigned to Captain Jack Doub of the 510th TFS, seen here climbing out of Bien Hoa.*

deployed gun-panel door. Even today, Osterhout, now Vice President of Legislative Affairs for Lockheed Martin Corporation, razzes Fogleman, now Air Force Chief of Staff, for losing 'his' aircraft.

The 510th TFS suffered another loss on 4 July 1969 when an F-100D (56-3253) was shot down in South Vietnam.

Fogleman returned to the 510th in mid-1969 when its commander was Lieutenant Colonel Robert H. McIntosh, who had been a member of the 'Thunderbirds' flight demonstration team a decade earlier.

531st Tactical Fighter Squadron

November 1965 – 31 July 1970

The 531st TFS, callsign RAMROD ('CP' tailcode; red), dubbed the 'Five Thirsty First', arrived at Bien Hoa as part of the 3rd TFW in November 1965, the first unit to be assigned PCS rather than TDY. The squadron inherited aircraft left behind by the departing 307th TFS/31st TFW, including an F-100D (56-3440) which later became a display at the National Air and Space Museum in Washington.

During the squadron's first few months in combat, there were problems. Captain Mark Berent, a fighter pilot with a decade of experience, arrived to find that the squadron commander had to return to the US due to a family emergency, no new commander was named, and "the ops officer was a poor leader and a coward, and the only man who could miss with napalm by 1,500 ft (464 m) on the side." Berent's point is that anybody can miss long or short, but missing to the side signifies reluctance to expose oneself to ground fire. "The 531st was an odd fighter squadron. I was surprised, shocked. A few of the so-called 'old heads' seemed reluctant to mix it up, to do what they got paid to do. The 531st initially suffered from poor leadership."

On 8 February 1966, Berent flew a close support mission to support South Vietnamese troops pinned against a canal in the Mekong Delta near Rach Gia, 130 miles (209 km) from Bien Hoa. The FAC (forward air controller) cleared Berent and his wingman to deliver 500-lb (227-kg) Mk 82 bombs. Berent's first was a dud, but the second hit the target. A load of CBUs (cluster bomb units) remained.

Dropping CBUs in the face of heavy ground fire was tougher: the CBUs had to be released while flying straight and level at Mach 0.71 and 300 ft (93 m). Before release on Berent's first run, his right windshield quarter panel was shattered by an AK-47 rifle round, showering his face and eyes with shards of glass and smashing his gunsight. "With the current brand of leadership, if you got hit, you went home. I couldn't even get my wingman to give me a visual check of the damage. I talked to the FAC. He said, 'If you go home, they're

dead,'" referring to the friendly troops. Berent 'shook things up' by badgering his wingman to press on with the mission. He wiped glass from his eyes, dumped cabin pressure, lowered his seat, pulled down his visor, and went in for a second pass, then a third. On the third, Berent was hit again, but he persisted and succeeded in relieving the pressure on the friendly ground-pounders. He was later awarded the Silver Star for the mission.

"We eventually turned that squadron around because of the willingness of us senior captains to make things work right. The success we eventually attained was the result of hard work by pilots like Captains Jack Ward, Bob Graham, Gene Armistead and Bob Putnam – and lieutenants like Ron Miller, Joe Howard, Brian Rockell and Phil Drew."

During Berent's era, the squadron suffered its first combat loss, an F-100D (55-3502), to ground fire in South Vietnam on 30 September 1966. Another (55-3809) went down on 12 October 1966. By the time of Berent's departure in December 1966 (he later became best-selling author of novels like *Phantom Leader* and *Storm Flight*), leadership changed for the better, while the quality of junior officers continued to be high.

The 531st TFS lost an F-100D (55-3514) in South Vietnam on 26 January 1967. It was during this period that Defense Secretary Robert S. McNamara denied that there was a "bomb shortage," yet fighter-bombers were going forth on combat sorties with as small a load as just one 500-lb (227-kg) bomb. The problem was more serious for F-105 pilots going north than for F-100 jocks fighting 'in-country', but all were affected. At least some of the aircraft lost during this period were going into battle with far less weaponry than they were capable of carrying. The next loss of a 531st F-100D (56-3027) came on 30 March 1967, and another (56-3285) on 21 May 1967. The roster of downed 'Huns' continued, with another F-100D (55-3549) downed on 12 July 1967 and another (56-3041) on 2 August 1967. The squadron lost an F-100D (56-2922) in South Vietnam on 22 December 1967 and another (55-3458) on 18 May 1968.

On 23 April 1969, a 531st TFS F-100D (56-3335) was shot down in South Vietnam. On 5 July 1969, the squadron lost an F-100D (55-3589) in the south. Losses for the 531st TFS continued with an F-100D (55-3889) on 5 July 1969 and another (56-3049) on 10 July 1969, both in the south.

By 1970, it was official US policy that the war was winding down and the US withdrawing its forces. The 531st TFS lost an F-100D (56-3097) over South Vietnam on

Captain Ronald R. Fogleman, now Air Force Chief of Staff, demonstrates how he clung on to the gun bay door of an Army AH-1G Cobra while being rescued. He was shot down on 12 September 1968, and was on the ground for 75 minutes before the Cobra came to pick him up.

Captain Mark Berent, 531st TFS, poses besides an F-100D armed with a 500-lb (227-kg) Mk 82 bomb at Bien Hoa in mid-1966. Berent was awarded the Silver Star for a 1966 air-to-ground mission.

14 January 1970 , then sustained its final combat casualty of the war when another F-100D (56-3242) went down in the south on 30 May 1970. The 531st ended its war and its assignment to the 3rd TFW on 31 July 1970.

Above: *The 531st TFS was one of three squadrons which made up the 3rd TFW at Bien Hoa. Here one of its aircraft is seen at Tuy Hoa, another major F-100 base.*

Two 531st TFS aircraft prepare to launch from Bien Hoa. The furthest aircraft is carrying a finned *BLU-27 napalm tank on its outboard pylon.*

Korat RTAFB, Thailand

Korat grew like topsy. At first, it was little more than a clearing in the jungle, later a sprawling installation. It went from having one US Air Force officer and 14 enlisted men in April 1962 to 4,000 Americans a decade later. Best known as home for the F-105- and F-4-equipped 388th TFW, Korat offered a world-class airfield with a 9,850-ft (3050-m) runway with 1,000-ft (310-m) overruns at each end, sitting at 600 ft (186-m) elevation. The base is located about 5 miles (8 km) south of Korat City, the third largest city in Thailand with a population of 80,000. It is 145 miles (233 km) north and slightly east of the capital, Bangkok.

6234th TFW (Wild Weasel detachment)

26 November 1965 – July 1966

On 26 November 1965, the first of four modified two-seat F-100F Wild Weasel I aircraft from Eglin AFB, Florida arrived at Korat, Thailand. Three more followed two days later. Led by Major Garry A. Willard, the super-secret Wild Weasel I detachment from Eglin's Tactical Air Warfare Center (not from the 33rd TFW as sometimes reported) was to conduct a 90-day evaluation of newly installed RHAW systems to counter the SAM threat. "For 'evaluation', read 'combat'," remembers Captain Maurice D. Fricke. The detachment may have reported to the provisional 6234th TFW, although participants do not remember this. The first combat mission was flown on 20 December 1965.

The F-100F Wild Weasel I was an electronic marvel but was not yet equipped with an anti-radar missile. "We were intended to work with Iron Hand F-105 SAM-suppression flights," says Fricke. The F-100F weasel modification included AN/APR-25 (also called Vector IV) radar homing and warning receiver, AN/APR-26 crystal receiver to detect missile guidance launch signals, IR-133 panoramic receiver to detect S-band signals at a distance, KA-60 panoramic strike camera, and a dual-track tape recorder. This equipment could only be operated by an EWO in the backseat. The Shrike anti-radar missile had not been developed for Air Force use: the F-100F, armed with napalm and rockets, would be 'hunters' teamed in a 'hunter/killer' package with included F-105 Thunderchiefs.

"One F-100F would troll for SAMs, leading three F-105s on a flight," remembers Fricke. "At first, we had the rollback concept. We'd start at the border and work north to Hanoi. This didn't work because the powers-that-be wanted to go up closer to Hanoi right away, so we bypassed some sites to go after those near [the capital]." The job was difficult, because "the North Vietnamese had excellent radar discipline. They would shut down when they knew we were near. It took us a month and a half to destroy our first site, though in the meanwhile we damaged their air defences by prevented sites from transmitting."

That first day, 20 December 1965, while trolling for SAMs, the F-100F (58-1231, callsign APPLE 01) flown by Captain Jack Pitchford and EWO Captain Robert D. Trier became the first two-seat 'Hun' to fall in battle. A single 37-mm anti-aircraft shell exploded in the rear fuselage of the F-100F. Pitchford had been able to fire his market rockets to pinpoint the SAM sites for the F-105s; they attacked the target, then followed the F-100F with the intent of observing the damage and, if necessary, directing a rescue of its crew.

APPLE 01 was in bad shape. Pitchford headed for the Gulf of Tonkin. The F-100F lost hydraulics and became uncontrollable. It pitched, then dived for the ground. There was no choice. Trier ejected first, then Pitchford. Pitchford was immediately captured and spent the rest of the war as a POW. Trier resisted capture and was killed by the North Vietnamese.

The first detachment of Wild Weasel fliers went home in February 1965, Fricke recalls (and most later went to Nellis AFB, Nevada to develop the weasel mission for the F-105). They were replaced by other F-100 crews, "kind of Wild Weasel I-A."

On 23 March 1966, the Wild Weasel I detachment suffered the loss of a second F-100F (58-1212) and the two crewmen were killed.

18 April 1966 saw the first USAF combat firing of an AGM-45 Shrike anti-radiation missile by an F-100F Wild Weasel I against an Active SAM site on a SAM search-and-destroy mission. Ironically, the arrival of the Shrike came as the F-100F effort was winding down. The USAF was in the process of obtaining converted F-105F Thunderchiefs to take over the weasel mission. The 'Huns' assigned to the job were depleted and dilapidated. Originally deployed for 90 days on 26 November 1965, the Wild Weasel I F-100Fs belatedly returned home in July 1966.

Two views of 58-1221 show the aircraft refuelling (right) and at Eglin (below). The aircraft carries a typical early Weasel load-out of napalm and 2.75-in rocket pods.

Above: Photographed in December 1965, this was the Wild Weasel detachment at Korat. The front row consists of the pilots and EWOs, who had been the original crews trained at Eglin AFB.

Right: Relaxing in front of the Wild Weasel detachment badge is the CO, Major Gary Willard.

Posed by their aircraft are Captain Al Lamb (pilot, on left) and Captain Jack Donovan (EWO, on right). This crew achieved the Wild Weasel's first SAM-site kill (in 58-1226) on 22 December 1965, using rockets and 20-mm cannon. The site was finished off by supporting F-105Ds.

Tuy Hoa Air Base, South Vietnam

A line-up of 'Huns' prepares to launch from Tuy Hoa, comprising aircraft of the 306th ('SD') and 309th ('SS') Tactical Fighter Squadrons.

Located on the coast 2.5 miles (4 km) south of a village by the same name, Tuy Hoa air base was sometimes jocularly called 'The Atlantic City of the South China Sea'. The base was built on sand, so it did not have the problem of humidity which plagued maintenance people at other bases.

With the largest number of assigned F-100 Super Sabres, Tuy Hoa for a time was the busiest of the F-100 bases during the Vietnam War. It operated five full squadrons, three that were the regular components of the 31st TFW and two 'gained' Air National Guard units. Initially with AM-2 aluminium-plank runway and parking facilities, the base acquired a 9,500-ft (2941-m) paved runway in April 1967, but a second runway and the ramp employed AM-2 until the base was abandoned in mid-1970. All fuel for the base arrived by sea and was piped in from Vung Ro Bay 15 miles (24 km) away.

31st Tactical Fighter Wing

In July 1965, the 31st TFW, home-based at Homestead AFB, Florida, with its 306th, 307th, 308th and 309th TFS, began a rotational cycle of TDY for typical 90-day periods at Bien Hoa air base. Bien Hoa was one of the most saturated air bases in South Vietnam, located just northeast of Saigon.

On Christmas Day 1966, the 31st TFW moved PCS from Homestead to Tuy Hoa with its 306th and 309th squadrons. The 308th TFS, having moved from Bien Hoa to Tuy Hoa on 15 November 1966, was assigned to the 31st TFW on 25 December. The wing's other squadron, the 307th, never served at Tuy Hoa (see Bien Hoa entry).

Beginning in June 1968, New York's 136th and New Mexico's 188th TFS (Air National Guard units called to active duty during the *Pueblo* crisis in Korea in early 1968) joined the 31st TFW at Tuy Hoa. They remained until May 1969 when they were replaced by the 355th and 416th TFS which transferred from Phu Cat.

During the Tet Offensive in January/February 1968, Viet Cong infiltrators got into the town of Tuy Hoa and inflicted many casualties while trying in vain to capture a friendly 105-mm artillery battery which would have been within range of the air base. 31st TFW F-100D pilots flew missions right into the village. "We carried Mk 82 high-drag bombs," remembers Captain Tom Barnes of the 306th TFS. "There were a lot of airplanes all queued up and ready to go. You usually didn't have a lot of airplanes ganging up on alert to take off, so this was an unusual sight. We flew with empty drop tanks, rather than removing the tanks and flying without them."

In July 1968, 31st TFW pilots flew 2,175 sorties, a figure which typified the build-up then under way. In December 1968, the 31st TFW flew its 50,000th combat sortie in Southeast Asia. On 12 September 1969, the wing recorded its 100,000th combat sortie.

The 31st TFW's first Vietnam-era commander, Colonel James Jabara, had been the first American ace of the Korean War; he was killed in an automobile mishap on 17 November 1966 while the wing's involvement in the conflict still consisted of temporary-duty postings. Commanders in Vietnam were Colonel Raymond C. Lee, Jr (1966), Warren R. Lewis (1966-67), William J. Evans (1967-68), Abner M. Aust, Jr (1968-69), Cuthbert A. Patillo (1969), William B. Yancey, Jr (1969-70), and Gilbert D. Hereth (1970).

On 15 October 1970, as part of the US policy of withdrawing forces from Vietnam (under the 'Guam doctrine', enunciated by President Nixon in August 1969), the 31st TFW flag moved 'without personnel or equipment' to Homestead. The 306th, 308th and 309th squadrons, however, transferred to England AFB, Louisiana, although this turned out to be a temporary move; the squadrons returned to Homestead later that month.

306th Tactical Fighter Squadron

25 December 1966 – 15 October 1970

The 306th TFS ('SD' tailcode, callsign LIMIT) moved to Tuy Hoa with the 31st TFW, transferring from Homestead, on 25 December 1966. While this squadron was flying the F-100 in combat, actor Jimmy Stewart (a B-24 pilot in World War II) visited the base to narrate an Air Force film. The squadron's first loss at Tuy Hoa came on 12 February 1967 when an F-100D (56-3451) was claimed by gunfire in South Vietnam. Apparently on a mission to Laos – where 'Huns' returned not to challenge the Pathet Lao but to attack North Vietnamese troops –

another F-100D (56-3451) was shot down on 12 February 1967. The 306th TFS lost an F-100D (56-3122) in action in South Vietnam on 2 July 1968.

No nose art was worn by 306th aircraft during 1966-68. The squadron lounge had artefacts from World War II, including a model of a Spitfire flown by the 306th in North Africa in 1942, together with captured AK-47s and Viet Cong flags.

On 24 August 1968 Major Forrest Fenn was flying one of many secret missions into Laos when small-calibre rounds riddled his F-100D (56-3019) from nose to tail, setting off the engine fire warning light. Wingman Captain Gary Van Valin escorted Fenn's crippled fighter as they attempted to put it down at the nearest airstrip, at Binh Thuy in the Mekong Delta. The barrier was deployed and Fenn was preparing to land with tail hook down when the engine belched, spat out gouts of smoke, and – a mile and a half from the air strip – died. Fenn dead-sticked the F-100D down and

Seen at Phu Cat in September 1970, this F-100F served with the 306th TFS. The two-seaters were used widely as FAC and BDA aircraft.

successfully engaged the wire. "The tail hook pretty much pulled the tail of the airplane off." Fenn's battered Super Sabre landed in less than 400 ft (124 m). The pilot was unharmed but the merit of salvaging the F-100D was questionable. That night, the issue was resolved when Viet Cong mortars damaged the F-100D still further. A month later, a second mortar attack destroyed the aircraft.

Another pilot of the 306th was badly injured after his Super Sabre sustained gunfire in the autumn of 1968. He made a 'precautionary landing' at Pleiku where the arresting-wire barrier had been set up for his emergency landing. He landed too fast – in the words of a squadron mate, "hotter than a two-dollar pistol." The barrier did not

Two views show 306th TFS aircraft. Prominent on the aircraft at right are the unusual wing fences, which appeared on the F-100D and which featured a cut-out in the rear to accommodate the travel of the ailerons.

Left: The 308th TFS was one of three squadrons which made up the 31st TFW at Tuy Hoa between 1966 and 1968, when more arrived to bolster the force.

Above: 308th aircraft wore their green/white checkerboard markings for most of their assignment to Tuy Hoa. Most aircraft received nicknames painted on the nose.

work. The fighter went off the end of the runway, sheared its undercarriage off, ran into a rice paddy and came to a halt, stuck in full afterburner. A coupling link from the barrier system slammed into a guard shack nearby, nearly killing an airman. The pilot was unable to get out of the aircraft while his afterburner kept running. Men pulled him from his cockpit with a broken back. It was later determined that the fault lay not with the pilot, despite his touching down on afterburner with battle damage, but with US Army personnel manning the barrier. Thereafter, the device intended to catch the tail hook of a 'Hun' was operated by Air Force members.

On 20 December 1968, the squadron sustained another combat loss, an F-100D (55-3647) in Laos. Major Fenn, who was now being shot down for the second time, decided to record the entire event: "I had camera and tape recorder. I was going to photograph my chute opening and my plane going in." He ejected. Hanging from his parachute risers, Fenn photographed the F-100D as it flew into a vertical bluff and exploded. Fenn was down overnight and was rescued by an HH-3E 'Jolly Green' helicopter guided by a forward air controller he had known in flight school. The 1,500th man to be saved by Air Rescue forces in Southeast Asia, Fenn was in his home town in America by Christmas Eve, three days later.

The final combat loss for the 306th TFS was an F-100F (56-3945) shot down in Laos on 19 March 1970.

On 15 October 1970, the 306th (with the 308th and 309th) was reassigned from Tuy Hoa to England AFB, Louisiana, and subsequently to Homestead on 30 October 1970, ending its role in the war.

Above: Thor's Hammer was assigned to the 309th TFS. It wears the 31st's wing badge on the fin, which consisted of a wyvern above waves.

Below: M117-armed 309th aircraft make their way to the target. The aircraft in the foreground wears the 'Pair o' Dice' insignia on the fin, denoting previous assignment to the 90th TFS.

Below: 309th TFS F-100s nestle in their revetments at Tuy Hoa. Note the leading-edge slats.

308th Tactical Fighter Squadron

15 November 1966 – 15 October 1970
The 308th TFS 'Emerald Knights' ('SM' tailcode, green squadron colour, callsign LITTER) deployed to Tuy Hoa on 15 November 1966 (arriving from a temporary assignment at Bien Hoa). The squadron officially became part of the 31st TFW on 25 December 1966. Apparently, the squadron's first combat loss at Tuy Hoa was an F-100D (55-3618) shot down over South Vietnam on 10 May 1967.

Commander of the 306th in 1967-68 was Lieutenant Colonel John Rivers. 308th TFS aircraft wore green and white checkerboard fin tips. In small print in yellow on the nose, they wore nicknames such as *Jeanne Kay* on 56-2910.

The 308th lost an F-100D (55-3510) in combat over South Vietnam on 13 June 1967. Another (55-3765) was lost on 4 January 1968.

Rivers was succeeded in spring 1968 by Lieutenant Colonel Jack Smith, who took command after surviving an incident on his first sortie in-theatre, when his F-100F was hit, apparently by a Viet Cong rocket. Smith was typical of many who brought hard-won experience to the war in Vietnam: he had flown F-80 Shooting Stars with the 16th FIS in Korea (and on 8 November 1950 had loaned his F-80C 49-0713 to First Lieutenant Russell Brown who shot down a MiG-15 in history's first jet-versus-jet dogfight). Smith is generally given high marks for steering an outfit which inflicted major harm to the Viet Cong while sustaining modest casualties. The squadron did not suffer another loss until 18 March 1969 when an F-100D (55-3635) was shot down in South Vietnam. A 308th TFS F-100D (56-3090) was shot down in South Vietnam on 6 August 1969. The squadron lost another F-100D (55-3511) in the south on 28 December 1969. The final combat loss of the war for the 308th TFS was an F-100D (56-3278) shot down in Laos on 6 April 1970.

On 15 October 1970, the 306th, 308th and 309th TFS were reassigned from Tuy Hoa to England AFB, Louisiana, and subsequently to Homestead on 30 October 1970, ending their role in the war.

309th Tactical Fighter Squadron

ca. January 1966 – 15 October 1970
The 309th TFS ('SS' tailcode) operated as part of the 31st TFW at Tuy Hoa apparently from January 1966. The squadron's first combat loss seems to have been an F-100D (55-3714) shot down over South Vietnam on 15 February 1967, followed by an F-100D (56-2907) in Laos the next day, 16 February 1967.

Commander of the 309th in 1968 was Lieutenant Colonel David Renshaw. For reasons that are not clear, the squadron went for more than a year, including the busy Tet Offensive period, without sustaining a loss until an F-100D (56-3124) was lost on a mission in the south on 9 July 1968. Another gap followed and on 16 April 1969 a 309th TFS F-100D (56-3403) was shot down over Laos. The 309th TFS lost an F-100D (55-2849) in South Vietnam on 12 July 1969 and an F-100F (56-3567) in Laos on 24 October 1969. The final combat loss of the Southeast Asia war for the 309th TFS was an F-100D (56-3136) shot down in South Vietnam on 26 May 1970.

The squadron departed Tuy Hoa on 15 October 1970.

355th Tactical Fighter Squadron

15 May 1969 – 30 September 1970
On 15 May 1969, the 355th TFS ('HP' tailcode) began transferring to Tuy Hoa (from Phu Cat) where it joined the 31st TFW

to fill in for a departing Air National Guard squadron. The squadron lost an F-100D (55-3555) on 24 May 1969 when the Super Sabre was hit by ground fire in South Vietnam and went down at sea. Another F-100D (56-3332) went down in Laos on 10 December 1969.

The squadron flew operational missions until 20 September 1970, when its last sortie took place. Ten days later, the 355th TFS ended its part in the Southeast Asia conflict.

416th Tactical Fighter Squadron

28 May 1969 – 28 September 1970
The very busy 416th TFS 'Silver Knights', which could claim to have been in combat longer than any other Super Sabre squadron, transferred to Tuy Hoa (from Phu Cat) to become a component of the 31st TFW on 28 May 1969. During its stay at Tuy Hoa, the squadron lost two F-100Fs on Laotian missions on 19 January 1970 (56-3847) and on 8 May 1970 (56-3827). The latter appears to have been the final combat casualty of a squadron which was in the fight from the beginning. The 416th flew its final combat mission on 4 September 1970 and ended its stay in Southeast Asia on 28 September 1970.

136th Tactical Fighter Squadron

14 June 1968 – 25 May 1969
The 136th TFS 'Rocky's Raiders', an activated New York Air National Guard squadron, with 22 F-100Cs ('SG' tailcode) usually located at Niagara Falls International Airport, arrived to join the 31st TFW at Tuy Hoa in May 1968. Lieutenant Colonel Laverne J. Donner was commander.

In the immediate aftermath of the Tet Offensive, the 136th TFS lost an F-100C (54-1912) on 25 July 1968 and another (54-1775) on 2 August 1968, both in South Vietnam. The Guardsmen were hit with their third loss on 23 August 1968 when an F-100C (54-1922) was hit in South Vietnam and crashed at sea. Hardest hit among Guard squadrons, the 136th TFS suffered its fourth and final combat loss of an F-100C (54-1931) in South Vietnam on 15 December 1968.

The New York Guardsmen returned to Niagara Falls with their aircraft in May 1969.

188th Tactical Fighter Squadron

May 1968 – 5 June 1969
The 188th TFS or 'Enchilada Air Force' ('SK' tailcode, yellow squadron colour, callsign TACO) was an activated New Mexico Air National Guard squadron commanded by Lieutenant Colonel Fred J. Fink. In the spring of 1964, the squadron had converted from F-100As to F-100C/Fs.

On 26 January 1968 the squadron was called to active duty as a result of the Pueblo crisis in Korea. The squadron ferried its 22 aircraft (21 F-100Cs, one F-100F) from Albuquerque to Hawaii to Guam to Tuy Hoa. In May 1968, these New Mexico Guardsmen arrived at Tuy Hoa to begin combat operations. Members of the squadron learned that the radio callsign ENCHILADA was being used by a Marine Corps helicopter squadron so they began using TACO, and still use the latter callsign today.

188th TFS Super Sabres wore standard camouflage and had yellow squares beneath the windscreen on which crew names appeared. Nicknames such as *Tin Lizzie* (53-1775) appeared in white letters on the nose. The New Mexico 'road runner' silhouette appeared in yellow on the tail.

On 4 January 1969, the 188th TFS suffered the loss of two pilots and aircraft (54-2030, 54-2051). Captain Bobbie Neeld and First Lieutenant Mitch Lane were on a rough mission in bad weather. With the weather closing in, they elected to make a radar approach to Phan Rang rather than landing at Tuy Hoa. This decision was made for fuel considerations: the approach to Phan Rang was always understood to be the more difficult of the two options. Both

aircraft were lost. No one knows whether they collided in flight.

An F-100C (54-2041) was lost in action in South Vietnam on 31 January 1969. Pilot J. Williams ejected safely. However, the New Mexico squadron lost its most junior pilot, Second Lieutenant Michael Adams, on a 4 May 1969 mission into Laos in an F-100C (53-1741) which had previously been belly-landed at Da Nang by pilot Smith. Adams and another flier had taken very heavy fire the day before over the same target. This time, the folly of using predictable targets, routes and timing extracted its toll. Adams was observed to have a 'good chute' after ejecting.

Major Louis A. Bowerman remembers the loss of yet another F-100C in a non-combat mishap, although it does not appear on official records. When it became clear that the US had one war on its hands, not two – Korea began to settle down – the ANG squadrons went home. On 5 June 1969, the 188th returned to state control.

Above: The 355th TFS flew briefly from Tuy Hoa in 1969/70. Here one of its aircraft receives open-air maintenance.

Above: The 416th TFS flew for over a year from Tuy Hoa as part of the 31st TFW, with the tailcode 'SE' assigned.

Right: With its 31st TFW tailcode, an F-100C from the 136th TFS stands at Myrtle Beach. In the background are aircraft from the 113th TFS/DC ANG, this unit being activated in 1968 to act as a schoolhouse for F-100 pilots, and also to help man the active-duty 355th TFS at Tuy Hoa.

Below: A tin can serves a purpose as a pitot tube protector on this 188th TFS F-100C at Tuy Hoa. The base received two ANG squadrons during the Pueblo mobilisation, and two extra active-duty units afterwards.

Phan Rang AB, South Vietnam

Phan Rang was a city with a population of 240,000. Its airfield straddled level fertile ground which reached about three miles to the sea, while its building complex nestled at the base of rugged jungle-clad mountains that extended to the west. Near the main gate were ruins of a Cham Temple built in the 12th century. The construction of the airfield, like so much that happened during the build-up, occurred quickly. Early missions were flown from surfaces of AM-2 (aluminium matting) which was similar to, and replaced, the better-known PSP (pierced steel planking).

Initially, the combat wing at Phan Rang was the 366th TFW (from 20 March 1966) until it was replaced by the 35th TFW (on 10 October 1966). As the war expanded, the 35th TFW moved to this new airfield and brought with it no fewer than five combat squadrons – initially, three F-100D/F Super Sabre units plus attached Canberra squadrons. After construction, the airfield consisted of a 10,000-ft (3048-m) concrete runway with parallel taxiway, plus open and covered aircraft revetments located on asphalt and AM-2 matting aprons.

On 25 January 1969, two F-100 Super Sabres were destroyed by a Viet Cong rocket attack on Phan Rang.

366th Tactical Fighter Wing

20 March 1966 – 10 October 1966
The 366th TFW was the original combat wing at Phan Rang, arriving on 20 March 1966, and served for a time as the command for the 352nd TFS (15 August – 10 October 1966), 614th TFS (18 September – 10 October 1966), and 615th TFS (15 May – 10 October 1966). Commander during the period at Phan Rang was Colonel George S. Weart. On 10 October 1966, the 366th TFW designation was switched to an F-4 Phantom combat wing at Da Nang.

35th Tactical Fighter Wing

1 October 1966 –- 31 July 1971
The 35th TFW had been inactivated in October 1957 following combat in Korea and air defence duty in Japan. Then it was reorganised in April 1966 at Da Nang and moved in October 1966 to Phan Rang,

replacing the 366th TFW there.

On 1 October 1966, the 35th and 366th wings moved in name only, the 35th replacing the 366th at Phan Rang and becoming an F-100 operator. Squadrons included the 352nd TFS (20 October 1966 – 31 July 1971), and the 615th TFS (10 October 1966 — 31 July 1971). Two USAF B-57 Canberra squadrons (the 8th and 13th Bomb Squadrons), Australia's RAAF No. 2 Squadron with Canberras, and (in 1970) the A-37B Dragonfly-equipped 8th Special Operations Squadron were also components of the 35th TFW. When the Air National Guard was recalled in 1968, the 35th TFW gained the 120th TFS. Another component, actually a *de facto* squadron, was the F-100-equipped Detachment 1, 612th TFS. On 15 March 1971, the 612th TFS moved from Japan to Phan Rang in name only, replacing the detachment.

The 35th TFW was commanded in Vietnam by Colonels George S. Weart (who stayed on when the wing designation at Phan Rang changed, serving in 1966-67), James A. Wilson (1967-68), Herndon F. Williams (1968), and Frank L. Gailer, Jr (1968-69). Brigadier General Walter Galligan commanded the wing in 1969-70. Colonel Cregg P. Nolan, Jr was the final Vietnam-era commander in 1971.

The wing began phasing down for inactivation in April 1971 and stood down on 26 June 1971. On 8 July 1971, the *Pacific Stars and Stripes* reported the impending departure of the 35th TFW as the entire fighter wing prepared to ferry its F-100s back to the US, part of the gradual withdrawal begun by President Nixon the previous year. Remaining resources passed to the 315th Tactical Airlift Wing on 31 July 1971, when the 35th TFW inactivated. The wing reappeared on the US Air Force scene in later years beginning when it activated as an F-4/F-105 Wild Weasel operator at George AFB, California later in 1971.

352nd Tactical Fighter Squadron

15 August 1966 – 31 July 1971
The 352nd TFS ('VM' tailcode) was at Phan Rang as part of the 366th TFW from 15 August to 10 October 1966, and of the 31st TFW from 10 October 1966 to 31 July 1971. The squadron sustained its first combat loss on 13 January 1967 when an F-100D (56-3448) was shot down over South Vietnam.

Above: A 352nd TFS pilot and crew chief pose prior to a napalm mission in 1971. Nose art was restricted to 'hidden' places, such as inside the intake.

Below: This 352nd TFS F-100F visiting Udorn in 1971 was in use as a Misty FAC platform. Here it is seen carrying baggage pods, which were converted napalm bomb cases.

The squadron lost an F-100F (56-3980) on 2 May 1967.

The 352nd TFS lost an F-100D (56-3372) on 30 June 1968 and another (55-2900) on 4 July 1968, both in South Vietnam. On 2 October 1968, a squadron F-100D (55-3661) was hit over South Vietnam and lost at sea. Five weeks later, on 29 November 1968, Viet Cong gunfire claimed another F-100D (56-3237). The next loss came on 21 January 1969 when an F-100D (56-3113) was downed over South Vietnam, and then five months later another F-100D (56-3119) was hit over South Vietnam on 25 May 1969 and went down at sea.

The US bombing campaign over Cambodia took a toll on the 352nd TFS. The squadron lost five aircraft in 1970-71, more

The 'VM' tailcode and yellow/black checkerboard denote the 352nd TFS, which served at Phan Rang for five years. For the first few months it was assigned to the 366th TFW before the 35th TFW took over F-100 operations from the base.

than any other unit during this period, of which the final four went down in Cambodia. These F-100Ds were lost on 9 March 1970 (55-2890), 12 December 1970 (56-3132), 27 January 1971 (56-3197), 4 April 1971 (56-3120) and 15 April 1971 (56-2955). The last of these was the penultimate Super Sabre lost in combat in Southeast Asia.

Above: Parked at Phu Cat is a pair of Det. 1, 612th TFS aircraft. The following month the detachment officially became a squadron. The 'VS' codes were worn from 1969.

Below: Lucky Penny was assigned to the blue-tails of the 612th TFS late in the war. It is seen here carrying downward-ejecting submunition dispensers.

Right: The 612th TFS was best known as a Misty FAC unit, and one of its well-known aircraft was The Yellow Submarine, shown here while visiting Cam Ranh Bay.

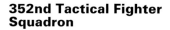

Above: Carrying SUU-7 dispensers, a pair of 614th TFS F-100Ds rests at Phu Cat in February 1971.

Right: The 35th TFW had good hangar facilities for maintenance. Here is a 614th TFS F-100F.

Detachment 1, 612th Tactical Fighter Squadron

15 May – 8 June 1967
14 April 1969 – 31 July 1971

Det. 1 612th TFS ('HS' tailcode) began as, in effect, a headquarters squadron situated at Phan Rang and flying F-100Fs belonging to other squadrons at that base. The detachment became a full squadron in all but name when it moved to Phu Cat on 8 June 1967 and commenced Misty FAC operations. On 14 April 1969, still a squadron in all but name, the detachment returned to Phan Rang with 'VS' codes.

Det. 1 612th TFS lost an F-100D (55-2895) on 23 August 1969 and another (55-3512) on 12 September 1969, both in South Vietnam. The Vietnam War's final combat losses for the 612th TFS detachment were F-100Ds on 10 February 1970 (55-3585), 21 August 1970 (56-3435) and 16 September 1970 (55-3806). The first of these was hit in South Vietnam and crashed at sea, the second went down in South Vietnam, and the third was hit in Cambodia and went down at sea.

When Misty FAC operations ended in the summer of 1970, the two-seat Super Sabre crews had logged 21,000 combat hours. Their mission was taken over by Wolf FAC (F-4Ds from Ubon), Tiger FAC (F-4Es from Korat), and Stormy FAC (F-4Ds from Da Nang) Phantom IIs.

The detachment officially became the 612th TFS on 15 March 1971. Like the rest of the F-100 operation at Phan Rang, it ended its role in Southeast Asia on 31 July 1971.

614th Tactical Fighter Squadron

18 September 1966 – 31 July 1971

The 'Lucky Devils' became part of the 35th TFW when the latter wing took over Phan Rang on 10 October 1966. The squadron's first combat loss occurred on 26 October 1966 when an F-100D (56-3167) was claimed by gunfire in South Vietnam. Another (56-3431) went down on 16 November 1966.

A 614th TFS F-100D (56-2927) was hit by gunfire over South Vietnam on 19 February 1967 and was lost at sea. The squadron lost yet another F-100D (55-2912) on 19 March 1967. Following almost a year without a loss, the squadron had another F-100F (56-3959) shot down over South Vietnam on 17 February 1968. An F-100D (56-3152) was shot down over North Vietnam on 23 March 1968. The next casualty for the 614th TFS was an F-100F (58-1226) downed north of the 17th Parallel on 5 July 1968. Six months later, on 24 January 1969, the squadron lost another F-100F (56-3731) on a mission in the south.

On 3 June 1969 the squadron lost an F-100D (55-3790) in the south. On 26 June 1969 another 614th TFS F-100D (55-3516) was hit over South Vietnam and crashed at sea. And on 8 August 1969, the squadron lost another F-100D (55-3581) in the south. The 614th TFS lost an F-100D (55-3803) on 29 May 1970 and another (56-3418) on 12 March 1971, both in South Vietnam.

In February/March 1971, the 614th TFS deployed temporarily to Phu Cat to bolster warplanes stationed there during a Viet Cong influx around the airfield. Upon its return to Phan Rang, the 614th TFS suffered its final two combat losses of the war: an F-100D (56-2937) in South Vietnam on 11 April 1971 and another (55-3749) in Cambodia two days later on 13 April 1971. Like the other squadrons at Phan Rang, the 614th wrapped up its war on 31 July 1971.

Carrying a load of four Mk 82 bombs, a 614th TFS aircraft flies over the base at Phan Rang before heading out for its target area.

615th Tactical Fighter Squadron

16 July 1966 – 31 July 1971

The 615th TFS ('VZ' tailcode) had already been blooded in early, pre-emptive action over Laos (see entry for Da Nang) when it began operations at Phan Rang, where it initially was part of the 366th TFW beginning 16 July 1966. Here the squadron lost an F-100D (55-3789) to ground fire on 25 July 1966 and another (56-2956) four days later on 29 July 1966. The squadron lost another F-100D (56-3071) on 13 September 1966. With the change in combat wing designation at Phan Rang, the squadron became part of the 35th TFW on 10 October 1966.

A pair of F-100Ds from the 615th TFS taxis for the Phan Rang runway in 1971, each carrying four cluster bomb dispensers.

Above: Start-up was accompanied by clouds of smoke. This 615th TFS aircraft carries the 90th TFS insignia. Note the nose-mounted RWR.

Below: Photographed in 1968, this 615th TFS aircraft carries a full load of four unfinned BLU-27 napalm tanks for a short-range mission.

Showing clear signs of battle damage repair, a 120th F-100C is armed with M117 bombs.

The 615th TFS lost an F-100F (56-4002) over South Vietnam on 1 July 1967. After months without another loss, Viet Cong gunfire claimed a 'VZ'-coded F-100D (55-2914) on 18 June 1968. On 9 September 1968, the squadron lost another F-100D (56-3446) in South Vietnam. Another F-100D (56-2935) went down in South Vietnam a week later on 16 September 1968. Nearly four months elapsed before the squadron had yet another F-100D (55-3704) shot down on 20 January 1969 and another (56-3150) the next day, 21 January 1969, both in South Vietnam. On 25 March 1969, a 615th TFS F-100D (56-2960) was shot down in South Vietnam, and one (56-3069) was lost in the south on 14 October 1969.

The busy 615th sustained three losses during 1970-71 as F-100 operations wound down. These included an F-100D in Laos on 9 March 1970 (56-3384), another in South Vietnam on 3 July 1970 (55-2943) and finally the very last Super Sabre to be lost in the years of Southeast Asia fighting, another F-100D (55-3550) on 28 April 1971.

The 615th TFS ended its role at Phan Rang on 31 July 1971.

120th Tactical Fighter Squadron

April 1968 – 11 April 1969

The 120th TFS, Colorado ANG ('VS' tailcode) was activated on 26 January 1968, three days after the seizure of the spy ship USS *Pueblo* (AGER-2) by North Korea created a threat of a second major war erupting in Asia – coinciding with the Tet Offensive in Vietnam.

The 120th, commanded by Lieutenant Colonel Robert Cherry, claims to be the first ANG organisation ever to be called to combat as a unit. In April, the squadron deployed to Phan Rang with 22 F-100Cs. This move preceded by two weeks deployment of Iowa's 174th TFS to Phu Cat and of New Mexico's 188th TFS to Tuy Hoa.

The first ground attack against Phan Rang by Viet Cong sappers occurred the night of the Colorado unit's arrival in Vietnam. The Guardsmen found themselves dodging bullets while ducking jeers from active-duty Air Force people, who called them F.A.N.G.s (F***ing Air National Guardsmen) or R.A.M.s (Rear Area MotherF***ers). The insults had little impact on a very experienced group

consisting of, in the words of Colonel Jack Wilhite, "22 airline pilots, three Air Guard technicians, and one struggling lawyer – all there because we wanted to be." The total complement was 21 officers and 345 enlisted men; since the latter figure far exceeded the 152 enlisted airmen routine for an active-duty squadron, many of the Coloradans were farmed out to wing support elements. Needless to say, 120th members seized hold of the taunting acronyms and referred to their airfield as FANG RAM Air Base.

The 120th flew difficult air-to-ground missions with considerable success and without a loss for nearly a year. Combat sorties began five days after arrival. On 29 December 1968, the squadron lost an F-100C (54-1973) but not its pilot. On 27 March 1969, Major Clyde Seiler became the squadron's first casualty, when his F-100C (54-1897) was downed by Viet Cong gunfire. A fellow Guardsman remembers, "We knew where Clyde went down but the area was completely controlled by the VC. It was a year before US forces could get in there and pick his body up." A week later, the 120th suffered its only other combat death when Captain Perry Jefferson failed to return from am observation mission in an O-1 Bird Dog.

The only problem that affected squadron operations was outside the control of the 120th or, for that matter, of any other F-100

Photographed in the US shortly after its return from Vietnam, Mumble Machine, a 120th F-100C, still carries its 'VS' tailcode.

unit in South Vietnam. Beginning in November 1968, the 120th began sending its aircraft – typically, three to four at a time – to Taiwan for replacement of the wing centre-section structure assembly, a modification that took the aircraft out of action for three weeks. But when they came back, their new wing centre-sections permitted the increase of their maximum limit in pullouts from 6 to 7.33 g. Before the modification programme, the squadron was averaging 24 combat sorties a day, a rate of about 1.1 sorties per aircraft, somewhat higher than the wing average. During the modification programme, a typical day saw the 120th flying 10 pre-planned missions and four from the alert pad, for a total of 14

The 120th flew more than 10,000 hours, including 5,905 combat missions. Its final mission came on 8 April 1969. According to number crunchers, the 120th TFS had delivered 14.3 million lb of bombs, 5.6 million lb of napalm, 423,000 rockets, 227,070 lb of cluster bombs, and 1.8 million rounds of 20-mm ammunition. On 11 April 1969, the squadron began returning to Colorado to revert to ANG status.

Phu Cat AB, South Vietnam

Phu Cat was located on flat, sandy ground along the coastal highway 20 miles (32 km) north of Qui Nhon and due west of Pleiku. It was built by the USAF for its exclusive use. Its new concrete runway was 10,000 ft (3048 m) in length and had a parallel taxiway. Covered and open aircraft revetments were located on asphalt and aluminium matting aprons which housed F-100s. A POL (petroleum, oil, lubricant) pipeline laid from the coast to Phu Cat could not be used because of sabotage and theft.

The 37th TFW was the combat wing at Phu Cat. In April 1969, the F-100 squadrons at Phu Cat began phasing out. On 13 April

1969, Det. 1 612th TFS moved to Phan Rang to become part of the 35th TFW. The 174th TFS returned to its status as an Iowa Air National Guard squadron. The 416th TFS moved to Tuy Hoa to become part of the 31st TFW. As for the base itself, Phu Cat continued to operate after the F-100s were gone. The base reverted to the Vietnamese air force in 1971 and was taken over by advancing North Vietnamese forces on 31 March 1975.

37th Tactical Fighter Wing

1 March 1967 – 31 March 1970

The 37th TFW was initially a Combat Support Group and was activated as a TFW

Left and below: The 416th TFS 'Silver Knights' served with the 37th TFW at Phu Cat for two of the war's toughest years. The squadron lost at least 13 aircraft to groundfire during this period.

on 1 March 1967. Personnel for the wing headquarters and tactical components were in transit from the United States and elsewhere, and actual operations did not begin until mid-April 1967. Its initial unit was the 416th TFS. It later gained the 355th TFS and, when Detachment 1 of the 612th TFS became a full squadron ('HS' tailcode), on 8 June 1967, it too was assigned to the 37th.

Wing commanders included Colonel Raymond C. Lee (from 6 May 1967) and Colonel Edwin A. Schneider (from 15 May 1967). Colonel LeRoy J. Manor, the 37th TFW wing commander (from 15 May 1968), went on to command the Son Tay raid (a commando effort aimed at freeing US prisoners of war) and retired at three-star rank. The wing's final combat commander was Colonel Harry B. Trimble (from 1 May 1969).

355th Tactical Fighter Squadron

3 February 1968 – 15 May 1969

The 355th TFS ('HP' tailcode, blue squadron colour) was apparently the very last Super Sabre squadron to join the fray in Southeast Asia. The squadron was 'attached' to the

The 416th served at Da Nang and Tan Son Nhut before joining the 37th TFW at Phu Cat.

37th TFW at Phu Cat from 3 February 1968 to 4 July 1968, and 'assigned' from 5 July 1968. The 355th TFS experienced its first combat loss, an F-100D (56-3261), on a mission into Laos on 25 February 1968. The squadron lost an F-100F (56-3784) in North Vietnam, the first 'Hun' to go down north of the 17th Parallel, on 18 March 1968.

As the year of the Tet Offensive unfolded, the 355th TFS suffered the loss of another F-100D (56-2905) on 21 July 1968, plus an F-100F (56-3834) on 17 August 1968 and another F-100F (56-3772) on 10 September 1968, both in South Vietnam. The July and September losses were in the south; the August casualty was hit up north and crashed at sea. Five months later, the 355th lost an F-100F (56-3886) which was hit over Laos and went down at sea.

On 5 March 1969, a 355th TFS F-100D (56-3174) was shot down on a mission in South Vietnam. The squadron ended its stay at Phu Cat on 15 May 1969 (at which time it moved to Tuy Hoa to become part of the 31st TFW).

416th Tactical Fighter Squadron

15 April 1967 – 27 May 1969
The 416th TFS 'Silver Knights' ('HE' tailcode), the most-travelled 'Hun' squadron of the era, served at Phu Cat as a component of the 37th TFW. The first combat loss for the 'Knights' at Phu Cat was an F-100D (55-3766) shot down over South Vietnam on 6 June 1967. On 8 November 1967, a squadron F-100F (56-3764) was hit by gunfire over North Vietnam and crashed at sea.

The 416th TFS had an F-100D (55-3606) shot down over North Vietnam on 20 March 1968. Further losses included an F-100F (56-3839) apparently in Laos on 7 April 1968, and an F-100D (56-2949) over South Vietnam on 17 April 1968. Another air-to-ground sortie in support of friendly forces battling the Viet Cong resulted in the loss of a 416th TFS F-100D (55-3536) on 25 June 1968. The squadron lost an F-100F (56-3775) over Laos on 20 November 1968. One month later, a 416th TFS F-100D (56-2968) was hit over Laos and went down at sea.

A 416th TFS F-100D (55-3562) was shot down in Laos on 3 February 1969. Ten weeks later, on 22 April 1969, an F-100D (55-3637) was shot down in Laos. Just days later, on 30 April 1969, the 416th TFS lost another F-100D (56-3075) to ground fire in South Vietnam. The squadron's losses continued with an F-100F (56-3734) on 9 August 1969 and another (56-3332) on 10 December 1969, both in Laos.

In May 1969, the 416th TFS began transferring from Phu Cat to Tuy Hoa where it joined the 31st TFW to fill in for a departing Air National Guard squadron.

Det. 1, 612th Tactical Fighter Squadron

8 June 1967 – 13 April 1969
Commando Sabre, the programme name for the use of two-seat F-100Fs as high-speed FACs, began on 28 June 1967. Using the callsign MISTY from the Errol Garner song and commanded by Major George 'Bud' Day, F-100F FACs operated in high-threat areas where 'slow-mover' FACs might not survive. As the mission evolved, Misty FAC aircraft were flown by two fully qualified, experienced pilots. From one sortie to the next, pilots routinely shifted from one seat to the other. The standard warload for a Misty FAC mission was KAU-59A rocket pods on the outboard stations and 355-US gal (1344-litre) drop tanks on intermediate stations; a few F-100Fs carried special fore/aft camera pods mounted inboard of the inboard ordnance station. All pilots belonged to Detachment 1 of the 612th TFS but most Misty FAC aircraft carried the 'HE' tailcode of the 416th TFS, a situation which makes it impossible to correctly identify some F-100F actions in historical records.

On 26 August 1967, Day's F-100F (56-3954) was hit by ground fire on a Misty FAC mission over North Vietnam. Day ejected, was captured and tortured, escaped, and was captured again. His valour in resisting his captors is not part of the F-100 story but it is one of the great sagas of the war, and he was later awarded the Medal of Honor for courage as a prisoner. Command of the Misty FAC detachment passed to

Although Det. 1/612th TFS is known as a fast-FAC unit, it also operated F-100D single-seaters on standard attack missions.

Above: While flying from Phu Cat, Det. 1/612th TFS used the 'HS' tailcode for its Misty FAC missions.

Lieutenant Colonel Alonzo W. Groves. The fast-moving Misty FAC took on new volunteers from other Super Sabre units, among them Major Merrill A. 'Tony' McPeak and Captain Ronald R. Fogleman. McPeak later became operations officer, then commander, of the Misty FAC detachment.

The record of losses in Southeast Asia shows a 612th TFS F-100D (56-2965) from Phu Cat struck by gunfire on a combat mission over South Vietnam and lost at sea on 21 October 1967. Another 612th TFS F-100F (56-4005) is listed as having been lost on 20 December 1967. Likewise, another F-100F (56-3878) on 22 December 1967. A 612th TFS F-100D (55-3619) was lost on 7 January 1968. Punishing air-to-ground missions in South Vietnam went on, through the Tet Offensive period early in the year, without another 612th TFS loss until 14 July 1968, when an F-100D (55-3722) was batted out of the sky by Viet Cong gunfire.

Det. 1 612th TFS lost an F-100F (56-3865) in North Vietnam on 16 August 1968. Another F-100D (55-2921) was hit over South Vietnam on 23 October 1968, then lost at sea. On 16 December 1968, the 612th TFS lost an F-100D (55-2920) over South Vietnam. On 21 January 1969, a squadron F-100D (55-3513) was hit apparently in Laos, and lost at sea. On 10 March 1969, a 612th TFS F-100D (56-3380) was shot down in South Vietnam. On 12 January 1969, an F-100F (56-3995) was shot down by North Vietnamese forces in Laos.

The history of the US Air Force would have been quite different had the Viet Cong succeeded in shooting down a Misty FAC F-100F (58-6837) which flew a combat observation mission on 4 March 1969. In the F-100F that day were McPeak and Fogleman, the two men later to serve as USAF chief of staff during the 1990s (McPeak was USAF chief of staff from 3 October 1990 through 25 October 1994; Fogleman has held the post since 26 October 1994).

According to General William 'Spike' Momyer, who commanded Seventh Air Force in Saigon, Misty FAC sorties repeatedly pinpointed targets in the lower portion of North Vietnam. For years, the North Vietnamese never learned the purpose of the F-100Fs which prowled the lower area of the country, nor linked them to the precision-guided strikes which followed their appearance.

174th Tactical Fighter Squadron

May 1968 – May 1969
The 174th TFS Iowa ANG ('HA' tailcode), commanded by Lieutenant Colonel Gordon Young and equipped with 22 F-100C and F-100F models, was activated during the *Pueblo* crisis in Korea and found itself in Vietnam by the spring of 1968. Reporting to his leadership back home, Young noted that missions from Phu Cat were "especially difficult" because of the heavy concentration of gunfire in the region near the Demilitarized Zone. Included on the 174th roster were 11 airline pilots who, like all activated Guardsmen, gave up their civilian careers for what was to become a year of fighting. In their first 30 days, Young's pilots flew 563 combat missions each averaging 1.5 hours.

The 174th TFS lost three aircraft in combat. One pilot was killed. A ground mishap caused a second fatality. The first loss was also the first F-100C claimed in the conflict (54-2004), shot down in South Vietnam on 14 July 1968. Another F-100C (53-1765) followed on 27 September 1968, hit in South Vietnam but lost at sea. On 14 March 1969, a 174th TFS F-100C (53-1740) was shot down in South Vietnam.

174th aircraft wore a variety of nicknames, usually in small letters on the

This photograph of the 612th TFS Misty FAC/Commando Sabre pilots includes two future Air Force Chiefs of Staff: Ronald Fogleman (back row, third from left) and Merrill 'Tony' McPeak (back row, second from left). Also in the group are Wilbur Creech (back row, far left) who would head TAC, Leroy manor (back row, far right) who would lead the Son Tay prison raid, and Lacy Veach (front row, second from right) who would become a Shuttle astronaut.

nose: *Karen, Carol's Crisis, Corrine's Corrupter, Loyal Linda, Darling D.,* and *Patty's Pumpkin.*

During its year of combat flying from Phu Cat, the 174th expended 12.9 million lb of bombs, 3.0 million lb of napalm, 154 tons of rockets, 512,000 lb of cluster bombs, and 1,864,801 rounds of 20-mm ammunition.

The squadron completed its active service and returned to Sioux City on 14 May 1969.

A Misty FAC F-100F of the 612th TFS is seen at Phu Cat in early 1969. The nickname, 'Protester's Protector', reflected the opinion held by many USAF personnel at the time.

Republic XF-12 Rainbow
All the Fours

Republic's four-engined beauty was one of that sizeable band of aircraft which were developed late in World War II and which, by circumstance, were robbed of their rightful places in aviation history. The end of the conflict and the ensuing post-war austerity combined with the advent of the jet engine to deny the Rainbow its chance to shine as what must be, arguably, the ultimate piston-engined aircraft ever designed. In terms of performance, its vital statistics were firmly in the '4' category: 40,000-ft altitude, 4,000-mile range and over 450-mph top speed – a combination of figures unmatched by any other piston-powered machine.

Left: Lowery Brabham (left) and Oscar Hass pose in front of the first XR-12. They were the pilot and co-pilot respectively on the type's first flight. Brabham is better known as the first man to fly the P-47 Thunderbolt.

In 1943 the US Army Air Forces were faced with a daunting prospect in the Pacific theatre – how to obtain photographic intelligence of the Japanese heartland. During August the head of the USAAF, General H. H. Arnold, had submitted an 'Air Plan for the Defeat of Japan', which outlined the use of B-29s to pound Japan into submission. Under the codename Matterhorn, the plan would initially see the Superfortresses operating from bases in India and China, and subsequently from purpose-built bases in the Marianas Islands after they had been captured. The latter became a major strategic priority, as did the question of providing reconnaissance for the massive bomber force.

Although the United States and Commonwealth forces were slowly pushing the Japanese back across the Pacific and Southeast Asia, the bases available to the Americans were all well over 1,000 miles (1610 km) from Japan, and it would be many months before they had airfields close enough to launch the reconnaissance aircraft then in the inventory. Clearly, what was needed was a fast, high-flying camera platform with exceptional range. A request for proposals was issued to industry, stipulating two of the '4's, namely a 40,000-ft (12192-m) ceiling and 400-mph (644-km/h) top speed.

Republic Aviation, of Farmingdale, New York, was one of two companies to answer the call. The rival was Hughes Aircraft, whose proposal was a twin-engined aircraft with a configuration inspired by the Lockheed P-38. By contrast, Republic began work on a massive machine whose dimensions were not far short of those of the Boeing B-29. In March 1944 both manufacturers were awarded a contract for

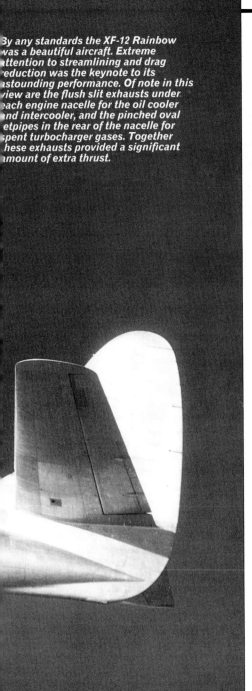

ended. Realistically, there was little chance of challenging Boeing, Convair and Douglas for large bomber and transport contracts, but the reconnaissance requirement was perfect: it was the first ever issued for a new aircraft dedicated to the mission (as opposed to a conversion of an existing fighter or bomber), leaving the field clear for new entrants into the large aircraft market. It was to be Republic's only major flirtation outside the fighter world.

Streamlining obsession

Heading Republic's design team was Alex Kartveli, well-known as the creator of the Thunderbolt and F-84. Hailed by many as an aerodynamic genius, he was obsessed by streamlining which, combined with enormous brute power, gave the new Rainbow both its shape and its performance. While Hughes chose a scaled-up version of his D-2 fighter design with two engines, Kartveli opted for four powerplants, allowing his team to create a much larger aircraft with considerable internal capacity for the carriage of photographic equipment or, it was eventually hoped, passengers. In examining the Rainbow as a technological marvel, it is difficult to find a starting place, so manifold were its strengths and innovations.

In its design 'culture' and basic configuration, the XF-12 design owed much to the B-29, which itself represented one of the biggest technological leaps ever achieved by one design. However, the Rainbow was built with performance as its priority, rather than load-carrying

The prototype XF-12 emerged from the Farmingdale factory in December 1945, the pressing need for its talents having long since passed. It should be remembered that the US forces were not expecting an invasion of Japan until 1946 at the earliest when production of the Rainbow was authorised.

capability. To start with, Kartveli and his team produced an almost perfect aerodynamic shape for the fuselage, which swelled gracefully from the shark-like nose to the central fuselage, and then tailed off to a point with a fineness ratio of nearly 10:1. Excrescences were kept to a minimum and, when the Rainbow eventually emerged, just a handful of radio aerials, an ADF loop antenna in a teardrop fairing and a shallow astrodome along the spine spoiled its lines. Construction was of a tough Dural alloy (75ST), maintaining Republic's reputation for strength, and the finish was of a very high standard, with flush riveting across the external surfaces.

With such a slick fuselage the vertical fin was huge out of necessity, but Republic produced an elegant elliptical shape also used to great effect on the F-84 Thunderjet. Moving aft, the profile of the fin actually started as a small fillet in line with the wing trailing edge, curving into the main upright portion before descending below and slightly behind the point of the tail-

As with most new aircraft types, the prototype Rainbow carried an air data instrumentation boom during its early flights. These showed the aircraft to have not only enormous performance potential, but no serious design flaws.

two prototypes, the Hughes design becoming the XF-11 and that from Republic the XF-12 Rainbow. In the interim, many B-29s were converted to F-13 (later redesignated RB-29) configuration with cameras, and in the event it was to be this aircraft which bore the brunt of US long-range reconnaissance operations, not only over Japan in the last year of World War II, but also for the first years of the Cold War and over Korea.

Republic had always been a fighter builder. From the corporation's roots in the Seversky company, through the wartime P-47, to the F-84 and F-105 of the post-war period, Republic's name was synonymous with big, tough, honest fighter aircraft. But in 1943/44 the company sought to diversify into large aircraft, no doubt with an eye towards the boom in civil transport expected once the war had

Shown to advantage in this view of ground running tests at Farmingdale are the leading-edge intakes for the engine accessories. These were very efficient, and removed the requirement for the drag-inducing inlets usually positioned above and below the engine cowlings.

cone, forming a small ventral fin. Owing to the small angular travel of just 6° 10' at rotation, a retractable tail bumper was mounted in the ventral fin. The dihedralled tailplane was mounted part-way up the fin to avoid turbulence from the wing.

At the other end of the Rainbow was an extensively glazed nose, but all was not what it seemed. The flight deck was situated in line with the row of small windows and quarterlights which wrapped round the top of the fuselage. Forward of this were two large Plexiglas curved panels (and associated panels underneath) which formed the streamlined shape and gave the pilots excellent visibility in most flight regimes. However, a key complaint voiced by B-29 pilots, who flew an aircraft which also featured curved windscreen panels, was that the reflections caused by the curvature when landing were at best distracting, and at worst dangerous, especially at night or in bad weather. Accordingly, Kartveli made the two upper panels retractable, able to slide down inside the lower portion of the nose to reveal a flat, angular and reflectionless windscreen immediately ahead of the pilots for landing.

Of high aspect ratio for aerodynamic efficiency, the tapered wings were of two-spar construction, set at 6° dihedral and with slightly rounded tips to confer benign stall characteris-

tics. Span was 129 ft 2 in (39.34 m). Well aware of the effects of compressibility at high transonic Mach numbers thanks to his work with fighters, Kartveli devised a new laminar-flow aerofoil section (Republic R-4). Another feature of previous fighter work was the setting of the wing in the lower-middle position on the fuselage so that the upper and lower joints were, in effect, at right angles to the fuselage. There was virtually no blending fillet around the joint, this configuration having earlier been proved to offer the least drag. Similarly, the engine nacelles were mid-set with no blending fairings.

Wing surfaces

Moveable surfaces on the wing included high aspect-ratio ailerons with tabs outboard, all surfaces having spring-feel servos to lighten stick loads. Three sections of flaps were located either side of, and between, the engine nacelles, the section between the outer nacelle and the

aileron being very small. Of double-slotted configuration, the powerful flaps provided significant extra lift. Although the Rainbow had a very high limiting Mach number of 0.8 (today's airliners cruise only slightly faster, at about M=0.84), this could easily be exceeded in a dive owing to the aircraft's 'slippery' contours. To avoid overstressing the airframe, speed brakes were fitted under the wing which were deployed automatically if the limiting speed was reached.

Part of the interspar area was given over to fuel, but the sections between the inner nacelle and the fuselage were used to house the mainwheels. Faced with a wheel well constrained by the thickness of the wing, Kartveli had no alternative but to use massive single mainwheels. Each wheel, some 5 ft 10 in (1.78 m) in diameter, carried a large door on the strut, the well being covered by a wing-mounted inner door. The twin-wheel nose unit retracted backwards into a bay covered by two sets of double doors. In addition to the wing tanks, fuel was held in the lower fuselage, total internal capacity being 5,505 US gal (20839 litres). Each nacelle contained an oil tank of 61 US gal (231 litres) capacity.

Searching for a suitable powerplant, both Republic and Hughes settled on Pratt & Whitney's new R-4360 Wasp Major, rated ini-

Left: The glazed nose of the XF-12 included upper sliding panels which reduced glare for the pilots on landing. The flight deck was protected by a flat-plate windscreen behind the curved panels.

Above and right: Each giant nacelle was built with as few excrescences as possible, and at its greatest diameter was barely wider than the engine itself. Noticeable are the sliding ring flaps at the rear of the cowling for dumping air, a function normally performed by cooling gills.

Above: In its day the XF-12 was, by a wide margin, the fastest four-engined aircraft in the world. The second aircraft made a famous coast-to-coast run, producing a continuous strip of film along the way.

Right: In landing configuration the XF-12 lost much of its elegance, thanks to the ungainly undercarriage. The nacelle design precluded the inclusion of the main undercarriage units, so that they had to be accommodated in the thin wing. This in turn demanded large single-wheel units.

tially at around 3,000 hp (2238 kW). Whereas most large radial engines had two rows each of nine cylinders, the R-4360 had four rows of seven. This had the advantage of massive power production with a small frontal area, but gave rise to cooling problems for the cylinders in the aft rows. In respect of the engine's configuration, the nickname 'corn-cob' was inevitably applied.

It was in the design of the propulsion system that Kartveli's team really excelled. Each nacelle was roughly the length of a P-47, and like the Thunderbolt most of the rear portion housed a mass of ducts for the complicated turbo supercharger system, yet its frontal cross-section was barely greater than that of the 'corn-cob' on the front. The streamlining was superb, with none

Captain William Elliot is seen nursing the first Rainbow on to Farmingdale's Runway 14, having lost the starboard undercarriage leg on the first landing attempt. The aircraft suffered relatively minor damage and was easily repaired and put back in the air once more.

of the auxiliary air intakes associated with standard installations. Large spinners enclosed the hub of the 16-ft 2-in (4.93-m) Curtiss propellers which, unusually for a piston engine, incorporated reverse pitch. Behind each prop was a very narrow annular intake for engine cooling air. To provide sufficient cooling for the four rows of cylinders, Republic designed a variable-speed fan at the front of the engine. This negated the need for drag-inducing cooling gills, allowing the Rainbow to have a sliding ring flap at the rear of the engine compartment to dump the cooling air, thereby retaining the streamlining under all flight conditions.

Also allowing the nacelles to be perfectly streamlined was the use of inlets in the wing leading edge, these providing air for the oil coolers and intercoolers. The slot inlets were very efficient, a figure of 98 per cent having been quoted for pressure recovery. Air from the slots was ducted to the oil coolers and intercoolers, and was dumped overboard through flush slit exhausts mounted in tandem in the bottom of the nacelle. These exhausts were angled backwards to extract a few horsepower from the heated waste air.

Jet thrust

More radical was the turbo supercharger arrangement in the rear of the nacelle. Two General Electric BM-4-5 units were fitted, although it was possible to engage only one in lower cruise settings. Spent exhaust gases from the turbines were ejected through a pinched oval jetpipe in the rear of the nacelle, providing extra thrust. In addition, exhaust gases which were not required by the supercharger's turbine, and which in other installations were merely dumped overboard, were also fed to the jetpipe. Approximately 250-300 hp (186-224 kW) extra thrust was recovered by this complex but efficient arrangement, raising the overall output of the R-4360-31 to 3,500 hp (2611 kW).

Farmingdale was buzzing in the first months of 1945. Thunderbolts were pouring from the production line and, surrounded by a veil of secrecy, the XF-12 was taking shape rapidly. Although the war in Europe was reaching the

Beyond the Frontiers

end game, that in the Pacific theatre seemed far from over, and an initial order for 20 F-12s was expected. Of course, no-one outside of the inner sanctum of government or the secret township of Los Alamos knew of the strangely titled Manhattan Engineer District Project, which was racing to produce the ultimate weapon which would, in effect, cut many months off the duration of the conflict with Japan. With two telling blows in early August, the A-bombs were unleashed on Hiroshima and Nagasaki, effectively concluding the war.

For Republic, the atomic bombs and the subsequent surrender also robbed the XF-12 of the mission for which it had been primarily designed: strategic reconnaissance of Japan. Hopes remained high for the type, for with peace would surely come a surge in commercial air transport. USAAF interest in the type did not end either, for, as the dust from the conflict settled, so the Soviet Union began to be eyed with ever greater mistrust.

However, with Japan defeated, the urgency and vigour with which the XF-12 programme had been pursued in its first 18 months waned considerably, and in the immediate post-war era there would be precious little funding for a highly specialised and expensive programme. Despite immediate assurances gained from the USAAF as to their continued commitment to the type, the first signs had appeared that there was not a crock of gold at the end of this particular rainbow.

Construction of the prototype (44-91002) continued, and it was rolled out in December 1945. In the same month, Republic had

The C-54 on the Wright Field ramp lends some scale to the Rainbow. It was the cheap post-war availability of the Douglas aircraft and of the Lockheed Constellation which effectively killed the Rainbow's chance of receiving orders for a commercial version.

received the USAAF's approval for discussions to begin with commercial operators. Pan Am's charismatic president Juan Trippe was the first to see the enormous potential of the sleek type. The Rainbow offered an unbeatable flight time of seven hours on the prestigious Los Angeles-New York service, and could fly New York-London non-stop in nine. Development of the commercial model was undertaken under the designation RC-2 (Republic Commercial Two) Rainbow.

Throughout January 1946 the Republic team carried out extensive ground tests on the completed prototype, receiving the all-clear for a first flight at the end of the month. On 4 February, 44-91002 lifted off for a successful maiden flight, crewed by Lowery Brabham (who had earlier performed the first flight of the P-47) as pilot, Oscar 'Bud' Hass in the right-hand seat and James Creamer as flight engineer. No major problems were encountered during initial flight trials, although the 'corn-cob' engines proved troublesome. This first aircraft was a true prototype insofar as it was heavily instrumented and did not carry any operational equipment.

Commercial orders

Despite Pan Am's initial interest, it was American Airlines which was the launch airline for the type, placing an order for 20 soon after the first flight. Pan Am swiftly followed suit with an order for six and an option for a further 12. The RC-2 was based very closely on the XF-12, but was configured to carry 46 passengers and a crew of seven, with the necessary cabin windows added. It was to have been slightly longer, at 98 ft 9 in (30.10 m) as opposed to the military model at 93 ft 9½ in (28.59 m). The weight was increased from the F-12's normal take-off weight of 101,400 lb (45995 kg) to 116,500 lb (52844 kg). The RC-

2 featured only one turbo-supercharger in each nacelle instead of the XF-12's two, and consequently had lower performance. Nonetheless, its projected cruise speed at 40,000 ft (12192 m) of over 400 mph (644 km/h) over a range (with reserves) estimated at 3,450 miles (5552 km) was nothing short of phenomenal, and its piston-engined rivals produced by Boeing, Douglas and Lockheed could not hope to match these figures.

As with many so-called 'foregone conclusions', the dramatic upsurge in commercial aviation never materialised, replaced in its stead by an era of considerable austerity. In such a climate, speed was seen as an unaffordable luxury while the airlines capitalised on the cheap availability of the DC-4 and Constellation. Subsequent post-war developments of these types were not only cheap but capacious – two adjectives which could not be applied to the Rainbow airliner. Faced with gloomy passenger revenue forecasts, American cancelled its order in February 1947 to continue its low-risk purchases of larger, slower aircraft with appreciably lower acquisition and operating costs.

The end of the airliner

By this time Republic had completed some 90 per cent of the tooling for the RC-2, and was able to recover some of its investment by way of penalty clauses. The six-aircraft Pan Am order was still intact, but the manufacturer had little choice but to raise the price to recoup some of its development costs, which had initially been spread across an order book of 26. Pan Am could not shoulder the additional burden, and reluctantly cancelled its order. This ended the RC-2's career before work had started on a single aircraft, and was highly embarrassing for Pan Am, which had embarked on a major promotion campaign featuring the Rainbow as its new flagship.

With little immediacy attending the barely-alive military programme, flight trials continued at a leisurely pace and it was more than a year before the prototype left Farmingdale for Wright Field, Ohio, where the Air Force began its service trials programme in June 1947. Despite the teething troubles associated with the R-4360, the Rainbow lived up to all its expectations with regard to performance.

A take-off run of 4,260 ft (1298 m) at the normal loaded weight of 101,400 lb (45995 kg) could be achieved and the initial climb rate was a spirited 2,200 ft (670 m) per minute. Service ceiling was set at 42,000 ft (12800 m) with a combat weight of 95,600 lb (43364 kg), and the XF-12 could fly a 1,755-mile (2824-km) radius mission at an average speed of 386 mph (621 km/h) with reserves, this distance being covered in just over nine hours. Total range was in excess of 4,000 miles (6437 km). In terms of speed, the Rainbow achieved an outstanding 462 mph (743 km/h) – making it the fastest four-engined piston-powered aircraft ever. Combined with the very high ceiling, the speed would theoretically allow the Rainbow to operate with impunity over enemy territory. Once back on the ground, the reverse-pitch feature ensured a commendably short landing run.

Camera installation

The R-12 would have carried a comprehensive suite of cameras for its strategic reconnaissance mission, augmented by electronic warfare equipment. The full camera system was fitted to the second prototype.

Right: This is the camera installation and operator's position in the rear of the cabin. The cameras were easily accessible for inflight repair and for the changing of lenses and film magazines.

Above: This was the main vertical camera. Between it and the camera operator's station was a sighting port for precise operation of the cameras.

Below: The split-vertical station had two cameras canted slightly inwards. Visible behind is the darkroom where the film was stored and processed.

Below: This is the camera control panel at the navigator's station. It also had photo-flash bomb controls.

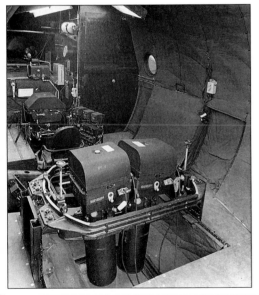

Above: The trimetrogon station had three cameras which exposed simultaneously to produce a combined panoramic image. Here only two of the cameras are fitted.

In its handling, the Rainbow was a thrill for any pilot accustomed to other four-engined aircraft. Many talked of "fighter-like handling", and it was certainly manoeuvrable and responsive at high altitude. The massive installed power allowed for aggressive manoeuvres, but also conferred a large safety margin if an engine was lost. Indeed, the Wright tests proved that the Rainbow could hold altitude and 150 mph (240 km/h) on the power of just one Wasp Major.

That power was called into use during an early flight, when Captain William Elliot was attempting a maximum-weight, minimum-length landing. He hit the runway so hard that the right main undercarriage was torn off. Elliot immediately applied full power and miraculously managed to pull the XF-12 away from the runway without the propellers striking the ground. After several anxious hours circling to

burn off fuel, Elliot then nursed the Rainbow back on to the ground at Farmingdale for a soft two-wheel landing which resulted in relatively minor damage to the right outer wing and one engine.

Following repair at Farmingdale, the aircraft returned to Wright Field only to be damaged again. This time a careless tow-truck driver failed to guide the aircraft's fin through a cut-out notch which was provided above the hangar door for the necessary clearance, causing considerable, yet repairable, damage.

Mission-capable prototype

Like the prototype, the second XF-12 was delayed considerably due to the low urgency attached to the Rainbow programme and it was not until 12 August 1947 that 44-91003 took to the air, piloted by 'Bud' Hass with Pete Collins as co-pilot and James Creamer again as flight

engineer. This aircraft was fitted out from the start with a fully representative equipment and interior fit, which catered for a standard crew of seven, although the capacious cabin could accommodate more reconnaissance specialists and more equipment if required. Behind the two pilots were stations for the flight engineer and navigator, while in the main cabin were stations for three mission specialists. The cabin was fully pressurised, holding an equivalent 10,000-ft (3050-m) altitude pressure at the maximum operating height above 40,000 ft (12192 m).

A comprehensive navigation and communications suite was fitted, including a bombing radar in a fully retractable radome under the belly. Although no record can be found, it is reasonable to assume that operational F-12As would have carried the extensive suite of electronic warfare and jamming equipment which

The second aircraft differed little externally from the first, but was fully equipped inside. On its intended mission the R-12 would have carried a basic crew of five, to which extra mission specialists could be added as required.

was fitted to some B-29s. The main camera equipment was carried in the rear of the cabin.

Three camera stations were provided. At the front was the vertical station, which usually mounted a large, long focal-length camera. The centre station was for the trimetrogon installation, which consisted of three cameras mounted in a transverse fan, each peering through a separate window. Frames were exposed simultaneously, and the cameras were arranged so that the three frames could be joined together to form a continuous horizon-to-horizon image, a function later handled by a single optical bar camera. The aft camera station was occupied by the split-vertical, which utilised two cameras peering downwards but canted slightly toward each other. By combining simultaneous frames from each camera a rudimentary three-dimensional image was formed.

Easy access

All of the camera stations were easily accessible in flight thanks to the low cabin floor, and film canister changes or camera maintenance could be undertaken from either a standing or kneeling position. Between the vertical and trimetrogon stations was a dedicated camera operator's station, consisting of a forward-facing seat on the centreline and a console mounted to the right. This console was repeated at the navigator's station. Between the camera operator's knees was a small porthole which could mount a sight for precise operation of the vertical camera.

To provide for night photography, the XF-12 was fitted with a small stores bay forward of the vertical camera which could hold 18 700,000-candlepower AN/M-46 photo-flash bombs, held either side of a central vertical rack. Instead of conventional outward-opening bay doors, which would inflict a severe drag penalty, the Rainbow had tight-tolerance flush fitting doors which slid up inside the fuselage when the bay was open. Similarly, the five camera ports (three along the centreline and two in the lower sides of the fuselage for the outer trimetrogon cameras) were fitted with flush sliding doors. When opened, each revealed a pane of optically flat glass.

Onboard processing

One problem which had dogged reconnaissance aircraft throughout history was the timeliness of the intelligence they had gathered. Visual sightings could be communicated by radio, but the photographic 'take' remained undeveloped in its canisters until the aircraft had returned to base. It then had to be processed and analysed before the material gathered could be regarded as useful intelligence; the results were available many hours after the photographs had been taken, especially on the type of long-range operations for which the XF-12 was designed. In a fluid situation, such delays could prove costly.

Although a far cry from today's near real-time digital datalinks and satellite relays, the Rainbow did attend to this problem by the simple expedient of providing an onboard darkroom. Located amidships on the starboard side of the cabin, the darkroom provided safe storage for film canisters in addition to full film processing capacity. This would have allowed the 'take' to be processed during the long return leg from the operational area, ready for immediate dispatch on the aircraft's landing. To further speed the intelligence process, reconnaissance specialists could be carried onboard to analyse the 'take' while still in the air. On an important long-range mission, the Rainbow's crew could effectively turn raw, undeveloped film into interpreted and prioritised military intelligence which could reach the hands of the generals in the time the aircraft took to reach a friendly airfield.

Owing to the considerable time lag between the two prototypes, the No. 1 aircraft had performed most of the aerodynamic and structural tests, so the No. 2 machine was assigned to equipment trials. After a short wringing out by the manufacturer it transferred to the Wright Field photo section. In late 1947 an order for six production F-12As was placed. During its tenure at the Ohio base, it was used for a headline-making coast-to-coast run which it undertook in less than six hours, producing a continuous photographic strip along the route. In October 1948 it transferred to Eglin AFB, Florida for operational evaluation by the Photo Test Squadron of the 3200th Proof Test Group. By then, the Rainbow had been redesignated the XR-12, the 'F' for 'Foto' classification having been replaced by 'R' for 'Reconnaissance'.

At this point in time the Rainbow was still eagerly awaited by the reconnaissance community, who were getting by with conversions of fighter and bomber types: the RB-29 offered the range but not the performance; the RP-80

The first Rainbow was used for flight testing throughout its short career. It is seen here in 1948, back at Republic's Farmingdale factory, shortly before it was dispatched to Aberdeen Proving Grounds for use as a gunnery target.

had the speed but not the range. In late 1948 the XR-12 still offered the best available platform for the job, and it caused considerable interest when it arrived at Eglin. With the Rainbow now finally in the hands of the customer, there seemed an outside chance that the type might justify the faith that Republic had placed in it.

Loss of the Rainbow

Perhaps inevitably, fate dealt its cruel blow within a few days of the aircraft's arrival. On its second flight from Eglin, the second Rainbow was lost while the crew were practising go-arounds after a photo run. During the final climb-out, some instruments for No. 2 began reading strangely, yet the engine was still producing full power. Instrument anomalies had been noted in the Rainbow before, and the flight engineer could not pinpoint any problem. Just as he reported this to the pilots, the No. 2 engine exploded, buffeting the aircraft and sending it into a diving left bank. Despite the efforts of both pilots the Rainbow would not recover, so the commander rang the 'Bail Out' alarm bell. With some effort the crew released the door and six bailed out. The seventh crewman refused to jump, and rode the Rainbow to a watery end in the Gulf of Mexico.

With the loss of the second XR-12, the programme came to an abrupt end. Soon after the XR-12 crash the remaining rival Hughes XR-11 arrived at Eglin, and despite showing impressive high-altitude performance, was inferior to the Rainbow in terms of versatility, handling, operability and speed. Meanwhile, the Air Force soldiered on with the RB-29 as its long-range reconnaissance aircraft, although jets began to assume an ever-greater burden on shorter-range missions. It was not until the service entry of the mixed-powerplant RB-36D in 1950 that the USAF strategic reconnaissance fleet had an aircraft which could rival the XR-12's performance.

Republic returned to its core business of building tough fighter-bombers, severely chastened by its one attempt to move into the large aircraft market. As if to rub salt into an already deep and painful wound, the first prototype Rainbow was to suffer perhaps the most ignominious fate that could befall such a beautiful and promising aircraft: it was taken to Aberdeen Proving Grounds in Maryland for use as a target, its perfect lines being reduced to a tangled mess by artillery fire. **David Donald**

Hughes XF-11: The Rival

Offered to meet the same specification, powered by the same engines and a close rival in the beauty stakes, the Hughes XF-11 might have been expected to look like the Rainbow, but the similarity ended with the opening statements. Howard Hughes' team of designers created an aircraft with exceptional looks and performance by taking a completely different avenue, basing the configuration on that of the Lockheed P-38, with an efficient wing mounting a tiny fuselage nacelle and two large booms which mounted both the tail surfaces and the engines.

Development of the XF-11 reached back to December 1939, when Hughes began a design study for a twin-boom warplane known as the D-2. Originally intended as a bomber, it subsequently became a long-range fighter, and was of Duramold (a moulded wood/plastic composite) construction. Hughes' fanatical secrecy surrounded the project, and although photographs were taken of the aircraft when it emerged, none have been published. With a span of about 60 ft (18.28 m), and powered by Pratt & Whitney R-2800-49 engines, the D-2 fighter was trucked to a rough wooden hangar on Harpers Dry Lake, California, for flight preparation.

With Howard Hughes at the controls, the D-2 made several high-speed taxi runs, including a few short airborne hops, before the first two full flights were undertaken on 20 June 1943. No record of it flying again has surfaced, but in 1944 it and its shelter were destroyed in a fire. Hughes workers swear that it was hit by a freak bolt of lightning from a clear blue sky, while more cynical observers have pointed to arson or malfunctioning equipment. The truth will probably never be known, adding more mystique to the Hughes 'mystery ship'.

During the development of the D-2, there were several proposals for long-range reconnaissance platforms, and when the USAAF requirement was issued Hughes was well placed to offer a design based on the D-2, known as the D-5 (military designation F-11). The original configuration was based on the D-2 fighter, with cameras held

in the nose of the fuselage nacelle and in the capacious rear booms. However, when the aircraft was actually built it was much larger than the D-2, with a wing span of 101 ft (30.78 m). Power was provided by two 3,000-hp (2238-kW) Pratt & Whitney R-4360-37 engines driving then-novel contra-rotating propellers, and the construction was of metal. The engines had underslung intakes and conventional cooling gills. The huge laminar-flow wing had virtually no dihedral, and featured small ailerons and spoilers for roll control. This allowed the fitment of aileron-to-aileron flap surfaces, interrupted only by the tail booms, these giving a stalling speed of just 80 mph (129 km/h). The beautifully crafted central nacelle had a glazed nose and camera windows. Fuel was held mostly in the long tailbooms.

On the basis of its performance potential, and the need for a reconnaissance aircraft to prepare for the invasion of the Japanese mainland, orders were placed for two prototypes and 98 F-11 production aircraft. With the sudden ending of the war, the production order was cancelled, but construction of the prototypes continued (there were actually three airframes built, the second being used for ground tests).

Hughes took the first XF-11 aircraft (44-70155) aloft from Culver City airport on 7 July 1946, but disaster struck. The rear propeller on the starboard engine went into reverse pitch, blanking airflow from most of the wing. The aircraft crashed into a Los Angeles suburb, nearly costing Hughes his life.

After a long recovery, which some would argue was never completed, and against the orders of his doctors, Hughes flew the second flying prototype (44-70156) for the first time on 5 April 1947,

The first XF-11 is depicted before its fateful flight. The contra-rotating propellers were most distinctive.

the aircraft having reverted to conventional four-bladed propellers. Its huge and highly efficient wing combined with the massive power available to give the XF-11 exhilarating climb performance, and a maximum altitude of about 48,000 ft (14630 m). Handling at high altitude and high speed was good, but was sluggish low down owing to the inadequate ailerons.

In late 1948 the aircraft (by then redesignated XR-11) followed the second XR-12 to Eglin AFB, Florida, for USAF testing with the Photo Test Section. By the time it had arrived the Rainbow had crashed, allowing no chance for truly competitive evaluation. However, the XF-11 was found to be slower than the Rainbow. Further comparisons revealed that it was nearly twice as expensive, and to 'productionise' the aircraft would have incurred huge cost, as many of the parts were custom-built. It was not an easy aircraft to operate, particularly with regard to ground access to the cameras and film magazines. Furthermore, the tiny size of the fuselage nacelle allowed no room for any form of inflight film processing, and certainly ruled out any development for other roles. With the loss of the Rainbow, and the shortcomings of the Hughes rival, the USAF lost its last shred of interest in this class of airplane, and the XR-11 was passed to a ground training school at Sheppard AFB.

XF-11 No. 2 was completed with conventional propellers following the accident to No. 1. The camera window in the side of the nose was for the trimetrogon installation.

VULCAN

A beautiful craft by any standards, the Avro
Vulcan was conceived for a deadly mission:
nuclear bombing at the heart of the Soviet Union.
In this role it carried the UK's nuclear deterrent
burden for over a decade. When it finally went
into action in the twilight of its career, it was in a
very different scenario – attacking a runway 8,000
miles from its home base.

Delta Force

Carrying the markings of No. 44 Squadron, a Vulcan B.Mk 2 of the Waddington Wing crosses the threshold at its base. Still held in awe by any who saw it in its final years, the aircraft was a technological marvel at the time of its debut. Optimised for high-altitude flight, where the bomber's handling and manoeuvrability were the stuff of legend, the Vulcan took the transition to low-level operations easily within its stride.

Among people who refuse to accept that an aircraft is merely a lump of aluminium bent into shape and filled with wires, there is a consensus of opinion that the Vulcan is high on the all-time list of the world's most beautiful aircraft. Despite a deadly *raison d'être*, aviation's first production delta-winged bomber charmed its crews with almost viceless handling, and beguiled air show crowds when demonstrating what seemed to be fighter-like manoeuvrability. As one of the trio of 'V-bombers' which symbolised Britain's status as a global power, the Vulcan was the final link in an unbroken chain of 'heavies' stretching back to the Handley Pages of World War I. A chapter of RAF history begun in 1918 with the first ventures in strategic attack from the air by Trenchard's Independent Force had its closing paragraph written in the skies above a windswept group of islands in the South Atlantic during 1982.

The Falklands War was a short, though triumphant,

valediction for the Vulcan – and not inappropriate, considering the varied career enjoyed by the aircraft which the RAF knew as the 'Tin Triangle' and its cousins in USAF Strategic Air Command dubbed the 'Aloominum Overcast'. Having begun in the role of high-level, free-fall nuclear attack, the Vulcan converted in part to stand-off missiles, then went low level into a very different operational scenario. The advent of a sea-based deterrent failed to dislodge the popular – if ageing – manned bomber, which branched out into maritime radar reconnaissance as well as providing a theatre-nuclear capability for NATO and CENTO. Epic long-range conventional bombing sorties almost literally on the delivery flight to the scrapyard, and a disfiguring conversion to aerial tanker, were all taken in the Vulcan's stride.

Combat missions were almost four decades in the future when, in May 1944, a study paper titled 'Future Bomber Requirements' was circulated in the Air Ministry. The

key to successful strategic attack with minimal casualties was identified by the paper as superiority over attacking fighters – such as that gained by the de Havilland Mosquito – and emphasis was accordingly placed on 'speed, height and evasive manoeuvre for protection against interception'. Long range and a weighty bomb load were viewed as equally important, and it was clear that the new jet engine, though still in its infancy, offered the best method of achieving these goals.

By 1946, bomber needs had crystallised into two Air Staff Requirements. Operational Requirement 229 covered a medium-range aircraft weighing up to 100,000 lb (45359 kg), and a more ambitious OR 230 stipulated a limit of 200,000 lb (90719 kg) for a longer-range machine. After some revision – not least to take into account Britain's plans for acquisition of the atomic weapon – OR 229 referred to carriage of a single 10,000-lb (4536-kg) 'special bomb' to a target 1,500 nm (1724 miles/2775 km) distant, or a still-air range of 3,350 nm (3855 miles/6504 km). OR 230 looked for 4,350 nm (5006 miles/8056 km) at 500 kt (575 mph; 926 km/h) with the same load, or a conventional cargo of 30,000 lb (13608 kg) over shorter distances. Both aircraft were to have a crew of five and no defensive guns. Only for a few months during 1953 was there brief flirtation with the possibility of retrospective addition of rear-firing armament.

The Bomb

In these modern times, when a nuclear device can be fitted into an artillery shell, it is important to stress that the best guess in 1946 for the operational British atomic bomb was a casing 24 ft 2 in (7.37 m) long and 5 ft 0 in (1.52 m) at maximum diameter, with its centre of gravity 6 ft 8 in (2.03 m) from the nose. These parameters were specified in OR 1001, dated 9 August 1946, describing the bomb which eventually entered service as Blue Danube. Interestingly, despite the awesome potential of the nuclear weapon, requirements included a stipulation that the resultant aircraft should be capable of large-scale production in the event of war. It is easy to conclude that this was the result of an inability to comprehend that nuclear conflict is likely to be of very brief duration. Such a judgement would be hasty: options were being kept open for a protracted conventional conflict in which the A-bomb was not used for reasons of choice or unavailability. Inevitable linking of the atomic weapon and B.35/46 tends to overshadow the fact that the RAF still needed a new heavy bomber, even if Britain shunned nuclear weapons research. The only variable would have been the funds assigned to the aircraft programme in the absence of atomic weapons. In other words, 'The Bomb' and the bombers were complementary, not components of one all-or-nothing plan.

At a time when the Avro Lincoln was the hottest

This five-man crew from No. 83 Squadron walks away from its B.Mk 2 aircraft after a training mission. The V-force became the élite of the RAF during the late 1950s, so important was their mission.

Above: This unusual view of a Vulcan B.Mk 2MRR was caught by a Canberra PR.Mk 9 sneaking up behind. At its maximum operating altitude few aircraft could reach the Vulcan, but the same could not be said of anti-aircraft missiles.

property in Bomber Command, ORs 229 and 230 represented a challenge of unprecedented proportions to the aircraft industry. Confident of their ability to build war-winning aircraft, the aircraft designers still baulked at the exceptionally high demands of the requirements. Strangely, however, in spite of the well-worn phrase 'post-war austerity', Britain's newly-elected Labour government showed no outward sign of wavering in its commitment to build both an A-bomb and the means to carry it with precision to a defended target. This was, no doubt, because

From almost any angle the Vulcan presented a menacing image, and when armed with nuclear weapons reality more than matched perception. In the conventional role the bomber was limited by bomb bay restrictions to a relatively light load of 21,000 lb (9526 kg).

Avro Atlantic

In September 1952, shortly after the Vulcan prototype had flown, Avro announced it was developing an airliner version, named Type 722 Atlantic, based on the wing and powerplant of the bomber. The airliner could accommodate 94 passengers in a basic configuration, or 113 in a tourist layout. Both versions featured rear-facing seats (as was common practice on RAF transports) and had a central bar area. The aircraft was intended to cover sectors of up to 4,000 miles (6440 km) at cruising speeds of over Mach 0.9, and at altitudes in excess of 40,000 ft (12190 m). The programme got little further than this impressive model.

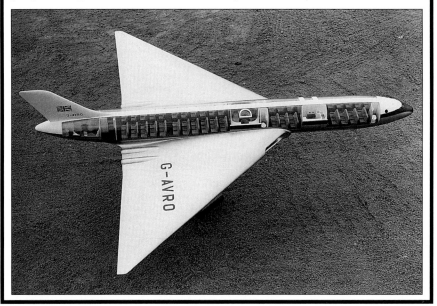

Above: VX790 was the 707B, a hasty concoction featuring the long, pointed nose of the high-speed 707A and the original 707 intake arrangement. Note the Vulcan-style airbrakes as it arrives at Farnborough air show on the day of its first flight.

Left: The ill-fated Type 707 prototype gets airborne for the first time at Boscombe Down. Less than a month later it crashed, killing Flt Lt Esler.

The Avro Type 707 was intended to be a trials aircraft for the impending Type 698 bomber, but in the event it did not reach hardware stage early enough to be of much use for direct design input. Despite this, the 707 and its

variants did much to dispel any doubts as to the validity of the delta-wing design, performing excellently throughout their test careers, with the exception of the early loss of the first aircraft.

A total of five aircraft was completed, the first flying on 4 September 1949. It was followed by a slow-speed 707B, two high-speed 707As and a single 707C with a side-by-side cockpit. The latter was intended to act as a pilot conversion trainer, but the full-size aircraft proved to have benign enough handling from the outset.

Right: The first high-speed Type 707A was much closer to the final bomber in configuration, including leading-edge engine exhausts.

Below: The second high-speed 707A is seen being towed through the Waddington fence having been transported from the Avro facility at Bracebridge Heath.

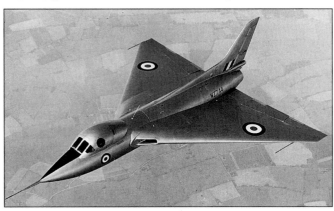

Above: The final 707 was the 707C, completed with a two-seat cockpit. Four of these trainers were originally ordered, but in the event only this single aircraft was procured.

While it has often been argued that the 707 programme was a waste of time, aircraft such as this 707A did provide much useful experience to aid the Vulcan flight-test programme, if not the final design process.

only a select few in the Cabinet – the six members of committee GEN 163 – were aware of the programme, although even they suffered from some clouding of vision. 'The Bomb' was seen as a means of ensuring a continued presence at the world's top table as one of the 'Big Three'; had anyone suggested dropping the weapon on another nation's cities, it is unlikely that the political will would have been present.

Discussion of the two ORs in committee on 17 December 1946 reached the inevitable conclusion: OR 229 was just possible, but OR 230 was beyond current means and had to be 'left open'. Specification B.35/46 was accordingly drawn up to cover OR 229. On 7 January 1947, the day before GEN 163 agreed to launch the British atomic bomb project, B.35/46 was formally issued. Armstrong Whitworth, Avro, English Electric and Handley Page received an invitation to tender on 24 January, although these and other firms had been given a

preliminary draft of B.35 options as agreed by a meeting on 7 November 1946. A planned closing date of 5 March proved optimistic and had to be extended to 30 April at the request of the aircraft industry. Vickers and Short Brothers made unsolicited tenders and Bristol maintained an interest in OR 230 which progressed as far as flying models to Spec E.8/47, before eventually withering as the requirement lapsed.

Weight struggles

It was immediately apparent that 100,000 lb was a low maximum weight if other criteria were to be met. Only Handley Page succeeded, offering 95,000 lb (43091 kg), but the aircraft's 43 ft 2 in (13.16 m) undercarriage track was deemed too wide for safety on the standard 50 ft 0 in (15.24 m) taxiways, and mainwheel loading was too high, so it was eliminated. Also ruled out were Vickers and Short. The former had just fallen within a revised weight limit of 115,000 lb (52163 kg) adopted in response to protestations from the industry, but track was 58 ft 0 in (17.68 m); Short's aircraft was the same weight and offered a 30 ft 6 in (9.30 m) track, yet was still turned down because of its airfield characteristics. This left AW, Avro and EE in the running, with offers of 113,000 lb (51256 kg)/31 ft 0 in (9.45 m), 104,000 lb (47174 kg)/30 ft 2 in (9.19 m) and 115,000 lb (51263 kg)/14 ft 0 in (4.27 m), respectively. Avro and HP were the only designs to feature four engines, AW and Short both proposing five and the other pair, six.

Avro was rated clear leader at the tender design conference of 28 July 1947 and a decision was reached to order its aircraft. AW and HP were runners up and allowed to proceed to a wind-tunnel 'fly-off' as a means of providing a second design for a final, full-scale show-

Above: For the 1953 Farnborough air show Avro compiled this truly memorable formation, comprising both Type 698 prototypes and the four surviving Type 707s. Here the sextet cruises over the West Sussex countryside near RAF Thorney Island.

Right: VX770, the Vulcan prototype, first flew from the company's Woodford airfield on 30 August 1952. During the flight two undercarriage door fairings fell off, but this did not affect the flight as the Vulcan was operating under speed restrictions.

down. At length, on 15 January 1948, the HP.80 design (later to become the Victor) was promoted to joint winner, and EE and Vickers were invited to produce (in a shorter timescale) a slightly lower-technology 'insurance'. This obviated the even more basic Short Sperrin – a 'long-stop' design, to OR 239 and Spec B.14/46 of 11 August 1947, of which two were built – and gave the RAF the Vickers Valiant, to B.9/48, two years before the first of the definitive aircraft entered service. De Havilland suggested a bomber version of the Comet airliner as a Valiant alternative, but the proposed DH.111 was not taken up. In the same month of January 1948, Avro was given a first instalment of £100,000 of the taxpayer's money and told to get on with the job of producing a strategic jet bomber.

Futuristic design

Avro's design offices in the Manchester suburb of Chadderton had begun preliminary studies under the project number 698. Like all the other five competitors, the Avro 698 featured swept wings and a pressure cabin for the crew, comprising two pilots, two navigator/bomb aimers and a radio/ECM operator. Meeting the stipulations of a 500-kt (576-mph; 927-km/h) cruise speed and achievement of 50,000 ft within 2.5 hours of take-off (as fuel was used and weight reduced) proved impossible with an aircraft of conventional shape. Chief Designer Stuart Davies and his small team then turned their attention to the large 'flying wing' concept that was enjoying some popularity at the time (with Armstrong Whitworth and the

American firm of Northrop, plus General Aircraft and de Havilland in smaller scale). This looked more promising, except that the required wing area demanded a large span, which in turn increased structural weight. So, span was reduced and the missing wing area added between the two trailing edges. The outcome was a triangle: the same symbol as the fourth letter of the Greek alphabet, delta.

Below: A pair of early Vulcans formate with two Valiant B.Mk 1s. It was the Valiant which performed most of the pioneering work for the V-force in terms of weapons and tactics.

Above: Painted in dazzling white and with high-visibility roundels, the prototype Vulcan was a truly futuristic sight in 1952/53. When it first flew, the prototype had only one pilot's seat fitted, the second being added after it had appeared at the September 1952 Farnborough show.

Right: The small engine nozzles of the first prototype's original Avons are readily apparent here.

Below: A development B.Mk 1 displays the eight-wheel main bogies, fence-type airbrakes and the finely-sculpted air intakes. Also of note are the large splitter plates to shield the engines from fuselage boundary layer air.

A delta was hardly innovative, as both Blackburn and Bristol had schemed similar bomber designs in the previous year. At this stage, the deep wing provided ample space for crew, weapons and fuel, plus two pairs of Bristol BE.10 turbojets in pick-a-back (Lightning) fashion, but it was not long before Avro departed from conventional wisdom. Prompted by RAE wind tunnel researches, it was concluded that the wing would have to be thinner in order to guarantee performance at high altitudes and Mach numbers. Internal equipment thus displaced had to be

found a new home, and so the Avro 698 took one step back towards more traditional shapes and added a fuselage. In this guise, with pairs of engines now side-by-side, the aircraft was accepted by the Ministry of Supply on 27 November 1947 and awarded its first official funding in the form of an 'Instruction to Proceed' two months later.

Two small changes were required before the design assumed its near-definitive form. Early in 1948, fins formerly located at the wingtips as the last vestige of 'flying wing' days were replaced by a single vertical structure, incorporating a rudder, at the rear of the fuselage. At about the same time, air intake trunks extending forward of the wing at the fuselage sides were removed in favour of apertures in the wing leading edge. By this means, Avro arrived at the aircraft familiar to future generations as a Vulcan – the name bestowed by the Air Council on 2 October 1952. It was still not quite the well-loved shape of later years, although that worrying discovery was not to be made for some time.

Small beginnings

More than a few projects begun energetically have as their epitaph the well-worn phrase, 'It seemed a good idea at the time'. That was almost the case with the series of Avro 707 trials aircraft – not because they were failures,

Prototypes

Two prototypes were authorised, the first flying on 30 August 1952. Two days later it went to Boscombe Down for general handling trials, and during the following week appeared several times at the Farnborough air show. After 32 hours it was grounded for various modifications, including the fitment of Sapphire engines in place of the original Avons. It resumed flying in July 1953. Later in its career VX770 received Conway engines, before being lost in a mid-air break-up in 1958 during an air show.

The second aircraft joined the programme on 3 September 1953, fitted with Olympus 100 engines. On 27 July 1954 it was damaged in a heavy landing at Farnborough, and during the rebuild Olympus 101s were fitted. Taking to the air again in February 1955, VX777 undertook engine tests, before being grounded again for fitment of the Phase 2 wing. Further test work included acting as the B.Mk 2 prototype.

Left: The second prototype touches down during one of the Vulcan's many appearances at Farnborough. During the winter of 1953/54 the aircraft was engaged on high-altitude test work at the edge of the bomber's envelope.

Above: VX770 displays the classic (almost) pure delta shape of the original design. When it resumed flying with Sapphires in July 1953, VX770 began the dedicated development work for the production aircraft, carrying out a wide range of trials.

Below: The first prototype streams its brake chute on landing at a snowy airfield. Much of the early test flying was undertaken at the A&AEE at Boscombe Down, or at Avro's Langar facility. Both prototypes carried Avro's house logo on the fin.

but because they were never sufficiently ahead of the 698 to be in a position to feed flight-test data back into the bomber's design. In fact, the serial numbers tell almost the whole story. The two prototype 698s ordered in June 1948 were assigned serials VX770 and VX777, while VX784 and VX790 were simultaneously reserved for one-third scale trials aircraft to Specification E.15/48. While later accomplishing some useful pure aerodynamic work, the 707s may even have slowed the 698 programme through diversification of effort.

Originally, it had been planned to prefix the prototype 698s by a single 707 of wooden construction for low-speed work; a twin-engined (RR Avons) Avro 710 capable of Mach 0.95 and altitudes of 60,000 ft (18290 m) to assess performance in the operational environment; and a 'flying shell' 698 devoid of all extraneous equipment. Within a short time, however, the two last-mentioned aircraft had been cancelled as unnecessary and the 707 recast in metal and optimised for the highest speed possible from its single 3,500-lb st (15.57-kN) RR Derwent: about Mach 0.85. Transported by road to the MoS experimental airfield at Boscombe Down after taxi trials at Avro's Woodford flight test base, 707 VX784 made the first flight of a tailless delta in British skies on the evening of 4 September 1949.

Losing no time in advertising the achievement, Avro demonstrated the aircraft at the Farnborough air show two days later, but tragedy struck soon afterwards when VX784 crashed near Blackbushe on 30 September, killing its project pilot, Flight Lieutenant Eric Esler. Examination showed the probable cause to be a control fault which locked the airbrakes open and provoked a stall. No blame was attached to the basic design which, in the three short hours it had accumulated in the air, showed every promise of being a winner.

May 1949 had seen a third mini-delta, WD280, ordered as a high-speed Avro 707A to Specification E.10/49. In order to make up for the early loss, its part-completed nose was borrowed to speed construction of the second low-speed aircraft, VX790, which then became the 707B. Wing Commander R. J. 'Roly' Falk lifted '790 off the Boscombe runway on 6 September 1950, and later in the same day delivered the all-blue aircraft to the static park at that year's Farnborough display (they were annual events at that time.) In spite of a curious, inefficient and unrepresentative spine intake, VX790 did useful work

XA891 was the third production Vulcan, seen here in pristine silver paint finish and with Phase 2 wing fitted. The first five B.Mk 1s flew with the original straight wing.

A trio of early Vulcan B.Mk 1s is seen prior to delivery. The kinked Phase 2 wing did not add to the Vulcan's performance, but allowed it to operate at high altitude and at high speed with a greater margin of safety.

during the next two years in dispelling many of the myths surrounding delta-winged flight. From February 1951, it was even persuaded to fly a little faster, thanks to intake modifications.

The true high-speed 707 eventually emerged with a replacement front fuselage. WD280, the 707A, had wingroot intakes as well as ailerons and elevators more faithfully representing the 698's control surfaces. 'Roly' Falk flew it for the first time at Boscombe on 14 June 1951, although he soon ran into pitching oscillations. Having taken up much research time and caused innumerable hours of lost sleep, the problem vanished

when powered flying controls were fitted in May 1952. As the 698 was intended to have power control from the outset, the earlier efforts at rectification became, in retrospect, a needless diversion.

Avro was by now in the curious position wherein the 698 development team was giving modification advice to the 707 project personnel, instead of vice versa, as the bomber design became 'frozen'. The one valuable discovery made in the course of trials was that the 707A encountered 'buzz' at high Mach numbers, yet so close behind was the 698 that early production aircraft had to suffer the same problem before the necessary modifications

Phase 2 Wing

Following early trials, it became apparent that the high Mach number buffet threshold of the original straight wing was uncomfortably close to the outer boundary of the Vulcan's performance, especially when fitted with later marks of Olympus. Accordingly, Avro and the RAE designed a leading-edge extension which added a

kinked, drooping section on the outer panels of the wing. This was first tested in scale on the Avro 707A WD280, before being fitted to the 698 second prototype. Successful clearance of the Phase 2 wing led to its incorporation on the production line and retrofit to the first five aircraft which had flown on the straight wings.

Below: XA889 was the first production aircraft and, as such, flew initially with straight wings. It was returned to Avro for fitment of the new leading edge, and became the first of the production B.Mk 1s to fly with the new wing. It spent most of its career as an engine testbed, flying with, successively, Olympus 101s, 102s and 104s.

Above: VX777, the second prototype, lifts off with the Phase 2 wing fitted. It was the main vehicle used for validating the new design.

Above: The Vulcan adopted a white paint scheme from XA901. The first deliveries to 230 OCU initially had Olympus 101 engines, while the first aircraft for No. 83 Sqn, the initial operational unit, had 102s from the outset.

could be passed into the manufacturing system. Three more 707s were ordered in November 1951, comprising a second 707A at the behest of RAE, and the first two of four 707C side-by-side seat conversion trainers. One of the trainers was cancelled when it was realised that the 698's flying characteristics did not warrant any special pilot indoctrination, and the other two flew several months after the prototype Vulcan. This pair has been preserved for posterity in British museums, while the first 707A (WD280) was saved by private initiative in Australia, when it had ended its days as a trials vehicle – ironically, at the low end of the speed spectrum.

Flight development

Throughout the entire development and early production phases of the Vulcan, Avro was spurred by the belief that the RAF would order only one B.35/46 contender into large-scale service. Considerable effort was expended in bettering the Handley Page on performance and delivery and, when 25 of both the Vulcan and Victor were ordered simultaneously, the Mancunians merely supposed that the ultimate decision had been postponed until after a period of squadron-level assessment. It transpired, of course, that the RAF could never bring itself to axe an aircraft which represented innumerable man-hours of devoted work by a leading manufacturer, so orders continued in parallel, and the Vulcan and Victor served alongside each other until the Royal Navy assumed responsibility for the strategic deterrent in 1969. The Victor was better aerodynamically, but the Vulcan evened the score by employing more powerful engines during its operational lifetime.

Determination to beat Handley Page into the air resulted in the 698 being fitted with unscheduled powerplants for its early test programme. While the BE.10 had its first bench run on 6 May 1950, it was still far from flyable by the time the first 698 was complete. Therefore, it was with the assistance of four 6,500-lb st (28.91-kN) RR Avons that Falk lifted VX770 off the Woodford runway on 30 August 1952, and two days later was able to deliver the impressive new shape to the A&AEE at Boscombe Down. Here it kept company with the prototype Victor – which might have beaten it into the air but for ill luck and some technical miscalculation – and made five flying appearances at the Farnborough show, escorted by the 707A and 707B.

The aviation press was still enthusing over the futuristic appearance of Britain's new bomber as VX770 was temporarily grounded at Boscombe after its public debut for instrumentation changes and minor modifications. Handling trials occupied it for the next few months until, after a total of 32 hours' flying, it had achieved as much as possible on the low-powered Avons. With the Olympus still not ready, VX770 took to the air in June 1953, supported by four Armstrong Siddeley Sapphire ASSa.6s, delivering 7,500 lb st (33.36 kN) each. Having been upgraded from its earlier spartan equipment standard, the aircraft now had pressurisation and the full wing fuel

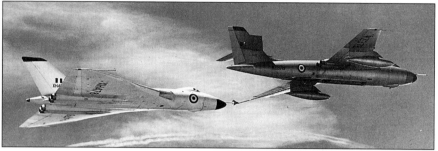

system which was designed to maintain a constant centre of gravity despite steadily reducing weight.

Adding further strength to the growing belief that Avro aircraft were primarily produced for the purpose of public exhibition at Farnborough, the second prototype, VX777, was first flown on 3 September 1953 – just in time for that year's show. Those fortunate enough to see it will never forget the sight of the two white Vulcans flanked by all four surviving, multi-coloured 707s sweeping over the Hampshire landscape in majestic formation. It was a truly show-stopping performance, yet as soon as the display was over, both Vulcans were immediately reabsorbed in the development programme. There was much still to do.

VX777 had been the first Vulcan to take aloft Olympus engines, which it did in Mk 100 form, with the rating of 9,750 lb st (43.37 kN). Grounded for six months of modifications, the aircraft began bombing trials, only to succumb to a serious landing accident soon afterwards, resulting in further hangar time. Some of its programme was reassigned to VX770, an urgent aspect being high-altitude/high-Mach number trials, begun early in 1955.

The 707s had shown some unacceptable behaviour in this region, and the prototype Vulcan confirmed that with engines of production power, the aircraft would closely approach the buffet threshold. Buffeting began before the

XH478 was used by the A&AEE for refuelling probe trials in 1958, validating the system used by the B.Mk 1A and B.Mk 2 fleet. Support was provided by Valiant tankers. Note the unusual tailcone fitted to the Vulcan: this may indicate some form of early tail-warning radar.

230 OCU at Waddington officially received its first two aircraft (XA895 and XA898) in January 1957. This aircraft (XA896) was the third, arriving with the unit on 3 March. From the outset, Waddington aircraft wore the City of Lincoln coat of arms on the fin.

Above: The second B.Mk 1 receives the finishing touches inside the giant assembly building at Woodford, with others following it down the line.

Right: The first production aircraft flew on 4 February 1955, and preceded the second by six months. Thereafter the line speeded up, although XA894 was held back to be the first fully representative B.Mk 1 with Phase 2 wing fitted from the start.

For ground crew, the Vulcan offered a new challenge in sophistication, and required many new skills to be learned. The sheer size of the aircraft posed access problems, chiefly solved by the ubiquitous 'Giraffe' telescopic platform. Here a B.Mk 1 undergoes a major overhaul with the Waddington Aircraft Servicing Flight.

Production

Much of the Vulcan airframe was built at Avro's Chadderton factory, also the site of the design office. Components were also built at Woodford, where final assembly and flight test was accomplished. Production was established with great haste in an attempt to keep the V-bomber programme abreast of strategic developments. Many modifications which would normally be made during the prototype stage were incorporated on the production line, with earlier aircraft being returned to the manufacturers for modification when possible.

Below: The flight line at Woodford groans under the weight of seven Vulcan B.Mk 1s. The date is late 1956: XA895 was at Boscombe Down and XA897 had recently crashed at Heathrow on return from New Zealand.

aircraft reached its cruising Mach number, thereby reducing not only range but also accuracy on the bombing run and the ability to make evasive manoeuvres. Additionally, the aircraft developed a nose-down trim at Mach 0.86 and became progressively more uncomfortable to fly as it approached the design Mach number of 0.95. Assessments showed that it could make perhaps only 43,000 ft (13106 m) over the target with a 10,000-lb (4536-kg) bomb – not good enough to guarantee immunity from fighters. A&AEE was not happy.

The wing comes right

Concern mounted as the faithful stand-by 'fixes' of vortex generators, fences and notches failed to rectify the onset of compressibility effects. At length, Farnborough came to the rescue. The RAE had already played a leading role in the Vulcan's wing design at the drawing board stage when the area of maximum thickness was moved forward to the leading edge (incidentally making more room for the later addition of bigger engines). Now, its scientists recommended a 'kinked' leading edge, in which the 52° sweepback was reduced by 10° at mid-span, but reinstated further outboard. This became the Phase 2 wing, and it worked wonderfully up to the maximum

output of the Series 100 Olympus, even though it did nothing for the ceiling. In production form, the Vulcan B.Mk 1 was 'red-lined' at Mach 0.98, and the Mk 1A limited to the slightly slower 0.95 as the result of its modifications.

Having been tested in miniature in 1954 on the 707A, WD280, the revised leading edge first flew on VX777 on 5 October 1955. The aircraft had recovered from its landing accident and resumed trials on the previous 4 February, the enforced grounding being an opportunity to fit pre-production Olympus Mk 101s of 10,000 lb st (44.48 kN), which were re-rated at 11,034 lb st (49.08 kN) in production form. Translation of the Phase 2 wing into metal was comparatively simple, although the first five production Vulcans made their initial flights with straight leading edges so as not to disrupt the development programme more than necessary.

For similar reasons of expediency, the first 25 production Vulcan B.Mk 1s were ordered to Specification B.129 in July 1952 – a month before the prototype's initial flight and six months prior to the final mock-up conference on the B.Mk 1. On straight-edged wings, and with Olympus 101s providing the power, XA889 took off at Woodford on 4 February 1955, wearing a colour scheme of overall silver. Not until 12 months later did it become the first production aircraft to receive Phase 2 leading edges. One of the aircraft's main duties was engine development, for which it was fitted with 12,009-lb st (53.42-kN) Olympus 102s in March 1957 and 13,500-lb st (60.05-kN) Mk 104s the following July. These marks of engine were introduced on the production line and retrofitted to aircraft in service as they were cleared for use. Extra power added another 1,500 ft (457 m) to the original over-target altitude of 43,000 ft (13106 m), which was still far from sufficient for the crew's peace of mind.

In spite of early concern, Avro had managed to get away with breaking the unwritten rule that manufacturers should never combine a new airframe with a new engine. This departure aside, the firm had been remarkably conservative with the Vulcan's engineering, its *avant garde* exterior hiding structural design which, if not old-fashioned, was certainly tried and trusted. Built around a two-spar wing, the aircraft was clad primarily in aluminium alloy, with sparing use of magnesium on the control surfaces, fin and bomb doors. Between the two gigantic spars was the capacious weapons bay, covered by inward-

opening doors which would not disturb the airflow on approach to the target. Blue Danube, the first British atomic bomb, conformed to the anticipated dimensions, although it had telescopic tailfins in order to fit inside V-bomber weapon bays. The Vulcan's doors were about 29 ft (8.84 m) long and 10 ft 6 in (3.20 m) wide. There were plans to carry up to two of the rocket-propelled Blue Boar TV-guided bombs – each weighting 10,000 lb (4536 kg) and mounted side-by-side – until the weapon was cancelled in 1954. Green Cheese, an anti-ship missile based on Blue Boar, would have given V-bombers a maritime strike capability, but it was also abandoned.

Fuel management

Outboard of the weapons bay were the engines, each pair boxed-in by three load-bearing ribs. The innermost of each trio were the supports for arches forming the upper fuselage and from which the bomb load was hung. Fuel tanks occupied much of the area outboard of the engines and also the fuselage between the weapons bay and the pressurised crew compartment. Fuel contributed 74,000 lb (33566 kg) to the Vulcan B.Mk 1's maximum take-off weight of 167,000 lb (75750 kg), and was the subject of a complex management system which ensured that only 10 per cent of capacity would be lost if one of the 12 tanks (two in the fuselage, plus five in each wing) were holed.

Sitting shoulder-to-shoulder in a cockpit which could most generously be described as 'cosy', the two pilots were covered by a blister canopy in which were set two small portholes and five forward-facing transparencies. No need was foreseen for a visual look-out, and in any event the paucity of glass minimised pressurisation problems. At the insistence of Falk, a fighter-type control column

mounted on the instrument panel replaced the 'spectacles' more normally associated with aircraft of the Vulcan's size, and after that pilot had demonstrated the aircraft's remarkable manoeuvrability with a legendary slow roll (in XA890) before the 1954 Farnborough crowds, nobody again asked why. Three remaining crew members faced rearwards on a lower deck behind the pilots, there being just enough extra room for a visual bombing station in the prone position and two jump-seats in what was only half-jokingly known as the 'coal-hole'. No 'sixth man' was

XA904 was the first production aircraft to feature the Olympus 102 engine, offering a significant thrust increase over the 101 engine of the early production machines. '904 became the second aircraft of No. 83 Sqn.

Engine testbeds

The large size, excellent ground clearance, high speed and outstanding altitude capability of the Vulcan made it a natural test vehicle for high-performance engines. It was to play a major part in the development of powerplant for three of the UK's most important aircraft programmes (TSR.2, Concorde and Tornado). Additionally, XA896 was to have tested the BS100 vectored-thrust engine for the P.1154, but the trials were cancelled following axing of the entire supersonic VTOL programme.

Left: XA894 tested the Olympus 22R for the BAC TSR.2. The unrepresentative intake system was bifurcated to accommodate the Vulcan's nosewheel, and portions of the rear of the aircraft had a stainless steel-covered acoustic blanket for protection.

XA894 first flew with Olympus 22R on 23 February 1962, the test engine later replaced by the 22R-1 with reheat. On 3 December, the 22R-1 broke up during ground running, causing the untimely end of XA894, although the crew escaped before it burned out completely.

Below: XA903's last assignment was as the testbed for the Tornado's RB199 engine, fitted on the starboard side with a representative Tornado intake, including cannon port. The aircraft undertook gun firing trials in early 1976. On 22 February 1979, XA903 made the last flight of a B.Mk 1.

Below: Fitted with an icing rig, XA903 test-runs Concorde's Olympus 593 engine. First flying in this guise on 9 September 1966, XA903 was heavily modified, with over 11 tons of test equipment and provision for a crew of seven.

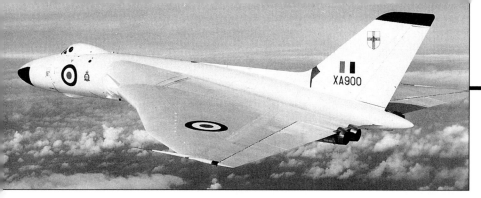

XA900

Above: The Vulcan schoolhouse was 230 Operational Conversion Unit, initially based at Waddington. The first squadron (No. 83) was formed by taking the first course to complete the OCU syllabus and assigning squadron status.

B.Mk 1 in service

The entry of the Vulcan into service progressed sporadically. The establishment of 230 OCU in early 1957 was the first priority, followed in July by the first squadron, No. 83. The second squadron, No. 101, received its first aircraft in October 1957, but it was not until May 1958 before No. 617 became the third Vulcan unit. The three initial squadrons were formed at three different bases (Waddington, Finningley and Scampton) to broaden operations and introduce a measure of force dispersal from a very early stage. Only two more squadrons (Nos 44 and 50) were to operate the B.Mk 1, these acquiring their aircraft when Nos 83 and 617 transitioned to the B.Mk 2 in 1960/61. The last B.Mk 1 was delivered to the RAF in April 1959.

Left: In addition to training crews, the OCU was also responsible for evaluating a wide range of operational tactics and servicing procedures. The first few aircraft were delivered in silver paint.

Below: XA896 was one of the OCU's first aircraft, seen here after repainting in the white scheme. In June 1960 it joined the ranks of No. 83 Sqn, and later passed to No. 44 Sqn before returning to the OCU.

Having earlier been officially assigned to the unit but used by A&AEE, XA895 was one of the first two permanently assigned aircraft for 230 OCU. On arrival in January 1957, it and XA898 were used for a period of intensive trials before crew training began on 21 February. The delivery of three further aircraft (XA900, 901 and 902) in March, April and May allowed the first course to graduate on 21 May.

available in the form of an autopilot for the Vulcan B.Mk 1, so some very careful handling of the engines and controls was necessary when lightly-loaded aircraft ventured above 50,000 ft (4645 m).

Beneath the nose, a dielectric panel covered the EMI-built ground-mapping radar. Up to the end of the Vulcan's long career, this remained the Model H2S, although the designation fails to explain that the equipment had been modified to a state far removed from the H2S which guided earlier Bomber Command aircraft over the Third Reich. In later days, the extreme nose sported a refuelling probe for contacts with Valiant tankers, and the diminishing physical size of nuclear weapons meant that additional tanks could be added in the bomb bay as a further means of extending range. In an early trial with only normal fuel, the Vulcan used 57,300 lb (25991 kg) of kerosene to cover 2,890 nm (3,326 miles/5352 km) in 5 hours 55 minutes, releasing a 10,000-lb (4536-kg) bomb load at the half-way point from 43,000 ft (13106 m). The sortie was representative of a mission from Lincolnshire to Moscow, but A&AEE was far too gentlemanly to point this out.

Twin nosewheels and two eight-wheel main bogies supported the Vulcan on the ground. When 'three greens' were showing, airbrakes could be fully deployed above and below the wing in the form of pairs of rectangular plates raised above the boundary layer and angled at 80° to the airflow. To prevent excessive nose-down pitching, one brake (the outer) on each side of the lower surface was permanently locked early in the aircraft's career. From the second B.Mk 1, extended and outward-angled jetpipes were introduced to further minimise transient trim changes, such changes resulting from throttle movements. A Mach trimmer had also been added to obviate Boscombe's earlier

XA895

criticism of a nose-down tendency at high Mach numbers, and in this modified guise with a newly-fitted Phase 2 leading edge, XA889 was tested for C(A) Release in March-April 1956. Official issue of the Release came on 31 May.

That same day, No. 230 Operational Conversion Unit formed at Waddington, immediately south of Lincoln, tasked with production of Vulcan aircrew. The OCU is popularly credited with having received its first aircraft, XA897, on 20 July, but the hand-over was merely a symbolic affair and '897 remained at Woodford. When

Below: Wearing No. 101 Sqn's badge on the fin, XA912 manoeuvres over mountainous terrain. The B.Mk 1 did not have an autopilot, necessitating careful handling at high altitude, although autostabilisation was added from the first production aircraft.

formally transferred to No. 230 on 2 September, it actually operated from Boscombe, making preparations for a record-breaking flight to New Zealand and back. Adorned with the City of Lincoln arms on the fin (a feature of all subsequent Waddington Vulcans), the aircraft left Britain on 9 September, but crashed on landing at London Airport (Heathrow) on 1 October, only seconds from a triumphal return.

Such a catastrophe might have blighted the career of lesser aircraft, but the Vulcan quickly put this sad beginning – for which the machine itself was not to blame – behind it. XA895, also on charge to the OCU, began a 150-hour reliability trial at Boscombe Down on 20 September 1956, flown by the Handling Squadron but maintained by No. 230's personnel. At last, on 18 January 1957, XA895 and XA898 were accepted by the OCU at Waddington and on the following day '895 began a short programme of intensive flying trials. The first course of 25 aircrew began training on 19 February, with the first Vulcan sortie taking place two days later. All the early Vulcan converts were

The B.Mk 1's angular wing and tip-mounted pitot probes were the most characteristic features of this variant. The undernose cupola was intended for visual bombing from a prone position, and incorporated an optically-flat glazed panel. It was rarely used, the H2S radar system usually providing sufficient cues for a systems release.

Blue Steel tests

The Avro Blue Steel missile had a long and difficult gestation, problems being encountered with the stainless steel construction, guidance system and rocket motor. The first airborne tests were accomplished by a Valiant dropping a 40 per cent scale model over Aberporth range in 1957. These were followed by full-scale tests using a Valiant, initially, and then Vulcan XA903. Full-size test-rounds included

the W.102 unpowered, uncontrolled vehicle, W.103/W.103A with power (from the de Havilland Double Spectre motor) and controls but with aluminium structure, and the W.100 stainless steel missile. The W.100A was a fully representative pre-production missile. Most test firings took place at Woomera in Australia, where the first full-range 100-mile flight of a W.100A was achieved in early 1962.

Three views show XA903 with Blue Steel test rounds carried in a semi-recessed bay. The main difference between this aircraft (the only B.Mk 1 to carry the missile) and the operational aircraft was the depth of the fuselage recess. On XA903 the bay was much shallower, with the result that the nose of the missile stood proud from the aircraft undersides. The aircraft undertook many missile launches, continuing work performed by Valiants WP199 and WP204.

Waddington Wing

In the late 1950s Waddington housed No. 83 Sqn and the OCU. The operational squadron was initially armed with the Blue Danube free-fall weapon, and this remained the primary equipment until late 1958, when Waddington began to receive US-made Mk 5 hydrogen bombs. In 1960/61 the original squadron left for Scampton, and two new units, Nos 44 and 50, were reformed to continue with B.Mk 1s, joined by No. 101 from Finningley. In February 1962 the first UK-made Yellow Sun Mk 1 bombs arrived, supplanting the Mk 5s. These were followed by the definitive UK hydrogen bomb, the Yellow Sun Mk 2, which remained the Waddington Wing's primary armament until 1966.

Above: While Scampton and Coningsby received B.Mk 2s, Waddington remained on B.Mk 1As until conversion in 1965/67. The Severn Bridge was a well-known landmark to Vulcan crews.

Below: A Waddington B.Mk 1A takes on fuel from a Valiant BK.Mk 1 of No. 90 Sqn. Anti-flash white with toned-down national insignia was the standard scheme in the early 1960s.

officers, and all were of above-average ability in their specialist areas. After three months of training, No. 1 Course was transformed by a stroke of the pen into 'A' Flight of No. 83 Squadron on 21 May. However, the OCU took the first six Vulcan B.Mk 1s delivered to the RAF (painted overall white from XA901) and No. 83 had to wait until 11 July for the first aircraft it could call its own: XA905. Five days later, XA904 arrived, the first Vulcan to be fitted on the production line with Olympus Mk 102s.

USAF competition

Initial tasks for No. 83 were a flypast at that year's Farnborough show and training (to participate with Valiants) for the SAC annual bombing competition. If the latter appears a curious priority for a new squadron, it should be seen in the context of the close relationship then being developed in nuclear targeting between Bomber and Strategic Air Commands. Having proved its capabilities, the RAF became a trusted partner, being incorporated in the USAF strike plan from 1 July 1958, and

Below right: A B.Mk 1A taxis in at a Middle East destination. The Mk 1A carried the Yellow Sun (OR1136) bomb as its main weapon, although it retained (and its crews practised for) conventional bombing.

Below: A B.Mk 1A displays the weapons bay of the type. This bay, indeed the whole aircraft, had been designed around Britain's first atomic weapon, the 10,000-lb (4536-kg) Blue Danube. As nuclear weapons shrunk in size, the bay was used to house additional fuel.

later that year benefitting from the supply of US-made nuclear weapons for the Canberras and V-force, under Project 'E'.

While No. 83 Squadron shared Waddington with the OCU, the next unit to form was based at Finningley, near Doncaster. XA909 arrived on 1 October 1957, and was technically without an owner until No. 101 Squadron was established with a further batch of OCU graduates on 15 October. Four aircraft – half strength – were received before the end of 1957, coincidentally completing deliveries from the first batch of 25. The RAF had authorised further Vulcans in 1954, these emerging as 20 Mk 1s, followed by the balance as Mk 2s. First of the former, XH475, had Olympus 104s and was delivered to 230 OCU for a week's familiarisation on 22 January 1958.

Others followed with speed and, before the year was out, only three of the 20 remained to be delivered. However, many of the batch were distributed between the existing units, and the only new squadron to form was No. 617, at Scampton on 1 May 1958. XH482 was assigned on the following day, the unit being up to strength with eight aircraft by 11 November. Discrete badges applied in the vicinity of the forward fuselage roundel (or on the fin for No. 101) proclaimed squadron identities prior to larger fin markings becoming fashionable on the Vulcan B.Mk 2. Like its companion bases, Scampton had been recently raised to Class One status for the V-bomber force with a 200-ft (61-m) wide, 9,000-ft (2743-m) long runway – plus a 1,000-ft (305-m) over-run area – with a bearing strength of 200,000 lb (90719 kg). There were also

B.Mk 1A

Towards the end of the 1950s there was considerable concern over the continued survivability of the Vulcan over Soviet territory. This was caused by the development of new, high-flying interceptors such as the MiG-19. While there was no hope of extending the B.Mk 1's ceiling, it was felt that its chances could be increased by fitting better countermeasures. The B.Mk 1 had featured just one jammer, Green Palm, and this was far from adequate to deter interception. A decision was taken to fit the ECM suite which had been developed for the B.Mk 2 into the Mk 1, creating the B.Mk 1A. The modification was characterised by the swollen tailcone which housed most of the jammers and tail-warning radar, and a flat-plate antenna situated between and underneath the starboard engine trunks.

A trio of Waddington B.Mk 1s overflies the Lincolnshire countryside. A major problem for the station (and for the Victors at Honington and Valiants at Marham) was that the US-owned Project 'E' weapons which armed the aircraft were held off base and could not be released for training purposes. This severely hampered both operational training and the effectiveness of dispersal.

hardstandings for at least 16 aircraft and much new infrastructure, including special storage and security facilities for weaponry.

Established squadrons claimed the later mark of Vulcan when it entered service. On 1 July 1960, 'B' Flight of No. 230 OCU began receiving Mk 2s, although its older aircraft continued in service with 'A' Flight until XA900 and '901 were retired in November 1965. No. 44 Squadron was created at Waddington on 10 August 1960 when No. 83 Squadron was renumbered in preparation for a rebirth with Vulcan B.Mk 2s. One year later, No. 617's old aircraft were ferried the short distance across Lincoln to stock No. 50 Squadron following its formation at Waddington on 1 August 1961. Associated with these changes was the movement of No. 101 Squadron to Waddington in June 1961, room having been made by posting the OCU in the opposite direction, to Finningley, at the same time. Thus, apart from training aircraft and those of Bomber Command Development Unit (also at Finningley), all the B.Mk 1s were concentrated at Waddington with Nos 44, 50 and 101 Squadrons.

Megaton weapons

A variety of nuclear weapons was, by now, available for the V-force. Blue Danube had arrived on RAF stations even before the Valiant entered service and was the Vulcan's primary armament. On 16 June 1954 the government had authorised development of the more powerful hydrogen bomb, resulting in the issue on 6 June 1955 of OR 1136 for a 'megaton range' bomb. (In fact, 'megaton' in UK parlance means anything over 500 kilotons, and when OR 1153 was issued in November 1956 for a 'multi-megaton' weapon, a yield of over 1 mT would have sufficed. This explains why alleged explosive power of British weapons consistently failed to meet official pronouncements of striking force.) The May 1957 H-bomb tests – Operation Grapple – showed that a modified warhead could be made in advance of the definitive new weapon and its associated casing and so, keen to get its hands on an 'interim megaton' bomb, the RAF placed an immediate order for 12.

Codenamed Violet Club, the stopgap weapon was first assembled by the Bomber Command Armament School at Wittering in March 1958. It was, in effect, a Blue Danube casing fitted with the new Green Grass warhead, weighing in at 9,000 lb (4082 kg), or 2,000 lb (907 kg) less than its progenitor. The intended Victor application never materialised and only the Vulcan wings at Finningley and Scampton were equipped, and then only until their Green Grass warheads could be removed and reinserted in the definitive OR 1136 bombs as they arrived.

In addition to the British bombs, US-made Mk 5 weapons were supplied under Project 'E' which began officially on 1 October 1958 (later encompassing Mk 28 and Mk 43 weapons, primarily for the tactical Canberras and Valiants). The Vulcan wing at Waddington received Mk 5s, as did the Victor and Valiant units at Honington and Marham. Each base had 24 of these 6,000-lb (2722-kg) bombs in a USAF-staffed secure compound but – as they could only be released from American control on the outbreak of war, and no British bombs were held at those stations – regular training, especially dispersal to other airfields, was severely inhibited, if not impossible.

Yellow Sun Mk 1, the eventual outcome of OR 1136, became available in 1960, apparently going first to Finningley and Scampton, as well as to Victor squadrons. Stocks began arriving at Waddington in February 1962,

allowing the Project 'E' bombs there to be supplanted from 17 March. In service only until 1963, Yellow Sun Mk 1 weighed 7,000 lb (3175 kg) and had a yield of 500 kT. Yellow Sun Mk 2 was similar, except that its Red Snow warhead (the same as in the Blue Steel missile) had been designed with the benefit of American technical information.

Introduced in 1961 and only 250 lb (113 kg) heavier, it

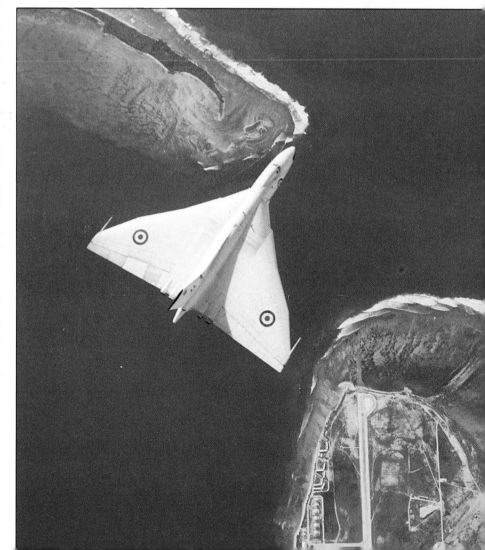

Below: A B.Mk 1 from Waddington overflies the UK outpost at Gan, an island in the Indian Ocean. Gan was an important stop-over for aircraft deploying to the Far East.

Phase 2C wing

The Vulcan B.Mk 2 was planned around the far more powerful Olympus 200 series powerplant. It was calculated that the 'fixed' Phase 2 wing could not handle the extra performance of the new engines, and a return to dangerous buffet conditions at high altitude would result.

A new outer wing was designed, designated Phase 2C. This featured rounded wingtips and a much-increased area, resulting from a span increase, a more pronounced kink on the leading edge and also a kink on the trailing edge which extended the wing rearwards.

Above and right: Two views show the second prototype in its third major incarnation, testing the Phase 2C wing and acting as aerodynamic prototype for the B.Mk 2. The original aileron/elevator configuration of the Phase 2 wing was ditched in favour of combined elevons on the new surfaces.

Above: As befitted the initial operational recipient of the Vulcan, No. 83 Sqn was also first to get the B.Mk 2. The arrival of the B.Mk 2 coincided with the delivery of the first Yellow Sun Mk 1 weapons to Scampton.

had a destructive power of 1 mT. Blue Danube and Violet Club shared the same streamlined casing, and due to the constraints of the V-bombers' bomb bays and requirements for stabilisation during free-fall they were fitted with pop-out rear fins. The Yellow Sun casing had a bluff front end, which restricted free-fall velocity to subsonic levels. This in turn reduced the requirement for fin area and the bombs could be fitted into the Vulcans and Victors without the need for pop-out fins.

Waddington received 24 Yellow Sun Mk 2s to equip its Vulcan B.Mk 1As, while similar numbers went to Coningsby's Vulcan B.Mk 2s and to the Victor station at Honington. Plans were also made for Vulcan and Victor bases to have a small stock of the Red Beard tactical free-fall bomb which weighed 1,750 lb (793 kg) and had a yield of 15 kT. It was used by some Valiants, but it is unclear whether it ever became a full part of the Vulcan/Victor armoury.

A sting in the tail

If the Vulcan B.Mk 1 could not be persuaded to fly higher, it could, at least, be fitted with countermeasures equipment to make hopeful interceptor pilots work harder for their pay. An ECM suite devised for the B.Mk 2 in 1956 was earmarked for fitment to the B.Mk 1s in squadron (though not OCU) service and operated by a turbine-driven alternator, the trials installation being made in XA895 during 1958.

The main elements of the electronic suite were an ARI 18074 Green Palm voice communications jammer, ARI 18075 Blue Diver metric frequency jammer, ARI 18076 Red Shrimp centimetric jammer, ARI 18105 Blue Saga radar warning receiver, ARI 5919 Red Steer rear-facing radar (adapted from the night-fighter Meteor's equipment), and ARI 18051 chaff dispensers. These were carried forward into the Vulcan B.Mk 2, with minor variations on those aircraft equipped to launch Blue Steel.

A flat plate aerial between the starboard jetpipes and a bulged tailcone characterised the modification, raising the designation to Vulcan B.Mk 1A. Armstrong Whitworth's facility at Bitteswell was responsible for 'production' conversions, although it received some assistance from Vickers in the case of the first two aircraft (XH500 and '505), which were received in July 1959 and redelivered to No. 617 Squadron in September and October of the following year. When XH503 returned to Waddington on 6 March 1963, it concluded the Mk 1A programme after modification of eight 'XA' and all 20 'XH' aircraft, excluding XA895.

In 1963, the V-force was assigned to NATO and given a part in the Alliance's nuclear strike plan, but with full powers of reversion to national control for conventional or nuclear tasks. In the case of the Waddington Wing, that responsibility included being prepared for deployment to

Illustrating the might of UK airpower in the 1960s, a lone Vulcan leads a quartet of Lightning interceptors from No. 5 Squadron. Vulcans regularly provided inviting (and challenging) targets for the NATO interceptor forces, and at extreme altitude could usually out-manoeuvre their intended pursuers.

B.Mk 2 development

Design of the B.Mk 2 had begun in late 1955, and ministerial approval was gained on 31 May 1956. The new variant was introduced on the production line as early as was possible, resulting in the paper conversion of the last 17 aircraft on the B.Mk 1 line. Increased survivability was the key to the B.Mk 2's development, key areas being the new ECM installation and extra altitude performance provided by more powerful engines and the Phase 2C wing. An over-target altitude of 55,000 ft (16764 m) was the requirement, easily met by the new aircraft. Most of the trials were accomplished with VX777 and B.Mk 1 machines, there being no B.Mk 2 prototype as such.

Above: The fourth B.Mk 2 lands at Farnborough during one of the Vulcan's many appearances at the SBAC show. The first few aircraft originally flew with a B.Mk 1-style short tailcone. XH534 tested the ECM-equipped tail.

the Middle East to support British interests and protectorates in a conventional role. Victors were mainly assigned to the Far East, yet small Vulcan B.Mk 1 detachments, codenamed Profiteer, were dispatched to Butterworth and Changi in 1959-60 during operations against the Communist guerrillas in Malaya, although they were never called into action.

Operational criteria introduced in July 1958 required V-bomber stations to have 20 per cent of their aircraft operational within two hours of an emergency notification, 40 per cent in four hours, 60 per cent in eight hours, and 75 per cent in 24 hours – every day of the year. The last-mentioned corresponded to the Strategic Warning status, while Tactical Warning required bases to be capable of launching a maximum strength attack at 40 minutes' notice and remaining on standby at this state for one month, or keeping up a 15-minute readiness for a week. In these cases, Bomber Command expected to have 91 per cent of the V-bombers operational within 72 hours. From 1 January 1962, each squadron maintained one Vulcan at 15 minutes' QRA (Quick Reaction Alert) readiness, its crew dressed in flying suits and occupying a caravan close to their bombed-up aircraft.

Following rejection of a 1965 proposal to replace SACEUR's fatigue-grounded Valiants with 24 early Vulcans, B.Mk 2s began arriving at Waddington in 1966. The first of the wing's Mk 1As departed to No. 19 MU at St Athan on 11 March for recovery of useful equipment before scrapping. On 10 January 1968, XH506 similarly flew to South Wales and XH481 was handed over to the Waddington firemen, completing the run-down of the Vulcan B.Mk 1A force. (Those in trials use survived longer: XH478 was delivered to Akrotiri, Cyprus, in March 1969 for static instruction: and XA903 – one of two engine testbed Vulcans – made its final touch-down at Farnborough on 22 February 1979, having managed to remain overall white throughout its long career.)

B.Mk 2 development

Some might view it as an act of betrayal or an admission of no confidence, but in the world of military aviation it is an accepted fact that work begins on designing the successor to an aircraft even before it enters service. Thus it was that a year before the Vulcan B.Mk 1 received

C(A) clearance, the Avro drawing office at Chadderton had an improved model on the drawing boards. The Mk 1 had risen to the challenge of its 1946 specification, meeting it in most respects, but the problem was simply that times had changed. The Soviet Union was now clearly the potential target if the V-bomber force was ever to be called into action, and it had made rapid progress in establishing a large force of jet interceptors. It would not be long before effective missiles increased the fighters' reach and proliferated in surface-to-air form.

Bomber Command saw a supersonic aircraft as the long-term means of maintaining its effectiveness. Unfortunately, such a machine was out of the question for a further 10 years (and in the event, it – the Avro 730 – was cancelled). However, persuading the existing aircraft to fly above 60,000 ft (18288 m) and fitting jamming equipment presented itself as a viable interim solution. Protected by a battery of defensive aids, and with height on its side, a subsonic bomber still had an excellent chance of evading the Soviet defences.

More power was the key to increased ceiling, and with Bristol Siddeley planning a 20,000-lb st (88.97-kN) version of the Olympus – compared to 13,500 lb st (60.05 kN) offered by the Olympus Mk 104 which B.Mk 1s ultimately received – the means to defeat the Soviet air defence force appeared to be within the RAF's grasp. First, a new wing would be needed to harness the extra thrust, since the Phase 2 design with its distinctive 'kinked' leading edge

XH533 was the first of 89 B.Mk 2 airframes built by Avro, first flying on 19 August 1958. The first 11 aircraft were used for a variety of service clearance trials, and it was not until July 1960 that the RAF received a B.Mk 2.

Naturally, 230 OCU was the first unit to get B.Mk 2s, based alongside B.Mk 1s at Waddington. As further B.Mk 2s arrived for operational squadrons a considerable upheaval took place in the Vulcan force. The training unit moved out to Finningley in June 1961, making room for No. 101 Sqn which made the reverse journey. Once at its new base, 230 OCU rapidly applied the white rose of Yorkshire to its aircraft.

Coningsby Wing

Vulcans were introduced to a new base in 1962 with the establishment of the Coningsby Wing with three squadrons (Nos 9, 12 and 35). Initially assigned free-fall duties with Yellow Sun Mk 2 weapons, the entire wing moved out to Cottesmore in 1964, where it became the first user of the WE177B lay-down strategic weapon. Prior to cancellation of the Skybolt missile, the wing was the intended first recipient of the weapon. In 1969, with the ending of the RAF nuclear deterrent tasking, the wing was broken up.

Sitting on the Coningsby ORP (Operational Readiness Platform), this quartet of B.Mk 2s comprises examples from each of the resident squadrons. No. 35 Sqn is represented by the aircraft in the foreground, No. 9 by the second and fourth aircraft, with No. 12 in the third slot.

B.Mk 2s of No. 83 Sqn line up at Scampton. From 1960 the V-force commanders were obsessed with force readiness, and many no-notice dispersal exercises were held. In 1961 No. 83 Sqn also flew on the large-scale Exercise Skyshield, a test of the SAC/NORAD air defence system. Operating from Lossiemouth, the squadron's aircraft penetrated US airspace at very high level.

For a few months after January 1965, when the Valiant fleet was prematurely grounded, the RAF was without refuelling support. In July the first Victor K.Mk 1 squadron (No. 55) became operational, followed closely by Nos 57 and 214. Here the recipient is a Vulcan of the Cottesmore Wing.

began losing its anti-buffet properties as installed power increased. Also, with the massive leap promised by the new variant of Olympus, the Vulcan would have been plagued by the old problem without some wing redesign.

The wing known as the Phase 2C was envisaged for higher-powered aircraft, maintaining the earlier model's fine handling qualities by increasing in area from 3,446 sq ft (320.14 m²) to 3,965 sq ft (368.36 m²) to accommodate a greater all-up weight and defeat the buffeting which became acute when *g* was pulled at height. A further 12 ft 0 in (3.66 m) was added to the span, to produce a new figure of 111 ft 0 in (33.83 m), and in combination the new wing and engines were expected to increase range by up to 300 miles (483 km). Elevons were simultaneously added to the training edge, one of their effects being to extend the potential for aerodynamic braking after touch-down by keeping the nose high until ground speed reached 80 kt (92 mph; 148 km/h) – or lower, if a crowd was watching! Approaching the runway at 135-145 kt (155-167 mph; 250-269 km/h), the Vulcan B.Mk 2 would halt within 4,000 ft (1219 m) with the additional help of a powerful braking parachute which produced as much drag as the engines did thrust.

Above 50,000 ft (15240 m) Vulcans turned like ballerinas as clod-hopping fighters attempted to out-manoeuvre, or floundered thousands of feet below at their operational ceilings. Heights of 65,000 ft (19812 m) were achieved under optimum conditions, although the margin there between cruise speed and the onset of compressibility was but a few knots. From the 40th B.Mk 2, wings were strengthened to take an underslung Douglas Skybolt nuclear missile on special attachment points, while further modifications ultimately added up to an incredible 10,000 lb (4536 kg) of reinforcement to keep the sturdy wing ahead of the ravages of fatigue. Designed for a life of 5,900 hours in the calm upper air, many aircraft exceeded this figure in the far more demanding low-level regime, the record being over 7,250 hours. If the scrapping order had not been issued, the B.Mk 2 fleet could have been flying for many more years.

The Mk 2 emerges

Other changes were introduced to the revised Vulcan. There was a stronger undercarriage with shortened (by 18 in/46 cm) nosewheel leg; a flight refuelling probe in the extreme nose; an autopilot (Smiths Mk 10A); more reliable and versatile 200V AC electrics in place of 112V DC; a Plessey 'pop-out' ram-air turbine and Rover airborne auxiliary powerplant (next to the starboard outer engine) for emergency power; and the ECM suite first installed in Mk 1As, although some of the first aircraft to be produced (including B.Mk 2 prototype XH533) did not have the extended tailcone fitted in their early test careers.

The Olympus reached its full potential in two stages. Early production Vulcan B.Mk 2s were fitted with four Olympus B.O.16 Mk 201s rated at 17,000 lb st (75.66 kN) each, and featured the larger intakes designed to provide the additional airflow for the definitive 20,000-lb st (88.97-kN) B.O.121 Olympus Mk 301. Having flown in the outboard bays of the 11th production B.Mk 2 on 19 May 1961, Mk 301s were introduced to the production line with the 34th airframe, early in 1962. After eight aircraft powered by this engine had been produced, 12 with Mk 201s were inserted before the later engine was fully established. This appears to have been part of a plan to standardise Mk 201s on Scampton-based aircraft, a scheme that misfired upon the disruption caused by cancellation of Skybolt (as related later).

Plans for a Mk 301 retrofit to these and earlier aircraft came to nothing when the change to low-level operations made the increased operational ceiling they conferred superfluous. The power differences remained in the fleet until the retirement of the aircraft (practised ears could apparently differentiate between engine types by the

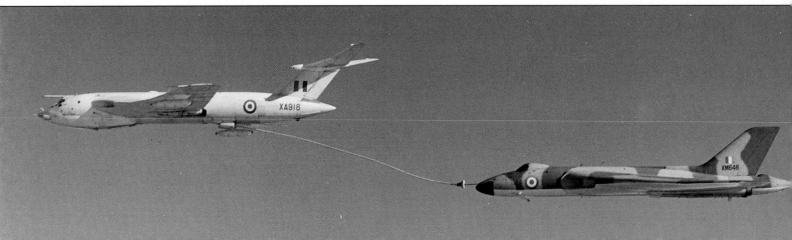

Powerplant

Although there were many exceptions, the Scampton Wing standardised on the Bristol Siddeley B.O.16 Olympus 201-powered aircraft, while Waddington operated the B.O. 121 Olympus 301-powered machines. The 201 provided 17,000 lb (75.65 kN) thrust, while the 301 was rated at 20,000 lb (89 kN).

Camouflage and markings

This aircraft wears the scheme adopted during the mid-1960s with the shift to low-level operations. The undersides remained in anti-flash white, but the topsides featured a two-tone disruptive pattern. The radome was subsequently camouflaged, and the roundels reduced to two colours. A second topside roundel later appeared on the starboard wing. The aircraft wears the panther's head badge of No. 1 Group, and the breached dam tail markings of No. 617 Sqn.

Engine intakes

The rectangular intake had a simple dividing fence downstream from the inlet. Air was fed in a straight line to the compressor face, structural wing members forming rings around the circular intake ducts. Next to the fuselage was a fixed splitter plate.

Avro Vulcan B.Mk 2
No. 617 Squadron
RAF Scampton

With the relinquishing of the nuclear deterrent to the Polaris force, the Scampton Wing gave up its notoriously difficult Blue Steel missiles and adopted the WE177B as its primary weapon. With these it flew the Vulcan as a tactical theatre nuclear strike force dedicated to NATO operations, with a secondary conventional attack role. The Vulcans also remained available for UK national roles.

Fuselage

The Vulcan's vestigial fuselage was arranged in five main sections. From nose to tail these comprised the nosecone with housing and supports for the H2S radar. Next came the five-man crew compartment, aft of which were two large fuel cells. Behind these was the weapons bay. The extreme rear fuselage consisted of a section at the base of the fin which housed oxygen and the rudder power control unit, with ECM equipment and the brake chute in the tailcone.

Airbrakes

Two sections of airbrakes were deployed above and below each wing. The brakes were held on vertical beams at each side, straddling the intake ducts. These were thrust vertically upwards, with the brake section rotating from the flush position to provide surface area.

Undercarriage

The Vulcan had Dowty undercarriage, the main units each supporting eight Dunlop wheels with high-pressure tyres. The wheels were fitted with Maxaret anti-skid braking units. The main undercarriage retracted forwards into the wing structure.

XM600

rougher, more rasping tone of the Mk 201 when it was at full power). In general, when the aircraft subsequently operated from only two bases, Scampton had the 200 series aircraft and Waddington the 300s.

These monsters could be brought to life within seconds by an external battery-powered simultaneous starting system more sophisticated than the old 'trolley-acc'. When first in service, having started one engine, the Mk 1 could begin taxiing and wind up the remaining three within 105 seconds while on the move, and the Mk 2 took 35 seconds for the same feat. With 'Simstart', trialled by No. 83 Squadron in April 1960 and generally introduced throughout the Vulcan force during 1963, all engines would be started almost at once by involved electrical switching, flight instruments erected and powered flying controls brought on line within 20 seconds. If parked on the operational readiness platform by the runway's edge (another 1963 innovation), four times 80+ tons of Vulcan would be blasting down the runway in a cloud of black smoke for a stream take-off well within the worst-case 'four-minute warning' of a pre-emptive missile attack.

From a standing start, Olympus 301-powered models would unstick at the 3,500-ft (1067-m) point, reaching 156 kt (180 mph; 289 km/h) in just 23 seconds and an altitude of 5,000 ft (1524 m) in one minute. Nine minutes later, at over 40,000 ft (12,192 m), the giant delta would throttle back to 86 per cent RPM and cruise-climb steadily to 50,000 ft (15240 m) at Mach 0.84. The Vulcan 'scramble' (not technically correct, for the crew was at Cockpit Readiness, already strapped in) was the show-stopper at many a Battle-of-Britain display. Had it been for real, the white-painted V-bombers would have turned east and sought their assigned targets behind the Iron Curtain, hoping for 59,000 ft (17983 m) as they entered Soviet territory.

Service deliveries

After the two prototypes and a small flock of Avro 707 scale test aircraft came an initial contract in August 1952 for 25 Vulcan B.Mk 1s, followed in September 1954 by 37 more, then eight in March 1955. Anxious to introduce the new Mk 2 model as quickly as possible, the RAF amended the contract on 1 June 1956 and had the 46th and subsequent aircraft built as B.Mk 2s, placing later contracts for 24 in February 1956 and 40 (later 39) in January 1958. In all, therefore, Avro (Hawker Siddeley after July 1963) built 45 Mk 1s and 89 B.Mk 2s.

Fitted with the span-increasing outer panels, second prototype Avro 698 (VX777) first flew in Phase 2C wing configuration on 31 August 1957. This was just in time for display at Farnborough, and eight months after the first

Four Vulcans wait for the call to action on the Waddington ORP. The Operational Readiness Platform situated the aircraft on the runway's edge, correctly positioned for a minimum-interval stream take-off if the alert was sounded.

B.Mk 1 had been delivered to No. 230 Operational Conversion Unit (OCU) to begin crew training. Other Mk 1s assisted the programme by testing Olympus Mk 200 engines (XA891), AC electrics (XA893) and the intended Avro Blue Steel stand-off bomb (XA903). When the first contracted B.Mk 2 (XH533) took to the air on 19 August 1958, it did so in advance of the last six Mk 1s and without the ECM tailcone.

The usual pre-service trials occupied the early aircraft, so it was not until 1 July 1960 that the first RAF delivery took place when No. 12 (XH558) was ferried to Waddington to begin formation of 'B' Flight of No. 230 OCU. Scampton was the first assigned operational base, however, and it was to No. 83 Squadron there that XH563 was delivered at Christmas 1960 to start the working-up process. No. 83 had formerly flown the Vulcan B.Mk 1, but when No. 27 Squadron formed at Scampton on 1 April 1961, it was the initial 'green' Mk 2 operator, accepting XJ823 on 21 April. Finally, No. 617 Squadron disposed of its Mk 1s and

A crew rushes to its Vulcan in a practice scramble. In real times of tension, they would have been at Cockpit Readiness.

Scramble!

A feature of any V-bomber crew's life was the scramble start. Initially this consisted of a run and bus ride to the aircraft, but in the QRA (Quick Reaction Alert) era this meant at least one aircraft from each unit at Cockpit Readiness, with the crew strapped in. Using the 'Simstart' equipment, one crew demonstrated the ability to get airborne 57 seconds after the alert sounded. QRA was introduced to the Vulcan force on 1 January 1962, stipulating a 15-minute readiness for one aircraft from each squadron, later increased to two. Readiness was regularly tested by exercises such as Mayflight and Micky Finn, these involving force-wide scrambles, dispersals and sustained operations.

Few sights in aviation were more dramatic than a full four-aircraft launch from the ORP, as demonstrated here by Blue Steel-carriers. The impressive climb performance of the Vulcan was used to the full during these exercises.

Upon reaching the aircraft, the scrambling crew's first priority was to get the engines started. Before the 'Simstart' system was introduced, standard practice was to get one engine started and begin taxiing, winding up the other three on the move. 'Simstart' allowed all four to be started together, greatly reducing response times.

began receiving the new mark, starting with XL318 on 4 September 1961.

The entire Vulcan force was administered by Bomber Command (Strike Command after 1968) via the No. 1 Group HQ at Bawtry HQ, whereas the Victor and Valiant units came under No. 3 Group at Mildenhall. No. 1 Group next assigned Vulcan B.Mk 2s to Coningsby, where Nos 9, 12 and 35 Squadrons all formed from scratch on 1 March, 1 July and 1 December 1962. The latter wing moved to Cottesmore, a former Victor base, on 7 November 1964, at which it took delivery of the last production Mk 2 (XM657) on 15 January 1965.

Nuclear weaponry

The three wings had different weaponry and an accordingly varied standard of aircraft. Scampton's Vulcans, fitted with Olympus 201s, were designated B.Mk 2A, for they had provision for Blue Steel semi-recessed in special bomb bay doors. To accommodate Blue Steel, the front bomb bay spar had to be cranked and the rear spar partly cut away – changes brought in with aircraft No. 26 (XL317, the first ordered from the outset as a Mk 2). No. 617 Sqn received its first modified aircraft in

September 1961, as previously noted, and the other Scampton units passed on their earlier equipment as more new Vulcans arrived.

Scampton's 26 Blue Steel Vulcans (eight per squadron, plus two spares) were aircraft Nos 26-33 and 42-59. When Skybolt failed to appear, Cottesmore's aircraft (Nos 61-89 plus some earlier machines) were equipped instead with the WE177B lay-down strategic nuclear weapon. Finally, in

Conventional bombing practice was regularly undertaken, and with the change to low-level operations often involved ballute-retarded weapons, as demonstrated here by a No. 12 Sqn aircraft over Salisbury Plain.

Above: Resplendent in its gloss camouflage finish, XM649 from the Waddington Wing cruises over the Lincolnshire countryside. The enormous wing provided considerable buffet at low level, but the Vulcan made a satisfactory transition to the new regime when tactics dictated.

Right: Eight Cottesmore Vulcans line the ramp at one of the two main deployment bases in the Far East, Tengah or Butterworth. The first major rapid reinforcement exercise, Spherical, was undertaken in April 1965, involving eight aircraft deploying to the Malayan peninsula. A simulated arming was carried out at the stop-over at Gan, and the bombers demonstrated that they could have hit targets in Indonesia within 48 hours of a request from FEAF commanders.

A Vulcan B.Mk 2 of No. 617 Sqn drifts across the threshold. The Vulcan had benign landing qualities thanks to the large wing. A favourite procedure for air shows was to hold the nose high during much of the rollout.

1966-67, the Waddington Wing of Nos 44, 50 and 101 Squadrons relinquished B.Mk 1As and Yellow Sun Mk 2 in favour of Vulcan B.Mk 2s armed with WE177B free-fall nuclear weapons. Reallocation of aircraft was made possible by a reduction in squadron strengths and disbandment of No. 12 Squadron. Its companions, Nos 9 and 35, then spent six years in Cyprus having been freed of the nuclear deterrent tasking, splitting up on return to the UK to reside at Waddington and Scampton (where No. 83 had disbanded in 1969).

Based within sight of Lincoln Cathedral since 1975, the eight surviving Vulcan B.Mk 2 units (OCU included)

remained in the forefront of the RAF's strike forces until the run-down began in 1981, having cost £5 million per year to operate since 1969. Taking into account the low-level flying task, losses were remarkably light, at 0.33 per 10,000 flying hours – consistently below the average for all types of RAF aircraft, which was around 0.45.

Whenever a Vulcan was lost, much was made of the lack of ejection seats for the three rear crew of nav radar, nav plotter and air electronics officer (AEO). While pilot and co-pilot could eject to safety, the rear crew had to exit via the hatch in the cabin floor, and this could be difficult or impossible if the aircraft was reeling out of control. If the undercarriage was down, there was the further complication of obstruction by the nosewheel leg. It was a case of the best being the enemy of the good. The original intention of B.35/46 had been to provide a wholly jettisoning, parachute-suspended cockpit as a crew escape module or, failing that, a jettisoning system for all seats. When both proved impractical, airframe design was too far advanced for explosive hatches to be incorporated above the three back seats and OR 229 was amended in January 1953 to include a blast-protected escape hatch for the rear crew.

After the V-bombers were in service, Martin-Baker was asked to devise a method of upward ejection for the rear occupants, but it seemed to officialdom at the time that the Vulcan would be withdrawn when Polaris submarines became operational, so it was not pursued. In truth, there were precious few cases in which the pilots were able to eject while leaving the remainder of the crew to its fate. Although much was made in the media of the 'moral dilemma' in which they were supposedly placed, the survivors of such accidents received no criticism from their fellows. Having tried everything to save the aircraft, it was their duty to eject, for the air force does not subscribe to the naval tradition of captains perishing needlessly with their ships.

Blue Steel

Following cancellation of Blue Boar, fresh steps were taken towards the goal of providing V-bombers with a stand-off weapon so that they need not hazard themselves by exposure to the air defences of a high-value target. Under Air Staff Requirement (ASR) 1132 – issued on 3 September and better known by its codename of Blue Steel – Avro and a team of sub-contractors produced a weapon powered by a Bristol Siddeley BSSt.1 Stentor rocket engine and capable of a variable flight profile. Blue Steel would be launched at around 40,000 ft (12220 m), from where the 16,000 lb st (71.20 kN) of the Stentor's main combustion chamber accelerated it to Mach 2.3 and over 70,000 ft (21340 m), when momentum was maintained on the secondary chamber's 4,000 lb st (17.80 kN). Normal range was 115 miles (185 km), culminating in a Mach 1.5+ dive on the target, but this could be doubled if a high subsonic penetration were selected.

Powered by highly volatile fuel and notoriously difficult to integrate with its carrier aircraft, Blue Steel attained an interim ('national emergency' only) operational capability with No. 617 Squadron on 24 September 1962, the aircraft/missile combination being in satisfaction of ASR 367. First rounds had been delivered in July for a trial launch at Woomera, Australia, although initial formal acceptance was not until the following December. Finally, in February 1963, the weapon was declared fully operational when seven missiles had been accepted and six more were undergoing acceptance tests. Nos 27 and 83 Squadrons were similarly equipped before the end of 1964, and shared the 57 production Blue Steels with 12 Victor B.Mk 2s of Nos 100 and 139 Squadrons at Wittering. The total – reduced from the planned 75 – included five spare rounds and four for proof firing; there were also 16 ground loading/training rounds. Victors launched two of

Vulcans in the US

To illustrate the close relationship between the RAF's V-force and Strategic Air Command, Vulcans were regular visitors to the United States. In addition to participation in many USAF exercises, the Vulcans undertook Western Ranger navigation exercises which usually terminated at Offutt AFB, Nebraska. Permanent servicing parties were established both at Offutt and the usual staging post at Goose Bay, Labrador.

Right: XA901 is seen in November 1957 returning to Waddington after participation in the SAC bombing competition at Pinecastle AFB, Florida. Two Vulcans were involved, flying alongside two Valiants from No. 138 Sqn.

Below: Two delta-winged bombers of very different characters meet at Offutt AFB. The Convair B-58 Hustler was hugely expensive, and had only a limited career with Strategic Air Command.

Left and below: As SAC and Bomber Command had joint targeting plans, the main bombers of the two organisations regularly came face-to-face. At left, operational aircraft meet at Offutt, while below the third B.Mk 2 (XH535) flies with the sixth B-52H (60-0006) near Edwards AFB.

Bottom: Aircraft of the Scampton Wing often took training rounds of the Blue Steel missile with them on training deployments. Here, one poses over the US side of the Niagara Falls.

the proof rounds, the balance being fired by Vulcan XL390 over the Aberporth range on 31 May and 7 July 1967. Servicing of Blue Steel was undertaken in an air of secrecy by No. 92 Maintenance Unit at Faldingworth, east of Scampton.

From mid-1964, the weapon was adapted for low-level launching (below 1,000 ft/305 m). Both combustion chambers then fired together, though with the penalty that range was reduced to one-quarter of that at high level. A Mk 2 version, capable of flying up to 690 miles (1110 km), was abandoned early in the development phase. Blue Steel Mk 1 continued in its curtailed, though still vital, role throughout the 1960s.

Carefully concealed during the early period was a fundamental weakness of the Blue Steel concept. Although unarmed and unfuelled missiles were fitted to aircraft standing QRA from August 1963, at least 30 minutes' work was required for them to be made serviceable. Safety considerations precluded the routine, peacetime fitment of ready-to-launch Blue Steel, because of both the proximity of volatile fuel and nuclear material and dangers inherent in leaving thermal batteries permanently in the detonation mechanism. Naturally, weapons would have been armed in the event of a deteriorating political situation, but in response to a no-notice nuclear attack, the QRA Vulcans and Victors armed with Blue Steel were impotent until new safety procedures were introduced a year later, allowing the nuclear warhead to be armed in 10 seconds.

Finally, on 30 June 1969, the Royal Navy's Polaris-equipped submarine fleet assumed the mantle of deterrence; QRA was discontinued at midnight and the Scampton Wing began to break up. No. 83 Squadron disbanded at the end of August and, by 1 January 1970, No. 27 was operational in the free-fall nuclear bombing regime. First 'in', No. 617 was also last 'out' when it flew the final Blue Steel sortie on 21 December 1970, prior to converting to free-fall.

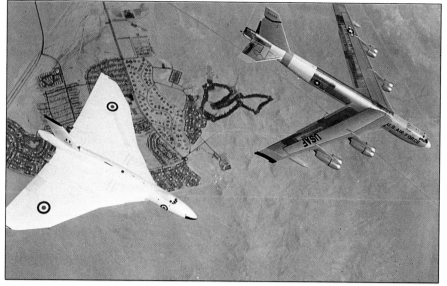

Scampton Wing

Established as the third Vulcan base, Scampton initially used the Vulcan B.Mk 1 armed with Blue Danube, followed in 1958 by the interim Violet Club thermonuclear weapon. This was superseded by Yellow Sun Mk 1 (the same warhead in a new casing) in 1960. In 1961 the base, by now boasting three squadrons (Nos 27, 83 and 617), began to receive B.Mk 2A aircraft equipped for the carriage of the Blue Steel missile, with which a limited capability was achieved in September 1962. Blue Steel operations consumed most of the wing's activities until 1969/70, when the aircraft returned to free-fall bombing with WE177B and conventional bombs. In 1969 No. 83 Sqn was disbanded, its place at Scampton taken by 230 OCU which moved in from Finningley. Further changes in the 1970s saw No. 27 Sqn reborn as a reconnaissance unit, and the arrival of No. 35 Sqn from Cyprus.

Above: With a pale blue-coloured Blue Steel clutched to its belly, a No. 617 Sqn aircraft displays the toned-down markings of the early 1960s period.

Below: Blue Steel missiles were serviced by No. 92 Maintenance Unit at Faldingworth, close to Scampton. Here, the carrier aircraft is from No. 27 Sqn.

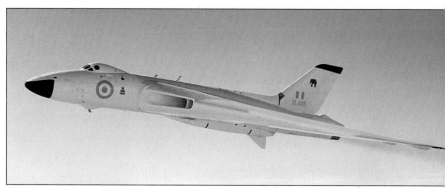

Right: This view provides an excellent view of the Blue Steel carriage, and of the flat plate ECM antenna under the starboard engine nacelles.

Below: XL360 sits on the Scampton ramp. The base had a special pit over which Vulcans could taxi in order to dump the volatile missile fuel in an emergency. Similarly, water baths were provided near the aircraft for any personnel who accidentally came into contact with the fluid.

There might have been no Polaris had not the RAF backed a loser when looking for a second air-launched strategic missile. Meeting ASR 1149, the Douglas AGM-87A Skybolt missile promised a range of 1,000 miles (1609 km) and was seized upon in 1960 as a replacement for the cancelled British ICBM, Blue Streak, as well as Blue Steel Mk 2. Unfortunately, after a troublesome initial trials programme, the US government took similar action with Skybolt in November 1962. At a stroke, the whole future of the RAF's airborne deterrent was swept away, leaving purchase of Polaris submarines as the only alternative. Up until then, all Bomber Command's planning had revolved around the building of an eventual force of 72 Vulcan B.Mk 2s (ground clearance on the Victor was insufficient), each carrying two Skybolts as a replacement for the existing fleet of 144 V-bombers with a single bomb or Blue Steel.

Despite plans for an enlarged Vulcan carrying up to six Skybolts and a relief crew, no attempt was made to emulate the SAC system of airborne alerts. True, the Vulcans did have refuelling probes, but these were for overseas deployment, not standing patrols. The wings of early production Vulcan B.Mk 2s had even been retrospectively modified with Skybolt attachment points, which were to find a use later.

Lay-down weapon

Skybolt's dramatic disappearance caused RAF planners to do some rapid thinking. On 2 January 1963 – a fortnight after the supply of Polaris had been agreed – the Defence Research Policy Committee reported that only a high-yield, low-level release bomb to supplement Blue Steel could maintain the deterrent value of the V-force until the new submarines became available in 1969. A potential answer was immediately forthcoming when it was suggested that a new tactical bomb, the WE177 then in development, could be uprated for strategic use. The product of Naval & Air Staff Requirement 1177, this weapon was optimised for low-level delivery by parachute from the Blackburn Buccaneer and BAC TSR.2. The tactical version became the 600-lb (272-kg) WE177A,

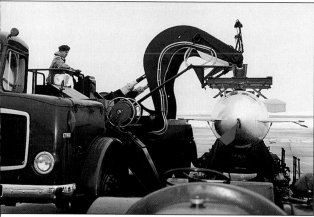

Above: Road transport of the Blue Steel was accomplished using the AEC Mandator, specially equipped with a hoisting gantry and with stabilising legs to hold the vehicle steady when lifting the missile.

Below: Fuelling the Blue Steel was one of the most potentially hazardous occupations in the RAF, and full protective clothing was worn as a matter of course. The floors were washed down before in case of spillage.

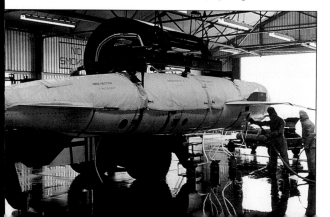

Blue Steel missile

The production W.105 Blue Steel missile was powered by a Bristol Siddeley Stentor rocket engine, fuelled by a mixture of kerosene and HTP (High Test Peroxide). The latter was a mix of hydrogen peroxide and water, and was extremely volatile, necessitating very careful handling. From front to rear the missile consisted of a pitot tube, flight rules computer, autopilot, kerosene tank and forward HTP tank, Red Snow megaton warhead, main HTP tank, alternator and electronic power control unit and finally the Stentor motor. The latter had a main chamber for the boost phase, and a smaller chamber for sustained flight. Other components included a fuel pump, gearbox and equipment to fold the lower fin to provide sufficient ground clearance.

Right: Blue Steels are seen undergoing maintenance in the Scampton shed. The twin chambers of the Stentor motor are clearly visible, the main one providing 16,000 lb (71.2 kN) thrust for the initial climb phase.

Right: The B.Mk 2A modification for Blue Steel carriage required several internal structural changes to accommodate the recess. The cockpit had some new instruments for missile launch.

Above: After transport to the ramp on the Mandator, the missile was lowered on to a trolley to be pushed under the aircraft for hoisting into the cut-out.

Skybolt

XH537 was Avro's Skybolt development aircraft, used for a series of dummy drops at the West Freugh range.

The Douglas AGM-87A Skybolt missile (known originally as WS138A) was intended as a replacement for the Blue Steel Mk 2, and offered a range of over 1,000 miles, a far cry from the 100-mile stand-off achievable with the Blue Steel Mk 1 then in service. Discussions with the US started in early 1960, and a Memorandum of Understanding was signed on 6 June. The intention was to procure 144 missiles, carried two per Vulcan, to maintain what was deemed a sufficient deterrent capability. The use of Skybolt would make Vulcan bases even more attractive targets, and so an airborne alert was contemplated. In the event, the missile was cancelled by President Kennedy in November 1962, a fact that was officially communicated to Prime Minister Macmillan on 19 December.

Above: XH537 first flew with the dummy Skybolts in November 1961, and made the first drop on 1 December. In the US, XH538 was used by the British Joint Trials Force at Eglin AFB, and made four powered launches.

Right: The motor section of the dummy Skybolt was covered with a fairing to maintain aerodynamic properties. Hardpoints for the wing pylons were incorporated on the production line from the 61st aircraft and retrofitted to others.

Below: After Skybolt's cancellation, the programme was offered to the UK, but Macmillan opted for Polaris. If Skybolt had been adopted, the six-missile Vulcan B.Mk 3 would have been developed to enable the RAF to undertake an airborne alert deterrent with 84 Skybolts airborne at any one time.

while the strategic WE177B tipped the scales at 950 lb (431 kg). Both types were 12 ft 0 in (3.65 m) in length, 16.5 in (42 cm) in diameter and had a tailfin span of 2 ft 0 in (60 cm).

Meanwhile, Bomber Command was forced to change tactics, using what equipment it had. A policy document on the new direction was drafted on 10 January and quickly approved by the Cabinet's Defence Committee, while on the following day the Defence Research Policy Committee debated the change to low-level penetration. Its recommendations were sanctioned by the Air Council on 14 March and written up and issued as Standard of Preparation 54 on 3 May. One year later, on 5 May 1964, Air Staff Requirement 380 was published to describe in full terms the new doctrine.

Air Council approval was but a formality, as the first low-level training sortie had been flown two days before (on 12 March 1963) by a No. 44 Squadron Vulcan B.Mk 1A. Transition was eased by advice from Marham Valiant crews who had been flying low-level for SACEUR for two years. Initially, Vulcans transited low-flying routes at 1,000 ft (305 m) before being cleared down to 500 ft (152 m) when they became proficient, and even lower at the captain's discretion. ASR 380 envisaged 50 ft (15 m) under extremely favourable conditions.

The new tactics were introduced in two stages. Mk 1As converted first, their mission being hi-lo-hi delivery with a low-level penetration phase of up to 1,100 miles (1770 km). However, this would have to be punctuated by a climb to 12,000 ft (3660 m) to release Yellow Sun Mk 2. In the short term, Mk 2s continued their high-level missions and would have been tasked against peripheral targets. Only in 1964 did Mk 2s also descend to low altitude.

Coincident with the change came a coat of green and grey disruptive pattern camouflage on the Vulcan's vast upper surfaces. First applied to Waddington's Mk 1A XH505 in April 1964, this replaced the overall 'anti-flash'

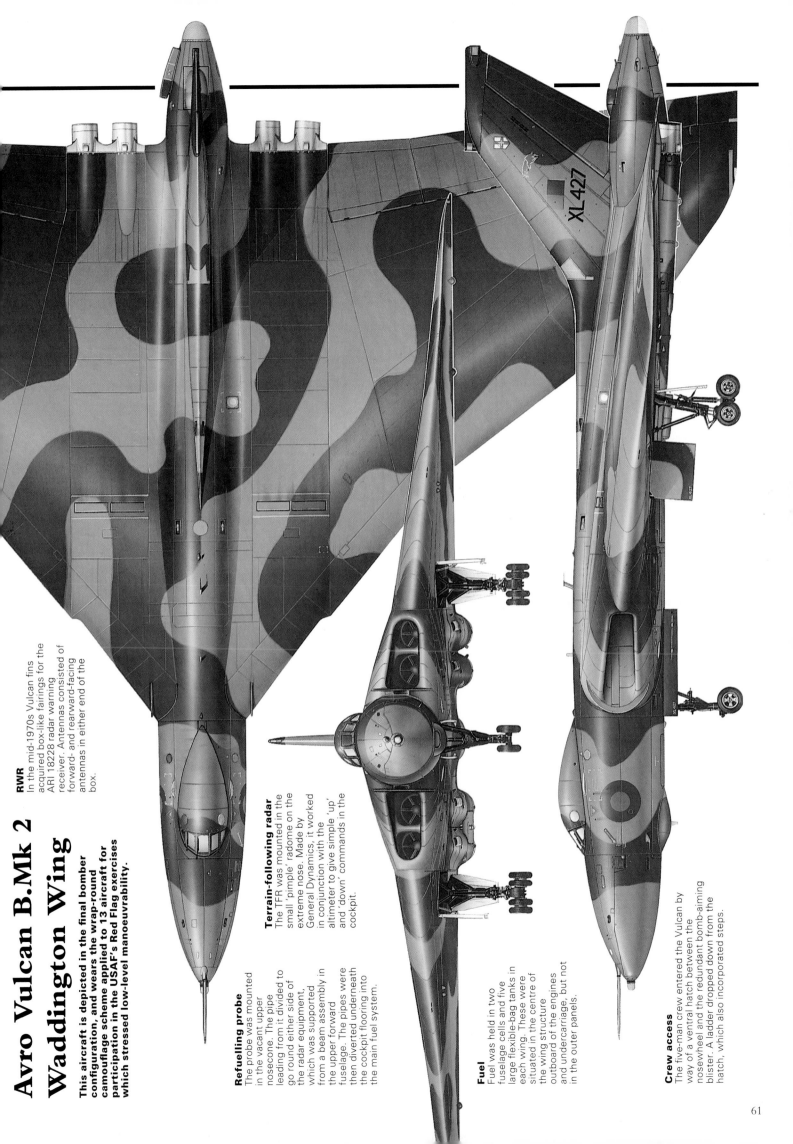

Avro Vulcan B.Mk 2 Waddington Wing

This aircraft is depicted in the final bomber configuration, and wears the wrap-round camouflage scheme applied to 13 aircraft for participation in the USAF's Red Flag exercises which stressed low-level manoeuvrability.

RWR
In the mid-1970s Vulcan fins acquired box-like fairings for the ARI 18228 radar warning receiver. Antennas consisted of forward- and rearward-facing antennas in either end of the box.

Refuelling probe
The probe was mounted in the vacant upper nosecone. The pipe leading from it divided to go round either side of the radar equipment, which was supported from a beam assembly in the upper forward fuselage. The pipes were then diverted underneath the cockpit flooring into the main fuel system.

Terrain-following radar
The TFR was mounted in the small 'pimple' radome on the extreme nose. Made by General Dynamics, it worked in conjunction with the altimeter to give simple 'up' and 'down' commands in the cockpit.

Fuel
Fuel was held in two fuselage cells and five large flexible-bag tanks in each wing. These were situated in the centre of the wing structure outboard of the engines and undercarriage, but not in the outer panels.

Crew access
The five-man crew entered the Vulcan by way of a ventral hatch between the nosewheel and the redundant bomb-aiming blister. A ladder dropped down from the hatch, which also incorporated steps.

61

Low-level operations

The cancellation of Skybolt and the proliferation of Soviet surface-to-air missiles combined to render the existing high-altitude operations ineffective, at least beyond 1965. This created Britain's own 'missile gap' until such time as the Polaris force could become operational, expected in 1969. Bomber Command was without any alternative other than to transition to low-level operations to maintain the V-force's survivabilty, this beginning in March 1963. This caused serious problems: until the WE177B strategic lay-down bomb could be fielded it had less than ideal weapons. The Yellow Sun and Red Beard weapons required a pop-up to at least 12,000 ft (3660 m) for release, while Blue Steel launched at low level was limited in range. At first the Yellow Sun force went low-level against primary targets, leaving the Blue Steel carriers to attack fringe targets.

Above: The most obvious change associated with the switch to low-level operations was the adoption of camouflage, initially applied to Waddington's B.Mk 1As in a high-gloss finish. Here a Cottesmore B.Mk 2 is seen in company with a white-scheme aircraft from the Finningley OCU.

Left: In the early 1970s, matt paint was introduced on the upper surfaces.

Below: With the shadow of the Jet Provost photo-platform joining that of the Vulcan, the last aircraft built demonstrates its low-level capabilities. The pimple on the nose housed terrain-following radar.

white with its pale-coloured serialling and insignia, although it was not until some years later that the white component was deleted from national identity markings.

Unit badges also disappeared by the spring of 1964 as bases fully implemented a centralised servicing system introduced on 1 March 1963, under which aircraft were pooled and issued to squadrons as required by the day's tasking. Because of the changing role of its components, the Scampton Wing reverted to individual allocations from 1971 and resumed the practice of applying badges during the following year. Waddington retained the pooling system up to disbandment of the Vulcan force, although for reasons of *esprit de corps* its aircraft also wore badges from 1972.

To assist study of the increased fatigue likely from operations in denser air, XM596 was taken off the production line in the spring of 1963 and placed in a static test rig, thereby reducing the final contract to 39 aircraft. Following service trials at Cottesmore between 28 February and 6 July 1965 (during which the second weapon was flown for 50 hours) and at Akrotiri from October 1965, WE177B was finally cleared for V-bomber QRA fitment in September 1966. Yellow Sun Mk 2 was withdrawn almost immediately and the final WE177B of the contract was received in or around May 1967.

Avionics and self-defence systems were also revamped for low level. In addition to the jammers and sensors already mentioned as carried forward from the Mk 1A to Mk 2 were an ARI 18205 L-band jammer and an upgrade of rear-facing fighter detection radar from ARI 5919 Red Steer to ARI 5952. Mk 2s also gained a Mk 6 version of GPI (ground position indicator), had their Green Satin Doppler sets modified for lower altitudes and received the Mk 4 Decca roller map. ASR 3600 was initiated for sidescan radar capability and a requirement issued for

A pair of Vulcans flies past the Ballistic Missile Early Warning System radar site at Fylingdales, Yorkshire. The BMEWS was vital to the V-force's ability to launch effectively, as it provided the main warning of incoming nuclear missile attacks.

terrain-following radar. The latter materialised in July 1965 when 158 sets of General Dynamics TFRs were ordered for all Mk 2 V-bombers and fitted from the following year, taking the form of a small 'thimble' radome in the extreme nose. Linked to the altimeter, TFR provided the pilots with visual 'up' and 'down' signals which they followed to keep the aircraft at a chosen height above the ground.

Ageing avionics

It is probably little exaggeration to say that the bombing and navigation system which kept three crew gainfully occupied with a plethora of dials, screens, fuses, valves, wheels and pulleys in the darkened rear compartment of a Vulcan could now be tucked away in a small black box. That must not be allowed to cloud the fact that the Vulcan retained a credible theatre-nuclear strike capability from July 1969 to its dying day. The avionics were old and labour-intensive, but that did not prevent a trained crew from finding its target. This was amply demonstrated when the RAF won the Mathis Trophy and Navigation Trophy in the 1974 Strategic Air Command bombing competition (Giant Voice). Until the advent of the Tornado, English-based USAF F-111s and RAF Vulcans were the only fully all-weather theatre-nuclear aircraft assigned to SACEUR's Strategic Reserve.

The five men responsible for taking the Vulcan to war included pilot and co-pilot side-by-side in a compact cockpit. Below and to the rear, the navigation and bombing systems were managed by the three remaining members in a line of backwards-facing seats: nav radar (starboard), nav plotter (centre) and air electronics officer (port). The trusty H2S Mk 9A radar provided just one source of information fed by the nav radar into the Vulcan's NBS (navigation and bombing system). Other data came from Green Satin, which was a Doppler speed and drift indicator and which continuously updated the GPI, a dial readout of the aircraft's predicted latitude and longitude.

An electro-mechanical computer, the NBC Mk 2, integrated the inputs to produce a corrected position fix, accurate to within 150 ft (46 m). When Blue Steel was being carried, its inertial navigation system was so accurate that it became the prime navigation sensor, although a radar cross-check and other data updated its position information just before release.

The NBS worked equally well at low level and could be backed up by map-reading if circumstances permitted. For bomb release at this height, the pilot had the option of over-riding the systems and releasing visually. His sighting equipment was no more complex than a hastily-designed device made of perspex, for the ventral bomb-aiming blister remained unused in the Mk 2 Vulcans. Defensive aids remained largely unaltered apart from the addition of a Marconi ARI 18228 radar warning receiver from 1975. The RWR occupied a distinctive fin-top position,

In the conventional role the Vulcan carried up to three clips of seven bombs each (19 of the full load are visible here). The bombs were sequenced to drop singly from each clip in the order front, centre and rear, repeating the sequence seven times.

The Blue Steel was largely overtaken by events, and operationally its use, especially from low level, would have been restricted to peripheral targets.

Low-level Blue Steel

The transition to low-level occurred almost simultaneously with the full entry into service of the Blue Steel missile, and the test unit's work at Woomera reflected this, undertaking both high- and low-altitude tests. The first low-level launch of a W.100A pre-production round took place from a Vulcan on 19 November 1963. Only small modifications were necessary for low-level launches, which entailed firing both chambers of the Stentor motor together. This provided sufficient power but greatly reduced the range. Controller (Aircraft) release for an emergency low-level capability came on 1 July 1964. As recounted elsewhere, four of the 57 Blue Steel missiles ordered by the RAF were reserved for proof testing, and these were launched (two from a Victor and two from a Vulcan) at 1,000 ft (305 m) altitude over Aberporth range in the early summer of 1967.

Rangers

In addition to the regular scrambles and QRA operations, Vulcans also often practised long-range deployments, usually singly. These were known as Rangers, and were designed to test not only the mobility of the Vulcan and its crews, but also their ability to operate self-sufficiently from airfields not equipped with specialised support equipment. Lone Ranger flights headed eastwards, to Wildenrath, Luqa, El Adem or Muharraq, or southwards to Nairobi or Salisbury, the African destinations requiring a stop at Luqa. Western Rangers headed across the Atlantic with a stop at Goose Bay before continuation to Offutt AFB, where the force maintained a permanent servicing party. The Blue Ranger flights were special trips to deliver Blue Steel missiles for testing at the Woomera range. The Vulcan was no stranger 'down under', with regular deployments and visits to both Australia and New Zealand.

Left: A Vulcan from the Waddington Wing stops over at a snowy Goose Bay during a Western Ranger flight.

Right: In addition to its Cold War mission, the Vulcan had a non-NATO global mission, resulting in the type appearing at many distant bases. Here, a pair is seen at a USAF deployment base, with a C-124 and a WB-50 in the background.

Left: Not an RNZAF Vulcan, but the victim of some serious Kiwi 'zapping' at a New Zealand air show. Other well-known rebadged aircraft included Akrotiri's BDA aircraft, which wore large 'Fly Navy' titles and an 809 Naval Air Squadron badge.

Above: Although its primary purpose was far more concerned with the 1960s world of superpower stand-off, the Vulcan also represented a bygone era in which Britain could claim an Empire. The arrival of a Vulcan 'down under' would invariably spark some sort of Imperial pride and suitably irrational behaviour, hence the RNZAF bagpiper to welcome the new arrival from Blighty.

having first been fitted to XM597 in 1972 for trials at Boscombe Down with the A&AEE and at Waddington. In earlier, high-level days, a modification codenamed Fishpool enabled the H2S to locate a fighter climbing to intercept the bomber from the front. This was by no means as reliable as today's airborne early warning systems, but it was later sophisticated enough to spot the launch of an air-to-air missile by a pursuing interceptor.

Right: Back home, the serious business of training for the Cold War continued unabated, broadened to include more conventional sorties once the deterrent was passed to the Royal Navy. In 1975 the ARI 18228 radar warning receiver began to make an appearance in the characteristic rectangular fairing at the fin's top.

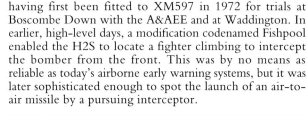

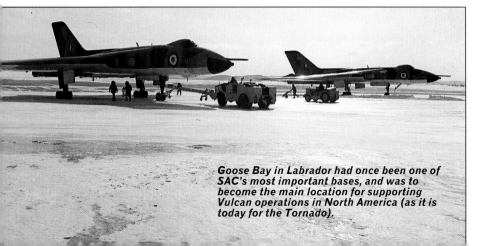

Goose Bay in Labrador had once been one of SAC's most important bases, and was to become the main location for supporting Vulcan operations in North America (as it is today for the Tornado).

Although widely travelled overseas, the Vulcan was not permanently stationed abroad until Nos 9 and 35 Squadrons began leaving Cottesmore for the British sovereign base at Akrotiri, Cyprus, on 15 January 1969. Assigned to CENTO as a replacement for four squadrons of Canberras, they formed the Near East Air Force Bomber Wing of 16 aircraft. Additionally, having greater range than their predecessors, they also were able to operate in the UK national interest (with WE177B) against Soviet targets from dispersed bases at Muharraq (Bahrain, three aircraft) and Masirah (Oman, six aircraft). Reductions in overseas commitments brought the units home again in January 1975: No. 9 to Waddington and No. 35 to Scampton, both being redeclared to SACEUR on 1 March. Meanwhile, on 20 January, four of No. 50 Squadron's Vulcans deployed to Akrotiri at the start of a programme of regular detachments.

Prior to 1982, the nearest approach to an operational deployment by the Vulcan force took place in the Far East. British defence responsibility for Malaysia, under threat of invasion from Indonesia, resulted in the assumption from the Victor force of this theatre by Nos 9, 12 and 35 Squadrons when they moved into Cottesmore in 1964. Beginning with No. 12 Sqn on 1 October, each unit took it in turns to base four aircraft in the Far East, for 3.5 months at a time, in what was known as the Matterhorn Rotation. The Indian Ocean island airfield of Gan was the rear base, although aircraft were usually based forward at Butterworth and Tengah. The offensive capability was, of course, strictly conventional. Rapid reinforcement of the

Profiteer, Chamfrom and Matterhorn

In the last years of the Malayan Emergency, Bomber Command dispatched V-bombers to Butterworth under Operation Profiteer. Valiants were sent initially, but in October 1959 one No. 617 Sqn aircraft was sent, to be followed by four from No. 101 in January 1960, and four from No. 83 Sqn in February 1960. The V-bombers played no part in the emergency. In the 1963-66 Indonesian Confrontation, Vulcans and Victors were sent to Malaya under Operation Chamfrom to man the

Matterhorn Medium Bomber Rotation, and they acted as a significant deterrent to Indonesian aggression. Vulcan squadrons involved were No. 12 (October to December 1964), No. 9 (from August 1965) and No. 35 (March to August 1966). In April 1965, No. 35 Sqn had also demonstrated the ability to deploy eight aircraft to the theatre very rapidly under Exercise Spherical. With the end of the confrontation in 1966, the Matterhorn rotation was ended.

Above: A pair of No. 83 Sqn B.Mk 1s is seen at RAAF Butterworth, Malaya, during an Operation Profiteer deployment. The aircraft exercised with RAAF Sabres during their deployment.

detachment was practised until the Indonesians shelved their plans in August 1966 and all aircraft returned home, the last on 30 August. When the Cottesmore Wing broke up in 1969, No. 44 Squadron at Waddington assumed the Far East rapid deployment brief, testing its capabilities with a deployment to Tengah in the following year.

It was with North America that the Vulcan established its closest links. Since the late 1950s, the USAF had permitted RAF use of its range facilities. A permanent RAF servicing echelon was based at Offutt AFB, Nebraska, from where detached V-bombers operated for 25 years until the RAF's corner of a foreign field closed in July 1982. At Goose Bay, Canada, the nearby immense, unpopulated wastes provided a virtually featureless exercise area for low-level training.

Akrotiri Wing

In May 1968 it was decided that two squadrons of Vulcans, Nos 9 and 35, would replace the Near East Air Force's Canberra Wing (with Nos 6, 32, 73 and 249 Sqns) at Akrotiri. The 16 aircraft would continue the main tasking of providing nuclear (with WE177B) and conventional bombing in support of both CENTO and UK national interests. In addition to operations from Akrotiri, the wing also manned the Pedigree detachment on Masirah island, Oman, and undertook detachments

and Rangers to places such as Muharraq (Bahrain), Sharjah, Tengah, Peshawar, Teheran and Nairobi. The wing was required in time of tension to immediately deploy six aircraft to Masirah and three to Muharraq. When Turkey invaded the northern half of Cyprus on 20 July 1974, the Akrotiri Wing found more difficulty in continuing its training operations, and in the following January the squadrons returned to the UK. Four-aircraft detachments from the UK continued to meet CENTO obligations after that.

Above: A Vulcan from the Akrotiri Wing overflies its adopted home. During the Turkish invasion of the island the Vulcans flew maritime radar reconnaissance missions, and also acted as communications relay posts. However, for most of their tenure on Cyprus they provided nuclear muscle to the CENTO organisation.

Below: A young Cypriot watches a Vulcan landing at Akrotiri. The force was in residence for six years.

Above: Servicing Vulcans in the hot Mediterranean sun was a far cry from working at rainswept Cottesmore. The badges on the crew access door were the Akrotiri station badge and those for Nos 9 and 35 Sqns. The legend read 'Near East Air Force Bomber Wing'.

Sixteen operational Vulcan B.Mk 2s were assigned to the NEAF Bomber Wing, operating from two large ramps (below) interconnected by a taxiway, and clearly visible on approach (above) to Akrotiri's single runway.

Above: Wearing the Red Flag wrap-round scheme, XM575 passes Spurn Head, a distinctive spit of land jutting into the Humber estuary and a regular landmark for Vulcans operating from Waddington and Scampton.

Right: The Vulcan airframe took quite a pounding in the low-level regime, especially in Cyprus where aircraft on training flights took off in the cool early morning to reduce fatigue-inducing buffet at heavy weights. When the force went low-level, one airframe was taken off the production line for fatigue testing.

Solo exercises, known as Rangers, also took the Vulcan over the Atlantic, as did the USAF's highly realistic Red Flag training exercise, run by Tactical Air Command at Nellis AFB, Nevada. First deployed for a Red Flag in 1977, Vulcans were soon operating down to 200 ft (61 m) over the vast Nellis weapons range, often completing their mission without being 'hit' by a single defending fighter or simulated SAM site, despite the crystal-clear flying conditions. After that, no one questioned the ageing bomber's ability to penetrate the Iron Curtain in the murky European weather, or at night. For even greater concealment during tight turns at low level, 13 Vulcans received wrap-round camouflage, on which the lower surface pattern was a mirror image of that above.

Even at high level, the Vulcan was not an easy target for, apart from the vertical fin, it coincidentally adopted what would today be called a 'stealthy' shape. Vulcans were always harder to locate by radar than their fellow bombers, as Mk 1s proved in 1961 when they tested the mighty US air defence network. One even had the effrontery to land at Plattsburgh AFB, New York, underlining the point that if it were war, the United States' second city would have been no more. In fact, in the joint targeting plan adopted in 1958, the RAF would act as an advance guard for Boeing B-52s striking at the Soviet heartland.

Other roles

A reduction in nuclear responsibilities freed Vulcan B.Mk 2s for other duties. No. 27 Squadron disbanded at Scampton in March 1972 but reformed at the same base on

Red Flag

Red Flag is the USAF's most realistic warfare training exercise, and Vulcans were invited to participate from 1977. Tight turning in the mountain ranges during these exercises was the driving force behind 13 aircraft receiving a wrap-round camouflage, as the Red Flag fighter opponents would see as much of the undersides of the aircraft as the topsides.

Left: With No. 44 Sqn (Waddington Wing) markings, a Vulcan gets airborne smartly from the Nellis runway. In the background are an F-111 and Martin EB-57s, the latter used for target facilities and EW training.

Above: A gaggle of Vulcans, including a No. 617 Sqn/Scampton aircraft in the standard camouflage, taxis out at the start of a Red Flag mission. The Vulcans were highly successful in these exercises.

Above: XH558, the last flying Vulcan, is seen during an earlier time when it was a B.Mk 2MRR wearing the 'Dumbo' badge of No. 27 Sqn. The gloss paint offered greater protection against corrosion in the overwater role than the matt finish employed by bomber Vulcans.

Reconnaissance had been a role assigned to the V-force since its inception, with Valiants and Victors performing the task with No. 543 Sqn. The mission had substantially changed from photo-recon to radar reconnaissance, and the emphasis had shifted to maritime operations. With the release of surplus Vulcan airframes caused by the run-down of the airborne nuclear force, the type became available for long-range maritime radar reconnaissance sorties, using the aircraft's bomb/nav radar (which had received a much greater sidescan capability on the introduction of the low-level role) as the primary sensor, backed up by cameras. The Vulcan's long range and good low-level handling made it ideal for the task. No. 27 Sqn was reformed as the dedicated MRR squadron, although the other two units of the Scampton Wing also had MRR as a secondary tasking.

The discovery and subsequent exploitation of North Sea oil made the area one of strategic importance to the UK, warranting special attention from the Vulcan MRR fleet.

Left: The Skybolt pylon attachments were reactivated on the B.Mk 2MRR to carry air-sampling 'sniffer' pods. These may have been modified from surplus fuel tanks.

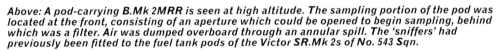

Above: A pod-carrying B.Mk 2MRR is seen at high altitude. The sampling portion of the pod was located at the front, consisting of an aperture which could be opened to begin sampling, behind which was a filter. Air was dumped overboard through an annular spill. The 'sniffers' had previously been fitted to the fuel tank pods of the Victor SR.Mk 2s of No. 543 Sqn.

1 November 1973 in the maritime radar reconnaissance (MRR) role. Its aircraft partially replaced the Victor SR.Mk 2s of No. 543 Squadron when they retired in the following May. Initially, four (XH534, XH558, XH560 and XH563) were converted to B.Mk 2(MRR) standard by Hawker Siddeley with the addition of Loran C navigation equipment and removal of TFR from the nose. They also retained the gloss polyurethane camouflage paint when their bombing companions converted to a matt finish. Standard Vulcans were operated until four more MRR models (XH537, XJ780, XJ823 and XJ825) were added in 1976-78, although only XH537 and the first four had their underwing pylons activated for the occasional carriage of upper-air sampling pods.

Tasked with patrol of the waters around the United Kingdom (with emergency assistance from Nos 35 and 617 Squadrons, which were assigned a secondary MRR task), No. 27 would operate one of three basic missions at high level: 'Instow', a wide area search; 'Crisp' (Continuous Radar Intelligence Surface Plot) to monitor traffic passing through a pre-determined 'box'; or 'Aspid' (Airborne

Below: The giant wing of the Vulcan is shown off to great effect by this B.Mk 2MRR at low level. A small characteristic of this variant was the deletion of the TFR 'pimple' from the nose.

Above: XL391, in Black Buck camouflage, is seen carrying an AN/ALQ-101 ECM pod (starboard) and anti-radar Martel acquisition round (port) during a trials flight from Waddington in 1982.

Vulcan colours

The first few production Vulcans were delivered to 230 OCU in this silver scheme. These were subsequently painted white, as below

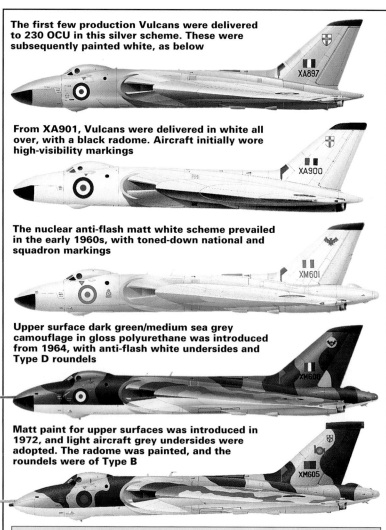

From XA901, Vulcans were delivered in white all over, with a black radome. Aircraft initially wore high-visibility markings

The nuclear anti-flash matt white scheme prevailed in the early 1960s, with toned-down national and squadron markings

Upper surface dark green/medium sea grey camouflage in gloss polyurethane was introduced from 1964, with anti-flash white undersides and Type D roundels

Matt paint for upper surfaces was introduced in 1972, and light aircraft grey undersides were adopted. The radome was painted, and the roundels were of Type B

The wrap-round scheme of dark green and dark sea grey was applied to XH561, XL389, XL425, XL426, XL427, XL444, XL445, XM575, XM605, XM648, XM652 and XM657 for Red Flag participation

XL391, XM597, XM598, XM607 and XM612 received dark sea grey undersides for Falklands War operations

K.Mk 2 aircraft had the trailing edge and centre-section undersurfaces painted white, with centreline alignment marks in black and Dayglo

A.V. Roe Ltd, Woodford
While on test with the manufacturers, the prototype Vulcans and some early production examples wore Avro's winged logo on the fin.

No. 9 Squadron
No. 9 Squadron's bat was adopted early in the unit's career to signify its nocturnal bombing role. Its motto is 'Per noctem volamus' ('Throughout the night we fly'). At Coningsby the bat was originally worn as a simple motif (left), but when the markings resurfaced at Waddington, the bat was presented on a yellow circle. There were two variations, one being a representation of the cartoon character Batman (right), the other being based on the traditional motif.

No. 12 Squadron
One of the best-known badges in the RAF, 'Shiny Twelve's' fox's mask represents the squadron's use of the Fairey Fox light bomber between 1926 and 1931. The marking was worn only briefly at Coningsby before centralised servicing was adopted, and the squadron was disbanded before tail markings were readopted.

This Coningsby Wing aircraft wears a badge depicting Tattershall Castle, a landmark which is visible from the Fenland country many miles around the town of Coningsby.

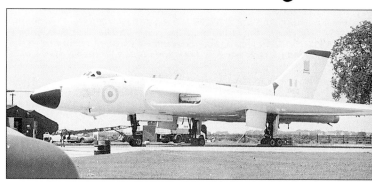

No. 27 Squadron
The elephant was adopted in World War I to preserve the memory of the squadron's use of the Martinsyde Elephant. In the inter-war years it was of special importance as the unit was based in India. The elephant motif is consequently of the small-eared Indian variety. The original presentation on Blue Steel-carrying Vulcans was similar to the official badge (right), but when the unit reformed with a maritime reconnaissance tasking the cartoon character Dumbo was adopted. One version had the flying elephant wearing goggles; another with a blue hat.

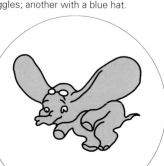 

No. 35 Squadron

The winged horse badge of No. 35 Sqn signifies the unit's co-operation with the cavalry in World War I, and was applied to its Vulcans while at Coningsby. When the unit returned to Scampton, it adopted a numerals device, at first worn plain but subsequently mounted on a green oval.

No. 44 Squadron

No. 44 Sqn's official badge depicts an elephant, similar to that of No. 27. Consequently, when the Waddington Wing reintroduced squadron badges on its aircraft, No. 44 adopted this numerals device.

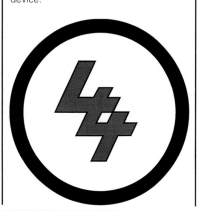

No. 50 Squadron

The two running dingoes badge of No. 50 Sqn was first applied in World War I, and is believed to stem from the unit's callsign. It was revived on the Vulcans in the early 1970s.

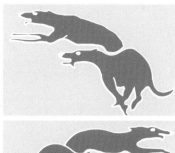

No. 83 Squadron

The antler fin marking appeared on No. 83 Sqn B.Mk 2s at Scampton. In addition to signifying the unit's close early ties with Scotland, it had six tines to represent the six DFCs awarded to unit personnel during one successful operation on the night of 14/15 June 1918.

No. 101 Squadron

When first established as a Vulcan squadron, No. 101 applied its squadron crest to the fin. Markings disappeared until Waddington introduced fin badges in the early 1970s, at which time the turret and lion badge was revived (left). This was subsequently revised (right). The badge commemorated the use by the squadron of the Boulton Paul Overstrand turreted bomber.

No. 617 Squadron

The 'Dambusters' derived their fin markings from the unit's badge. The early lightning bolt (left) was usually worn in low-visibility paint. The later version (right) was more similar to the official breached dam crest.

230 Operational Conversion Unit

The OCU's official badge is a golden sword on a wave background, and this marking (below) was worn in the unit's later life. Between 1961 and 1969 the OCU operated from Finningley, and adopted the Yorkshire white rose (right) as its fin badge.

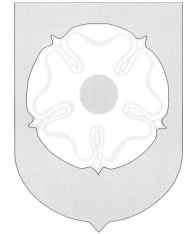

Bomber Command Development Unit

The handful of aircraft assigned to this unit did not wear tail markings as a rule, although the long-term BCDU 'inmate', XA895, carried the unit's title above the fin-flash.

XA907 was with the BCDU for a short period in 1964/65, long enough to gain the unit's badge on the crew access hatch.

No. 1 Group

The group's badge of a black panther's head was applied to the forward fuselage sides for aircraft participating in bombing competitions on the group's behalf. Aircraft going to US exercises also often wore the Union Jack on the fin. The panther was adopted to commemorate No. 1 Group's codename (Panther) at the time of its mobilisation in August 1939 to serve as the Advanced Air Striking Force in France.

Waddington Wing

All Waddington Wing aircraft wore the crest of the City of Lincoln on the fin, this practice persisting after the introduction of squadron tail markings. In the early days the badge was occasionally presented with a blue background.

XA905 was a B.Mk 1 assigned to 230 OCU at Finningley. In 1964 it was transferred to No. 9 School of technical Training (SoTT) at Newton, where it is seen wearing the markings of its previous owner.

Vulcan cockpit

Left: The nav/radar's position in the K.Mk 2 tanker featured a control panel on the side of the cockpit to control the HDU, refuelling indicators and floodlights. Visible in the main panel is the ARI 5928 radar display with associated control stick in the table below, above which is a camera installation. Beneath the table was the master stores control panel.

Above: The Vulcan's flight deck featured a central bank of engine instruments and thrust levers, flanked by identical displays of flight instruments for pilot and co-pilot. Noteworthy for this size of aircraft was the fighter-style stick, indicative of the aircraft's agility. More switches were located in side panels. Visibility was restricted by the high dashboard and small windows.

Below: During the Vulcan's long career there were many variations of the aft crew dashboard, depending on role (free-fall, Blue Steel or tanker) and modification programmes. Accommodation was provided for the nav-plotter in the centre, with nav-radar to his left and AEO to his right. The latter's task was to work the extensive EW and warning suite, with displays for radar and RWR.

Below: At work in the 'coal-hole': conditions in the aft compartment were cramped, but did foster close co-operation between the individual members. The adjustable lamps were originally of the angle-poise type, but were replaced by these more versatile flexible mounts.

Above: The Plessey **TRA** 170/26 turbine provided airborne emergency power by being lowered into the airstream.

The entire canopy was removable for ease of maintenance and to remove seats and equipment. The small fairing forward of the rear cabin porthole allowed a sextant to be used for celestial navigation. On the port side was a similar air-locked aperture for the use of a flare pistol.

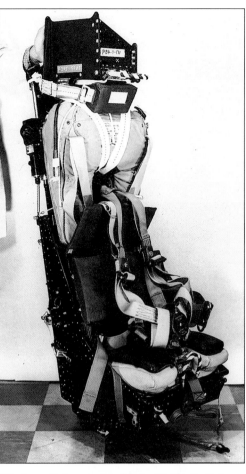

The two pilots were provided with Martin-Baker Type 3**KS** ejection seats, which fired after the canopy had been blown off. The two seats were 'handed' and could not be interchanged.

In the 'coal-hole' the nav-radar and **AEO** sat in swivelling seats, while that of the nav-plotter was fixed. Each had an 'assistor cushion' to help the occupant egress quickly and correctly.

A view through the access hatch shows the integral ladder which dropped down from the bottom of the door. In flight, the ladder was removed to allow a quick exit.

Nosewheel steering was activated by a push-button on the stick and controlled by the rudder pedals. Travel was 47¼° to either side and the wheels were automatically centred once airborne.

The eight-wheel main units were extended hydraulically, but had an emergency nitrogen system. Microswitches in the bogies held the struts locked until weight was off the wheels.

Black Buck – Bombing

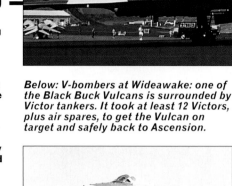

Fighting a war in a small island group 8,000 miles from home called for some desperate measures, and among the British responses to the Argentine invasion of the Falklands was the hasty modification of five Vulcans for long-range bombing missions and their dispatch to Ascension Island, the nearest available base.

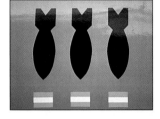

Left: XM607 carried three bomb symbols for its missions to the Falklands.

From here three bombing raids were launched against the islands, the first two (30 April/1 May and 3/4 May) aimed at Port Stanley airport with the aim of preventing the Argentine air force from basing potent combat aircraft there. In this the RAF was successful, despite the fact that only one of 42 bombs dropped actually hit the runway. The third Black Buck bombing raid followed much later on 11/12 June, involving an airburst strike against the airfield facilities four days before the eventual surrender.

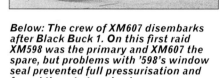

Below: V-bombers at Wideawake: one of the Black Buck Vulcans is surrounded by Victor tankers. It took at least 12 Victors, plus air spares, to get the Vulcan on target and safely back to Ascension.

Below: The crew of XM607 disembarks after Black Buck 1. On this first raid XM598 was the primary and XM607 the spare, but problems with '598's window seal prevented full pressurisation and forced them to turn back.

Above: A crowd gathers at Wideawake to welcome back the crew of XM607 on the morning of 1 May 1982, after the first Black Buck raid. Note the collection of Sea Harriers in the background.

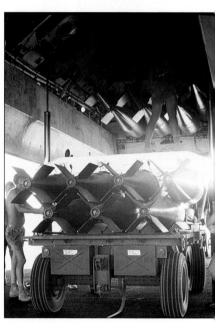

Above: Photographed on 14 May, XM612 is being loaded with 21 1,000-lb (454-kg) bombs for the aborted Black Buck 3 raid. The bombs were held in clips of seven, which were individually hoisted into the bomb bay.

Above: XM607 lands back at Wideawake after a Black Buck sortie. Seven raids were planned, of which two (Black Buck 3 and 4) were cancelled. Black Buck 1, 2 and 7 were the bombing raids against Port Stanley airfield.

Below: XM612 was one of the five aircraft converted for Black Buck missions. It replaced XM598 at Wideawake after the first two bombing raids.

Surface Plot Indicating Direction) to investigate a choke point, such as the Iceland-Faroes Gap. Visual identification and photography of vessels was a regular feature of operations, using either the modified F95 strike camera taking eight frames per second or a hand-held Canon AE-1. In time of conflict, the Vulcan would more prudently have called in a Buccaneer, or possibly a Canberra, to

investigate a plot, and was also capable of co-ordinating an attack by the former aircraft.

No. 27 Squadron flew the last Scampton Vulcan sortie with XJ782 (its sole 'straight' B.Mk 2) on 31 March 1982 – disbandment day – and handed its duties over to the Nimrod fleet. The running-down process had first claimed No. 230 OCU in August 1981, closely followed by No. 617 in December and No. 35 in February 1982. Waddington was expected to continue flying Vulcans for a couple of years, until the Tornado was firmly established in service, but in November 1981 it was revealed that No. 9 would go in April 1982, followed by Nos 44, 50 and 101 before the end of June. Economy was the sole reason, for the Vulcan had already far exceeded its planned span of service and many 'good for a lifetime' components were

Below: XM607 and XM612 are seen on 16 May 1982, the day the pair should have launched as primary and secondary respectively for Black Buck 3. The raid was cancelled because of high winds which would have reduced fuel safety margins beyond limits.

beginning to wear out. Unfortunately, they were generally in inaccessible places and would have required prohibitively costly work to replace. Paradoxically, therefore, the Vulcan's rapid run-down was the direct result of its remarkable longevity.

Final fling

At the very moment that XJ782 was overflying Scampton in salute, ships of the Argentine navy were closing on the Falkland Islands, carrying an occupation force. Having exhausted diplomatic possibilities in the four weeks which followed, Britain took steps to eject the invaders by force. Five Vulcan B.Mk 2s (XL391, XM597, XM598, XM607 and XM612) were singled out for missions against the occupied islands by virtue of the fact that they retained both the Skybolt attachment points and the refrigeration ducting for that missile in the wings. This enabled them to be fitted with a Westinghouse AN/ALQ-101(V)-10 jamming pod under the starboard wing, with the associated wiring running through the ducts.

Above: The first attempt to provide an anti-radiation capability employed the AS37 Martel missile, used by the Buccaneer force. At the time it was the only defence suppression weapon in RAF service. XM597 took the missile aloft from Waddington for the first time on 4 May, and made a live firing at Aberporth the following day.

Below: Another weapon considered during the Falklands conflict was the 1,000-lb (454-kg) laser-guided bomb, with a laser designator in the bomb-aimer's cupola. Drop tests were undertaken but it was not deployed.

At the same time, a Carousel inertial navigation system was fitted and a coat of dark grey was applied to the undersides for reduced conspicuity at night. The long-disused air-to-air refuelling system was refurbished, although the panic to provide serviceable probes for Vulcans, VC10s, Hercules and Nimrods caused a small crisis. Even XM605, a B.Mk 2 consigned the previous year to the Castle AFB museum in California, had its probe removed by an RAF team and later replaced after hostilities had ended.

Operating at an overload weight of 210,000 lb (95256 kg) from Ascension Island on the night of 30 April/1 May 1982, Flight Lieutenant Martin Withers and his crew in XM607 were aided by a fleet of Victor K.Mk 2 tankers on an unprecedented sortie. Rising to 10,000 ft (3048 m) after a 300-mile (483-km) low-level run in under the radar, XM607 released 21 1,000-lb (454-kg) bombs at 04.46 hours local (07.46 GMT), the first cratering the

Chinook, Wessex and Hercules are visible in this scene at Wideawake. The AGM-45 Shrike missile on the Skybolt pylon has been hastily camouflaged. The initial Shrike raid, Black Buck 5, involved the carriage of just two missiles.

Below: The second Black Buck raid saw XM597 carrying four Shrike missiles. The AGM-45 was much lighter than the Martel, and offered less integration problems. Nevertheless, the launch rails were by necessity of haste a very inelegant lash-up. The stencilled message on the undercarriage door is from a USAF C-5 unit, the 436th MAW, and reads 'Ascension 82: 436 MAW: Go Brits'.

Black Buck – Shrike

The targets for Black Buck 4, 5 and 6 were the Argentine radars in use on the Falklands, which included a TPS-43F, a TPS-44 and Skyguard and Super Fledermaus gun-tracking units. Black Buck 4 launched on the night of 28 May, the day after the Shrike-equipped Vulcan had arrived at Wideawake. However, a faulty HDU on one of the Victor tankers caused the mission to be abandoned, although it was launched again two nights later as Black Buck 5. This caused some damage to the primary TPS-43F target. Black Buck 6 was flown

on 2/3 June, and destroyed a Skyguard radar, although the Vulcan made a dramatic diversion into Rio de Janeiro after its refuelling probe broke.

Above: XM597 wore two Shrike silhouettes for its radar raids, and a Brazilian flag for its unscheduled visit to Rio.

Below: XM597, the Shrike carrier, is seen after its return to the UK. Following its emergency landing at Rio, it was impounded by the Brazilian authorities until the end of hostilities, being released on 10 June.

Tanker

Above: XM571 trails the hose from its single Flight Refuelling Mk 17B hose-drum unit. Part of the undersides were painted white and given receiver alignment marks.

Below: A Vulcan of No. 50 Sqn refuels a No. 29 Sqn Phantom. Occasionally carried under the Vulcan's wing was a small localiser pod to facilitate rendezvous with receivers.

Right: XM571 is seen in the Woodford factory being prepared for conversion to tanker configuration. Noteworthy are the number of cylindrical tanks lying around: these were fitted into the redundant bomb bay.

Above: The packaging of the Mk 17 HDU was driven more by haste than elegance. Nevertheless, the Vulcan was considered a good and stable tanker.

Below: XM575 cruises over Waddington near the end of the Vulcan's career. Today the base houses Sentries and Sigint Nimrods.

Like the Valiant and Victor before it, the Vulcan adopted the role of tanker in the twilight of its career. In 1982, with the Falklands campaign in full swing, a large percentage of the Victor tanker force was needed at Ascension Island, leaving the UK-based fleet sorely depleted. The only means to partially restore the situation was the hasty conversion of six Vulcan bombers, a task carried out in record time at Woodford. Originally known as the B.Mk 2K, by the time the tanker entered service it was designated K.Mk 2. The type served until March 1984, by which time sufficient VC10s had been converted to take over the tanker role.

runway of Port Stanley Airport. Black Buck 1, as the mission was codenamed, lasted 15 hours 45 minutes for the 7,500-mile (12070-km) round trip. Black Buck 2 on 3/4 May just failed to hit the runway with its bombs, while Black Buck 7, on 11/12 June, delivered airburst bombs.

At the time, Black Buck missions were certainly the longest bombing missions in history based on straight-line distances, although some of the B-52D/G Linebacker II raids from Guam against North Vietnam in December 1972 probably covered greater actual distances because of the circuitous nature of the target approaches. (Both were soundly beaten in January 1991 by B-52Gs flying Secret Squirrel non-stop missile-launching attacks against Iraq from Louisiana.)

In parallel with the anti-runway bombing missions, attempts were made to silence the Argentine radars with Texas Instruments AGM-45A Shrike missiles fitted under the wings of XM597. Black Buck 5, with two missiles aboard, narrowly missed its target on 30/31 May. Raid 6 (2/3 June) carried four Shrikes, one hitting a Skyguard gun control radar. A broken probe sustained during refuelling forced '597 to land at Rio de Janeiro, where it was temporarily impounded by the Brazilian authorities. The two other Black Buck raids were cancelled or abandoned.

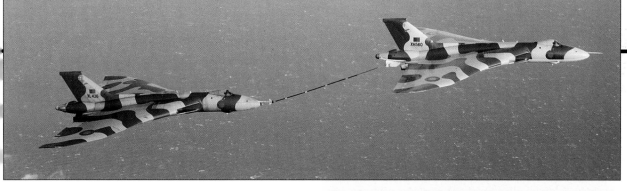

Several other weapons almost found their way into the Vulcan's armoury during this period of hectic improvisation. Before the United States made Shrike available, the Anglo-French AS37 Martel was borrowed from the Buccaneer force as the sole anti-radar missile on hand. It first flew on a Vulcan's underwing pylon on 4 May 1982 and was launched (with inert warhead) over the Aberporth weapons range the following day. Also during the first week of May, 1,000-lb Paveway II laser-guided bombs were test-dropped and studies conducted into the possibility of fitting AIM-9 Sidewinder AAMs to the wing pylons for self-defence.

The results of Black Buck

None of these schemes came to fruition, and thus ended the Vulcan's finest hour. Little material damage had been caused by the raids, despite the immense tanker effort (at least 14 sorties each) and expense required to mount them. However, the 1 May attack had been a spectacular opening to the British recapture effort and a warning that – even though the runway was swiftly repaired – basing of combat aircraft at Stanley would be unwise. Denial by the Argentine government that the raids had taken place was proof enough of the damaging psychological effect they had upon the defenders.

Left: As originally envisaged, the Vulcan tanker carried the HDU in the rear of the bomb bay, but this was felt to place the receiver dangerously close to the tanker, and consequently the old EW bay was chosen as the location for the equipment. Note the 'traffic light' system positioned on the flanks of the HDU.

Although hard to prove, it is generally accepted that, following the first Black Buck raid, Argentina feared bombing attacks on its mainland airfields. Consequently, Mirage IIIs were withdrawn from southern bases after the opening air battles on 1 May to defend the more strategically important north of the country. This in turn denied the Argentine war effort in the south its only dedicated air superiority force.

Black Buck was not the end of the Vulcan by any

Above: This was the first B.Mk 2, XH533, which was raided of parts and eventually scrapped at St Athan. This Welsh base was the central servicing location for the Vulcan fleet, and the last resting place for many of the airframes.

Above: A common sight around RAF airfields in the 1970/80s was the carcass of a Vulcan on the base dump. Here they were plundered for spares, set ablaze for fire practice or pulled to bits for battle damage repair training. These are the remains of XL384, which spent the best part of a decade on the Scampton dump.

Scrapping

The vast majority of Vulcans met their end at the hands of the scrapper's torch at St Athan, as trainer airframes with base fire sections and battle damage repair flights, or at the central fire school at Catterick. The first tranche of scrappings occurred with the retirement of the B.Mk 1A fleet, which assembled at St Athan in 1966 for disposal and sale as scrap. A similar fate greeted many B.Mk 2s in 1981/82 as the Vulcan force wound down. Thankfully many others survived owing to their low disposal price (£5,000), and there were several donations to museums. Many more nose sections were also saved while the rest of the airframe was turned into washing machines. By 1996, 20 aircraft were still in existence, all B.Mk 2s. Sadly, no B.Mk 1s have survived, the last two being XA903 (the

engine test-bed) which languished at Farnborough for many years before succumbing to the torch in 1984, and XA900, which had been a ground instructional airframe with 2 SoTT at Cosford before being transferred to the co-located museum in 1975. This was unceremoniously cut up in 1986, shortly after the museum received a B.Mk 2.

Left: VX777, the second prototype, survived until scrapped in 1963. After its work as the aerodynamic prototype for the B.Mk 2, it was used for bombing-up trials at Farnborough, where it is seen in derelict condition in 1962.

Below: On 20 September 1992, XH558 gave the last public performance of a Vulcan at Cranfield, the bomb bay doors carrying a suitable message. A hard-fought 'Save the Vulcan' campaign was waged to keep '558 in the air, but the Ministry of Defence would not entertain any offers of private sponsorship. On 23 March 1993 the aircraft was delivered to its new owner, David Walton, at Bruntingthorpe, the last flight to be made by the 'Tin Triangle'.

Vulcan Display Team

For 25 years the Vulcan had been the star attraction at many an air show. When the type retired in 1984, the MoD decided to keep XL426 flying for air display purposes under the auspices of the Vulcan Display Team (later raised to Flight status). When '426 began to run out of hours before a major servicing was due, XH560 was slated as its replacement, but it was found to have only 160 hours left, whereas XH558, then being reduced for spares at Waddington, had 600. Accordingly, XH558 was converted from tanker to bomber status, and was flown by the VDF until 1992. Although parented by No. 55 Sqn (Victors) at Marham, the aircraft flew from its ancestral home at Waddington.

Above: For eight years after the operational demise of the Vulcan, the VDT/VDF continued to thrill air display crowds with an awesome demonstration of the Vulcan's low-speed power and manoeuvrability. Most of the flying was performed by Squadron Leaders David Thomas and Paul Millikin.

Above: XH558 thunders skywards during an air show at Hurn. The aircraft was given a high-gloss finish for added protection, and wore the markings of No. 1 Group and the Waddington Wing. It had never worn the wrap-round scheme during its operational career.

Above: During its career '558 had been both an MRR aircraft and a K.Mk 2 tanker. For display flying the original bomber tailcone was fitted, albeit without the ECM gear installed. A feature which set the aircraft apart from other B.Mk 2s was the lack of the starboard ECM cooling intake.

means. No. 9 Squadron had disbanded on schedule, but No. 101 was retained until early August and No. 44 was granted a six-month stay of execution. Seven aircraft of this unit mounted Waddington's last Vulcan bomber flypast on 17 December 1982, touring the aircraft's former stamping grounds at Coningsby, Cottesmore, Finningley and Scampton. The qualification 'bomber' is important, for No. 50 was still in business – although a very different business from that of a few months previously.

Tankers bow out

The Falklands War, and the need to maintain a sizeable proportion of the Victor force on Ascension after the British victory, sorely pressed the home-based tanker fleet. A crash programme was launched to meet the extra demand by converting Vulcans to tankers. XH561, the first of six aircraft earmarked, arrived at Woodford on 4 May 1982, flying again on 18 June – four days after the Argentine surrender. Delivered to No. 50 Squadron on 23 June, it undertook its first operational sortie on 30 June.

Most obvious of the modifications which produced the Vulcan K.Mk 2 – first known as B.Mk 2(K) – was the removal of ECM and fitment of a large, entirely unaerodynamic box below the tail to house an FRL Mk 17B hose-drum unit. The bomb bay was filled with three auxiliary tanks of 1,000-Imp gal (4546-litre) capacity each, complementing the aircraft's normal load of 9,200 Imp gal (41823 litres) in the wing tanks. (It is of passing interest to note that the bay designed to take a single example of Britain's first atomic bomb could later accommodate a thermonuclear weapon, plus two fuel tanks.)

No. 50 Squadron operated only in the northern hemisphere during its short career as a tanker unit. It was also issued with a trio of standard B.Mk 2s for training. Tankers were easily identified from far below by their special underside markings. Initially the wing control surfaces were painted white, the prototype having the last 12 in (30 cm) of the starboard trailing edge and 32 in (81 cm) of the port thus coloured. Later, the last 14 ft 6 in (4.42 m) of the wing appeared in white.

It was with much regret that No. 50 Squadron disbanded on 31 March 1984. It had flown 3,000 hours on the tanker Vulcans, but was already depleted by the removal of hose-drum units to feed the VC10 tanker conversion line at BAe Filton. At the same time, the RAF bade farewell to a stalwart which had served it well in two marks and two additional sub-variants for almost 28 years. It proved impossible to make a clean break, with the inevitable result that two aircraft (XH558, a former tanker, and

Right: During XH558's conversion from tanker status for display work, the rear bomb bay tank was left in place. This offset a shift in centre of gravity caused by the removal of the HDU and the non-fitment of the original ECM gear. It was fitting that XH558 was the last flying Vulcan, for it had been the first B.Mk 2 delivered to the RAF, arriving at Waddington on 1 July 1960.

Below: A head-on view graphically illustrates the thick section of the huge wing. Apart from the large fin, the Vulcan was a surprisingly stealthy shape, giving ground radars considerable problems during air defence exercises.

XL426) were selected for flying preservation at Waddington, with only one being normally airworthy at a time. They were operated at many an air display by the Vulcan Demonstration Team, which was later raised to the status of a Flight and parented by Marham-based No. 55 Squadron, a Victor K.Mk 2 unit. (Sir Roy Dobson, Avro's fiercely anti-HP Managing Director, was doubtless rotating in his grave.)

Last flight of the Vulcan

As a cost-reducing measure, XL426 was sold in December 1986, its companion remaining on RAF charge for air display appearances until further funding cuts forced its disposal. XH558 made a final show participation at Cranfield on 20 September 1992 before being sold to C. Walton Ltd at Bruntingthorpe. Its delivery flight on 23 March 1993 included a tour of Woodford and former Vulcan bases, since which time it has been preserved in serviceable condition for fast taxiing displays. Three others achieved similar status during 1995, but the economics and certification rules surrounding former military jets have defeated hopes of putting a Vulcan back into the air.

Many others have been bought by museums and even private individuals for static display. Some were presented by the RAF to the US and Canadian air bases at which they spent much of their overseas deployment time. At around £1,500 as a scrapped hulk, or £5,000 complete and delivered by air, the Vulcan fleet was disposed of at a knock-down price, considering each cost over £1 million when new.

Of the Vulcan's former haunts, both Finningley and Scampton have been abandoned as flying bases; Cottesmore provides the initial training stage for crews who will eventually fly the V-bombers' successor – the Tornado GR.Mk 1; Coningsby houses Tornado F.Mk 3 interceptors; Waddington is still in the large aircraft business with Boeing Sentry AEW.Mk 1s and the intelligence-gathering Nimrod R.Mk 1s of No. 51 Squadron.

The dispersals on which the giant deltas once stood in splendour, awaiting the call to action, have not all fallen silent, but they will never again see such a majestic and well-loved aircraft as the Vulcan.   **Paul Jackson**

The Vulcan take-off was a sight and sound inextricably linked with the Lincolnshire countryside, and one which will remain embedded in the memories of all who witnessed it.

Museum Pieces

Upon retirement, Vulcans were offered for as little as £5,000 each. Many were saved by museums and groups throughout the country, and others were donated by the RAF. In 1996, four aircraft were still in theoretical flying condition, although constricted by many factors to occasional taxiing: XH558 at Bruntingthorpe, XL426 at Southend, XM603 at Woodford and XM655 at Wellesbourne Mountford.

XA900: Cosford museum, scrapped 1986

XJ823: Solway Aviation Society, Carlisle

XJ824: Imperial War Museum, Duxford

XL361: CFB Goose Bay

XL426/G-VJET: taxiing condition, Southend

XM575: East Midlands Airport

XM594: Newark Air Museum

XM603: The '603 Club, Woodford

XM605: Castle AFB museum

XM607: static display, RAF Waddington

XM655/G-VULC: Wellesbourne Mountford

Individual aircraft details

Abbreviations

A&AEE: Aeroplane & Armament Experimental Establishment, Boscombe Down
AW: Akrotiri Wing
AWA: Sir W. G. Armstrong Whitworth Aircraft Ltd (later Whitworth-Gloster division of Hawker Siddeley Aviation Ltd), Bitteswell
Aw/cn: awaiting collection from manufacturer
BCDU: Bomber Command Development Unit, Finningley
BLEU: Blind Landing Experimental Unit, Bedford

BSE: Bristol-Siddeley Engines, Filton (Patchway)
C(A): Controller (Aircraft)
Cat 3 FA: Category 3 flying accident (requires repair by RAF Maintenance Unit)
Cat 4: damage or unserviceability requiring manufacturer's repairs
Cat 5: written off
Cat 5C: withdrawn for salvage of useful components
ConW: Coningsby Wing
CotW: Cottesmore Wing
ETPS: Empire Test Pilots' School,

Farnborough
F/f: First flight
Major: major overhaul
Mfrs: Manufacturers. A.V. Roe & Co Ltd, Woodford (Avro division of Hawker Siddeley Aviation from 1.7.63, British Aerospace from 1.1.77). All manufacture at Woodford, overhauls at Woodford unless Bitteswell specifically indicated
MinTech: Ministry of Technology
MoA: Ministry of Aviation
MoD(PE): Ministry of Defence (Procurement Executive)
MU: Maintenance Unit

NEA: Non-Effective Airframe
ntu: not taken up
RAE: Royal Aircraft Establishment (Bedford, Farnborough, etc)
RR: Rolls-Royce Ltd
SoC: Struck off Charge
SoTT: School of Technical Training
St Athan: RAF Engineering Wing, St Athan, Glam
SW: Scampton Wing
VDF: Vulcan Display Flight (ex-VDT)
VDT: Vulcan Display Team, Waddington
WW: Waddington Wing (Nos 44, 50 and 101 Squadrons from 2.63 onwards)

Avro 707 production

To Spec E.15/48 on contract of 22 June 1948

VX784: Avro 707 first prototype

VX784: Model 707; taxi trials at Woodford; F/f at Boscombe Down 4.9.49 by Flt Lt Eric 'Red' Esler; crashed near Blackbushe 30.9.49 apparently due to control circuit failure (airbrakes locked open). Flt Lt Esler killed

VX790: Model 707B (originally intended as Avro 710 with two RR Avon engines); first with ejection seat; F/f at Boscombe Down 6.9.50 by Wg Cdr R. J. 'Roly' Falk; blue overall; operated from Dunsfold by Mfrs; Boscombe Down 9.51; ETPS; RAE Bedford Aerodynamics Flight; dumped at Bedford 1960

To Spec E.10/49 and contract 6/Aircraft/3395/CB.6(a), ordered 6.5.49.

WD280: Model 707A (ordered as unspecified variant; completed as 707A); F/f at Boscombe Down 14.6.51 by R. J. Falk; red overall; power control trials; replica of Phase 2 wing, 1954; Australia 1956 for airflow research; retired 1967; preserved by G. Mallet, Williamstown, Melbourne, Australia; up for sale 1996

To Spec E.10/49 and contract 6/Aircraft/7470/CB.6(a), ordered 13.11.51

WZ736: Model 707A; F/f 20.2.53; orange overall; RAE, automatic throttle and other trials; withdrawn 1964; 7868M at Colerne for preservation 7.12.64; Finningley;

Cosford Aerospace Museum; Waddington; Manchester Museum of Science and Industry 8.9.82; current
WZ739: Model 707C; not built

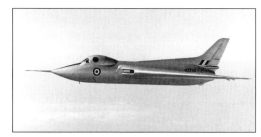

WZ744: Avro 707C with Vulcan-style cabin

WZ744: Model 707C; assembled at Bracebridge Heath, Lincoln; F/f at Waddington 1.7.53 by Sqdn Ldr J. B. Wales; silver overall; A&AEE; RAE; 7932M at Colerne for preservation 1.67; Finningley; Topcliffe; Cosford Aerospace Museum 13.4.73

Vulcan B.Mk 1/1A production

Contract 6/Aircraft/1942 of 22 June 1948: two Avro 698 prototypes

VX770: Avro 698 Vulcan first prototype

VX770: F/f 30.8.52 with RA.3 Avon engines; A&AEE 1.9.52 for handling trials; Mfrs for Sapphire ASSa.6 installation, reflown 6.53 and retained for trials to C(A) charge 5.1.55, remaining with Mfrs; Avro, Langar 17.8.56 for R-R Conway RCo.5 installation; R-R, Hucknall 24.8.57 as engine testbed (Malta, tropical trials 11.57); refitted with Conway RCo.IIs (as intended Victor B.Mk 2 powerplant); broke up in mid-air due to wing structural failure during low-level flypast for Battle of Britain Day display at Syerston 20.9.58. Crew killed

VX777: Avro 698 Vulcan second prototype

VX777: F/f 3.9.53 with Olympus 100 engines; A&AEE 10.9.53 and grounded for modifications for six months; RAE Farnborough for bomb-dropping trials (first mission 16.7.54); undercarriage collapse on landing at Farnborough 27.7.54 resulting from high-speed landing with jammed rudder; repaired and fitted with Olympus 101s, reflown 4.2.55; to Mfrs on C(A) charge 15.3.55;

A&AEE for four months' engine trials; Mfrs for Phase 2 wing mods (extended, drooped outer leading edge) and reflown 5.10.55; Mfrs trials; Mfrs mods 8.56 (Phase 2C extended-span B.Mk 2 wing and Olympus 102s) and reflown 31.8.57; Mfrs trials; RAE Farnborough (Armaments Section) 27.4.60 and grounded for bombing-up trials; SoC 10.62; scrapped 1963

Contract 6/Aircraft/8442/CB .6 (a) of 22.7.52: 25 Vulcan B.Mk 1s

XA889: first production B.Mk 1

XA889: F/f 4.2.55 on 'straight edged' wings and with Olympus 101s; silver overall; Mfrs trials; Aw/cn 10.6.55; Mfrs trials on C(A) charge from 10.6.55; first production aircraft with Phase 2 wing, 2.56; A&AEE 16.3.56 gaining C(A) release 29.5.56; Mfrs 13.7.56 for trials, fitted with Olympus Mk 102s from 3.57; BSE, Filton, 19.7.57 for Olympus Mk 104 trials; Mfrs 5.8.57; BSE, Filton, 3.4.58 for engine trials; Mfrs 28.10.58; A&AEE 9.11.62 for armament trials; SoC 22.8.67; sold to B. A. Taylor Ltd, West Bromwich, for scrap 12.67 and dismantled at Boscombe Down
XA890: F/f 24.8.55 on 'straight edged' wings (and with extended jetpipes adopted as standard on all

subsequent Vulcans); Aw/cn 31.8.55; Mfrs radio and radar trials – on C(A) charge from 31.8.55; A&AEE 27.4.56 (Mfrs 5.6-18.7.56); Mfrs for trials 18.9.56; RAE Farnborough 17.12.57 (still on Mfrs trials); RAE Farnborough Armaments Department 7.2.58 for bombing-up trials (Mfrs mods 2.2-22.7.59); RAE Farnborough Radio Department 1.6.62; RAE Bedford Aero Flight for aerodynamics trials 27.1.64; A&AEE 24.10.68 for ground trials; SoC 5.5.69; Boscombe fire training aircraft 19.3.71; dismantled by RR in January 1973 (Retained Phase 1 wing throughout)

XA891: third production B.Mk 1

XA891: F/f 22.9.55 on 'straight edged' wings; Aw/cn 23.9.55; Mfrs trials on C(A) charge from 23.9.55; retrofitted with Phase 2 leading edge and flown to Langar (Avro test airfield) for further mods; Mfrs engine and fuel system trials; R-R, Filton for installation of Olympus 200s; Mfrs 20.6.58 for engine trials; caught fire in mid-air following electrics failure and crashed near Walkington, Humberside 24.7.59

XA890: B.Mk 1, Farnborough air show

XA892: 1956 Farnborough air show

XA892: F/f 23.11,55, on 'straight edged' wings; Aw/cn 30.11.55; Mfrs trials, on C(A) charge from 30.11.55; RAE Farnborough 27.4.56; Mfrs 30.5.56 for fitment of Phase 2 leading edges; A&AEE for armament development 28.11.56; Mfrs 23.6.58; A&AEE 4.11.58; Mfrs 12.2.59; A&AEE 15.5.59; Mfrs 18.2.60; RAE Farnborough Armaments Department 20.9.60; assigned instructional serial 7746M 14.3.62; delivered to No. 1 SoTT, Halton, 21.6.62; coded '16'; scrapped July 1971

XA893: F/f 16.1.56 on 'straight edged' wings; Mfrs trials, on C(A) charge from 24.1.56; fitted with Phase 2 leading edges and Vulcan B.Mk 2 electronic system (200V AC in place of 112V DC); scrapped at Dishforth by No. 60 MU 1964; nose to No. 71 MU, Bicester, for travelling exhibition; RAF Exhibition Flight, Abingdon, 1977; belatedly assigned instructional serial 8591M 3.78; Cosford Aerospace Museum 1986

XA894: TSR2 engine testbed

XA894: F/f 9.1.57 (held back on production line; first fully representative B.Mk 1 with Phase 2 wing from outset); Aw/cn 18.1.57; C(A) on six months' loan from 18.1.57, but eventually extended to 31.12.60; initially with Mfrs, but A&AEE from 29.3.57 (apart from Mfrs 2.5-5.9.57, 4.10-31.10.57, 18.11.57-14.10.58, 9.7-27.11.59); BSE, Filton 19.7.60 for fitment with Olympus 22R in weapons bay for TSR2 development; MoA charge 11.60; f/f with Olympus 23.2.62; burnt out during ground running 3.12.62 after engine explosion – no casualties; SoC 14.9.65

XA895: F/f 12.8.56; Aw/cn 17.8.56; No. 230 OCU 16.8.56 (on charge 18.8, but operated at A&AEE); RAF Handling Squadron, Boscombe Down, on loan 31.12.56; No. 230 OCU 19.1.57 (Cat 3 repair on site by Mfrs 25.2-28.2.57); Mfrs 5.3.58; A&AEE 6.3.58 on 9 months' MoA loan (extended to 31.10.60) and converted to prototype **B.Mk 1A** for ECM trials; (allocated to No. 101 Sqn 7.11.60, but transfer cancelled); BCDU 8.6.61; loan MoA 11.5.65 for 1 month, later extended to 30.9.66,St Athan (No. 19 MU) 12.12.66; NEA 13.1.67; sold as scrap to Bradbury & Co., Bournemouth, 8.68 and broken up on site

XA896: F/f 30.1.57 (held back on production line); Aw/cn 4.3.57; No. 230 OCU 4.3.57 (on charge 7.3); No. 83 Sqn 27.6.60; No. 44 Sqn 10.8.60 (Cat 3 work on site by Mfrs 16.1-13.3.61 and 1.6-14.8.61); No. 230 OCU 6.9.61 (Cat 3 work on site by No. 60 MU 30.4-24.6.64) RR, Hucknall 24.6.64 (on MoA charge from 25.6.64) for fitment of BS100 vectored thrust in weapons bay for P.1154 trials; installation abandoned on P.1154's cancellation 2.65; deteriorated and scrapped at Hucknall

XA897: F/f 10.7.57; Aw/cn 20.7.56; C(A) 20.7.57 at Woodford; No. 230 OCU 2.9.56 operated from A&AEE; ex UK to New Zealand 9.9.56; crashed on return to London Airport (Heathrow) 1.10.56 – four killed, two ejected; SoC 3.10.56; remains assigned to No. 71 MU 25.10.56

XA898: F/f 26.11.56; Aw/cn 31.12.56; No. 230 OCU 3.1.57 (Mfrs mods 24.4-29.6.59, loaned to No. 101 Sqn 19.11-25.11.59; Cat 3 work on site by No. 60 MU 29.12.60-23.1.61; Cat 3 work on site by Mfrs 18.9.61-7.3.62, Cat 3 work on site by No. 60 MU 21.8-28.10.63); allocated instructional serial 7856M 23.7.64; No. 1 SoTT, Halton, 26.8.64; coded '30'; broken up and burnt, August 1971

XA899: F/f 16.2.57; Aw/cn 28.2.57; C(A) at Mfrs 28.2.57 on long-term loan; A&AEE 15.5.58 (on MoS charge from 2.7.58); BLEU, Bedford (via Farnborough) 26.2.59 for autopilot trials; world's first four-engined automatic landing 22.12.59; RAE Farnborough; Mfrs 9.2.62; returned to RAF 17.10.62 for disposal; allocated instructional serial 7812M 22.5.63 for No. 1 SoTT, Halton; delivered instead to No. 2 SoTT, Cosford, 26.6.63; sold J. Shackleton Ltd, Siddal, and removed from site 30.8.73

XA900: F/f 7.3.57; Aw/cn 20.3.57; No. 230 OCU 22.3.57 (on charge 25.3; Cat 3 work on site by Mfrs 4.3-23.4.59); No. 101 Sqn 22.6.60; No. 230 OCU 6.2.62; No. 101 Sqn 21.2.62 – allocation not taken up; Mfrs at

XA900: B.Mk 1, 230 OCU, Waddington

Coningsby for mods 22.2.62; No. 230 OCU 24.8.62 (Cat 3 works on site by No. 60 MU 18.12.62-17.1.63; again 2.10-30.10.63; and again 23.6-11.8.64); allocated instructional serial 7896M 17.11.65; No. 2 SoTT, Cosford 19.11.65; Cosford aerospace museum 12.75 (formally assigned 24.2.66); scrapped early 1986

XA901: F/f 19.3.57 (first production aircraft in overall white colours); Aw/cn 31.3.57; No. 230 OCU 4.4.57 (loaned No. 617 Sqn 19.11-25.11.59); No. 83 Sqn 27.6.60; No. 44 Sqn 8.60 (Cat 3 works on site by No. 60 MU 2.4-6.4.62; mods at Coningsby by Mfrs 9.7-17.12.62); No. 230 OCU 17.12.62 (Cat 3 flying accident 20.1.64 and repair on site by No. 60 MU 24.1-13.4.64); allocated instructional serial 7897M 17.11.65; RAF College Cranwell 19.11.65 (formally allocated 26.11.65); sold to J. Shackleton, Siddal for scrap 9.72

XA902: F/f 13.4.57; Aw/cn 7.5.57; No. 230 OCU 9.5.57 (on charge 10.5; landing accident at Waddington 28.2.58, originally assessed as Cat 5; SoC 3.3.58; reassessed as Cat 3; repaired on site by Mfrs 6.3.58; loaned to C(A) from 21.10.58 at Mfrs for installation of RR Conway RCo.ll engines and transferred on repayment terms 4.59 (still with Mfrs); RR, Hucknall 17.7.59 (replacing VX770); RB.163 Speys installed in outboard bays (Conways inboard) and f/f as such 12.10.61; RAF for disposal 14.10.62; dismantled by No. 60 MU and removed to Dishforth dump 3.63; SoC 6.63

XA903: Concorde engine testbed

XA903: F/f 10.5.57; Aw/cn 31.5.57; Mfrs at Langar on C(A) free loan 31.5.57; Mfrs at Woodford 27.1.58 for Blue Steel trials; (transferred to MoA on repayment terms 4.59); Mfrs at Edinburgh (Australia) 12.11.60; Mfrs at Woodford 7.2.61; temporarily grounded; BSE, Filton 1.64 and fitted with Olympus 593 engine beneath weapons bay for Concorde trials; f/f as such 9.9.66; fitted with underslung RR RB.199 at Filton for MRCA (Tornado) trials; f/f as such 19.4.73; RAE Farnborough 22.2.79 (last flight of a Vulcan Mk 1/1A); scrapped 9.84; nose to Wales Aircraft Museum, Cardiff Airport, then to Sidcup, Kent, 1993 for restoration by Colin Mears

XA904: Aw/cn 13.7.57 (first production with Olympus 102); No. 83 Sqn 16.7.57; Mfrs 19.10.59 for **B.Mk 1A** conversion; No. 44 Sqn 20.1.61; Cat 4 crash-landing at Waddington 1.3.61 – ran out of fuel after being 'stacked' for 1.5 hours; reassessed as Cat 5 and SoC 10.5.61; scrapped at Church Fenton by No. 60 MU; nose section allocated instructional 7738M 12.12.61; nose to Finningley 15.12.61 but since removed

XA905: Aw/cn 11.7.57; No. 83 Sqn 11.7.57 (Mfrs mods 23.2-24.3.59; Cat 3 brake failure 7.7.59; on-site repair by No. 60 MU 14.7-16.10.59); No. 44 Sqn 8.60 (Cat 3 work on site by Mfrs 10.8-14.10.60 and 23.2-26.6.61); No. 230 OCU 23.8.61; allocated instructional serial 7857M 23.7.64; assigned WW for ferrying 10.9.64; No. 9 SoTT, Newton 14.9.64; sold for scrap 29.1.74

XA906: Aw/cn 19.7.57; No. 83 Sqn 12.8.57 (Cat 3 work on site by Mfrs 1.1-31.3.59); No. 44 Sqn 8.60 (Cat 3 work on site by No. 60 MU 24.1-21.2.61; Cat 3 work on site by Mfrs 4.7-3.8.61; and by No. 60 MU 18.12.61-8.1.62); AWA 5.3.62 for **B.Mk 1A** conversion; No. 44 Sqn 16.8.62; WW 1963 (Cat 3 work on site by No. 60 MU 11.4-23.4.63); St Athan (No. 19 MU) 3.3.67; NEA 10.3.67; sold as scrap to Bradbury & Co., Bournemouth, 8.11.68

XA907: Aw/cn 29.8.57; No. 83 Sqn 29.8.57 (on charge 30.8; Mfrs mods 11.3-10.4.59; Cat 3 work on site by Mfrs 21.7-17.12.59); No. 44 Sqn 8.60 (Cat 3 work on site by No. 60 MU 24.2-17.3.61); AWA for **B.Mk 1A** conversion 29.10.61; No. 44 Sqn 4.5.62; WW 1963 (Cat 3 work on site by No. 60 MU 19.9-13.10.63); BCDU 2.2.65; St Athan (No. 19 MU) 12.10.66; NEA 3.11.66; sold as scrap to Bradbury & Co., Bournemouth, 20.5.68

XA908: Aw/cn 17.9.57; No. 83 Sqn 17.9.57; crashed near Detroit, USA 24.10.58 following electrical failure; five killed; SoC 27.10.57

XA909: Aw/cn 30.9.57; No. 101 Sqn 1.10.57 (Cat 3 work on site by No. 60 MU 19.10-6.11.61 and 18.12.61-12.1.62); AWA for **B.Mk 1A** conversion 19.1.62; No. 50 Sqn 25.6.62; WW 1963; crashed at Gwalchmai, Anglesey 16.7.64 following engine explosion – no fatalities; SoC 23.7.64

XA910: Aw/cn 31.10.57; No. 101 Sqn 31.10.57 (on charge 1.11; Cat 3 work on site by No. 60 MU 1.2-25.3.60); No. 230 OCU 21.6.60 (Cat 3 work on site by No. 60 MU 17.3-29.3.61); No. 101 Sqn 22.1.62; AWA 2.2.62 for **B.Mk 1A** conversion; No. 50 Sqn 19.7.62; WW 1963 (Cat 3 work on site by Mfrs 21.5-27.8.63); Cottesmore for instructional use 10.11.67 and allocated serial 7995M 12.67; subsequently scrapped

XA911: B.Mk 1, 230 OCU, seen in Canada

XA911: Aw/cn 31.10.57; No. 83 Sqn 1.11.57 (Mfrs mods 18.3-17.4.59); No. 230 OCU 27.6.60 (Cat 3 work on site by No. 60 MU 6.3-17.3.61 and 28.12.61-

12.1.62); AWA 17.7.62 for **B.Mk 1A** conversion; WW 19.2.63 (Cat 3 flying accident 31.12.63, rectification on site by Mfrs 15.1-20.7.64); St Athan (No. 19 MU) 9.2.67 (having been NEA 8.2.67); sold as scrap to Bradbury & Co., Bournemouth 8.11.68

XA912: Aw/cn 30.11.57; No. 101 Sqn 2.12.57 (Cat 3 work on site by No. 60 MU 24.6-7.8.58; Mfrs mods 4.3-7.4.59; Cat 3 work on site by Mfrs 24.6.59-5.2.60); AWA 3.10.60 for **B.Mk 1A** conversion; No. 101 Sqn 19.3.61 (Cat 3 work on site by No. 60 MU 12.6-10.7.61, also 30.8-12.9.61; Cat 3 work on site by Mfrs 3.1-5.3.62, and by No. 60 MU on site 2.4-16.4.62, and by Mfrs on site 10.5-28.5.62); WW 1963 (Cat 3 work on site by 60 MU 10.5-7.8.63); St Athan (No. 19 MU) 6.3.67; NEA 9.3.67; sold as scrap to Bradbury & Co. Bournemouth, 20.5.68

XA913: Aw/cn 18.12.57; No. 101 Sqn 19.12.57; work on site by Mfrs 17.12.58-20.3.59) AWA 21.3.61 for **B.Mk 1A** conversion; No. 101 Sqn 29.11.61; Cat 3 work on site by Mfrs 17.10.62-27.2.63; WW 27.2.63 (Cat 3 work on site by No. 60 MU 18.3-14.4.65); St Athan (No. 19 MU) 21.12.66; NEA 21.12.66; sold to Bradbury & Co., Bournemouth 20.5.68

Contract 6/Aircraft/11301 CB.6(a) dated 17.9.54: 37 aircraft, subsequently amended to 20 Mk 1s and 17 Mk 2s

XH475: B.Mk 1A, No. 101 Sqn, seen at Aldergrove

XH475: Aw/cn 10.1.58, with Olympus 104s; No. 230 OCU 22.1.58; No. 101 Sqn 28.2.58 (Cat 3 work on site by Mfrs 19.6-2.10.58; Mfrs mods 14.4-20.5.59; Cat 3 work on site by No. 60 MU 11.2-10.3.60; Cat 3 work on site by Mfrs 17.1-4.5.61 and 27.9-1.12.61); AWA 27.4.62 for **B.Mk 1A** conversion; No. 101 Sqn 24.9.62 (Cat 3 work on site by No. 60 MU 11.10-25.10.62; loaned to A&AEE 4.3-24.4.63); WW 1963; declared Cat 5 for ground instruction 6.11.67; allocated instructional serial 7996M on 20.11.67 for use at Waddington; to fire dump; sold for scrap 2.4.76

XH476: Aw/cn 3.2.58; No. 101 Sqn 4.2.58 (on charge 5.2; Mfrs mods 2.4-21.5.59; Cat 3 flying accident 29.5.60; repair on site by Mfrs 27.7-6.12.60); AWA 29.11.61 for **B.Mk 1A** conversion; No. 44 Sqn 7.5.62; WW 1963 (Cat 3 work on site by No. 60 MU 6.8-28.8.64); St Athan (No. 19 MU) 2.5.67 ; NEA 4.5.67; sold for scrap to Bradbury & Co., Bournemouth 21.1.69

XH477: Aw/cn 17.2.58; No. 83 Sqn 18.2.58; No. 44 Sqn 8.60; AWA 3.11.60 for **B.Mk 1A** conversion; No. 44 Sqn 14.7.61 (Cat 3 work on site by No. 60 MU 1.3-26.3.62); WW 1963 (Cat 3 work on site by No. 60 MU 1.4-23.4.63); crashed into St Colm Hill, Aboyne, Aberdeen 12.6.63 – five crew killed; SoC 13.6.63; sold as scrap to G. Williamson, Quarrywood

XH478: Aw/cn 28.3.58; C(A) at Woodford 31.3.58 on 6 months' loan (extended to 28.2.61) A&AEE 9.10.58 for refuelling probe trials; Mfrs 8.12.58; A&AEE 15.6.59; Mfrs 7.59 (detached to A&AEE 11.59 and 5.60); AWA 25.7.61 for **B.Mk 1A** conversion; No. 9.2.62; WW 1963 (Cat 3 work by No. 60 MU 5.9-7.10.63); A&AEE 20.4.66 on 6 months' loan to MoA for armament trials (extended to 31.7.67); Akrotiri Station Flight 27.3.69 – delivered 28.3.69 for ground instruction (weapon loading); allocated instructional serial 8047M 5.5.69; SoC 1.11.70

XH479/7974M: B.Mk 1A, 1 SoTT, Halton

XH479: Aw/cn 27.3.58; No. 101 Sqn 28.3.58 (on charge 31.3; Cat 3 work on site by Mfrs 3.2-15.3.60); AWA 12.5.61 for **B.Mk 1A** conversion; No. 101 Sqn 25.1.62; WW 1963 (Cat 3 work on site by No. 60 MU

7.10-22.10.63; Cat 3 work on site by No. 60 MU 19.1-18.2.65); No. 1 SoTT 13.6.67 for ground instruction; allocated 7974M 21.6.67 and coded '21'; SoC as scrap 23.7.73

XH480: Aw/cn 18.4.58; No. 83 Sqn 22.4.58; No. 44 Sqn 8.60 (Cat 3 work on site by Mfrs 12.12.60-19.1.61; Cat 3 work on site by No. 60 MU 13.11.61-15.1.62); AWA 22.6.62 for **B.Mk 1A** conversion; No. 44 Sqn 23.11.62; WW 1963; St Athan (No. 19 MU) 10.11.66; NEA 10.11.66; sold to Bradbury & Co., Bournemouth 19.9.68

XH481: Aw/cn 25.4.58; No. 101 Sqn 30.4.58 (Mfrs mods 19.1-24.2.59, Cat 3 work on site by No. 60 MU 5.5-24.6.59); AWA 7.10.60 for **B.Mk 1A** conversion; No. 101 Sqn 8.5.61 (Cat 3 work on site by Mfrs 21.9-24.10.61; Cat 3 work on site by No. 60 MU 4.1-14.2.62 and 31.8-25.9.62); WW 1963 (Cat 3 work on site by No. 60 MU 5.4.65-9.9.66); assigned to Cottesmore fire dump 8.1.68, but handed over instead to Waddington 10.1.68; removed 1977

XH482: Aw/cn 30.4.58; No. 617 Sqn 2.5.58 (on charge 5.5); No. 50 Sqn 1.8.61; AWA 30.3.62 for **B.Mk 1A** conversion; No. 101 Sqn 3.9.62; No. 50 Sqn 12.10.62; WW 1963; St Athan (No. 19 MU) 14.10.66; NEA 3.11.66; scraped 19.9.68; sold as scrap to Bradbury & Co. 19.9.68

XH483: Aw/cn 16.5.58; No. 617 Sqn 29.5.58 (Cat 3 work on site by No. 60 MU 19.9-7.10.60); AWA 20.1.61 for **B.Mk 1A** conversion; No. 50 Sqn 28.8.61 (Cat 3 u/s on Malta 27.10.62; part-repaired and to Waddington 1.11.62; Cat 3 work on site by No. 60 MU 4.1-24.2.63); WW 1963; RAF Fire Service Central Training Establishment, Manston and SoC 3.8.67 for crash rescue training; burnt and scrapped 1977

XH497: B.Mk 1, No. 617 Sqn, Scampton

XH497: Aw/cn 28.5.58; No. 617 Sqn 30.5.58 (Cat 3 3.7.58 landing minus nosewheels); No. 50 Sqn 1.8.61; AWA 9.1.62 for **B.Mk 1A** conversion (work on site – i.e. Bitteswell – by Mfrs 23.5-18.6.62); No. 50 Sqn 19.6.62; WW 1963; St Athan (No. 19 MU) 6.4.66; NEA 17.5.66; sold as scrap to Bradbury & Co., Bournemouth 21.1.69

XH498: B.Mk 1, No. 617 Sqn, damaged at Ohakea

XH498: Aw/cn 27.6.58; No. 617 Sqn 30.6.58 (Cat 4 25.10.59 damaged port undercarriage at Wellington, New Zealand during undershoot and leg collapsed in emergency landing at Ohakea; repair in NZ by Mfrs 6.1.60; restored to No. 617 Sqn 21.6.60; Cat 3 repair on site by Mfrs 21.12.60-16.3.61); No. 50 Sqn 1.8.61; AWA 6.10.61 for **B.Mk 1A** conversion; No. 50 Sqn 30.3.62; WW 1963 (Cat 3 work on site by No. 60 MU 18.3-1.4.63); assigned to No. 2 SoTT at Cosford, but allocation changed to Finningley for crew drill practice and aircraft SoC 19.10.67; assigned instructional serial 7993M 11.67; sold for scrap 9.2.70

XH499: Aw/cn 16.7.58; No. 617 Sqn 18.7.58 (Cat 3 work on site by No. 60 MU 13.8-16.9.59 and 28.10-14.11.60); No. 50 Sqn 1.8.61; AWA 10.5.62 for **B.Mk 1A** conversion; No. 44 Sqn 12.10.62; WW 1963 (Cat 3 work on site by No. 60 MU 20.6-3.7.63); MoA on indefinite loan 16.9.63 with A&AEE; AWA Bitteswell

31.1.64; A&AEE 16.4.64; Bitteswell 13.10.64; SoC 11.11.65 at Bitteswell and scrapped; declared Cat 5 for components recovery 1.12.65

XH500: Aw/cn 14.8.58; No. 617 Sqn 15.8.58 (on charge 18.8; Mfrs mods 25.3-26.4.59); AWA/Vickers 13.7.59 for **B.Mk 1A** conversion; No. 617 Sqn 30.9.60 (Cat 3 work on site by No. 60 MU 24.5-2.6.61); 5C Sqn 1.8.61; WW 1963 (Cat 3 work on site by No. 60 MU 18.7-16.8.63 and 30.12.63-5.6.64); Scampton 28.11.67 (not officially assigned until 1.1.68) for weapon loading practice, allocated instructional serial 7994M; Scampton fire dump 29.9.76 and burnt

XH501: Aw/cn 2.9.58; No. 617 Sqn 3.9.58; AWA 7.3.61 for **B.Mk 1A** conversion; No. 44 Sqn 2.11.61; WW 1963; St Athan (No. 19 MU) 12.10.66; NBA 3.11.66; sold as scrap to Bradbury & Co., Bournemouth, 8.11.68

XH502: Aw/cn 31.10.58; No. 617 Sqn 11.11.58; No. 50 Sqn 1.8.61 (Cat 3 work on site by No. 60 MU 30.8-6.10.61); AWA 14.8.62 for **B.Mk 1A** conversion; WW 25.2.63 (Cat 3 work on site by No. 60 MU 6.2-24.3.64); Waddington fire dump 10.1.68; nose for crew training at Waddington; removed

XH503: Aw/cn 18.12.58; No. 83 Sqn 31.12.58 (Mfrs mods 2.2-4.3.59); No. 44 Sqn 8.60 (Cat 3 work on site by No. 60 MU 12.10-2.11.60); AWA 30.8.62 for **B.Mk 1A** conversion; WW 6.3.63 (last Mk 1A conversion; Cat 3 work on site by No. 60 MU 11.12.64-16.1.65); St Athan (No. 19 MU) 6.12.66; NEA 6.12.66; sold as scrap to Bradbury & Co., Bournemouth 8.11.68

XH504: B.Mk 1, 230 OCU, Waddington

XH504: Aw/cn 19.12.58; No. 230 OCU 31.12.58 (loan No. 83 Sqn 19.110-25.11.59); AWA 21.8.61 for **B.Mk 1A** conversion; No. 101 Sqn 2.3.62; WW 1963 (Cat 3 work on site by No. 60 MU 21.6-9.7.63); Cottesmore 4.1.68 for instructional use, subsequently to fire dump; burnt 18.6.69

XH505: Aw/cn 31.12.58 but retained by Mfrs; No. 230 OCU 13.3.59 (on charge 16.3); AWA/Vickers 16.7.59 for **B.Mk 1A** conversion; No. 617 Sqn 6.10.60 (Cat 3 engine malfunction 24.11.60; repair on site by Mfrs 28.11.60-25.1.61; Cat 3 work on site by No. 60 MU 30.5-12.6.61 and 19.7-31.7.61); No. 50 Sqn 1.8.61; No. 44 Sqn 16.8.61; WW 1963 (loaned to BCDU 9.63 only; Cat 3 work on site by No. 60 MU 18.11.63-13.1.64 and 23.9-6.10.64); camouflaged 4.64 (first Waddington aircraft); Finningley 9.1.68 for fire-fighting; removed

XH506: Aw/cn 27.1.59 but retained by Mfrs; No. 101 Sqn 17.4.59 (on charge 20.4); AWA 25.1.60 for **B.Mk 1A** conversion; No. 617 Sqn 2.11.60; 50 Sqn 1.8.61 (Cat 3 work on site by No. 60 MU 14.12.61-3.1.62 and 18.3-2.4.63); WW 1963 (Cat 3 work on site by No. 60 MU 21.8.6-17.9.63); St Athan (No. 19 MU) 10.1.68; NEA 10.1.68; sold as scrap to Bradbury & Co., Bournemouth 8.11.68

XH532: Aw/cn 31.3.59; on C(A) loan at Woodford 31.3.59 for Mfrs trials; No. 230 OCU 30.4.59 (loan No. 101 Sqn 19.11-25.11.59; Cat 3 work on site by Mfrs 19.10-5.12.60, also 6.2-23.2.61 and 22.6-3.8.61); No. 101 Sqn 15.3.62; AWA 28.5.62 for **B.Mk 1A** conversion; No. 101 Sqn 15.11.62 (Cat 3 work on site by No. 60 MU 6.6-19.6.63); WW 1963; St Athan (No. 19 MU) 11.3.66; NEA 17.5.66; sold as scrap to Bradbury & Co., Bournemouth 8.11.68

NOTES

Remarks in parentheses refer to events that occurred while the aircraft was with the unit noted, and in each case the aircraft is returned to the same operator after maintenance or repair. Category 3 refers in most instances to scheduled servicing or replacement of a failed component. Flying accidents and incidents are recorded as such. Work 'on site' refers to the base of the operating squadron, not the outside unit brought in to undertake the servicing or repair. Travelling servicing parties were provided by Avro, mainly from its out-station at Bracebridge Heath, near Lincoln, and No. 60 MU. The latter was based at Rufforth until transferred to Church Fenton in July 1959; to Dishforth in February 1962; and Leconfield in February 1966.

Vulcan B.Mk 2 production

Contract 6/Aircraft/11301/CB.6(a) dated 30.9.54: 20 B.Mk 1s and 17 B.Mk 2s

XH533: first production B.Mk 2

XH533: First flight 19.8.58; Mfrs; aw/cn 26.3.59; C(A) 26.3.59 at A&AEE; St Athan 1968 and scrapped; reverted to RAF charge 1.10.69 at 7 Engineering Sqn, St Athan; allocated 8048M, ntu; Sold Bradbury & Co., Bournemouth for scrap 15.10.70

XH534: B.Mk 2MRR, No. 27 Sqn, Scampton

XH534: Aw/cn 17.7.59; Mfrs; C(A) 4.3.60 at A&AEE; ground collision with Gannet XL452 7.8.62; Mfrs for mods 4.1.65; 230 OCU 6.12.66; (Mfrs mods 1.3-3.5.68) Mfrs for storage 7.4.72; Mfrs major overhaul and **B.Mk 2MRR** conversion 8.73; 27 Sqn 14.8.74; St Athan 7.4.81 as Cat 5C; Harold John & Co., Gwent, 16.2.82 for scrap

XH535: third B.Mk 2, Avro/A&AEE

XH535: Mfrs aw/cn 27.5.60; C(A) 27.5.60 at A&AEE; Crashed near Chute, Andover 11.5.64 (four killed, two pilots ejected)

XH536: Avro, seen at Farnborough

XH536: Aw/cn 17.7.59; C(A) 16.12.59 at A&AEE; MoA 31.5.60 as Olympus engine testbed; WW 24.11.65; crashed into Fan-Bwlchchwtyth, Hedl Senni, Wales 11.2.66 on TFR trials (9 Sqn crew), no survivors; SoC 14.2.66

XH537: A&AEE Skybolt trials

XH537: Aw/cn 27.8.59; Mfrs; MoA 31.8.60 at A&AEE for Skybolt trials; 230 OCU 31.5.65 (Mfrs mods 23.9-13.12.65, 27.2-2.4.69 and 14.1.72-17.6.74); St Athan 14.2.78 for conversion to **B.Mk 2MRR**; 27 Sqn 8.5.78; Abingdon 24.3.82 for exhibition use as 8749M; scrapped 5.91; nose to Barry Parkhouse, Ottershaw; current 1996

XH538: Aw/cn 23.9.59; MoA 30.1.61 for Mfrs/A&AEE Blue Steel trials; SW 14.5.69 (Mfrs/Bitteswell mods 27.6-20.8.69); WW 29.4.70; 230 OCU 21.4.71; 27 Sqn 3.12.73 (27 Sqn/230 OCU 9.1-8.3.74); 230 OCU 15.1.75; Mfrs mods 9.2.76; 35 Sqn 28.7.77; WW 16.8.78; 35 Sqn 23.11.79; St Athan 11.3.81 as Cat 5C; W. Harold & Co. for scrap 31.8.81

XH539: A&AEE Boscombe Down

XH539: Aw/cn 30.9.59; MoA 25.5.61 for Mfrs/A&AEE Blue Steel trials; A&AEE (Mfrs/Bitteswell mods 4.10.68-13.11.69) withdrawn 12.71; sole white B.2 remaining; Waddington 7.3.72 for crash rescue training; painted olive drab; expired 1987

XH554: Aw/cn 29.10.59; Mfrs; 83 Sqn 10.4.61; 230 OCU 1.11.62 (Mfrs for retrofit 6.3.63-5.11.64, and mods 28.6-2.9.65 and 17.3-27.7.71) (Cat 3R FA 13.9.73); RAF Fire Fighting & Safety School, Catterick (fly-in) 9.6.81; 8694M allocated; destroyed by 2.84

XH555: 230 OCU, seen at RAAF Edinburgh air show

XH555: 27 Sqn 14.7.61; 230 OCU structural damage at Finningley, 1968 following heavy landing – Cat 5 – no injuries; Mfrs for fatigue tests; St Athan for structural integrity tests and cut-up; Struck off 5.10.71; scrapped 1977

XH556: 27 Sqn 29.9.61; 230 OCU; undercarriage collapsed at Finningley on start-up 18.4.66, no injuries; struck off 19.4.66; Finningley dump

XH557: Aw/cn 13.5.60; MoA 21.6.60 for Bristol-Siddeley engines; first flight with Olympus Mk 301 in outboard nacelles 19.5.61; Mfrs mods 1.7.64; CotW 6.12.65; WW 8.2.66 (Mfrs for mods 24.2-28.4.67 and 30.12.71-4.5.72); AW 19.4.74; WW 15.1.75 (9 Sqn marks) (Mfrs/Bitteswell major 20.3.79-1.2.80) (50 Sqn marks 3.81); declared Cat 5C 10.9.82 at Waddington with 5,013.30 flying hours; sold to Bird Group as scrap 8.12.82

XH558: Aw/cn 30.6.60; 230 OCU 1.7.60 – first B.Mk 2 service delivery (Cat 3R FA 10.8.62) (Mfrs for retrofit 11.2.64-29.6.65, mods 15.12.66-23.2.67); WW 26.2.68 (101 Sqn marks 5.72); Mfrs for mods 4.6-14.10.69 at Bitteswell, 2.10-31.10.72) (Cat 3R FA 3.12.69); Mfrs for conversion to **B.Mk 2MRR** 17.8.73 (Cat 3R FA 6.11.75); 230 OCU 18.10.76; 27 Sqn 29.11.76; WW 31.3.82 (44 Sqn marks 4.82); Mfrs for B.Mk 2(K), later **K.Mk 2** conversion 30.6.82, flown 3.9.82; 44/50 Sqns 12.10.82 (50 Sqn marks); (C(A) at A&AEE 25.10-30.11.82); Waddington Station Flight 1.4.84 (VDT 1984); Marham 18.9.84; allocation cancelled; VDF Waddington 14.11.84 parented by 55 Sqn; returned to B.Mk 2 standard (less some avionics); airworthy 1987; sold to C. Walton Ltd and delivered to Bruntingthorpe 23.3.93; retained in theoretically airworthy state and registered G-VLCN 6.2.95

XH559: Aw/cn 30.7.60; 230 OCU 24.8.60; (Mfrs mods 7.8.63-6.5.64 and 4.8.69-27.2.70 at Bitteswell) St Athan 27.5.81 as Cat 5C; Harold John & Co. 29.1.82 as scrap

XH560: Aw/cn 30.9.60; 230 OCU 3.10.60; Mfrs 28.11.60; loan MoA 13.1.61; Mfrs mods 16.3.62; 12 Sqn 26.9.62; 230 OCU 29.11.63; Mfrs for retrofit 2.6.64; CotW 23.8.65 (Mfrs mods 4.2-2.3.66, 12.1-22.3.67); WW 10.4.67; CotW 2.2.68; Mfrs/Bitteswell 19.5-26.6.68; AW 15.1.69; Mfrs for storage 20.10.71; major overhaul and **B.Mk 2MRR** conversion 1.2.73; 27 Sqn 15.3.74; WW 25.3.82 (44 Sqn marks 4.82); Mfrs for B.Mk 2(K), later **K.Mk 2** conversion 15.6.82, flown 16.8.82; 44/50 Sqns 23.8.82 (50 Sqn marks); 50 Sqn 1.83; Waddington Stn Flt 4.84 as VDT reserve; Marham 29.11.84; assigned to spares recovery 5.1.85; fire dump; scrapped 10.90; nose to Nigel Towler, Rayleigh

XH561: Aw/cn 31.10.60; 230 OCU 4.11.60 (Cat 3R FA 1.5.63 and 15.1.65 – wheels-up landing); Mfrs for retrofit 28.3.66; WW 7.8.67; CotW 8.5.68 (Mfrs mods 23.8-30.9.68); AW 19.3.69; (Mfrs mods 18.9.70-22.1.71 and 17.4.74-6.3.75); 35 Sqn 6.3.75; (Mfrs/Bitteswell 14.5.80-6.2.81); 50 Sqn 4.9.81; Mfrs for prototype B.Mk 2(K), later **K.Mk 2** conversion 4.5.82, flown 18.6.82; 50 Sqn 18.6.82 at Woodford; to Waddington 23.6.82; Waddington Station Flight 1.4.84; allocated 8809M 22.3.84 for RAF Fire Fighting & Safety School and delivered Catterick 14.6.84; expired by 1987

XH562: Aw/cn 30.11.60; 230 OCU 9.12.60; 35 Sqn 1.3.63; 230 OCU 11.3.63; 35 Sqn 30.4.63; 230 OCU 19.9.63; Mfrs for retrofit 2.4.64-30.7.65; CotW 1.8.65; 50 Sqn 8.3.66; Mfrs mods 15.12.66; WW 10.2.67; CotW 24.4.68 (Mfrs mods 9.8-18.9.68); AW 15.1.69 (Mfrs mods 7.8.70-12.1.71) (Cat 3R FA 21.3.74); Mfrs mods 16.7.74; WW 9.5.75 (44 Sqn marks); St Athan, major 6.7.77; 230 OCU 27.9.77 (Mfrs/Bitteswell 15.2-1.12.80); 35 Sqn 16.12.80; WW 19.6.81 (9 Sqn marks 7.81; 101 Sqn marks 6.82); RAF Fire Fighting & Safety School, Catterick (fly-in) 19.8.82 as 8758M with 5,978.20 hours; destroyed by 1984

XH563: Aw/cn 22.12.60; Waddington 23.12.60; 83 Sqn 28.12.60; 12 Sqn 26.11.62; Mfrs retrofit 6.6.63; 230 OCU 5.3.65; WW 6.8.68; 230 OCU 18.3.69 (loan MinTech 8.4-11.6.69 and 19.8-2.10.69); SW 3.5.71; 230 OCU 7.5.71; Mfrs mods 25.10.71-9.2.73 then Mfrs/Bitteswell for B.Mk 2MRR conversion 9.2.73; 27 Sqn 17.12.73; last flight 23.3.82; total time 6,637 hours; assigned to preservation at Scampton as 8744M, 31.3.82; broken up for scrap 11.86; nose to Donald Milne at Banchory

XH558 of the Vulcan Display Flight partners the 'Red Arrows' for a classic formation. The VDF continued as a valuable PR/recruiting tool long after the Vulcan was retired from front-line service until it, too, became a victim of ever-shrinking budgets.

Vulcan individual aircraft details

Contract 6/Aircraft/11830/CB.6(a) dated 31.3.55: 8 B.Mk 2s

XJ780: Aw/cn 10.1.61; 83 Sqn 16.1.61; 12 Sqn 26.11.62; 230 OCU 16.8.63 (Mfrs for retrofit 2.3.64-26.7.65, and mods 7.3-17.5.67); WW 10.10.67; CotW 6.12.68; WW 18.4.69 (Mfrs mods 4.7-3.9.69); AW 12.1.70 (Mfrs mods 16.7-8.12.70 and Cat 3FA 19.7.72); WW 17.1.75 (9 Sqn marks 1.75) (Mfrs mods 9.7.75-31.3.76); 27 Sqn 23.11.76; **B.Mk 2MRR** standard declared Cat 5 for spares 31.3.82 at Scampton; sold Bird Group as scrap 11.82

XJ781: Aw/cn 20.2.61; 83 Sqn 23.2.61; 12 Sqn 29.10.62; 230 OCU 4.2.64; Mfrs retrofit 1.3.65; WW 10.2.66 (Mfrs mods 26.4.67-30.6.67); CotW 22.4.68; AW 18.4.69 (Mfrs mods 5.12.70-7.4.71); damaged beyond repair at Shiraz, Iran, 23.5.73, landing on foam carpet with port mainwheel leg retracted, no fatalities; SoC 27.5.73

XJ782: 83 Sqn 2.3.61; 12 Sqn 23.10.62; 230 OCU 20.12.63; Mfrs retrofit 29.3.65; WW 25.3.66 (Mfrs mods 6.4-26.6.67); CotW 9.4.68 (Mfrs mods 9.12.68-20.1.69); AW 19.3.69 (Mfrs mods 11.11.72-17.5.73); WW 8.1.75 (44 Sqn marks 8.75); 27 Sqn 15.2.77 – remaining in B.Mk 2 configuration, last Scampton Vulcan sortie 31.3.82; allocated Scampton for scrap 31.3.82; cancelled and to WW 22.5.82 (101 Sqn marks 6.82); Finningley 4.9.82 for display as 8766M; 6,461.05 hours flown; SoC 6.9.82; scrapped 6.88

XJ783: No. 83 Sqn, Scampton

XJ783: Aw/cn 6.3.61; 83 Sqn 13.3.61; 9 Sqn 7.11.62; 230 OCU 28.2.64 (Cat 3 FA 23.2.64); Mfrs retrofit 25.9.64; WW 3.1.66 (Mfrs mods 10.5-14.7.67); CotW 22.3.68; AW 15.1.69 (Mfrs mods 6.12.71-28.3.72); 35 Sqn 16.1.75; 230 OCU 11.8.76; 35 Sqn 23.8.76; Mfrs/Bitteswell mods 7.3.78; 617 Sqn 23.11.78; 35 Sqn 3.4.81; declared Cat 5C 1.3.82; sold Bird Group for scrap 11.82

XJ784: Aw/cn 30.3.61; MoA 29.3.61 [sic] for A&AEE; Mfrs mods 15.9.66; 230 OCU 22.12.66 (Mfrs retrofit 12.5-13.6.69); AW 21.7.70; WW 16.12.70; AW 18.8.71 (Mfrs mods 31.1-23.8.73); WW 15.1.75 (9 Sqn marks 2.75, 44 Sqn marks 6.79, 101 Sqn marks 6.80) (Mfrs/Bitteswell 3.7.79-14.5.80); Declared Cat 5C 10.9.82 with 4,770.55 hours; sold Bird Group for scrap 8.12.82

XJ823: Aw/cn 20.4.61; 27 Sqn 21.4.61; 35 Sqn 2.1.63 becoming CotW 3.64; 230 OCU 11.5.64; Mfrs retrofit 28.6.65; WW 1.11.66 (loan MinTech 29.11-4.12.67); Mfrs mods 16.2.68; CotW 29.4.68; AW 5.2.69 (Cat 3 FA 5.2.70, Mfrs mods 13.3-14.8.70); WW 17.1.75 (9 Sqn marks 2.75); 27 Sqn 27.4.77; **B.Mk 2MRR** standard 35 Sqn 2.4.81; WW 1.3.82 (9 Sqn 3.82 but not marked, 50 Sqn marks 4.82); Holding Flight, Waddington, 4.1.83; sold Tom Stoddart 21.1.83 and delivered to Solway Aviation Society, Carlisle, 24.1.83; 5,953.30 hours flown; currently on display at Carlisle Airport

XJ824: Akrotiri Wing

XJ824: Aw/cn 11.5.61; 27 Sqn 16.5.61; 9 Sqn 25.2.63; 230 OCU 2.12.63; Mfrs retrofit 28.5.65; CotW 4.7.66; WW 4.10.66 (Mfrs mods 3.7-31.8.67); CotW 19.6.68; AW 5.2.69 (Mfrs mods 20.4-8.9.70); 35 Sqn 24.1.75 (Mfrs mods 5.6.75-26.2.76); 230 OCU 14.2.77; WW

XL320 was first assigned to No. 617 Sqn before becoming part of the pooled Scampton Wing.

10.79 (44 Sqn marks 10.79, 101 Sqn marks 7.82) (Mfrs/Bitteswell mods 18.9.80-8.6.81 – last Vulcan to leave Bitteswell); Imperial War Museum, Duxford, 13.3.82 as gift, 6,291.30 hours flown; current 1996

XJ825: Aw/cn 27.7.61; 27 Sqn 28.7.61; 35 Sqn 4.2.63; 230 OCU 30.4.64; Mfrs retrofit 18.8.64; CotW 3.9.65; Mfrs mods 3.2.67; WW 11.4.67; CotW 19.2.68; AW 26.2.69 (Mfrs mods 15.10.70-3.3.71); 35 Sqn 16.1.75; (Mfrs mods 7.3.75-13.1.76) 27 Sqn 15.12.76 – **B.Mk 2MRR** standard; 35 Sqn 6.4.81; WW 1.3.82 (101 Sqn marks 3.82); Mfrs for conversion to B.Mk 2(K), later **K.Mk 2** 11.5.82, flown 29.6.82; 50 Sqn 25.6.82 and to Waddington 1.7.82; allocated 8810M 22.3.84, for battle damage repair training at Waddington; SoC 5.4.84; broken up 1.92

Contract 6/Aircraft/13145/CB.6(a) dated 25.2.56: 24 B.Mk 2s

XL317: Aw/cn 14.7.61 (first production aircraft with Blue Steel carrying mods); MoA 13.7.61; 617 Sqn 7.6.62 becoming SW 1964 (Mfrs retrofit 18.2-29.10.65, Mfrs mods 22.3-11.5.67 and 21.1-28.5.71) (617 Sqn marks 1971); 230 OCU 24.4.74; 617 Sqn 1.5.74 (Mfrs mods 10.11.75-18.10.76); Akrotiri 1.12.81 for crash rescue training, allocated 8725M; scrapped late 1986

XL318: Aw/cn 30.8.61; 617 Sqn 4.9.61 (Mfrs mods 2.4.64-21.4.65, 9.11.65-14.1.66, 18.4-6.6.67 and 9.9-18.11.69); 230 OCU 22.5.72 (Mfrs mods 17.10.72-4.4.73); 27 Sqn 31.1.74; 230 OCU 1.2.74; WW 18.6.75; 230 OCU 5.8.75; WW 7.11.79; 230 OCU 21.2.80; 617 Sqn 1.7.81; last sortie by a 617 Sqn aircraft, 11.12.81; assigned RAF Museum 4.1.82 as 8733M, road transported to Hendon in three loads beginning 12.2.82; current 1996

XL319: Aw/cn 19.10.61; 617 Sqn 23.10.61 becoming SW 1964 (Mfrs mods 4.5.64-22.7.65, 9.5-29.6.67, 12.1-28.4.70); 230 OCU 14.5.70; SW 12.11.70; 617 Sqn 22.4.71; Mfrs mods 8.5.72; 230 OCU 19.9.72; 35 Sqn 16.10.78 (Mfrs/Bitteswell mods 22.5.79-25.3.80); WW 1.3.82 (44 Sqn marks 3.82); sold North East Aircraft Museum 20.1.83; delivered Sunderland 21.1.83; flew 6,644.10 hours; current 1996

XL320: Aw/cn 30.11.61; 617 Sqn 4.12.61 becoming SW 1964 (Mfrs retrofit 21.8.64-30.9.65, Mfrs mods 26.1-21.3.67 and 30.9-25.11.69); wearing 83 Sqn badge 6.71; 27 Sqn 9.71; 230 OCU 29.3.72 (Mfrs mods 20.10.72-22.2.73); flew 500,000th Vulcan hour 18.2.81; St Athan as Cat 5C 2.6.81; sold W. Harold & Co. 31.8.81 for scrap

XL321: Aw/cn 10.1.62; 617 Sqn 11.1.62 becoming SW (Mfrs retrofit 12.3-21.12.65, and mods 9.12.66-25.1.67, 8.4-19.8.71) (27 Sqn marks 1.71); 230 OCU 29.3.72; 617 Sqn 15.9.72; 230 OCU 11.10.72; 617 Sqn 13.4.73; 230 OCU 17.4.73; SW/230 OCU 6.12-17.12.73; 230 OCU 17.12.73; WW 8.6.76 (44 Sqn marks 7.76); 230 OCU 8.11.76; 35 Sqn 1.7.81; 617 Sqn 14.9.81; 35 Sqn 6.10.81; 50 Sqn 21.1.82; RAF Fire Fighting and Safety School, Catterick (fly-in) 19.8.82, allocated 8759M; 6952.35 hours; burnt by 1987

XL359: Aw/cn 31.1.61; 617 Sqn 1.2.62 becoming SW (Mfrs retrofit 9.12.64-3.9.65, and mods 5.8-11.11.66,

23.1-21.5.70); 27 Sqn marks 3.71; 230 OCU 21.10.71 (Mfrs mods 3.7-22.11.72); 35 Sqn 1.7.81; Scampton 1.3.82 (for gate but dumped instead); sold Bird Group 11.82 for scrap

XL360: Aw/cn 28.2.62; 617 Sqn 2.3.62 becoming SW (Mfrs retrofit 1.2-19.10.65, and mods 5.6-13.7.67, Cat 3 FA 5.3.69, Mfrs mods 7.1-12.5.71); adopted 617 Sqn marks 5.71; 230 OCU 13.7.71; WW 18.8.75; 230 OCU 21.10.75; Mfrs mods 24.2.77; 617 Sqn 5.12.77; 35 Sqn 31.5.78; 101 Sqn 5.1.82; sold Midland Air Museum 26.1.83 and delivered to Coventry/Baginton 4.2.83; 6,467.10 hours flown; current 1996

XL361: Aw/cn 14.3.62; 617 Sqn 15.3.62 (MoA loan 3-15.7.63 and 14.8.63-2.4.64); SW 2.4.64 (Mfrs retrofit 25.3.65-20.1.66, and mods 13.10-1.12.66 and 14.10-8.12.69); 230 OCU 7.10.70; SW 19.11.70; 230 OCU 30.11.70; SW 5.4.71; 230 OCU 12.5.71 (Mfrs mods 13.8-29.12.71 and ground accident 18.5.72); 27 Sqn/230 OCU 14.1.74 (wearing 230 marks); MoD(PE) at A&AEE 16.12.74; 230 OCU 10.1.75; 617 Sqn 14.1.75; MOD(PE) at A&AEE 7.8.75; 617 Sqn 3.9.75; 35 Sqn 3.8.77 (Mfrs/Bitteswell mods 5.9.78-6.7.79); WW 13.4.81 (9 Sqn marks); Cat 3 accident at Goose Bay (Canada) 13.11.81; declared Cat 5 21.12.81; 5,246.45 hours flown; placed on display at CFB Goose Bay 7.6.82; current 1996

XL384: Aw/cn 30.3.62; 230 OCU 2.4.62; Mfrs 7.8.63; SW 5.8.64 for Chaff ('Window') trials (Mfrs mods 26.4-21.6.66, 4.4-22.5.67 and 2.2-5.6.70); WW 23.3.70; SW/230 OCU 27.11.70; heavy landing 12.8.71 and assessed Cat 3R 13.8.71; on site repairs by No. 71 MU from 18.8.71 and Mfrs from 19.9.71; abandoned and declared Cat 5 14.1.75; escape trainer at Scampton assigned 18.3.76; allocated 8505M 30.9.76; transferred to crash rescue training and allocated 8670M 29.1.81; removed 1983; SoC 23.5.85; survived in badly burnt form until finally scrapped 3.94

XL385: Aw/cn 17.4.62; 9 Sqn 18.4.62; Mfrs retrofit 1.10.63; SW 9.10.64 (Mfrs mods 29.10-30.12.65); burnt-out 6.4.67 at Scampton (Nos 1 and 2 engines blew up on take-off), no fatalities; SoC 7.4.67

XL386: No. 9 Sqn, Coningsby/Cottesmore

XL386: Aw/cn 11.5.62; 9 Sqn 14.5.62 (Mfrs retrofit 4.11.63-7.12.64, and mods 28.5-12.8.65); SW 16.8.65 (Mfrs mods 21.12.66-13.2.67 and 27.8-31.10.69); 230 OCU 1.4.70 (Mfrs mods 5.3-21.10.74); WW 30.9.77 (44 Sqn marks 3.78, 101 Sqn 5.81, 50 Sqn 10.81); Central Training Establishment, Manston 26.8.82, allocated 8760M; 5,916.45 hours flown; scrapped 8.93, nose to Hanningfield Metals Ltd

XL387: 230 OCU, Finningley

XL387: Aw/cn 31.5.62; 230 OCU 4.6.62; Mfrs retrofit 2.12.63; SW 5.2.65 (Mfrs/Bitteswell 13.8-27.10.65, mods 10.11.66-2.1.67, 13.5-21.9.71) (Cat 3R FA 26.3.70) (617 Sqn marks 12.69); SW/230 OCU 5.7-9.8.72; 230 OCU 10.8.72; WW 10.1.73 (101 Sqn marks 8.73, 50 Sqn marks 8.75) (Mfrs/Bitteswell 26.1-3.11.78); St Athan for rescue training 28.1.82; 5,807.20 hours flown; sold for scrap to T. Bradbury 2.6.83

XL388: No. 9 Sqn, Coningsby

XL388: Aw/cn 13.6.62; 9 Sqn 14.6.62 (named 'Mayflower III' for US visit, Cat 3R bird ingestion 27.7.63) becoming ConW; Mfrs retrofit 2.1.64; SW 22.2.65 (Mfrs mods 21.7-22.9.65, 31.1-20.3.67, 18.5-27.7.70); 230 OCU 19.4.71; SW/230 OCU 10.5.71; Mfrs mods 28.1.72; 230 OCU 24.5.72; 617 Sqn 15.9.72; 230 OCU 29.9.72; 617 Sqn 2.2.73; 230 OCU 14.5.73; 617 Sqn 1.11.73; 230 OCU 5.3.74; 617 Sqn 6.3.74; WW 1.4.74 (44 Sqn marks 5.75) (Cat 3R FA 18.6.74) (Mfrs/Bitteswell 19.11.76-7.9.77); Honington fire dump 2.4.82; allocated 8750M; 5,597.20 hours flown; scrapped and sold to Swefeling Engineering Group 13.6.85; nose to Blyth Valley Aviation Collection, Walpole, Halesworth; current 1996

XL389: Aw/cn 11.7.62; 230 OCU 13.7.62; Mfrs retrofit 4.2.64; SW 20.5.65 (Mfrs mods 20.10-2.12.66 and 7.1.70-13.5.70); 230 OCU 11.11.70; 617 Sqn 12.70; 230 OCU 7.4.72; 617 Sqn 30.6.72; 230 OCU 12.1.73; 617 Sqn 16.1.73; WW 26.6.74 (9 Sqn marks 6.76, 44 Sqn 7.79, 101 Sqn 6.80); St Athan 6.4.81 as Cat 5C; 5,741.05 hours flown; sold W. Harold & Co. for scrap 31.8.81

XL390: (first production with Skybolt hardpoints) Aw/cn 19.7.62; 9 Sqn 20.7.62; Mfrs retrofit 2.3.64; SW 27.5.65 (617 Sqn marks 9.69, 27 Sqn marks 3.71, 617 Sqn marks 3.73) (Mfrs mods 5.12.66-6.2.67, 16.12.69-17.4.70); 230 OCU 30.4.71; 617 Sqn 3.6.71; 230 OCU 31.5.74; 617 Sqn 4.6.74 (Mfrs mods 6.2-3.10.75); failed to recover from wing-over and crashed near Glenview Naval Air Station, Chicago, 12.8.78 during practice for air display – all crew killed; SoC 21.8.78

XL391: Waddington Wing, Black Buck reserve

XL391: Aw/cn 22.5.63; MoA 22.5.63 at A&AEE; BCDU 15.6.65; MoA 6.1.66 at A&AEE; Mfrs mods 2.5.67; CotW 31.7.68; AW 5.2.69 (Cat 3 FA 11.8.70, Mfrs mods from 28.12.73); WW 17.1.75 (9 Sqn marks 1.75, 101 Sqn marks 6.80, 44 Sqn marks 7.82) (Mfrs/Bitteswell mods 2.11.78-31.7.79); sold Manchester Vulcan Bomber Society 11.2.83; flown to Blackpool 16.2.83; total 4,612.35 hours; current 1996

XL392: Aw/cn 31.7.62; 83 Sqn 2.8.62 becoming SW 1964 (Mfrs retrofit 1.4.65-23.2.66, and mods 12.7-

10.10.66, 25.6-13.11.70); 230 OCU 11.12.70; SW 21.12.70; 230 OCU 12.1.73; 617 Sqn 15.1.73 (Mfrs mods 21.5.76-25.2.77); 35 Sqn 4.1.82; Valley 24.3.82 for crash rescue training, allocated 8745M; scrapped 8.93

XL425: Aw/cn 30.8.62; 83 Sqn 31.8.62 becoming SW (Mfrs retrofit 14.5.65-2.3.66, mods 2.5-26.6.67, 12.1-23.3.70, and 17.5-30.11.72) (Cat 3 FA 8.4.69); 617 Sqn 30.11.72; 27 Sqn 1.11.73; 617 Sqn 1.4.74; declared Cat 5C 4.1.82; sold as scrap to Bird Group 4.82

XL426: Vulcan Display Team, Waddington

XL426: Aw/cn 7.9.62; 83 Sqn 13.9.62; becoming SW (Mfrs retrofit 21.6.65-11.3.66, and mods 18.7-18.10.66, 28.10-18.12.69); 230 OCU 29.3.72; 617 Sqn 7.4.72; 230 OCU 28.6.72; 617 Sqn 4.7.72; 230 OCU 11.7.72; 617 Sqn 1.8.72; 230 OCU 13.4.73; 617 Sqn 16.4.73; Mfrs mods 27.7.73; 27 Sqn 6.2.74; 617 Sqn 21.2.74 (Mfrs/Bitteswell 17.11.77-21.6.78); 50 Sqn 5.1.82; Waddington Station Flight 1.4.84; VDT 1984; 55 Sqn/VDF 1985-86 Scampton 7.86; sold Roy Jacobsen and delivered by air to Southend 19.12.86 for preservation in airworthy condition, 6,236 hours; registered G-VJET on 7.7.87; acquired by Vulcan Restoration Trust 28.7.83 and refurbished to taxiing condition, 1995; current 1996

XL427: Aw/cn 29.9.62; 83 Sqn 2.10.62 becoming SW (Mfrs mods 13.8.65-13.4.66, 14.2-5.4.67, 17.6-10.11.71) (617 Sqn marks 9.69, 27 Sqn 3.71); 230 OCU 29.6.72; 617 Sqn 5.7.72; 230 OCU 25.9.72; 27 Sqn 4.1.74; 230 OCU 11.8.76; 27 Sqn 27.8.76; WW 2.5.77 (9 Sqn marks 6.77, 50 Sqn 4.81, 9 Sqn 10.81, 44 Sqn 6.82); Macrihanish for crash rescue 13.8.82 as 8756M; 6,133.30 hours; dumped 1986; scrapped 4.95

XL443: Aw/cn 4.10.62; 83 Sqn 8.10.62 becoming SW (Mfrs retrofit 7.9.65-23.2.67, Cat 3 FA 8.12.69, Mfrs mods 4.3-7.7.71); AW 12.4.72; 35 Sqn 24.1.75 (Mfrs/Bitteswell mods 9.5.78-5.2.79); allocated RAF Museum 4.1.82 but sold to Bird Group for scrap 4.82

XL444: Aw/cn 29.10.82; 27 Sqn 1.11.62 becoming SW (Mfrs retrofit 13.9.65-30.5.66); 230 OCU 18.6.66; SW 19.6.67 (Mfrs mods 23.6-10.8.67 and 27.8-31.12.70); 230 OCU 5.4.71; SW 11.5.71 (27 Sqn marks 6.71, 617 Sqn 9.71); 617 Sqn/230 OCU 19.7.72-5.12.73; 617 Sqn 18.12.73 (Mfrs mods 25.1-17.11.77); 35 Sqn 31.5.78; WW 6.4.81 (9 Sqn marks 5.81); declared Cat 5C 10.9.82, with 6,001.40 hours; sold Bird Group 8.12.82 for scrap

XL445: Aw/cn 19.11.62; 27 Sqn 26.11.62 becoming SW (Mfrs retrofit 22.11.65); WW 30.9.66 (Mfrs mods 20.10-12.12.67); CW 18.4.68; AW 15.1.69 (Cat 3R FA 6.5.69) (Mfrs mods 1.2-19.6.72); 35 Sqn 16.1.75; WW 16.6.77; 35 Sqn 1.10.77; 230 OCU 16.10.78 (Mfrs/Bitteswell 2.3-21.12.79); 35 Sqn 1.7.81; 44 Sqn 18.11.81; Mfrs for B.Mk 2(K), later **K.Mk 2** conversion 25.5.82, flown 22.7.82; 50 Sqn 22.7.82 (same sortie); allocated 8811M 2.3.84; for crash rescue training at Lyneham 1.4.84; delivered 5.4.84; scrapped 1987; nose

XL445: No. 44 Sqn/Waddington Wing

to Blyth Valley Aviation Collection, Walpole, Halesworth; current 1996

XL446: Aw/cn 19.11.62; 27 Sqn 30.11.62 becoming SW (Mfrs retrofit 18.10.65-18.6.66); WW 16.9.66 (Cat 3 FA 10.11.66); Mfrs mods 2.11.67; 230 OCU 28.12.67 (Mfrs mods 31.5-2.7.68, 15.12.71-18.4.72); SW 18.4.72; AW 31.7.72; 35 Sqn 16.1.75 (Mfrs/Bitteswell mods 7.9.77-10.5.78); WW 24.5.78; 617 Sqn 31.10.78; 35 Sqn 4.1.82 declared Cat 5C 1.3.82; sold to Bird Group 11.82 for scrap

XL446: No. 35 Sqn, Scampton

Contract KD/B/OI/CB.6(a) dated 22.1.58: 40 B.Mk 2s

XM569: Aw/cn 4.1.63; 27 Sqn 1.2.63 becoming SW (Mfrs retrofit 16.12.65-29.8.66); WW 17.11.66; Mfrs mods 4.12.67; CotW 19.1.68; AW 26.2.69 (Mfrs mods 3.4.73); 27 Sqn 4.7.74; WW 23.11.76 (9 Sqn marks 1.77, 50 Sqn 6.79, 101 Sqn 9.81, 44 Sqn 8.82); sold Wales Aircraft Museum 21.1.83; delivered to Cardiff 2.2.83; 5,599.40 hours; current 1996

XM570: Aw/cn 26.2.63; 27 Sqn 27.2.63 becoming SW Mfrs retrofit 13.1.66; WW 2.1.67; Mfrs mods 12.12.67; CotW 26.1.68; AW 26.2.69 (Mfrs mods 8.9.72-7.3.73); 27 Sqn 8.3.74; 35 Sqn 8.12.76; 230 OCU 28.2.77; 35 Sqn 2.3.77; 617 Sqn 4.9.78; 35 Sqn 31.10.78; St Athan as Cat 5C 11.3.81; sold Harold John & Co. 29.1.82 for scrap

XM571: Aw/cn 20.2.63; 83 Sqn 22.2.63 becoming SW; Mfrs retrofit 22.2.66; CotW 20.1.67; WW 3.7.67; CotW 13.9.67; WW 15.12.67 (Mfrs mods 18.1-29.2.68); AW 19.3.69 (Mfrs mods 10.8.72-13.1.73); 27 Sqn 3.1.75; 35 Sqn 9.4.75; WW 16.6.75; 35 Sqn 3.11.75; WW 15.6.76 (50 Sqn marks 7.76); 35 Sqn 15.11.76 (Mfrs/Bitteswell 28.3.77-17.4.78); St Athan 9.1.79; 617 Sqn 27.3.79; WW 20.8.79; 617 Sqn 4.12.79; 101 Sqn 8.1.82; Mfrs for B.Mk 2(K), later K.Mk 2 conversion 11.5.82, flown 13.7.82; C(A) at A&AEE 14.7.82; 44/50 Sqns 25.8.82; A&AEE 3.9.82; 44/50 Sqns (50 Sqn marks) 26.10.82; 50 Sqn 1.83; Waddington Station Flight 4.84; allocated 8812M 22.3.84; Gibraltar 9.5.84 for preservation; scrapped 9.90

Vulcan individual aircraft details

XM572: Scampton Wing

XM572: Aw/cn 28.2.63; 83 Sqn 28.2.63 becoming SW (Mfrs retrofit 28.2.66-8.1.67); Mfrs mods 15.2.68; CotW 5.4.68 (Mfrs mods 25.11.68-7.1.69); AW 19.3.69 (Mfrs mods 7.7.71-14.12.71); 35 Sqn 24.1.75 (Mfrs mods 27.10.76-23.8.77); 9 Sqn 2.9.81; declared Cat 5C 10.9.82, with 5,525.25 hours; sold Bird Group for scrap 30.11.82

XM573: Aw/cn 26.3.63; 83 Sqn 28.3.63 becoming SW; Mfrs retrofit 11.3.66; WW 25.4.67; 230 OCU 15.2.68 (Mfrs mods 1.4-14.5.69); AW 26.6.70 (Mfrs mods 1.5-23.11.73); 27 Sqn 17.4.74; WW 9.3.77 (44 Sqn marks 3.77); 230 OCU 18.12.78; WW 7.4.81 (9 Sqn marks 5.81); Scampton 22.5.82; delivered Offutt AFB (USA) 7.6.82, with 5,533.45 hours; presented to USAF 12.6.82; current 1996

XM574: Aw/cn 12.6.63; 27 Sqn 21.6.63 becoming SW (Mfrs mods 28.1-13.6.66, 21.3-1.5.67, 10.5-17.6.68 and 2.12.69-30.1.70); 230 OCU 3.5.71; SW 12.5.71 (27 Sqn marks 9.71); WW 3.11.71 (101 Sqn marks) (Mfrs mods 12.12.72-19.6.73); AW 24.8.73; 35 Sqn 24.1.75; 617 Sqn 14.8.75; St Athan as Cat 5C 31.8.81; sold Harold John & Co. for scrap 29.1.82

XM575: Aw/cn 21.5.63; 617 Sqn 22.5.63 becoming SW (Mfrs mods 20.11.64-22.3.65, 1.3-18.4.67 and 12.8-21.10.69); WW 28.7.70; SW 27.11.70; 230 OCU 3.5.71; SW 7.5.71 (617 Sqn marks 5.72); Mfrs mods 22.12.72; 617 Sqn 28.6.73; WW 15.3.74 (101 Sqn marks 5.75, 50 Sqn 6.78, 44 Sqn 8.79); sold Leicestershire Air Museum 25.1.83; delivered Castle Donnington 28.1.83; 5,389.30 flying hours, registered G-BLMC; current with East Midlands Airport Volunteers Association, 1996

XM576: Aw/cn 14.6.63; SW 21.6.63 (Mfrs mods 4.1-29.3.65); crash-landed Scampton 25.5.65 during asymmetric landing practice; estimated Cat 4, but declared Cat 5 6.12.65

XM594: Aw/cn 9.7.63; 27 Sqn 19.7.63 becoming SW (Mfrs mods 30.12.65-16.5.66, Mfrs/Bitteswell 19.5-7.7.67, Mfrs mods 17.6-8.7.68, 13.4-14.7.70 and from 29.3.72); WW 24.8.72 (101 Sqn 6.75, 44 Sqn 5.77, Mfrs/Bitteswell mods 9.7.76-31.3.77); sold Newark Air Museum 19.1.83; delivered Winthorpe 7.2.83; 5,316.30 hours; current 1996

XM595: Aw/cn 21.8.63; 617 Sqn 21.8.63 becoming SW (Mfrs mods 8.10.64-4.2.65, 14.7-30.8.67, Cat 3 FA 4.7.68 Mfrs mods 21.10-25.11.68, 11.11.69-14.1.70); 617 Sqn 1970; Mfrs mods 11.2.74; 27 Sqn 16.8.74; 617 Sqn 9.75; 35 Sqn 11.76; 617 Sqn 2.78; 35 Sqn 4.1.82; declared Cat 5S 1.3.82; sold to Bird Group for scrap 11.82

XM596: 60th production B.Mk 2; not completed; used for static fatigue tests at Woodford in connection with low-level operations; scrapped 1972

XM597: Waddington Wing, Black Buck aircraft

XM597: Aw/cn 26.8.63; Mfrs 28.8.63; 12 Sqn 27.8.63 becoming ConW; Mfrs mods 4.9.64; CotW 18.12.64 (Cat 3 FA undercarriage collapse 23.6.66) (Mfrs mods 17.1-17.3.67); WW 18.4.68 (Mfrs mods 2.1-3.2.69 and 22.10.73-25.4.74, Bitteswell 8.4.78-6.3.79) (loan MoD(PE) at A&AEE 29.11.71-11.9.72 and 4.10.72-12.2.73 for trials of ARI 18228 RWR) (101 Sqn marks 8.73, 44 Sqn 9.75, 50 Sqn 4.76, 9 Sqn 5.79, 44 Sqn 10.81, 101 Sqn 7.82); Ascension Island 1982; Shrike ARM carrier, Port Stanley raids 31.5 and 3.6.82; impounded, Brazil 3.6-10.6.82; 44 Sqn 1.7.82; 50 Sqn 24.12.82; Royal Scottish Museum of Flight, East Fortune 12.4.84; current 1996

XM598: Waddington Wing, Black Buck reserve

XM598: Aw/cn 30.8.63; 12 Sqn 4.9.63 becoming ConW; CotW 11.64 (Mfrs mods 1.12.64-5.1.65, 29.1-25.2.66, 29,12.66-13.3.77); WW 9.4.68 (101 Sqn marks 5.72, 44 Sqn 8.75, 50 Sqn 4.78, 9 Sqn 10.79, 50 Sqn 10.81, 44 Sqn 6.82) (Mfrs mods 14.10-19.22.68, 20.5-8.10.71, 29.9.75-9.7.66, 27.3-24.7.79); Ascension Island 1982 – reserve; allocated 8778M 4.1.83; delivered Cosford Aerospace Museum 20.1.83; 5,428.05 hours; current 1996

XM599: Aw/cn 30.9.63; 35 Sqn 1.10.63 becoming ConW (Mfrs mods 1.12.64-15.1.65, Cat 3 FA 7.4.65, Mfrs mods 11-28.1.66, 18.8.66-31.1.67); WW 9.1.68 (Mfrs/Bitteswell mods 24.4-29.5.68, Mfrs mods 4.11.71-7.3.72, 3.12.74-8.8.75, Mfrs/Bitteswell 5.11.79-15.8.80) (101 Sqn marks 5.72, 50 Sqn 3.77, 44 Sqn 6.79); St Athan as Cat 5C 27.5.81; 5,272.10 hours; sold H. John & Co. for scrap 29.1.82

XM600: Aw/cn 30.9.63; 35 Sqn 3.10.63 becoming ConW (Mfrs mods 23.6-14.9.65, 1.8.66-20.1.67); WW 30.5.68 (Mfrs mods 31.7-12.9.68, 14.5-24.9.70, Cat 3 FA 8.1.71, Mfrs mods 25.1.74-4.12.74) (101 Sqn marks 8.73); crashed Spilsby, Lincs after engine bay fire 17.1.77; no fatalities; SoC 18.1.77

XM601: No. 9 Sqn, Coningsby

XM601: Aw/cn 31.10.63; 9 Sqn 5.11.63 becoming ConW; crashed 7.10.64 on Coningsby approach – all crew killed; SoC 8.10.64

XM602: Aw/cn 11.11.63; 12 Sqn 13.11.63 becoming ConW; CotW (Mfrs mods 29.3-9.6.65, 17-3-24.5.67); WW 24.4.68 (Mfrs mods 6.1-7.2.69, 22.5-7.10.70, 26.3-5.12.75) (9 Sqn marks 12.75); 230 OCU 19.10.76; 35 Sqn 29.10.76; WW 1.11.76 (Mfrs/Bitteswell 3.7.80-31.3.81) (101 Sqn 5.80); St Athan as Cat 5C 7.1.82; 5,300.15 hours; transferred Historic Aircraft Museum, St Athan 16.3.83 as 8771M; broken up 10.92 and nose to Woodford 11.93 for Avro Aircraft Restoration Society

XM603: Aw/cn 29.11.63; 9 Sqn 4.12.63 becoming ConW; CotW 11.64 (Mfrs mods 12.7-4.10.65); WW 18.1.68 (Mfrs mods 30.11.70-16.3.71, 19.8.74-5.6.75, Bitteswell 20.12.79-18.9.80) (50 Sqn marks 8.75, 101 Sqn 12.80, 44 Sqn 7.81); sold BAe, Woodford, for preservation by The '603 Club and delivered 12.3.82; 5,733.20 hours; current 1996 in original (white) condition, fully restored

XM604: Aw/cn 29.11.63; 35 Sqn 4.12.63 becoming ConW; CotW 11.64 (Mfrs/Bitteswell 9.8-9.11.65, 22.5-27.7.67); crashed Cow Close Farm, near Cottesmore, after loss of control overshooting 30.1.68; three rear crew killed; SoC 31.1.68

XM605: Aw/cn 17.12.63; 9 Sqn 30.12.63 becoming ConW; CotW 11.64 (Mfrs mods 6.9-14.12.65, 28.7-29.9.67); WW 16.2.68 (Mfrs mods 20.1-24.2.69, 2.7-1.12.71, 23.12.75-30.9.76) (101 Sqn marks 8.73, 50 Sqn 5.79); Castle AFB (USA) 1-2.9.81; 5,392.35 hours; presented USAF 8.9.81; current 1996

XM606: Aw/cn 18.12.63; 12 Sqn 30.12.63 becoming ConW; Mfrs mods 30.10.64; CotW 18.2.65; MoA 14.6.65 (Mfrs mods 2.5.67; CotW 5.4.68; WW 13.5.68 (Mfrs mods 3.2-6.3.69, 13.4-25.8.72, Bitteswell 6.10.77-27.7.78) (101 Sqn marks 12.75, 9 Sqn 6.79); Barksdale AFB (USA) 7.6.82; 4,879.15 hours; presented to USAF 14.6.83; current 1996

XM607: Waddington Wing, Black Buck aircraft

XM607: Aw/cn 30.12.63; 35 Sqn 1.1.64 becoming ConW; CotW (Mfrs mods 12.64-26.3.65); WW 24.5.68 (Mfrs mods 20.11-30.12.68, 21.12.70-23.4.71, 14.6.74-25.3.75, Bitteswell 25.3-18.12.80) (44 Sqn marks 4.76, 9 Sqn 5.79, 101 Sqn 3.81, 44 Sqn 7.81); Ascension Island 1982; bombed Port Stanley airport 1.5, 4.5 and 12.6.82; 44 Sqn 14.6.82; withdrawn from use 17.12.82 with 5,514.40 hours; allocated 8779M 4.1.83; assigned to static display at Waddington 19.1.83; current 1996

XM608: Aw/cn 28.1.64; 9 Sqn 29.1.64 becoming ConW; CotW 11.64 (Mfrs mods 18.1-8.4.65, 2.6-30.8.67); WW 23.2.68 (Mfrs mods 10.2-24.3.69, Cat 3 FA 23.2.71, Mfrs mods 8.3-13.9.73) (50 Sqn marks 4.75); St Athan as Cat 5C 6.4.81; 4,884.10 hours; sold Bird Group for scrap 2.12.82

XM609: Aw/cn 28.1.64; 12 Sqn 29.1.64 becoming ConW; Mfrs mods 30.10.64; CotW 3.3.65 (Mfrs mods 24.1-3.4.67); 230 OCU 7.8.67; CotW 1.10.67; WW 8.3.68 (Mfrs mods 30.9-4.11.68, 8.10.70-26.2.71, 28.3.74-5.2.75, 30.7.79-7.7.80) (9 Sqn marks 9.75, 44 Sqn 4.76); St Athan as Cat 5C 12.3.81; 5,594.20 hours; sold W. Harold & Co. for scrap 31.8.81

XM610: Aw/cn 10.2.64; 9 Sqn 12.2.62 becoming ConW; CotW 11.64 (Mfrs mods 15.10.65-27.1.66, Bitteswell 24.5-8.8.67); WW 5.2.68 (Mfrs mods 7.3-21.4.69); crashed Wingate, Co. Durham, 8.1.71 after engine fire; no fatalities; SoC 11.1.71

XM611: Aw/cn 12.2.64; 9 Sqn 14.2.64 becoming ConW; CotW 11.64 (Mfrs mods 29.3-18.7.66); WW 28.5.68 (Mfrs mods 20.7-11.12.72, Bitteswell 28.9.76-24.6.77) (101 Sqn marks 5.72); St Athan as Cat 5C 27.1.82; 5,660.55 hours; sold for scrap to T. Bradbury 2.6.83

XM612: Aw/cn 28.2.64; ConW 3.3.64 – initially 9 Sqn; CotW 11.64 (Mfrs mods 1.9-16.11.65, 13.4-16.6.67);

XM612: Waddington Wing, Black Buck reserve

MinTech 5.3.68 at A&AEE; WW 4.4.68 (Mfrs mods 18.4-22.5.69, 8.3-19.7.72, Bitteswell 24.1-10.10.77, Bitteswell 15.8.80-7.5.81) (101 Sqn marks 5.75, 44 Sqn 7.81); Ascension Island 1982 – reserve; 44 Sqn 23.5.82; sold Norwich Aviation Museum 19.1.83; delivered 30.1.83; 5,800.10 hours; current 1996

XM645: Aw/cn 10.3.64; ConW 12.3.64 (Cat 3 FA 12.6.64); CotW 11.64 (Mfrs mods 8.12.65-17.2.66, 3.4-31.5.67); WW 15.12.67; 230 OCU 5.8.68 (Mfrs mods 1.11-9.12.68); WW 21.4.71 (Cat 3 FA 15.9.72, Mfrs mods 20.8.73-28.2.74) (101 Sqn marks 8.73); AW 12.3.74; WW 15.1.75 (9 Sqn marks 2.75); exploded over Zabbar, Malta, 14.10.75 following structural damage in heavy roller landing; all crew killed; SoC 15.10.75

XM646: Aw/cn 7.4.64; ConW 8.4.64 – initially 12 Sqn; CotW 11.64 (Mfrs mods 1.2-14.4.65, 1.3-15.7.66, 11.10-29.12.67, 26.3-13.5.68); AW 5.2.69 (Cat 3R FA 2.9.69) (Mfrs mods 31.8.73-22.3.74); WW 17.1.75 (9 Sqn marks 1.79, 101 Sqn 6.81); St Athan as Cat 5C 26.1.82; 4,651.00 hours; sold for scrap to T. Bradbury 29.6.83

XM647: Akrotiri Wing

XM647: Aw/cn 15.4.64; ConW 15.4.64 – initially 35 Sqn; CotW 11.64 (Mfrs mods 5.10.65-6.1.66, 17.5-1.9.66, 21.9-27.11.67, 27.6-5.8.68); AW 26.2.69 (Cat 3R FA 3.2.70) (Mfrs mods 31.8.72-23.1.73); WW 15.1.75 (Mfrs/Bitteswell 21.7.78-31.5.79) (9 Sqn marks 1.75, 44 Sqn 9.79, 50 Sqn 9.81); Laarbruch 17.9.82 for ground instruction; 5,244.30 hours; allocated 8765M; sold Solair UK, Wallsend 25.2.85; scrapped 1.3.85

XM648: Aw/cn 5.5.64; ConW 6.5.64 – initially 9 Sqn; CotW 11.64 (Mfrs mods 16.12.65-16.3.66, 6.7-21.9.77); WW 25.1.68 (Mfrs mods 29.4-3.6.69, 26.2-2.7.71, Bitteswell 22.3.76-11.1.77) (101 Sqn marks 5.72, 44 Sqn 5.75, 101 Sqn 3.77, 9 Sqn 9.80, 101 Sqn 10.81); declared Cat 5C 10.9.82; 5,384.25 hours; sold Bird Group for scrap 8.12.82

XM649: Aw/cn 12.5.64; ConW 14.5.64 – initially 9 Sqn; CotW 11.64 (Mfrs mods 9.4-27.6.65, Bitteswell 11.5-18.8.66, Mfrs mods 30.8-31.10.67); WW 18.1.68 (Mfrs mods 28.5-30.6.69, 24.1-27.7.73) (loan MinTech 2.12.69-21.1.70) (101 Sqn marks 8.73, 9 Sqn 4.76, 101 Sqn 8.79); St Athan as Cat 5C 2.9.81; 5,384.25 hours; sold Bird Group for scrap 2.12.82

XM650: Waddington Wing, seen at Abbotsford, 1969

XM650: Aw/cn 27.5.64; ConW 5.6.64 – initially 12 Sqn; CotW 11.64; (Mfrs retrofit 5.3-14.5.65, and mods 13.4-21.7.66, 2.10-19.12.67); WW 20.12.67 (Mfrs mods 27.4-2.9.71, 27.1-16.11.76) (44 Sqn marks 5.75, 50 Sqn 1.77); St Athan as Cat 5C 28.1.82; 5,837.55 hours; allocated 8748M at St Athan 16.3.83; sold for scrap to Bournewood Aviation 22.3.84

XM651: Aw/cn 19.6.64; ConW 22.6.64 – initially 12 Sqn; CotW 11.64 (Mfrs mods 10.6-23.8.65, 25.7-28.12.66); WW 24.4.68 (Mfrs mods 9.9.71-24.1.72, 7.8.75-21.5.76) (101 Sqn marks 5.72, 50 Sqn 9.75, 101 Sqn 9.79); declared Cat 5C 10.9.82; 5,602.50 hours; sold to Bird Group as scrap 30.11.82

XM652: Aw/cn 12.8.64; ConW 17.8.64 – initially 9 Sqn; CotW 11.64 (Mfrs mods 21.4-9.7.65, 15.6-12.9.67); WW 24.12.67 (Mfrs mods 21.6-14.12.73, Bitteswell 3.12.77-5.9.78 and 6.12.78-28.2.79) (44 Sqn 9.75, 9 Sqn 10.81) (first in overall camouflage 9.79); 50 Sqn 10.82; sold to Boulding Industrial Supplies 20.2.84 and dismantled 3.84; nose to Sheffield 7.5.84, then Burntwood, Staffs, 1985; remainder disposed as scrap 2.85

XM653: Aw/cn 31.8.84; ConW 4.9.84 — initially 9 Sqn; CotW 11.64 (Mfrs mods 3.5-16.7.65, 17.2-14.4.67); WW 24.1.68 (Mfrs mods 16.6-22.8.69, 31.5-20.10.72, Bitteswell 21.6.77-27.1.78) (101 Sqn marks 5.72, 44 Sqn 5.75, 9 Sqn 9.75, 101 Sqn 10.78, 9 Sqn 5.79, 101 Sqn 7.79); unserviceable as Cat 3 9.8.79; St Athan 10.9.79; reassessed as Cat 5C 19.9.80; 4,391.30 hours; dumped 18.12.80; sold for scrap 28.7.81

XM654: Aw/cn 22.10.64; ConW 26.10.64 – initially 12

Sqn; CotW 11.64 (Mfrs mods 21.7-18.10.65, Cat 3 FA 29.10.65, Cat 3 FA 15.11.67); WW 30.4.68 (Cat 3 FA 1.9.72) (Mfrs mods 17.12.73-4.6.74, Bitteswell 5.2-6.11.79) (101 Sqn marks 8.73, 50 Sqn 9.75, 101 Sqn 9.81, 50 Sqn 10.81); declared Cat 5C 29.10.82; 5,127.30 hours; sold Bird Group for scrap

XM655: Aw/cn 19.11.64; CotW 23.11.64 – initially 9 Sqn (Mfrs mods 24.11.65-9.2.66, 8.9.66-27.2.67); WW 12.1.68 (Mfrs/Bitteswell 29.6.73-18.1.74 and 23.6.78-26.3.79) (101 Sqn marks 5.72, 44 Sqn 5.75, 50 Sqn 8.82); 50 Sqn 3.83; sold Roy E. Jacobsen 11.2.84; delivered Wellesbourne Mountford 11.2.84; registered G-VULC 27.2.84; cancelled 3.9.85; re-registered N655AV 1985 but not taken up; to Delta Engineering Association 7.92; restored to taxiing condition

XM656: Aw/cn 11.12.84; CotW 15.12.64 – initially 35 Sqn (Mfrs mods 18.5-6.8.65, Bitteswell 5.5-29.7.66, Mfrs 12.9-17.11.67); WW 2.2.68 (Mfrs mods 24.3-8.5.69, 3.9.70-15.1.71, 21.10.74-2.7.75, Bitteswell 1.2-13.10.80) (101 Sqn marks 9.75, 9 Sqn 12.80); Cottesmore for display 9.8.82; 5,423.15 hours; allocated 8757M; sold Bird Group for scrap 30.3.83

XM657: Aw/cn 14.1.65; CotW 15.1.65 – initially 35 Sqn (Mfrs mods 22.9-29.12.65, 27.4-5.7.67); WW 19.3.68 (Mfrs mods 19.7-20.8.68, 30.9.71-4.2.72, 21.4.76-24.1.77) (101 Sqn marks 5.72, 50 Sqn 8.75, 9 Sqn, 101 Sqn 3.77, 44 Sqn 4.80); allocated Central Training Establishment 5.1.82 and delivered to Manston 12.1.82 for crash rescue training; 5,100.50 hours; allocated 8734M; scrapped late 1990

NOTES

1: Aircraft Nos 26-33 (XL317-321, 359-361) and Nos 42-59 (XL392, 425-427, 443-446, XM569-576 and 594-595) became B.Mk 2A variants on completion of modifications required to carry Blue Steel. They reverted to Mk 2 standard in 1969-70.

2: Aircraft Nos 1-10, 12-33 and 42-53 (XH533-539, 554-556, 558-563, XJ780-784, 823-825, XL317-321, 359-361, 392, 425-427, 443-446, XM569-572) were powered by Olympus Series 200 engines, all other aircraft having Series 300s.

3: Dates quoted above are those of official allocation and may differ slightly from those of physical movement.

4: Dates and locations in parentheses – normally recording servicing or modifications – refer to aircraft returned to the unit last mentioned. Details in parentheses of Waddington Wing squadrons refer to badges applied to fins and the date on which they were first noted. Such unit data does not appear on official records.

5: Details of aircraft visits to RAF St Athan for servicing are not given unless the aircraft returned to a different squadron. Similarly, no details are included of regular servicing and repair undertaken on the aircraft's home base by an MU or the manufacturer, except for mention of occurrences in flight requiring rectification. Visits of aircraft to St Athan were too numerous to mention, the 500th such overhaul to a Vulcan being undertaken on Mk 2 XM573 in September 1978.

XM657 was the final Vulcan built, seen here in No. 44 Sqn marks landing at Waddington. Production accounted for two prototypes, 45 B.Mk 1s and 89 B.Mk 2s.

Vulcan operators

With its headquarters at High Wycombe, RAF Bomber Command consisted of two groups which operated the V-bombers, Thor missiles, home-based Canberra squadrons and related training establishments. While No. 3 Group (HQ: Mildenhall) was primarily composed of Victor, Valiant and Thor squadrons, the main equipment of No. 1 Group (HQ: Bawtry) was the Vulcan force. In addition, the group controlled the northern Thor squadrons, Canberra and Vulcan OCUs, a Valiant squadron (No. 18) and the Bomber Command Bombing School at Lindholme. On 30 April 1968 Fighter and Bomber Commands amalgamated to form Strike Command, although control of the Vulcan force by No. 1 Group was unaffected.

A total of five squadrons (and the operational conversion unit) was equipped with the Vulcan B.Mk 1. A further four were established to operate the B.Mk 2, to which the original five also converted. Vulcans served at six bases, although not simultaneously:

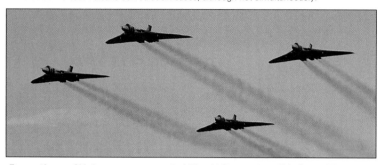

Formations of Vulcans were rare, but No. 44 Sqn put up this four-ship on 17 December 1982, four days prior to the disbandment of the squadron, an event which marked the passing of the Vulcan from the bomber role. The formation toured previous Vulcan bases, and included both Black Buck aircraft.

Akrotiri	9 Sqn	January 1969 – January 1975
	35 Sqn	January 1969 – January 1975
Coningsby	9 Sqn	March 1962 – November 1964
	12 Sqn	July 1962 – November 1964
	35 Sqn	December 1962 – November 1964
	adopted aircraft pooling March 1964	
Cottesmore	9 Sqn	November 1964 – January 1969
	12 Sqn	November 1964 – December 1967
	35 Sqn	November 1964 – January 1969
	aircraft pooled throughout	
Finningley	101 Sqn	October 1957 – June 1961
	230 OCU	June 1961 – December 1969
Scampton	27 Sqn	April 1961 – March 1972 and November 1973 – March 198?
	35 Sqn	January 1975 – February 1982
	83 Sqn	October 1960 – August 1969
	617 Sqn	May 1958 – December 1981
	230 OCU	December 1969 – August 1981
	adopted aircraft pooling April 1964. Squadron allocations resumed from January 1971. Individual markings re-applied from May 1972. 230 OCU remained separate from Scampton Wing for purposes of aircraft assignment.	
Waddington	9 Sqn	January 1975 – April 1982
	44 Sqn	August 1960 – December 1982
	50 Sqn	August 1961 – March 1984
	83 Sqn	May 1957 – August 1960
	101 Sqn	June 1961 – August 1982
	230 OCU	May 1956 – June 1961
	adopted aircraft pooling pre-B.Mk 2. Individual markings re-applied from May 1972, but aircraft remained in station pool, with a few exceptions.	

No. 9 Squadron

A mainstay of the RAF bomber force since 1916, when the young unit switched from army liaison work, No. 9 Squadron operated the Avro Lincoln and English Electric Canberra in the post-war years, having adopted the jet bomber in 1952. The squadron flew bombing raids during the Suez crisis. Canberras were flown from Binbrook until 2 June 1959, and Coningsby thereafter. The squadron disbanded there on 13 July 1961 in preparation for revival with the Vulcan.

This occurred officially on 12 March 1962, No. 9 being the first of the three Vulcan units activated to fly the B.Mk 2 and form the Coningsby Wing. The entire wing moved to Cottesmore on 7 November 1964. Initially, No. 9 Sqn had a high-level tasking with Yellow Sun Mk 2, although the squadron was earmarked for Skybolt carriage. After the switch to low-level operations, the WE177B became the primary weapon, the Cottesmore Wing being the first to receive the lay-down parachute-retarded weapon.

With the removal of the strategic deterrent tasking, No. 9 was dispatched to Akrotiri to replace Canberras of the Near East Air Force Bomber Wing. The unit returned to the UK, being assigned to the Waddington Wing until disbandment on 29 April 1982. In recognition of the unit's long and proud tradition, it was chosen to be the first Tornado GR.Mk 1 squadron, receiving the aircraft during June at Honington. No. 9 Squadron now serves with Tornados within RAF No. 2 Group (in Germany) at Brüggen, specialising in Alarm anti-radar missions.

Right: Coningsby Wing aircraft wore squadron markings only briefly. No. 9's wore an outsize bat emblem on the fin.

Below: When squadron badges returned to the Waddington Wing, No. 9 adopted a much smaller bat, usually worn on a yellow circle. In fact, all of the base's aircraft were held in a pool, with badges applied equally throughout the fleet.

No. 12 Squadron

No.12's pre-war claim to fame was as the sole operator of the outstanding Fairey Fox, in its time the fastest aircraft in the RAF, and inspiration for the unit's badge and nickname. Wartime saw 'Shiny Twelve' flying Battles over France in 1940 (Flight Lieutenant Garland and Sergeant Gray being awarded the Victoria Cross for their efforts), Wellingtons and Lancasters. Post-war, No. 12 joined No. 9 in flying the Lincoln and Canberra from Binbrook and Coningsby before disbanding at the latter base on 13 July 1961.

Just under a year later, No. 12 was reactivated as the second of the Coningsby wing squadrons, flying the B.Mk 2. It subsequently moved to Cottesmore on 7 November 1964, continuing in the free-fall bombing role with Yellow Sun and later WE177B, the intended Skybolt having been cancelled. A review of British nuclear deterrent forces, together with the impending entry into service of the Polaris submarine deterrent, created a surfeit of capacity, and No. 12 was the first casualty

of the slow run-down of the Vulcan force. It disbanded on 31 December 1967.

Less than two years later the unit was back in business, flying the Blackburn Buccaneer from Honington (from October 1969). The squadron moved to Lossiemouth to undertake the anti-shipping role, switching to the Tornado GR.Mk 1B in 1994.

'Shiny Twelve's' fox insignia appeared only briefly on the Vulcan, being worn from mid-1962 to early 1964 during the Coningsby era.

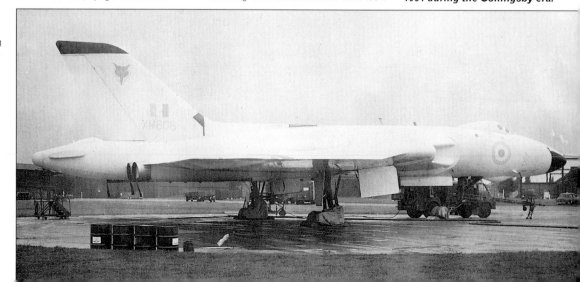

Vulcan Operators

No. 27 Squadron

In late 1915 No. 27 Sqn was formed to operate the new Martinsyde G.100 scout, his aircraft being nicknamed the 'Elephant' (hence the squadron's official badge). From 1920 to 1946 the unit was in India and the Far East, reforming briefly as a transport squadron before adopting the bombing role with the Canberra B.Mk 2 from 1953 until disbandment on 31 December 1956.

Having lain dormant for some while, the unit was chosen as the first of the four new squadrons to operate the Vulcan B.Mk 2, with which it was officially reformed on 1 April 1961. With these it joined the

Scampton Wing, flying free-fall sorties initially before receiving Blue Steel. From 1969 it reverted briefly to free-fall missions until disbandment on 29 March 1972.

It was not out of business for long, for it reformed at Scampton on 1 November 1973 to operate primarily in the MRR (maritime radar reconnaissance) role, equipped with Vulcan B.Mk 2MRRs and supplanting the

Wyton-based Victor SR.Mk 2s of No. 543 Sqn. It served in this important tasking until disbandment on 31 March 1982.

No. 27 Sqn subsequently reformed as the second of Marham's Tornado GR.Mk 1 squadrons. In the early 1990s the Tornados

In its first Vulcan phase, No. 27 was in the bombing and Blue Steel business at Scampton. The simple Indian elephant badge appeared in varying sizes during this period.

moved to Lossiemouth to adopt the numberplate of No. 12 Sqn, while the No. 27 Sqn identity, with its famous elephant, was transferred to the Chinook/Puma OCU at Odiham, from where it now operates as No. 27 (Reserve) Squadron.

Above and right: From late 1973 No. 27 performed maritime reconnaissance missions, occasionally carrying sampling pods (illustrated). The aircraft above is seen on the unit's last flying day, 23 March 1982.

No. 35 Squadron

No. 35 Sqn, one of the 'Madras Presidency' units, was well-known as the first operational user of the Handley Page Halifax, and it fought for much of World War with these aircraft. Lancasters arrived in 1944, and the squadron was part of the Tiger Force. Lincolns, Washingtons and Canberras followed, the squadron disbanding at Upwood on 11 September 1961.

After a year's dormancy, No. 35 Squadron was reformed as the third of the Coningsby Wing Vulcan units on 1 December 1962, its winged horse's head insignia gracing the B.Mk 2 from the following January. It was the last of the nine RAF squadrons to be formed on the Vulcan.

Like its sister squadrons, No. 35 moved to Cottesmore on 7 November 1964, and flew free-fall missions, being among the first to be allocated WE177B. When Polaris submarines adopted the UK national deterrent mantle in 1969, the Cottesmore wing was freed from its UK taskings and was reassigned to NEAF/CENTO, moving to Akrotiri alongside No. 9 Sqn in January 1969. Operations from here continued until withdrawal back to the UK in January 1975. The two Akrotiri Vulcan squadrons split up, No. 35 going to Scampton to operate in the primary free-fall role with a secondary MRR tasking. It was disbanded there on 26 February 1982, now permanently consigned to the history books.

Above: The last of the Vulcan squadrons to form, No. 35 flew from four different bases. The aircraft above is seen at the unit's first home: Coningsby. Subsequent moves took the unit to Cottesmore, Akrotiri and finally Scampton.

Right: On return to Scampton in 1975, No. 35 adopted this stylised numeral badge, rather than its traditional winged horse's head (which signified its co-operation with the cavalry in World War I).

No. 44 Squadron

Like No. 27 Sqn, No. 44 has the elephant as its badge, but in this case it is the large-eared African variety, No. 44 being (from September 1941) a 'Rhodesia' squadron. In 1942 it became the first user of the Avro Lancaster, later re-equipping with the Lincoln, Washington and Canberra. It disbanded at Honington on 16 July 1957.

On 10 August 1960 No. 44 Sqn was reincarnated as a Vulcan B.Mk 1 operator, this being achieved by the renumbering of

No. 83 Sqn (which in turn resurfaced at Scampton). The first modified B.Mk 1A was received on 14 July 1961, and the unit continued with these aircraft (and Yellow Sun Mk 2 weapons) until 1967, when B.Mk 2s arrived. Waddington squadrons were the first to transition to low-level operations in 1964, although their weapons still required a 12,000-ft (3660-m) 'pop-up' to be delivered safely. No. 44 Squadron disbanded for the last time at Waddington on 21 December 1982.

Above: Wearing No. 44's numeral badge, XM603 receives maintenance at Waddington in late 1981. The unit was the last to operate the Vulcan in the pure bomber role, although the type continued as a tanker for some time with No. 50 Sqn.

Left: In the wrap-round camouflage adopted for Red Flag exercises, XM575 also sports the Lincoln crest and No. 44's numerals device. Along with Nos 50 and 101 Sqns, No. 44 provided crews for Black Buck.

Vulcan Operators

No. 50 Squadron

After service as a Home Defence unit in World War I, No. 50 Sqn lay dormant until 1937, when it reformed as a bomber squadron with Hinds. Whitleys followed, and subsequently Manchesters and Lancasters. Lincolns and Canberras were flown in the post-war period before the squadron disbanded on 1 October 1959.

It was reformed on 1 August 1961 to complete the three-squadron Waddington Wing, equipped from the outset with Vulcan B.Mk 1As (with a few unmodified B.Mk 1s also) inherited from No. 617 Sqn at nearby Scampton. As with other Waddington units, it was swift to adopt low-level tactics in 1964, and was the first of the Waddington squadrons to receive the B.Mk 2, which first arrived in December 1965. These aircraft served in the free-fall role until 1982, when the panic requirements of the Falklands War saw the unit's aircraft hastily converted to K.Mk 2 standard. It flew successfully on tanker missions until final disbandment on 31 March 1984.

No. 50 Sqn flew from Waddington throughout its Vulcan career, at first in the bomber role (right) and then as a tanker unit (below). In the latter guise it was the last Vulcan unit.

No. 83 Squadron

No. 83 began its active career as a night-bomber outfit in France in 1918, although it fell victim to the dramatic cutbacks of the 1920s and early 1930s. Reborn during the Expansion period, it reformed as a Hind squadron, subsequently flying Hampdens, Manchesters, Lancasters and Lincolns (which it used in anger over Malaya) before disbandment on 1 January 1956.

When officially reformed at Waddington on 21 May 1957, the squadron leapt to prominence as the first operator of the Vulcan B.Mk 1, having been formed from the first course to graduate from 230 OCU. The first aircraft arrived on 11 July. The unit was heavily involved in evaluating operational procedures for the Vulcan, and in proving the aircraft's worth in bombing competitions and long-range deployments. It rapidly worked up to full operational capability to take its place in the airborne deterrent line-up, equipped initially with Blue Danube weapons, followed later by Violet Club.

In 1960 the squadron prepared to become the first operator of the B.Mk 2 variant. This was achieved by leaving behind the B.Mk 1s at Waddington for use by the

newly activated No. 44 Sqn (which stood up on 10 August 1960), and moving the squadron to Scampton. No. 83 then stood up as a B.Mk 2 operator on 10 October. After initial operations with free-fall weapons, No. 83 was subsequently

assigned Blue Steel missiles, and these were the allocated weapons until formal disbandment on 31 August 1969, the squadron being the major victim of the shift of nuclear deterrent to the Royal Navy's Polaris submarine fleet.

No. 83 Sqn was the first Vulcan squadron, and went on to be the first to receive B.Mk 2s. The red deer's antler badge (signifying ties with Scotland) was rarely seen.

No. 101 Squadron

A famous night-bomber squadron in World War I, No. 101 Sqn was also the only RAF squadron to operate the Boulton-Paul Sidestrand and Overstrand bombers. The latter was the world's first aircraft with an enclosed power turret, and was the

No. 101 settled at Waddington until disbandment soon after the Falklands campaign. Seen in 1975, this aircraft wears a variation in tail markings consisting of the squadron badge inside the number.

inspiration of the unit's lion and turret badge. In World War II No. 101 flew Blenheims, Wellingtons and Lancasters, the latter including 'Airborne Cigar' EW aircraft. Lincolns were received post-war, before 101 became the first Canberra unit. With B.Mk 6s, it was the first to use the Canberra in action, during the Malayan campaign, and subsequently flew bombing missions over Suez. It disbanded on 1 February 1957 to prepare for the forthcoming Vulcan.

These came in the form of B.Mk 1s, the first aircraft arriving at Finningley on 1 October and the squadron officially reforming on the type on 15 October 1957 to become the second Vulcan user.

Above: No. 101 Sqn followed No. 83 as a Vulcan operator, and became the only front-line unit to be based at Finningley. Aircraft such as this B.Mk 1 wore the full squadron crest on the fin.

Squadron aircraft accompanied the Secretary of State for Air during a major South American tour in May 1960. On 19 March 1961 the first modified B.Mk 1A was taken on charge, shortly before the squadron moved to Waddington. From here the aircraft operated as a Yellow Sun Mk 2 free-fall squadron, slowly adopting the B.Mk 2 from 1967 to become the last operator to adopt the later variant.

No. 101 Sqn became the penultimate Vulcan operator, having contributed crews to the Ascension detachment during the Falklands campaign. Official disbandment occurred on 4 August 1982.

On 1 May 1984 No. 101 Sqn reformed as a tanker unit at Brize Norton to operate the VC10 K.Mk 2. It now operates K.Mk 3 and K.Mk 4 aircraft.

No. 617 Squadron

Immortalised on film, No. 617 Sqn – the 'Dambusters' – is undoubtedly the best-known RAF squadron. Formed specifically on 21 March 1943 to deliver the 'bouncing bomb' against the Ruhr dams in Operation Chastise, No. 617 subsequently conducted pioneering work on the Tallboy and Grand Slam weapons. After the war it flew Lincolns and Canberras, the latter in action over Malaya, before disbanding on 15 December 1955.

On 1 May 1958 the 'Dambusters' were officially reformed as a Vulcan operator at

Although the deterrent role was lost in 1969, when this aircraft was seen, No. 617 continued on Blue Steel missions well into 1970.

Scampton. They were the first unit at this base, and the third squadron to get the Vulcan. From 30 September 1960 the squadron began receiving B.Mk 1As. The mixed complement of B.Mk 1/1As was sent to Waddington on 1 August 1961 to equip No. 50 Sqn, while No. 617 remained at Scampton to operate newly-arrived B.Mk 2s from September onwards. They were operated throughout the 1960s on Blue Steel operations, which continued for a year

or so beyond the date when the Royal Navy assumed deterrent responsibilities. During the 1970s the Vulcans operated on free-fall bombing missions (with WE177B as the prime weapon), although the squadron also had a secondary MRR tasking to augment the dedicated reconnaissance aircraft of No. 27 Sqn. No. 617 Sqn was disbanded at Scampton on 31 December 1981.

With Victors in the background, Blue Steel-carrying B.Mk 2s display No. 617's early flamboyant lightning flash markings.

No. 617's lightning flash now adorns the Panavia Tornado, the unit having been the second unit to form on the GR.Mk 1, at Marham on 16 May 1983. The squadron has since moved to Lossiemouth (to replace No. 208 Sqn), flying GR.Mk 1Bs in the maritime strike role.

In its final Vulcan years, No. 617 Sqn adopted a diamond-shaped representation of the official squadron crest.

No. 230 Operational Conversion Unit

230 OCU was formed in March 1947 by the renumbering of 1653 Heavy Conversion Unit at Lindholme. In February 1949, it moved to Scampton and continued to fly Lancasters and Lincolns until disbanded on 1 May 1953, the requirement for Lincoln aircrew having dried up.

230 OCU was reformed at Waddington

on 31 May 1956 to prepare for service entry of the Vulcan B.Mk 1. A symbolic hand-over of the first aircraft was undertaken on 20 July 1956, although this aircraft then went straight back to Avro. It was not until 2 September that an aircraft was officially assigned to the OCU, and even then it was the aircraft used for the fateful New Zealand

flight. The first real OCU aircraft did not arrive at Waddington until 18 January 1957. The OCU swiftly set about training the first course of crews with which 'A' Flight of No. 83 Sqn was formed on 21 May 1957.

On 1 July 1960 'B' Flight was formed to begin training operations with the B.Mk 2, shortly before the OCU moved to Finningley on 18 June 1961. B.Mk 1s served alongside the newer variant until November 1965. No OCU aircraft were updated to B.Mk 1A

standard. A further move was made in December 1969, this time to Scampton. The OCU remained here until the force rundown removed the requirement for new Vulcan crews: it disbanded on 31 August 1981.

After a spell at Finningley, the OCU moved into Scampton, although it remained outside of the Scampton Wing assignment pool.

In the early days, 230 OCU aircraft made many overseas trips. This aircraft was the first to visit Canada, seen at RCAF Uplands.

Miscellaneous units

In addition to work by the A&AEE and RAE, evaluation of some Vulcan systems was undertaken by the Bomber Command Development Unit. This unit had its roots in the Bomber Development Unit established at Boscombe Down in 1940, and was revived at Wittering in 1956 to evaluate aircraft systems for the new V-force jets and Canberras. Its early work was largely

connected with the Valiant, but as the accent shifted to the Vulcan, so the BCDU moved to Finningley in February 1960. Aircraft were occasionally borrowed as required from the OCU or front-line units, although one B.Mk 1A (XA895) was permanently assigned (joined briefly by XA907). The BCDU disbanded on 31 December 1968.

Finningley was also home to other support units, such as the Bomber

Command Vulcan Servicing School. No. 1 Group Communications Flight (with, initially, Meteors, Canberras, Ansons and Chipmunks) was present, while from 1 November 1965 Finningley also parented the US Vulcan servicing organisations.

V-force navigators/bombardiers trained at the Bomber Command Bombing School, based at Lindholme. This unit was equipped with Valettas and Lincolns, the latter used for H2S radar training. These were replaced

by 10 Hastings T.Mk 5s with H2S Mk 9 radars in a large ventral radome. When Lindholme closed, the unit (now known as Strike Command Bombing School) moved to Scampton on 1 September 1972. The school was disbanded on 1 January 1974, but the surviving aircraft carried on with the Hastings Radar Flight until July 1977, parented by 230 OCU. The unit was known unofficially as '1066 Sqn', a reference to the famous 11th Century Battle of Hastings.

BCDU stalwart B.Mk 1A XA895 is seen at St Athan, prior to scrapping. The words 'Bomber Command Development Unit' can just be seen above the fin-flash.

The Hastings T.Mk 5 was used to train Vulcan 'coal-hole' crews, the aircraft having H2S radar in a ventral radome. This '1066 Sqn' example wears the parent 230 OCU badge on the fin.

Fighter Combat over Korea

PART 3

A YEAR OF MIGS

The year of 1951 was the pivotal time frame that set the pace for the remainder of the Korean War. The front lines had stabilised, the Chinese air force (Soviet-operated) had made a major attempt to gain control of the skies over North Korea, and the Peace Talks had begun at Panmunjon. As 1951 faded, it would have been hard to imagine that this dirty regional war had only reached its halfway mark. What was to happen during those final 18 months would be a world-class game of 'cat and mouse', sponsored by the Chinese military.

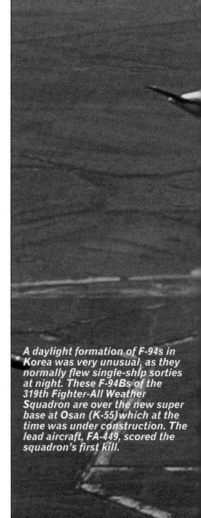

A daylight formation of F-94s in Korea was very unusual, as they normally flew single-ship sorties at night. These F-94Bs of the 319th Fighter-All Weather Squadron are over the new super base at Osan (K-55) which at the time was under construction. The lead aircraft, FA-449, scored the squadron's first kill.

The fact that the war could not be won by the Chinese was probably realised by their leadership in the spring of 1951. They had absolutely no chance of gaining air superiority over the United Nations. To withdraw and admit defeat was never a subject for discussion. Therefore, the Communist forces had to buy some time and try to initiate a successful build-up of supplies and forces to gradually inch the front lines as far south of the original line at the 38th Parallel as possible. This would be a bargaining chip for the Communists at the truce talks. There was only one drawback to this ... the most destructive and effective weapon that had been brought to bear on the People's Army was that of the fighter-bombers. These aircraft had destroyed a significant percentage of the supplies and troops that were being shuttled in from the staging areas just north of the Yalu River.

In figures that were compiled on 30 June 1952, it was shown that the FEAF had flown 87,552 interdiction missions which accounted for over 34,000 vehicles being destroyed. However, the Chinese were getting sufficient supplies through and they had shown no interest in getting serious at the peace talks. Radio Peking had been airing the news that despite the massive UN effort of 2,000 military aircraft, they had not been able to cut off the supply line. One fact alone will attest to this: in July 1951, the People's Army ground forces had fired an approximate total of only 8,000 artillery and mortar rounds at UN positions. One year later, in July 1952, they fired about 102,000 rounds.

It was obvious that they had the supplies to mount a serious offensive, but this was not evidence that air power had failed to do its

Below: **Atomic Tom** *of the 19th Bomb Group was one of the first B-29s to fly combat over Korea and one of the few to actually bomb targets in Seoul after its overrun.*

Below: 307th **BG** *aircraft fly in close formation en route to targets in North Korea. The group's aircrews had a great deal of experience from World War II.*

job. In mid-1951, the Chinese were in terrible shape and things looked bad for their chance of military survival in Korea. By bringing their enemy to the bargaining table, they had brought about a few short ceasefires. This gave them the time to bring in large quantities of supplies, and put them in a much stronger position in 1952.

In the past few years, it has been revealed that once the Soviets realised they could not take control of the airspace over North Korea, they used the war as a training ground for their own fighter squadrons, those of the Warsaw Pact countries and, to a limited extent, the Chinese and North Koreans. The latter were much more prevalent in 1953. So, the air battles raged and the quantity of MiG-15s

As in World War II, smaller aircraft-carriers were pressed into service to ferry Air Force aircraft to the war zone. USS Cape Esperance weathers rough seas on its way to Japan with a load of new F-86Es for the 51st Fighter Wing in late 1951.

that were available did not diminish. The one factor that widened the 'kill' ratio for the US Air Force was the fact they now had two fully complemented fighter wings with which to engage the enemy. There were a total of 205 kills confirmed in 1951. The total for 1952 almost doubled to 395 kills. This training ground for the Soviet Union might have moved their experience level much higher, but the experience gained by American pilots can never be overstated.

Early 1952
MiG TRAP

The MiGs were always interested in the slower fighter-bomber types and, of course, their favourite was the lumbering B-29. From time to time, the Soviet-built fighters would venture down below Pyongyang in hopes of catching some fuel-low friendlies making their way back to the south. However, this was not a tactic used as frequently as it had been in 1951. Major William K. Thomas,

an F-86 pilot in the 335th Squadron, relates a mission in which he was flying wing for Captain Cliff Jolley (a future ace who would achieve seven kills).

"This was a mission in which I did not get a kill, but became a member of the Six O'Clock Club. We were sitting alert at the end of the runway at Kimpo. Our helmets and chutes were in the 86s and the power units were hooked up to each aircraft. At about 15.00 hours local time, we were scrambled and were airborne in just over a minute. After checking in with radar, we were told

that they had a bandit flight at about 25,000 ft near Pyongyang. Since the MiGs seldom came that far south, I suspected a trap and climbed left to be in the sun. Slightly south of Pyongyang, Jolley called out four bandits high at our 5 o'clock position. Looking around and identifying the four MiGs, I spotted four more that were above the first flight. I called out the second group and we closed on them.

"At this point, I knew the top group was coming down so I called out to drop tanks as we started a slow climbing turn into them. The MiGs came ripping through our flight with all guns firing. We immediately turned back to the north to pick up the low flight. Again, we closed on them as the flight that had just come through

Three of the 335th Fighter Squadron's sharpshooters signal their confirmed kills. Left to right, they are Lt Al Smiley, Capt. Jim Horowitz and Lt James Low, who was to become the 17th jet ace with nine kills.

our formation climbed back up for position. Just as I was getting into firing range, Jolley calls out for me to break left and, as I did, the MiG that was behind me tried to follow me through the turn and he snapped into a spin. Jolley went right down behind him with his guns firing. Another MiG came out of nowhere and got on my tail. The only thing I could do was take him downstairs, where it didn't take long to lose him. All of this happened in just a couple of minutes and, when the dust settled, Jolley had one confirmed kill and a probable. Most of the time, I had MiGs on my tail while I was dodging their fire. After recovering at Kimpo, I tried to analyse what had just happened and I believe that the MiGs we fought were all flown by experienced pilots and not some low timers being used to bait the trap." A few weeks after this mission, Major Thomas was credited with a confirmed MiG-15 kill.

Spring 1952 ▰
INVADERS AGAINST THE TRUCKS

During the spring of 1952, the night-flying B-26s were having more of their share of problems. It could not have come at a worse time, with the pressure on to stop the flow of supplies and replacements getting down to the MLR (Main Line of Resistance). The only way to accurately determine how effective they were was by the number of vehicles reported destroyed each night. The totals were diminishing steadily, and part of the reason was the fact that each squadron from both the 3rd and 452nd Bomb Wings were operating with less than their full complement of aircraft. Some of the replacement aircraft they were receiving from the US had the old 'flap top' canopies, which were totally unsatisfactory. With the aircrews wearing the heavy winter flight suits, it would have been impossible to exit the aircraft if they had to bail out.

This was a minor problem compared to the attrition rate caused by the Communist forces

A B-26 from the 729th BS makes a rare daylight bomb drop. Most Invader missions were at night and at low level, where the North Korean AAA was less accurate.

being able to put up increasingly accurate ground fire around its truck convoys and trains. The Director of Operations for 5th Air Force stated, "we are trading B-26s for trucks in a most uneconomical

manner." As a result of this trend, the USAF authorised that the 3rd Bomb Wing's squadrons would be brought up to full strength of 24 B-26s. The other bomb wing (the 452nd) would be able to operate with 16 of the bombers for each squadron. This put the total of B-26s in front-line service at 120. There would also be another 60 in theatre reserve.

A majority of the B-26 crews flew in a world of darkness. They combined their expertise with the Marine night-fighters and wreaked havoc on anything that moved southward after sunset. To an F-86 pilot, the ultimate fantasy was to shoot down a MiG-15; to a B-26 crew, it was to locate and destroy a locomotive. They perfected it to the extent that during the final 12 months of the war, only a small percentage of supplies were sent south by train. This was caused by a combination of rail cuts made during the day and truck and train hunting at night.

Spring 1952 ▰
TRAIN HUNTING

One of the top locomotive killers in FEAF was First Lieutenant Walt McGinnis, a B-26 pilot operating out of Pusan AB. He describes just what it was like on a night mission. "The most exciting types of missions I flew at night were the rail recces. These proved to be a real challenge because the railroads

in North Korea wound through the mountainous terrain and the visibility was poor. The trains always ran at night with no lights. The only way to spot them was to see the puffs of smoke or steam. This could not be accomplished at altitude. You had to get down to 500 ft or less to see them. Routes of attack were always determined

The 6th Chadwick was damaged in a massive secondary explosion following a rocket strike on a truck column, but made it back to Kunsan. As with the first five Chadwicks, it was assigned to the CO of the 13th BS.

Below: The B-26s of the 34th Bomb Squadron of the 17th Bomb Wing were a familiar sight to all the pilots who flew in and out of Pusan during the war. This Invader is returning through hilly terrain to Pusan, on the southeastern extremity of the Korean peninsula.

Hawker Sea Fury FB.Mk 11 WJ232, No. 802 Squadron, Fleet Air Arm HMS *Ocean*

On 9 August 1952, his 29th birthday, Lt Peter 'Hoagy' Carmichael became the only British pilot of the Korean War to score a kill in a British-built aircraft. On this day, Carmichael's flight of four Sea Furies flying from HMS Ocean in the Yellow Sea was on a rail interdiction mission when attacked by eight MiG-15s. The MiGs attempted to dogfight with the more manoeuvrable piston fighters and Carmichael scored fatal hits on one with his four 20-mm cannon. Two other MiGs were damaged by members of the flight.

The 8th Bomb Squadron fought from the beginning of the war to its end. They dropped the first bombs of the war and also the last, on 27 July 1953. Sweet Bettye was with the squadron at K-13 in spring 1952.

by the mountains, which usually restricted you to only one or two directions. This brought some serious problems of having to avoid the barely discernible hills, plus the possibility of anti-aircraft guns being located on the ridges. They could easily spot us from the flames emitting from the exhausts as we went below them.

"On one mission we had the assignment of running the roads north of Wonsan, North Korea. After about 30 miles, we spotted a train moving along about five miles south of Kowon. It was the same place that we had knocked out a locomotive and 20 boxcars a few weeks earlier. I immediately made a dive-bomb attack and dropped an M-47 fire bomb that landed on the engine. This stopped it dead."

February 1952 ■
THE LOSS OF MAJOR DAVIS

There were two months during 1952 that MiG activity was extremely low, and therefore the number of recorded kills for that month was below average. For the year, there were 395 kills. In February only 17 were confirmed and in July that figure dropped to 16. Comparing these totals to the 63 kills made in September gives an indication of how little activity there was. Although February was a quiet month, it brought about one of the most tragic events to be recorded in the 4th Wing's archives for the Korean campaign.

Major George Davis Jr from the 334th Fighter Squadron was one of the most talented fighter pilots that ever flew combat over 'MiG Alley'. On 10 February, Davis was leading a flight of Sabres over the Yalu River at altitude. He spotted a formation of MiGs on the south side of the river at 32,000 ft. They

were in very close proximity to some fighter-bombers, so he took his element down to attack. In a matter of seconds, Davis had bagged his 13th and 14th kills. There were still plenty of enemy fighters in the area, so Davis locked on to a potential third kill and, while he was doing this, another

MiG came up behind him at close range and hit him with a fatal burst of cannon fire. His loss was felt throughout FEAF. Davis was awarded the Medal of Honor for his heroics, and his accomplishments placed him in the history books as the fifth jet ace of the war.

The month of March proved to

be the third best of the year for recorded kills, with 40. The 4th Wing was credited with 25 of them and the 51st Wing got 14. The remaining kill was credited to an F-94B from the 319th All Weather Squadron. Two Marine Corps exchange pilots attached to Sabre wings had kills in the F-86 in March.

Colonel Francis Gabreski, commander of the 51st FG, prepares to fit himself and his parachute into his F-86E at Suwon. With 28 kills in World War II, and 6.5 in Korea, he finished his career with 34.5 to be the top living US ace.

Spring 1952
PUGNACIOUS PANTHERS

An F9F-2 Panther from VF-191 takes a breather on dry land at Taegu. On many occasions, aircraft that were operating off the carriers sustained battle damage to the extent that it was best to opt for the nearest friendly base.

The USAF had numerous front-line aircraft that saw action during the Korean War, ranging from the F-86 through all of the fighter-bomber types, the all-weather, reconnaissance and bomber aircraft. The US Marines and Navy were limited to three types that numerically carried the brunt of the responsibility: the F4U Corsair, the F9F Panther and the AD Skyraider. None of them were given the mission of air superiority, but if the MiGs pressed the attack it was the F9F that could dish out the most firepower, with its 20-mm cannon.

Major Louis Steman, a Marine F9F pilot with VMA-311, recalls a close encounter with several MiGs while on a mission 35 miles north of Pyongyang. "We were a flight of eight Panthers (two four-ship divisions) assigned to attack a supply dump and then divert on over to the Yalu to strafe some heavy AA positions. One of the aircraft in the second division had to abort and return to Pohang. This gave us seven F9Fs and a long haul, trying to conserve our fuel. We hit the target area and, as I

Reconnaissance aircraft flying over North Korea were often escorted by fighters of the same basic type, as witnessed by this F2H-2 of VF-11 with its charge, an F2H-2P of VC-61 returning to USS Kearsarge, late 1952.

started a high-speed dive, a MiG flashed by right in front of my nose. One of the guys in my division yelled to watch out for those F-86s! I called out, 'Hell, those aren't Sabres, they're MiGs!' By my quick count, there were eight MiGs and, for a brief second, I thought about all of us dumping our ordnance and giving them a

fight. But, we were at 25,000 ft and they would definitely have had the advantage. Instead, I pressed the attack on our original objective, radioing to the rest of the guys to use only minimum speed brakes in their dives so we could drop our bombs on target and immediately turn on the MiGs. If we could battle them at treetop level, using up their depleted fuel supply (they were quite a distance from their base in Manchuria), they would not be able to make any high side passes on us. Seconds after releasing my bombs, I heard one of our pilots call out that the MiGs were firing on him. I looked around and saw a lot of MiGs all over our guys. One of the F9Fs passed right under me, with one right on his tail. I tightened my turn to get a shot at him and, with

Left: As this VF-831 Panther prepares to spread wings and go into action, it shows off its load of four 5-in (82-cm) HVARs and two 6.5-in (107-cm) ATARs, an emergency weapon developed to counter Russian-built T-34 tanks.

Below: Pilots of Marine photo-recon squadron VMJ-1 mingle at Pohang. On most missions, the Banshees would pick up their F-86 escorts just north of the bomb line before heading into 'MiG Alley'.

no time to lose, allowing plenty of lead, I fired a burst that caught his attention. He quickly pulled up and broke off contact.

"I immediately saw another MiG right behind one of our aircraft, so I lined him up and this time he was a lot closer. I fired a short burst and all four of my guns jammed! It was a tough situation to be in because there were MiGs all over the place. Out of the corner of my eye, I spotted a MiG and an F9F coming right at me. I turned into the MiG and headed straight for him at tremendous rate of closure. It must have scared the hell out of him ... and me too. A moment later, the MiGs had disappeared and one of our aircraft was still calling for help. I told him to stay low and head for water as the MiGs tended to break it off if the action was going to be over water. My four-plane division joined up and headed back to K-3. The F9F that had the last contact with the MiG-15s was low on fuel so I radioed for him to land at the closest base, which was Suwon. After refuelling, he came on back to Pohang where we had a chance to look his plane over – he had lost half of his horizontal stabiliser and was lucky to be back in one piece. It had been a memorable mission.'

The USS Kearsarge displays its arsenal of warplanes as a launch is prepared against North Korea in 1952. VC-61 Banshees, VF-884 Corsairs and VF-721 Panthers can all be seen. The F9F squadron was on its second cruise of the war.

Grumman F9F-2 Panther, VF-781, USS *Oriskany*, November 1952

In one of the more unusual engagements of the Korean air war, Lt(jg) J. D. Middleton and his wingman, Lt E. R. Williams, shot down a pair of Russian MiG-15s over the sea southeast of Kangui, a city on the Russian side of North Korea's northeastern border. The MiGs had flown from a base near Vladivostok, and the whole incident was kept secret for several years after the war to avoid international repercussions. A third pilot, Lt(jg) D. M. Rowlands, was credited with damaging a MiG on this day, 18 November 1952.

May 1952
FIGHTER-BOMBERS

FEAF records reveal that for the March-May period a total of 110 MiG-15s had been destroyed. On the other end of the spectrum, the losses posted by the USAF for the same period were 12 F-86s, five F-84s, one F-80 and one F-51. The slower fighter-bombers were caught by the MiGs when they were most vulnerable, coming off their bomb runs. During this period, the 4th Wing was using a mixture of A models and E models. It was not until sometime in July when the last As were phased out. The 51st Wing had been using only E models since their conversion from the F-80C.

There was great enthusiasm shown by some individuals to use the F-86 as a fast close support fighter-bomber. This was finally tried by the 4th in mid-January of 1951, and enough sorties were flown the first few months to get a good feel for the F-86 in this new role. One of the biggest advocates of the concept was Colonel Walker H. Mahurin, the commander of the 4th Wing. However, his enthusiasm would prove to be

tragic. On 13 May 1952, the 4th loaded 1,000-lb bombs on some of their Sabres and headed to the big Communist airfield at Sinuiju. With their speed brakes open, the Sabres got in quickly before the AAA gunners knew what hit them. Later on that same day, Colonel Mahurin led more bomb-laden Sabres against the Kumu-ri rail yards. This time the AAA was not caught napping, and Mahurin was shot down and was a POW for the remainder of the war. It was a significant loss for the 4th Wing.

The overall experiment of using the F-86 as a fighter-bomber proved to be very successful, and it could not have come at a better time. The attrition rates for the F-84, F-80 and F-51 had been high. The F-84E had taken a beating during the intense railway interdiction campaign during the early months of 1952. FEAF had been expecting either more replacement Es or the new F-84G. The latter had been specifically designed for the role of fighter-bomber. For one reason or another, the USAF decided that it would be at least five months before the newer Thunderjet

The bright red store under this 9th Fighter Bomber Squadron F-84G Thunderjet is in fact a modified drop tank filled with survival equipment to be dropped to Lt Lyle Cameron, a pilot of the unit downed behind enemy lines, October 1952.

models would reach the forces in Korea. The only solution was to ship 102 F-84D models to be used in the interim. This was not a satisfactory arrangement for an F-84 pilot, because the Ds had less speed and range than the E. It would also prove to be a major problem when both models were used in the same formations.

An F-84D pilot, Lieutenant Edward A. Fernandes recalls one of those memorable encounters with the unexpected ... the MiG. "I

remember one close call we had while flying with the 111th Fighter Bomber Squadron in the early spring of 1952. Colonel 'Wild Bill' Halton, the 136th Group commander, was leading the strike on a rail cutting mission to the south of Kunuri. The 111th was to be the first squadron in on the target. I was flying the No. 2 slot in the second flight. After our bomb run we were rejoining in a shallow, left-climbing turn around the target area. My flight was in a loose trail formation behind the lead flight. All of a sudden, red golf balls arched across our formation, followed by a beautifully polished swept-wing MiG. It gleamed in the bright sunlight with a large red star on its vertical stabiliser. Until then, I never realised how dull and tired our F-84s looked. The MiG continued firing as he went through the formation and, as he got to the lead flight, he broke off in a near vertical climb to the right. All of our formation had scattered in every direction. One of the guys got in a few bursts at the MiG and may have scored a few hits. All of us were wishing that we had been in a faster airplane and could have gone after him. It was my only experience with a MiG and I was impressed with what I had seen."

With the ominous mountain terrain of North Korea ahead, these F-84s of the 182nd Fighter Bomber Squadron haul their bombs towards their targets. The 182nd was part of the 136th Group, an all-National Guard outfit from San Antonio.

Spring 1952
THUNDERJET REINFORCEMENTS

Regardless of what FEAF planners thought, the decision was final. There were two combat wings of F-84s based on Korean soil. It was decided that the 49th Wing would retain all of the Es and the 136th Wing would receive all of the Ds. There were numerous problems with the D, as had been predicted. The situation became so critical that the Air Force announced in May that they would ship the new F-84Gs to Korea in sufficient numbers to bring both wings up to full battle strength and to create a 50 per cent reserve force to be held in Japan to take care of combat losses. By September, the wings were up to full strength for the first time in over a year.

The fighter-bomber problem was not completely solved because the F-80Cs and F-51Ds had been getting beaten up and patched up for almost two years. This situation had to be addressed in the near future. The 8th Fighter Bomber Wing, operating out of Suwon AB, was the only outfit using the F-80. The 18th Fighter Bomber Wing, with its Mustangs, was operating out of two bases: Chinhae and Hoengsong. Following the combat proof of the F-86's potential as a fighter-bomber, these two wings would get the new F-86F models in early 1953. Both the 8th and the 18th had done the impossible, stretching the use of their aircraft to two and a half years under the worst of conditions.

Above: A formation of 69th Fighter Bomber Squadron F-84s returns to Taegu from a mission over North Korea in June 1952. The stark grey mountains that were all too familiar during the harsh winters have taken on a lush green hue. The 69th was part of the 58th FBW.

The 49th Fighter Bomber Group has never been bashful about its heritage. These pilots were F-84 drivers stationed at Taegu Air Base. The 49th was extremely aggressive in its close support role, flying two types of aircraft during the war: the F-80C and F-84.

April 1952
WESTCOTT'S WAR ON THE MiGS

While the interdiction war raged at ground level, the aerial duels over the Yalu River continued. The month of April proved to be a good month for the Sabres, with 44 MiGs shot down. One of the most outstanding performances of April was turned in by Major William Westcott, a pilot in the 25th FIS. From 1 to 26 April (19 missions) he shot down five MiG-15s, to become the 12th jet ace of the war. On two of his missions, he had double kills. Westcott's marksmanship was matched by his excellent knowledge of the F-86 and exactly what it could and could not do, and he had acquired some accurate knowledge of the MiG's capabilities. Major Westcott observed, "Some USAF pilots claimed the MiG-15 could fly at Mach 1.2 above 50,000 ft altitude. No MiG-15 built could reach

supersonic speed, but it could certainly operate above 50,000 ft! I observed many of them in that range.

"The MiG's main advantage was its high rate of climb, higher by an appreciable margin than the F-86F. This was achieved by a design that provided an overall lighter basic aircraft with a higher thrust-to-weight ratio than the Sabre. It also had a wing that provided more lift per square foot of wing. The fences on each wing were evidence of a boundary layer that needed straightening out at a high Mach number. The MiG was similar to the F-84E in that it reached its critical Mach number at about 0.87, when the airflow reaches Mach 1. At that point, Mach buffet begins and control degrades rapidly. At high altitude, when turning – and depending on the rate of turn

commanded – the critical Mach number decreases and buffet begins sooner. When the airflow goes supersonic, the boundary layer over the wing or a section of it separates and becomes turbulent. The wing loses lift and stability. A single modification that will counter this phenomenon is to reduce weight. Unnecessary weight in the F-86F was the self-sealing tank, forward armour plate etc. The following incident is an example of less weight versus performance.

"On a regular patrol mission near the Communist airfield at Antung, I tangled with a flight of MiG-15s. After the initial

A flight of three F-86Es (photographed from a fourth) crosses the Yalu river and heads over 'MiG Alley'. With drop tanks still aboard, these 16th FS aircraft had not yet encountered any MiGs.

jockeying for position, I found myself in a rat race with a single MiG. We yo-yo'd, turned and rolled until we were about 1,500 ft above the ground. All of a sudden, he broke off and headed for altitude, at a terrific speed, in the direction of Antung. There was nothing I could do. I had 600 lb of fuel remaining in my Sabre, and no oxygen! The F-86 was climbing over 4,000 ft per minute at Mach 0.9. Reaching 39,000 ft, I cut off the engine and glided to about 3,000 ft over Suwon AB. A total of about 190 miles. Normally, an

A 336th Fighter Interceptor Squadron, 4th Fighter Interceptor Wing Sabre heads north on a dawn patrol. The 4th FIW was to account for 54 per cent of all USAF kills in Korea.

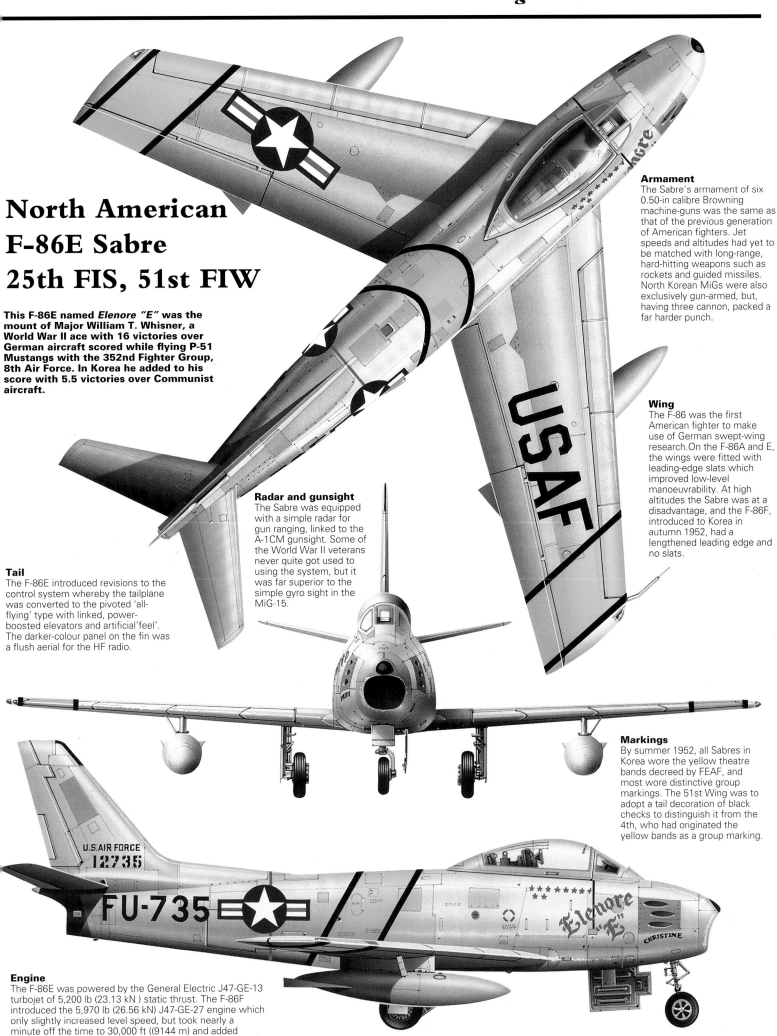

North American F-86E Sabre
25th FIS, 51st FIW

This F-86E named *Elenore "E"* was the mount of Major William T. Whisner, a World War II ace with 16 victories over German aircraft scored while flying P-51 Mustangs with the 352nd Fighter Group, 8th Air Force. In Korea he added to his score with 5.5 victories over Communist aircraft.

Armament
The Sabre's armament of six 0.50-in calibre Browning machine-guns was the same as that of the previous generation of American fighters. Jet speeds and altitudes had yet to be matched with long-range, hard-hitting weapons such as rockets and guided missiles. North Korean MiGs were also exclusively gun-armed, but, having three cannon, packed a far harder punch.

Wing
The F-86 was the first American fighter to make use of German swept-wing research. On the F-86A and E, the wings were fitted with leading-edge slats which improved low-level manoeuvrability. At high altitudes the Sabre was at a disadvantage, and the F-86F, introduced to Korea in autumn 1952, had a lengthened leading edge and no slats.

Radar and gunsight
The Sabre was equipped with a simple radar for gun ranging, linked to the A-1CM gunsight. Some of the World War II veterans never quite got used to using the system, but it was far superior to the simple gyro sight in the MiG-15.

Tail
The F-86E introduced revisions to the control system whereby the tailplane was converted to the pivoted 'all-flying' type with linked, power-boosted elevators and artificial 'feel'. The darker-colour panel on the fin was a flush aerial for the HF radio.

Markings
By summer 1952, all Sabres in Korea wore the yellow theatre bands decreed by FEAF, and most wore distinctive group markings. The 51st Wing was to adopt a tail decoration of black checks to distinguish it from the 4th, who had originated the yellow bands as a group marking.

Engine
The F-86E was powered by the General Electric J47-GE-13 turbojet of 5,200 lb (23.13 kN) static thrust. The F-86F introduced the 5,970 lb (26.56 kN) J47-GE-27 engine which only slightly increased level speed, but took nearly a minute off the time to 30,000 ft (9144 m) and added another 800 ft (244 m) to the stated maximum altitude.

103

Lt W. P. Dunbar Jr poses beside the famous 'Rocketeers' badge on his 336th Fighter Squadron Sabre. Dunbar scored no kills but was involved in numerous encounters with enemy aircraft, including the fight where Major Felix Asla had his wing blown off by a MiG.

F-86 pilot did not see 600 lb of fuel remaining until he was in the traffic pattern to land. Restarting the engine, landing, taxiing to the revetment area left an indicated 200-300 lb of fuel remaining. The point is that if the F-86 was able to fight against the MiG, weighing 1,400 to 1,500 lb less, the 'kill' rate would have at least doubled."

From the second half of 1951 through 1952, many F-86 pilots reported encountering MiGs with different colour schemes, many of which were painted in one solid colour. Major Westcott remembered an incident in which he and his wingman were streaking about 100 ft above the runway at Antung. Everything was just a blur, but he said that there were rows of MiGs parked with colour variations of polished metal and blue. Many sources have stated that the MiGs which were painted in a powder blue belonged to an all-weather squadron from East Germany.

Lieutenant W. P. Dunbar Jr, a pilot in the 336th FIS, states "There were several MiG paint jobs encountered during the length of my tour. Some were an all-powder blue, all silver, had red noses and tails, yellow trim, and I even saw some that were a Hawthorne green colour similar to the colour of a 1950 Ford car." This broad array of colour markings and the skills displayed by some of these MiG fliers indicated to Intelligence that they were flown by Russians and/or Warsaw Pact pilots. All of this was confirmed in the early 1990s when some details of the Soviet involvement in the Korean War were made public.

1 August 1952
MiGS ON CAMERA

One of the most spectacular and widely shown gun camera film to come out of the war was one in which a MiG was firing on an F-86. The MiG was, in turn, being shot at by an F-86 that was behind the MiG. The first F-86 was flown by Second Lieutenant Earl Brown of the 334th FIS. The Sabre in the rear that shot down the pursuing MiG was flown by Lieutenant Gene Rogge, also of the 334th. An observer to all of this action was Lieutenant Dunbar. He tells the story from his vantage point. "This mission was recalled while talking about how tough the Sabre was and the fact that it was able to take a lot of punishment. On a CAP mission in 'MiG Alley', I saw a MiG run up behind Earl Brown's Sabre and hit it in the left wing close to the main spar, with a 37-mm round. It was a hole big enough for you to stand up in. I saw the gun camera film afterwards and you could see the big puffs of smoke coming out of the MiG's cannon. There must have been five or six puffs before Rogge's hits stopped the firing. His F-86's 50-calibre tracers converged on and enveloped the MiG's cockpit area and the MiG exploded."

Lieutenant Gene Rogge remembers that particular mission in which he had a confirmed kill over a MiG. "I was the No. 3 man in a flight of four F-86s. The date was 1 August 1952. We were flying in a southwesterly direction, with my element on the left, in a tactical patrol formation. We were at 40,000 ft when I spotted a flight of four MiGs at 45,000 ft at our 10 o'clock position, heading in the opposite direction. I called them out, but our lead had not spotted them yet, so we continued on. The MiGs saw us and began a descending turn in behind us. I told lead that they were almost in firing range and that we needed to break left. Lead still hadn't seen them, so I called for my element to break to the left. I took on the No. 4 MiG, who was at a slight disadvantage. The fight raged for a short period and then, looking over for my wingman, I noticed that the lead MiG was locked on to him. They were ahead of me and slightly below. I tried calling out breaks to him, but he had already taken some hits and was in trouble. He had switched to the emergency

A pair of F-86s from the 334th Fighter Squadron prepares to take off from Kimpo. The squadron had fewer kills than its sister unit, the 335th, but boasted the number two US ace of the war, James Jabara.

channel and did not hear me. I was heading down toward them at a very high Mach and I pulled about 9 *g* trying to get a quick cut-off. I fired off a couple of bursts, out of range, in an attempt to distract the MiG and get him to break off. It did not work. I then closed in to range and put a long burst into his canopy area. The MiG burst into flames, rolled over and flew into the ground. I could not avoid flying through the fire and debris. When clear, I looked all over to see where the other three MiGs were and the sky was empty. I also could not find my wingman and, being low on fuel, I headed back to Kimpo. After landing, I noticed his F-86 parked over on the taxiway. He had made it back. The gun camera film was shown all over the world."

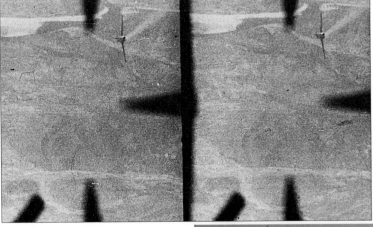

Above: With a Sabre in hot pursuit, a MiG-15 makes a dash for the Yalu River and safety. Already damaged by numerous 0.50-in calibre hits, the MiG did not make it.

Right: The building work at K-13 Suwon went on long after the 51st Fighter Group had taken up residence. In the first half of 1952, thousands of man-hours went into building earth revetments to protect the fighters.

Fighters of the Fifty-First

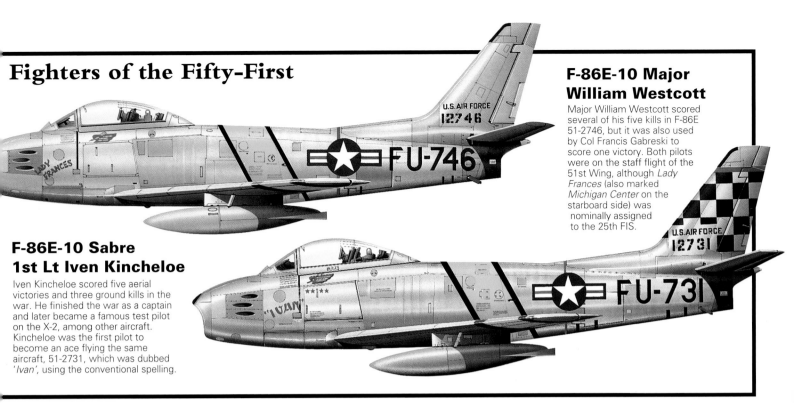

F-86E-10 Sabre
1st Lt Iven Kincheloe

Iven Kincheloe scored five aerial victories and three ground kills in the war. He finished the war as a captain and later became a famous test pilot on the X-2, among other aircraft. Kincheloe was the first pilot to become an ace flying the same aircraft, 51-2731, which was dubbed 'Ivan', using the conventional spelling.

F-86E-10 Major William Westcott

Major William Westcott scored several of his five kills in F-86E 51-2746, but it was also used by Col Francis Gabreski to score one victory. Both pilots were on the staff flight of the 51st Wing, although *Lady Frances* (also marked *Michigan Center* on the starboard side) was nominally assigned to the 25th FIS.

Mid-1952
MARINE AND NAVY OPERATIONS

For all of 1952, the US Marines and Navy aircraft worked up and down the coast of North Korea, and there were no targets that were not within their reach. They tended to work areas that were not frequented by the MiGs, unless they hooked up with an F-86 escort. The fast, straight-wing F9F was the closest air superiority type in the Navy's arsenal, but they were employed primarily in the close support role. At this time, the Marines were using four fully

The Marine night-fighters such as this VMF(N)-513 F4U-5N Corsair played as much havoc with the Chinese attempts to resupply their forces as did the night-flying B-26s.

complemented squadrons of F4U Corsairs: VMA-212, VMA-214, VMA-312 and VMA-323. All of these were involved in close support of Marine ground forces. They also used one squadron of night-fighter F4U-5N Corsairs (VMF(N)-513). During the final few weeks of the Korean War, VMA-312 'Checkerboards' would be replaced by VMA-332 'Polka Dots'. Both the Navy and Marines were heavy users of the AD

A good cross-section of Marine Corps aircraft is shown here at Kunsan in the spring of 1952. The F4U Corsairs are from VMF-323 'Death Rattlers', the AD Skyraiders are from VMA-121, and the F7F Tigercats are VMF(N)-513.

Skyraider, the F4U and the F9F.

Although these pilots very seldom had a crack at an enemy aircraft, the opportunity presented itself every now and then. On the night of 7 June 1952, First Lieutenant John Andre of VMF(N)-513 was on a night reconnaissance mission along the

west coast of North Korea. He was directed into the vicinity of an unidentified aircraft, where he locked onto the bogie, got into position and then shot down a World War II vintage Yak fighter. This marked the first time that a Yak type had been shot down at night, by a night-fighter type.

10 September 1952 ∎
MiG 1, CORSAIR 1

Three months later, one of the most spectacular missions flown by the F4U in Korea unfolded. Onboard the USS *Sicily*, the F4Us of VMA-312 were heavily tasked on interdiction, close support and CAP missions. Captain Jesse Folmar, USMC, relates the events that led to his MiG-15 'kill' on 10 September 1952. "On this particular day, my wingman Lieutenant Daniels and myself were scheduled to fly a strike mission. At 16.10 hours we launched to hit a target consisting of 300 North Korean troops located four miles from Chinampo, which was on the south side of the Taedong River. As we crossed over into unfriendly territory, we began executing a tactical weave at 10,000 ft. Upon arrival over our target we observed no activity, so we continued to fly reconnaissance in the vicinity of the Taejon Estuary. As we started a bank to weave over a small island off the coast, I caught a glimpse of two MiG-15s that were in the early stages of making a run on us. They were in loose section at the time.

"I steepened my bank, turning sharply into the MiGs and at the same time increased power, jettisoned all external ordnance and fuel tanks, and switched to the guard channel to report that we were being attacked by MiGs. I told Daniels to fly a tighter weave and not to let the MiGs out of his sight. In a matter of seconds, I saw two more MiGs closing very rapidly from my 8 o'clock position. I turned hard to the left and tried to get my guns to bear on them before they opened fire but, due to their rapid closing speed, I was unable to do so. Their tracers were overshooting us, so I reversed my bank to the right and turned inside one of the MiGs as he was starting

a climbing left turn. I pulled up, got him in my gunsight and gave him about 20 mils lead and held a five-second burst with my 20-mm cannon. I could tell that I had him boresighted by the blinking flashes along the left side of the fuselage. A grey trail of fuel vapour began to stream from his aircraft and it quickly turned into billowing black smoke. The MiG nosed over slightly and seemed to lose acceleration. Seconds later the pilot ejected, and as he tumbled through the air he appeared as a tumbling ball of smoke. When his parachute opened, I could see his *g* suit

Right: A very youthful 2nd Lt Robert Howard with his VMF-312 Corsair on the deck of USS Bataan. The ship and squadron were in a Japanese port before sailing for their battle station off the North Korean coast. On 16 October, the squadron (by now redesignated VMA-312) lost three Corsairs, for its costliest day of the war.

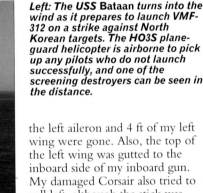

Left: The USS Bataan turns into the wind as it prepares to launch VMF-312 on a strike against North Korean targets. The HO3S plane-guard helicopter is airborne to pick up any pilots who do not launch successfully, and one of the screening destroyers can be seen in the distance.

Below: An F4U from VMF-312 'Checkerboards' prepares to launch from Bataan. This replacement aircraft has yet to receive the famous checked squadron marking on the cowl.

burning from head to foot. I glanced down and saw the flaming MiG hit the water in a vertical position.

"Lieutenant Daniels and I resumed our weave, and shortly thereafter I saw four more MiG-15s in addition to the original four. They were strung out in a loose column of two sections. Seeing the increased odds against us, I decided that it would be better to break it off. I transmitted 'Break hard left down' and made a diving turn to the left. I had just started picking up good diving speed when I saw balls of tracer rounds passing on my left and at the same instant felt a severe explosion in my left wing. Immediately, the left wing began to shudder as if in a high-speed stall. I glanced over and saw that

the left aileron and 4 ft of my left wing were gone. Also, the top of the left wing was gutted to the inboard side of my inboard gun. My damaged Corsair also tried to roll left, although the stick was placed in a full right position. This led to my decision that it would be too hazardous to attempt a landing on the carrier, so I decided to bail out. I transmitted the SAR distress signal and repeated my position prior to leaving the aircraft. As I finished my radio transmission, another MiG made a firing pass on me, but missed.

"At about 3,000 ft, I rolled out the right side of the cockpit and fell clear. As I pulled the parachute D-ring, I heard an ear-splitting cracking sound. I looked around and saw a MiG come by me and his guns were firing at my spinning Corsair. By my quick count, there were still seven MiGs in the area. Fortunately, they departed and I hit the water about a quarter of a mile southeast of a small island. Lieutenant Daniels flew over and circled my position, and the 'Dumbo' arrived and rescued me within eight minutes."

F4U-4B Corsair BuNo. 97201, flown by Capt. Jesse Folmar VMA-312

Captain Jesse Folmar of Marine attack squadron VMA-312 was able to claim the only Corsair vs MiG kill when his flight of two aircraft was attacked on the way to bombing troop concentrations on 10 September 1952. A MiG again made the fatal mistake of turning with the F4Us and Folmar hit one with a five-second burst of 20-mm cannon fire, causing it to dive out of control and the pilot to eject. Unfortunately, Folmar's aircraft was attacked by another group of MiGs and he was forced to bail out over the sea, where he was rescued by an SA-16 amphibian.

Summer 1952
TRANSPORT SUPPORT

For every military aircraft that flew north of the bomb line, there were scores of people that were responsible for getting it there. This included the ground crews, all enlisted personnel and wing headquarters. You have to go far beyond this echelon to realise just what was involved. The Military Airlift Command had one

The tower staff at Pusan would have to look up to see the tip of a C-124's tail, 48 ft (14.6 m) above the ground. Everything about the aircraft was big for its day, including its load of 200 fully-equipped troops or 127 stretchers, and 200,000-lb (91000-kg) maximum take-off weight.

of the most unpublicised missions of the war, yet they kept the ground and air forces in position to defeat the North Koreans and hold the Chinese People's Army at a stalemate along the original border at the 38th Parallel.

For the first 24 months of the war, the bulk of the air cargo was delivered by the C-54, C-47 and C-119. It was weight of these fully laden transports that kept tearing up the PSP and dirt runways at major bases such as Pusan, Taegu, Kimpo and Suwon. Due to the limited capacity of these aircraft, they were almost constantly in the air during the daylight hours.

A C-54 from the 'Bully Beef' 6th Troop Carrier Squadron leaves Japan en route to a base in Korea. These aircraft were replaced by the C-124s, but for the first two years of the war they lifted the bulk of troops and supplies.

Finally, during the summer of 1952, two squadrons of C-124 Globemasters began arriving, a few planes at a time. They would replace two C-54 squadrons from within the 374th Wing. The training programme was set up at Tachikawa AB, Japan. The instructors all came from the 62nd Troop Carrier Wing and a mobile training detachment brought in from Chanute AFB. The C-124 was definitely a more complex aircraft than the C-54. New, highly skilled positions such as load masters and scanners came into being. The conversion took months to complete. As the use of the C-124s intensified, the number of daily passengers climbed steadily until Tachikawa was averaging almost 2,500, to and from South Korea. One of the most unique

operations to come out of these airlift operations was the use of C-47s from Thailand. They were specialised in carrying the wounded from Tachikawa to the Camp Drew Hospital that was only 20 minutes away by air. The Globemasters airlifted all the wounded out of a central collecting area at Seoul. This would have included all personnel along the MLR who were wounded or needed medical attention. By the end of 1952, there was only one remaining C-54 squadron operating out of Japan.

The C-124 entered service in Korea in 1952, primarily on the troop shuttle to Japan. The increase in payload over the ageing C-54 was remarkable, but, with its great weight, the number of usable airfields in Korea was limited.

June – December 1952 ▬▬▬▬
AIR BASE CONSTRUCTION

No single factor hampered aircraft operations during the first two years of the Korean War as much as the lack of adequate air facilities. The only air bases in South Korea in June 1950 had been built by the Japanese during World War II, and there had been only minimal maintenance since the war. The problem was so acute that a significant percentage of operational aircraft had to launch and return from bases in Japan.

This put unnecessary strains on the fighters, especially the F-80s because they did not have the range to do a satisfactory job over the front lines. Those fighter groups that were fortunate enough to be allowed space at the limited number of South Korean air bases were running into severe problems from the beatings that the aircraft were taking from the rough runways, damaged PSP and mud. But it was not the lighter fighter types that were wrecking

The 9,000-ft (836-m) paved runway built at Taegu (K-2) and opened on 28 June 1952 was the first major step in modernising the crude air base strips that existed all over South Korea.

the airstrips. The heavy transport traffic was the culprit and there was nothing that could be done about it, at least not if the United Nations forces were to protect South Korea. On 28 June 1952, the engineers finished building a 9,000-ft concrete runway at

Taegu. From then, these airfield builders were able to show great progress and they built the superbase at Osan-ni (K-55). In December 1952 the base was ready for its tenant, which was the 18th Fighter Bomber Wing and its F-51 Mustangs. Just one month after the 18th arrived, they began transitioning to the new F-86Fs. Today, K-55 is still one of the most modern bases in South Korea.

Australia's No. 77 Squadron with its Meteor F.Mk 8s was attached to the 4th Fighter Wing out of Kimpo. The Meteors were considerably slower than the MiG-15 and did not fair too well in several dogfights with them. The squadron was much more successful in the close support role, often using rockets as seen here.

Kills list 1952

Date	Pilot	Aircraft/Unit	Enemy
6.1.52	Maj. Van E. Chandler	F-86, 25th FIS	MiG-15
6.1.52	Capt John M. Heard	F-86, 25th FIS	MiG-15
6.1.52	1st Lt Donald E. Little	F-86, 25th FIS	MiG-15
6.1.52	Col Walker M. Mahurin	F-86, 51st FIG	MiG-15
6.1.52	Maj. William T. Whisner Jr	F-86, 25th FIS	MiG-15
7.1.52	Capt. Ralph H. Ashby	F-86, 25th FIS	MiG-15
7.1.52	Capt. John M. Heard	F-86, 25th FIS	MiG-15
10.1.52	Capt. Nelton R. Wilson	F-86, 334th FIS	MiG-15
11.1.52	Col Francis S. Gabreski	F-86, 51st FIG	MiG-15
11.1.52	1st Lt Earl S. Payne	F-86, 16th FIS	MiG-15
11.1.52	1st Lt Thiel M. Reeves	F-86, 25th FIS	MiG-15
11.1.52	Maj. William T. Whisner Jr	F-86, 25th FIS	MiG-15
12.1.52	Lt Col George L. Jones	F-86, 51st FIG	MiG-15
15.1.52	Lt Col George L. Jones	F-86, 51st FIG	MiG-15
17.1.52	Lt Col James B. Raebel	F-86, 334th FIS	MiG-15
17.1.52	1st Lt Frank P. Robison	F-86, 16th FIS	MiG-15
17.1.52	Maj. William F. Sheaffer	F-86, 16th FIS	MiG-15
19.1.52	1st Lt Iven C. Kincheloe Jr	F-86, 25th FIS	MiG-15
20.1.52	Maj. Donald E. Adams	F-86, 16th FIS	MiG-15
20.1.52	1st Lt Lloyd D. Juhlin	F-86, 16th FIS	MiG-15
23.1.52	Maj. Donald E. Adams	F-86, 16th FIS	MiG-15
23.1.52	Capt. William C. Knoy	F-86, 16th FIS	MiG-15
25.1.52	1st Lt Frank J. Gately	F-86, 25th FIS	MiG-15
25.1.52	Capt. Mose W. Gordon Jr	F-86, 16th FIS	MiG-15
25.1.52	1st Lt William M. Guinther	F-86, 25th FIS	MiG-15
25.1.52	1st Lt Anthony Kulengosky Jr	F-86, 25th FIS	MiG-15
25.1.52	Capt. Robert T. Latshaw Jr	F-86, 335th FIS	MiG-15
25.1.52	1st Lt Robert H. Moore	F-86, 16th FIS	MiG-15
25.1.52	1st Lt Conrad F. Nystrum	F-86, 335th FIS	MiG-15
25.1.52	Maj. William F. Sheaffer	F-86, 16th FIS	MiG-15
25.1.52	1st Lt William C. Shofner	F-86, 25th FIS	MiG-15
30.1.52	Capt. Freeland K. Mathews	F-86, 336th FIS	MiG-15
10.2.52	Maj. George A. Davis	F-86, 334th FIS	MiG-15
10.2.52	Maj. George A. Davis	F-86, 334th FIS	MiG-15
11.2.52	1st Lt James E. Arnold	F-86, 16th FIS	MiG-15 ½
11.2.52	1st Lt Raymond E. Steinbis	F-86, 16th FIS	MiG-15 ½
17.2.52	Maj. Zane S. Amell	F-86, 335th FIS	MiG-15
17.2.52	1st Lt William M. Guinther	F-86, 25th FIS	MiG-15
17.2.52	Col Walker M. Mahurin	F-86, 25th FIS	MiG-15
17.2.52	1st Lt Russell H. Miller	F-86, 335th FIS	MiG-15
19.2.52	1st Lt John C. Friend	F-86, 16th FIS	MiG-15
19.2.52	Capt. Paul R. Henderson Jr	F-86, 25th FIS	MiG-15 ½
19.2.52	Col Albert W. Schinz	F-86, 25th FIS	MiG-15 ½
20.2.52	Maj. Van E. Chandler	F-86, 25th FIS	MiG-15
20.2.52	Col Francis S. Gabreski	F-86, 51st FIG	MiG-15 ½
20.2.52	Maj. William F. Sheaffer	F-86, 16th FIS	MiG-15
20.2.52	Maj. William T. Whisner Jr	F-86, 25th FIS	MiG-15 ½
21.2.52	1st Lt Billy B. Dobbs	F-86, 335th FIS	MiG-15
21.2.52	Capt. Brooks J. Liles	F-86, 336th FIS	MiG-15
23.2.52	Maj. William T. Whisner Jr	F-86, 25th FIS	MiG-15
27.2.52	Maj. Felix Asla Jr	F-86, 334th FIS	MiG-15
27.2.52	Maj. Van E. Chandler	F-86, 25th FIS	MiG-15
1.3.52	1st Lt John M. Marvin	F-86, 334th FIS	MiG-15
3.3.52	Maj. Donald E. Adams	F-86, 16th FIS	MiG-15 ½
3.3.52	Capt. Alvin R. Moorman	F-86, 16th FIS	MiG-15 ½
3.3.52	Capt. Jack C. Schwab	F-86, 335th FIS	MiG-15
5.3.52	1st Lt Gordon W. Atkinson	F-86, 25th FIS	MiG-15 ½
5.3.52	1st Lt Lloyd D. Juhlin	F-86, 16th FIS	MiG-15
5.3.52	Col Walker M. Mahurin	F-86, 25th FIS	MiG-15
5.3.52	Col Walker M. Mahurin	F-86, 25th FIS	MiG-15 ½
5.3.52	1st Lt Robert H. Moore	F-86, 16th FIS	MiG-15
5.3.52	1st Lt Dale W. Smiley	F-86, 25th FIS	MiG-15
5.3.52	Capt. Kenneth L. Swift	F-86, 51st FIG	MiG-15
5.3.52	Capt. Vincent K. Marzelo USMC	F-86, 16th FIS	MiG-15
6.3.52	Capt. Henry W. Frazier	F-86, 334th FIS	MiG-15
10.3.52	1st Lt Sabin L. Anderson	F-86, 25th FIS	MiG-15 ½
10.3.52	Capt. Ralph E. Banks	F-86, 336th FIS	MiG-15
10.3.52	Capt. Ralph E. Banks	F-86, 336th FIS	MiG-15
10.3.52	1st Lt Homer R. Charlton Jr	F-86, 25th FIS	MiG-15
10.3.52	Capt. Paul R. Henderson Jr	F-86, 25th FIS	MiG-15 ½
10.3.52	1st Lt Richard R. Martin	F-86, 16th FIS	MiG-15
10.3.52	Col Harrison R. Thyng	F-86, 335th FIS	MiG-15

F-86E-10 Sabre 51-2767 flown by Major Felix Asla Jr 336th FIS, 4th FIW

Despite the eight kill markings on *The Chopper*, Major Felix Asla only scored four kills before his death. One of these was when he was with the 334th FIS. Sharkmouths were found on a number of Korean War Sabres, but few were in the same style. The eye and brow design on Asla's Sabre gave the aircraft a distinctly bestial appearance.

Summer 1952
A TRAGIC LOSS

During the late summer of 1952, tragedy struck again within the ranks of the 4th Wing. The 336th Squadron commander, Major Felix Asla, was shot down and killed during a fight with the MiGs. Lieutenant W. P. Dunbar remembers the fatal mission. "We were in the middle of a lot of MiGs that day. Major Asla was chasing one and having a hard time closing on it. Somehow, his wingman had become separated from him as we heard Asla calling for his wingman to make sure he was clear as he pursued the MiG. From out of nowhere, a MiG popped in behind him and blew the Sabre's left wing off with direct

Capt. Sam and Ten Scents, a B-29 of the 19th Bomb Group, sports some of the most colourful nose art to come out of Kadena AB. As with a number of similarly painted B-29s, the cartoon characters represent the crew members.

hits from his 37-mm. Major Asla never took evasive action. My wingman and I talked about it later and the only answer we could come up with was that Asla saw the aircraft coming up behind him and assumed that it was his wingman. He was flying his regular F-86 named *The Chopper*. At the time of this incident, my wingman and myself were flying the oldest F-86s in the squadron, the

F-86A-5s. At the time of his death, the Major had 4.5 kills and if he had had a chance at the MiG he was after, he might have become an ace on that mission."

A ground crewman works in the cockpit of The Chopper, *Felix Asla's F-86E and the aircraft in which he was shot down and killed in the dogfight described here, on 1 August 1952.*

Date	Pilot	Aircraft/Unit	Enemy	Date	Pilot	Aircraft/Unit	Enemy
11.3.52	1st Lt Billy B. Dobbs	F-86, 335th FIS	MiG-15	3.4.52	Capt. Robert H. Moore	F-86, 16th FIS	MiG-15
11.3.52	Capt. Brooks J. Liles	F-86, 336th FIS	MiG-15	4.4.52	Capt. Conrad E. Mattson	F-86, 335th FIS	MiG-15
11.3.52	Capt. Conrad E. Mattson	F-86, 335th FIS	MiG-15	6.4.52	1st Lt Coy L. Austin	F-86, 335th FIS	MiG-15
11.3.52	1st Lt Kenneth H. Rapp	F-86, 336th FIS	MiG-15	6.4.52	Capt. Philip E. Colman	F-86, 335th FIS	MiG-15
12.3.52	Maj. Felix Asla Jr	F-86, 336th FIS	MiG-15	6.4.52	1st Lt Billy B. Dobbs	F-86, 335th FIS	MiG-15
12.3.52	Capt. Ralph E. Banks	F-86, 336th FIS	MiG-15	6.4.52	Capt. Iven C. Kincheloe Jr	F-86, 25th FIS	MiG-15
12.3.52	1st Lt Charles B. Christison	F-86, 336th FIS	MiG-15	13.4.52	Capt. William L. Craig	F-86, 25th FIS	MiG-15
12.3.52	Capt. Conrad E. Mattson	F-86, 335th FIS	MiG-15	13.4.52	Col Francis S. Gabreski	F-86, 51st FIG	MiG-15
16.3.52	Maj. Zane S. Amell	F-86, 335th FIS	MiG-15	13.4.52	1st Lt Donald J. Hemmer	F-86, 25th FIS	MiG-15
16.3.52	Capt. Philip E. Colman	F-86, 335th FIS	MiG-15	13.4.52	1st Lt James A. McCulley	F-86, 16th FIS	MiG-15
16.3.52	1st Lt Robert W. Smith	F-86, 335th FIS	MiG-15	13.4.52	1st Lt Robert L. Sands	F-86, 16th FIS	MiG-15
16.3.52	Lt Col J. S. Payne, USMC	F-86, 336th FIS	MiG-15	13.4.52	Maj. William H. Westcott	F-86, 25th FIS	MiG-15
19.3.52	Capt. Robert T. Latshaw Jr	F-86, 335th FIS	MiG-15	13.4.52	Maj. William H. Westcott	F-86, 25th FIS	MiG-15
20.3.52	Maj. Donald E. Adams	F-86, 16th FIS	MiG-15	18.4.52	Col Harrison R. Thyng	F-86, 335th FIS	MiG-15
20.3.52	Maj. Felix Asla Jr	F-86, 336th FIS	MiG-15	21.4.52	1st Lt Donald J. Hemmer	F-86, 25th FIS	MiG-15 ½
20.3.52	1st Lt Charles G. Carl Jr	F-86, 336th FIS	MiG-15	21.4.52	1st Lt James H. Kasler	F-86, 335th FIS	MiG-15
20.3.52	Capt. Robert J. Love	F-86, 335th FIS	MiG-15	21.4.52	Capt. Brooks J. Liles	F-86, 336th FIS	MiG-15
20.3.52	1st Lt James A. McCulley	F-86, 16th FIS	MiG-15 ½	21.4.52	Capt. Robert J. Love	F-86, 335th FIS	MiG-15
20.3.52	1st Lt Richard H. Schoeneman	F-86, 16th FIS	MiG-15 ½	21.4.52	Capt. Robert J. Love	F-86, 335th FIS	MiG-15
24.3.52	Capt. Robert J. Love	F-86, 335th FIS	MiG-15	21.4.52	Capt. Alvin R. Moorman	F-86, 16th FIS	MiG-15
24.3.52	Capt. Freeland K. Mathews	F-86, 336th FIS	MiG-15	21.4.52	1st Lt Percy L. Saunders	F-86, 25th FIS	MiG-15 ½
24.3.52	1st Lt James A. McCulley	F-86, 16th FIS	MiG-15 ½	21.4.52	1st Lt Robert L. Straub	F-86, 335th FIS	MiG-15
24.3.52	1st Lt Richard H. Schoeneman	F-86, 16th FIS	MiG-15 ½	22.4.52	Capt. Jere J. Lewis	F-86, 334th FIS	MiG-15
25.3.52	Capt. Brooks J. Liles	F-86, 336th FIS	MiG-15	22.4.52	Maj. Elmer W. Harris	F-86, 25th FIS	Ground kill
1.4.52	1st Lt Billy B. Dobbs	F-86, 335th FIS	MiG-15	22.4.52	Capt. Iven C. Kincheloe Jr	F-86, 25th FIS	Ground kill
1.4.52	Col Francis S. Gabreski	F-86, 51st FIG	MiG-15	24.4.52	Capt. Richard H. Schoeneman	F-86, 16th FIS	MiG-15
1.4.52	1st Lt James H. Kasler	F-86, 335th FIS	MiG-15	26.4.52	Maj. William H. Westcott	F-86, 51st FIG	MiG-15
1.4.52	Capt. Iven C. Kincheloe Jr	F-86, 25th FIS	MiG-15	30.4.52	1st Lt Arlan P. Brietenstein	F-86, 16th FIS	MiG-15 ½
1.4.52	Capt. Iven C. KincheloeJr	F-86, 25th FIS	MiG-15	30.4.52	1st Lt Duane K. Bryant	F-86, 335th FIS	MiG-15
1.4.52	Capt. Robert J. Love	F-86, 335th FIS	MiG-15	30.4.52	Maj. Deltis H. Fincher	F-86, 16th FIS	MiG-15 ½
1.4.52	Capt. Robert H. Moore	F-86, 16th FIS	MiG-15	30.4.52	Capt. Robert T. Latshaw Jr	F-86, 335th FIS	MiG-15
1.4.52	1st Lt Robert W. Smith	F-86, 335th FIS	MiG-15	30.4.52	Capt. Conrad E. Mattson	F-86, 335th FIS	MiG-15
1.4.52	Maj. William H. Westcott	F-86, 25th FIS	MiG-15	30.4.52	Capt. Charles D. Owens	F-86, 336th FIS	MiG-15
1.4.52	Maj. William H. Westcott	F-86, 25th FIS	MiG-15	30.4.52	Lt Col James B. Raebel	F-86, 25th FIS	MiG-15
2.4.52	Capt. Iven C. Kincheloe Jr	F-86, 25th FIS	MiG-15	3.5.52	Maj. Donald E. Adams	F-86, 16th FIS	MiG-15
2.4.52	Capt. Robert T. Latshaw Jr	F-86, 335th FIS	MiG-15	3.5.52	Maj. Donald E. Adams	F-86, 16th FIS	MiG-15
2.4.52	1st Lt Dale W. Smiley	F-86, 25th FIS	MiG-15	3.5.52	Capt. Robert T. Latshaw Jr	F-86, 335th FIS	MiG-15
3.4.52	1st Lt Charles G. Carl Jr	F-86, 336th FIS	MiG-15	3.5.52	Capt. Robert J. Love	F-86, 335th FIS	MiG-15

F-86E-10 Sabre flown by Capt. Clifford D. Jolley, 335th FIS, 4th FIW

Captain Clifford Jolley made full play on his surname with the decoration on his F-86. When the aircraft was passed on to 'Jolting' Joe Romack, he renamed it *Patricia II* but kept the vivid skull-and-crossbones insignia. Jolley was the 18th ace of the war and scored two of his seven victories flying one of six solid rocket motor-equipped F-86Fs evaluated by the 335th FIS in September 1952. These motors gave extra acceleration in combat, but at the expense of greatly impaired handling.

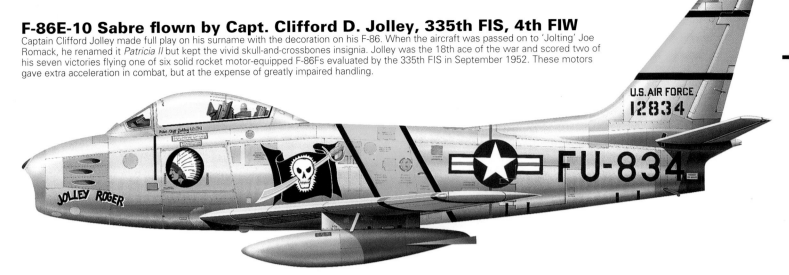

Late 1952
F-80 NEARS REPLACEMENT

Two of the most unique fighter-bomber groups were the 8th and 18th. They had flown only one aircraft type for the length of the war, which was now closing in on 30 months. The 8th had been operating all of the existing F-80Cs and the 18th had inherited all of the F-51Ds in Korea (with the exception of those of the RoK, which operated the Mustang for the entire war). As 1952 came to a close, it had already been decided by the Pentagon and FEAF

Above: The sun rises on another day of combat over Korea. This 35th Fighter Bomber Squadron F-80C is loaded with napalm and is destined for close air support of the UN ground troops from K-13, or Suwon as the locals knew it.

Below: During 1952, the number of squadrons operating the F-80 fighter-bomber in Korea were whittled down to three. The 8th Fighter Group and its three squadrons – the 35th, 36th, and 80th – were working their aircraft during all hours of daylight. This aircraft is from the 'Headhunters' of the 80th FBS at Suwon.

Date	Pilot	Aircraft/Unit	Enemy	Date	Pilot	Aircraft/Unit	Enemy
3.5.52	Lt Col James B. Raebel	F-86, 25th FIS	MiG-15	6.6.52	Maj. Felix Asla Jr	F-86, 336th FIS	MiG-15
4.5.52	Capt. Iven C. Kincheloe Jr	F-86, 25th FIS	Ground kill	6.6.52	Capt. Fred H. Barrett	F-86, 16th FIS	MiG-15
4.5.52	Capt. Iven C. Kincheloe Jr	F-86, 25th FIS	Ground kill	6.6.52	Capt. Paul R. Henderson Jr	F-86, 25th FIS	MiG-15
4.5.52	Capt. Iven C. Kincheloe Jr	F-86, 25th FIS	Ground kill	6.6.52	1st Lt Ramon L. Koenig	F-86, 25th FIS	MiG-15
4.5.52	Capt. Philip E. Colman	F-86, 335th FIS	MiG-15	6.6.52	Capt. Jere J. Lewis	F-86, 334th FIS	MiG-15
4.5.52	Capt. Clifford D. Jolley	F-86, 335th FIS	MiG-15	6.6.52	2nd Lt James F. Low	F-86, 335th FIS	MiG-15
4.5.52	1st Lt James H. Kasler	F-86, 335th FIS	MiG-15	6.6.52	1st Lt John H. Moore	F-86, 335th FIS	MiG-15
4.5.52	1st Lt James A. McCulley	F-86, 16th FIS	Yak-3	6.6.52	1st Lt Robert F. Ronca	F-86, 335th FIS	MiG-15
4.5.52	Capt. Richard H. Schoeneman	F-86, 16th FIS	Il-10	7.6.52	Lt John Andre	F4U-5NL, VMF(N)-513	Yak-9
4.5.52	Maj. Elmer W. Harris	F-86, 25th FIS	Ground kill	11.6.52	2nd Lt James F. Low	F-86, 335th FIS	MiG-15
4.5.52	Maj. Elmer W. Harris	F-86, 25th FIS	Ground kill	11.6.52	2nd Lt James F. Low	F-86, 335th FIS	MiG-15
8.5.52	2nd Lt James F. Low	F-86, 335th FIS	MiG-15	11.6.52	1st Lt Albert B. Smiley	F-86, 335th FIS	MiG-15
8.5.52	1st Lt Albert B. Smiley	F-86, 335th FIS	MiG-15	15.6.52	2nd Lt James F. Low	F-86, 335th FIS	MiG-15
13.5.52	1st Lt Sabin L. Anderson	F-86, 25th FIS	MiG-15	15.6.52	Lt Col Stephen A. Stone Jr	F-86, 334th FIS	MiG-15
13.5.52	Capt. Philip E. Colman	F-86, 335th FIS	MiG-15	15.6.52	Capt. Francis A. Williams	F-86, 25th FIS	MiG-15
13.5.52	Capt. Robert W. McKittrick	F-86, 336th FIS	MiG-15	20.6.52	Col Royal N. Baker	F-86, 336th FIS	La-9
13.5.52	Maj. Lewis W. Powers	F-86, 335th FIS	MiG-15	20.6.52	Capt. Frederick C. Blesse	F-86, 334th FIS	La-9
13.5.52	1st Lt Herschel D. Spitzer	F-86, 336th FIS	MiG-15	20.6.52	1st Lt George J. Wood	F-86, 336th FIS	La-9
15.5.52	1st Lt James H. Kasler	F-86, 335th FIS	MiG-15	21.6.52	1st Lt William D. Angle	F-86, 336th FIS	MiG-15 ½
15.5.52	1st Lt James H. Kasler	F-86, 335th FIS	MiG-15	21.6.52	1st Lt Donald A. McLean	F-86, 336th FIS	MiG-15 ½
15.5.52	1st Lt Albert B. Smiley	F-86, 335th FIS	MiG-15	21.6.52	1st Lt Asa S. Whitehead	F-86, 25th FIS	MiG-15
20.5.52	1st Lt Coy L. Austin	F-86, 335th FIS	MiG-15	25.6.52	1st Lt Robert L. Goodridge	F-86, 335th FIS	MiG-15
20.5.52	Capt. Cleve P. Malone	F-86, 335th FIS	MiG-15	27.6.52	Capt. John R. Spalding	F-86, 25th FIS	MiG-15
20.5.52	1st Lt Robert L. Straub	F-86, 335th FIS	MiG-15	4.7.52	1st Lt Sabin L. Anderson	F-86, 25th FIS	MiG-15
20.5.52	Col Harrison R. Thyng	F-86, 4th FIG	MiG-15	4.7.52	Col Royal N. Baker	F-86, 336th FIS	MiG-15
25.5.52	Capt. Frederick C. Blesse	F-86, 334th FIS	MiG-15	4.7.52	Capt. James A. Horowitz	F-86, 335th FIS	MiG-15
25.5.52	1st Lt James H. Kasler	F-86, 335th FIS	MiG-15	4.7.52	1st Lt Francis A. Humphreys	F-86, 39th FIS	MiG-15
25.5.52	1st Lt John H. Moore	F-86, 335th FIS	MiG-15	4.7.52	Capt. Clifford D. Jolley	F-86, 335th FIS	MiG-15
25.5.52	1st Lt Elbert W. Whitehurst	F-86, 334th FIS	MiG-15	4.7.52	1st Lt Frank O. Keller	F-86, 39th FIS	MiG-15
27.5.52	Maj. Donald E. Adams	F-86, 16th FIS	MiG-15	4.7.52	2nd Lt James F. Low	F-86, 335th FIS	MiG-15
28.5.52	Maj. Elmer W. Harris	F-86, 25th FIS	MiG-15	4.7.52	1st Lt Gerald E. Lyvere	F-86, 336th FIS	MiG-15
28.5.52	Maj. Elmer W. Harris	F-86, 25th FIS	MiG-15	4.7.52	Lt Col Carroll B. McElroy	F-86, 335th FIS	MiG-15
28.5.52	1st Lt Robert C. Ochs	F-86, 25th FIS	MiG-15	4.7.52	Capt. Alvin R. Moorman	F-86, 16th FIS	MiG-15
31.5.52	Maj. William K. Thomas	F-86, 335th FIS	MiG-15	4.7.52	Maj. Lewis W. Powers	F-86, 335th FIS	MiG-15
31.5.52	Lt Col Francis J. Vetort	F-86, 335th FIS	MiG-15	4.7.52	Capt. Raymond W. Staudte	F-86, 51st FIG	MiG-15

that both of these units would transition to the new F-86F models after the first of the year. The 18th was the first to go online with this speedy new close support jet fighter. The 8th Group's 80th Squadron 'Head Hunters' was the final fighter-bomber squadron to receive

the new Sabres. (That story will be expanded upon in the final 1953 portion.)

For a time the only F-80 squadron, the 80th FBS had kept its aircraft in action since the start of the war, and keeping them flying became a constant battle.

March - December 1952
NIGHT-FIGHTER WAR

The all-weather alerts had been handled by the F-82Gs of the 68th Squadron during the early months of the war. When the 68th All Weather Squadron, out of Itazuke AB, Japan, received their F-94Bs, they started sending two aircraft at a time up to Suwon to stand alert. This spread them too thinly to accomplish their primary mission of air defence of a large sector of Japan. This situation prompted the movement of the 319th All Weather Squadron and their F-94Bs from McChord AFB to Suwon (K-13). They became operational in March 1952, and operated from this base for the duration of the war.

The F-94B was strictly a stopgap measure. At first, they were not

F-94Bs like these 319th All Weather Squadron aircraft were front-line USAF interceptors. In Korea they flew barrier patrols for B-29s, but were ineffective against MiGs under careful GCI control.

allowed to go north of the bomb line because the aircraft contained some sophisticated radar equipment, and the possibility of one going down behind enemy lines had too many inherent risks. When high command realised that the F-94Bs could not be effective unless they went deep into North Korea, they were allowed to do so. The B-29 formations were under constant attack from night-flying MiG-15s that were vectored by the

precise ground control radar that the Soviets used so well. The radar used by the F-94 was not capable of giving the B-29s proper protection, so the 319th fighters would fly a barrier patrol, placing themselves between the Yalu River and the B-29s. This meant the MiGs would have to go through them to get to the bomber streams. On many occasions this did happen, and there were bombers that took some serious

battle damage as a result.

The MiG-15 night-fighter was used very effectively through its ground control intercept. This duo proved to be much more effective than the F-94 could counter. However, all was not lost. In May 1952, the Marines of VMF(N)-513 received the new F3D Skyknights, although only 12. They began the task of protecting the B-29 formations. The AN/APQ-35A radar on the F3D was unique in that it would allow the night-fighter to mingle in the formation of bombers with no danger of collision, thereby allowing a more effective pursuit of the enemy in the most threatening part of his attack. In other words, the enemy's GCI could not discern where the Marine night-fighters were. For one reason or another, the Communist pilots were coming up after the B-29s in a very aggressive, reckless manner. Apparently, they realised that the shortcomings of the F-94 had opened up a weak spot and they were determined to get as many B-29 kills as quickly as they could. Several 513 pilots have stated that there was a good possibility the MiGs did not know about the F3D.

Date	Pilot	Aircraft/Unit	Enemy	Date	Pilot	Aircraft/Unit	Enemy
4.7.52	Capt. Francis A. Williams	F-86, 25th FIS	MiG-15	20.8.52	1st Lt William A. Korbel	F-86, 39th FIS	MiG-15
12.7.52	Maj. .Elmer W. Harris	F-86, 25th FIS	MiG-15	29.8.52	1st Lt Charles A. Gabriel	F-86, 16th FIS	MiG-15
14.7.52	F/L Lawrence E. Spurr, RCAF	F-86, 51st FIG	MiG-15	30.8.52	1st Lt Ronald A. Berdoy	F-86, 334th FIS	MiG-15 ½
16.7.52	Capt. Arthur H. McCarthy	F-86, 25th FIS	MiG-15	30.8.52	Capt. Lewis R. Blakeney	F-86, 334th FIS	MiG-15 ½
20.7.52	1st Lt Ronald A. Berdoy	F-86, 334th FIS	MiG-15	30.8.52	Capt. Paul R. Henderson Jr	F-86, 25th FIS	MiG-15
1.8.52	Capt. Daniel J. Dennehy	F-86, 336th FIS	MiG-15	30.8.52	Capt. Leonard W. Lilley	F-86, 334th FIS	MiG-15
1.8.52	Capt. Karl K. Dittmer	F-86, 335th FIS	MiG-15	30.8.52	1st Lt Robert L. Sands	F-86, 16th FIS	MiG-15
1.8.52	1st Lt Alfred M. Miller	F-86, 335th FIS	MiG-15	30.8.52	Capt. Francis A. Williams	F-86, 25th FIS	MiG-15
1.8.52	1st Lt Gene F. Rogge	F-86, 334th FIS	MiG-15	4.9.52	1st Lt Martin J. Bambrick	F-86, 335th FIS	MiG-15
4.8.52	1st Lt Henry A. Crescibene	F-86, 335th FIS	MiG-15	4.9.52	Maj. Frederick C. Blesse	F-86, 334th FIS	MiG-15
5.8.52	F/L Claude A. Lafrance, RCAF	F-86, 39th FIS	MiG-15	4.9.52	Capt. Norman L. Box	F-86, 25th FIS	MiG-15
5.8.52	1st Lt Charles G. Cleveland	F-86, 334th FIS	MiG-15	4.9.52	Capt. Leonard W. Lilley	F-86, 334th FIS	MiG-15
5.8.52	2nd Lt William W. Cook	F-86, 39th FIS	MiG-15 ½	4.9.52	1st Lt Justin W. Livingston	F-86, 335th FIS	MiG-15
5.8.52	2nd Lt Ronald W. Hartrim	F-86, 39th FIS	MiG-15 ½	4.9.52	1st Lt Justin W. Livingston	F-86, 335th FIS	MiG-15
5.8.52	Capt. Robinson Risner	F-86, 336th FIS	MiG-15	4.9.52	Capt. Arthur H. McCarthy	F-86, 25th FIS	MiG-15
5.8.52	Capt. Walter G. Savage	F-86, 39th FIS	MiG-15	4.9.52	1st Lt Ira M. Porter	F-86, 335th FIS	MiG-15
6.8.52	1st Lt Robert E. Barnes	F-86, 334th FIS	MiG-15	4.9.52	1st Lt Ira M. Porter	F-86, 335th FIS	MiG-15
6.8.52	Maj. Frederick C. Blesse	F-86, 334th FIS	MiG-15	4.9.52	1st Lt Robert L. Sands	F-86, 16th FIS	MiG-15
6.8.52	Capt. William S. Borders	F-86, 16th FIS	MiG-15 ½	4.9.52	1st Lt Laverne G. Strange	F-86, 25th FIS	MiG-15
6.8.52	Maj. Westwood H. Fletcher Jr	F-86, 334th FIS	MiG-15	4.9.52	Capt. John E. Taylor Jr	F-86, 335th FIS	MiG-15
6.8.52	Capt. Samuel T. Rohrer	F-86, 16th FIS	MiG-15 ½	4.9.52	1st Lt Garry A. Willard Jr	F-86, 25th FIS	MiG-15
6.8.52	Capt. William J. Ryan	F-86, 334th FIS	MiG-15	5.9.52	Maj. Richard L. Ayersman	F-86, 334th FIS	MiG-15
6.8.52	Capt. William J. Ryan	F-86, 334th FIS	MiG-15	5.9.52	Capt. Norman L. Box	F-86, 25th FIS	MiG-15
7.8.52	2nd Lt John A. Inferrera	F-86, 39th FIS	MiG-15	5.9.52	Maj. Aubrey C. Moulton Jr	F-86, 25th FIS	MiG-15
7.8.52	Capt. Clifford D. Jolley	F-86, 335th FIS	MiG-15	5.9.52	Capt. Robinson Risner	F-86, 336th FIS	MiG-15
7.8.52	Capt. Clifford D. Jolley	F-86, 335th FIS	MiG-15	7.9.52	1st Lt Cecil G. Foster	F-86, 16th FIS	MiG-15
7.8.52	Maj. Charles D. Owens	F-86, 336th FIS	MiG-15	7.9.52	2nd Lt Paul A. Kauttu	F-86, 16th FIS	MiG-15 ½
8.8.52	Capt. Clifford D. Jolley	F-86,335th FIS	MiG-15	7.9.52	1st Lt Edgar N. Powell	F-86, 16th FIS	MiG-15 ½
8.8.52	Capt. James E. Tilton	F-86, 16th FIS	MiG-15	7.9.52	1st Lt William E. Powers	F-86, 16th FIS	MiG-15 ½
8.8.52	Maj. Philip H. Van Sickle	F-86, 335th FIS	MiG-15	7.9.52	Capt. John E. Taylor Jr	F-86, 335th FIS	MiG-15 ½
9.8.52	1st Lt Heber M. Butler	F-86, 16th FIS	MiG-15	8.9.52	Maj. Richard L. Ayersman	F-86, 334th FIS	MiG-15
9.8.52	Lt Peter Carmichael, RN	Sea Fury FB.Mk 11 802 Sqn	MiG-15	8.9.52	Maj. Frederick C. Blesse	F-86, 334th FIS	MiG-15
9.8.52	Lt Carmichael and flight	Sea Fury FB.Mk 11 802 Sqn	MiG-15	8.9.52	Maj. Frederick C. Blesse	F-86, 334th FIS	MiG-15
20.8.52	Maj. Edward P. Ballinger	F-86, 334th FIS	MiG-15	8.9.52	Capt. William B. Craig	F-86, 334th FIS	MiG-15
20.8.52	Maj. Frederick C. Blesse	F-86, 334th FIS	MiG-15	8.9.52	F/L Ernest A. Glover, RCAF	F-86, 334th FIS	MiG-15

F3D-2 flown by Maj. Willam Stratton and MSgt Hans Hoglind, VMF(N)-513
The first conclusive combat between jet aircraft at night took place just after midnight on 2 November 1952, when Marine pilot Bill Stratton and radar operator Hans Hoglind picked up a contact which they followed to a visual identification as a 'Yak-15' (a straight-wing Russian-built jet fighter not confirmed as having ever served with the North Koreans). The enemy aircraft received three bursts of cannon fire and fell in flames, the Skyknight narrowly avoiding damage when it flew through debris from the falling jet.

November 1952
FIRST KILL FOR THE F3D

The first night kill by the Skyknight was recorded on 2 November, when Major W. T. Stratton shot down a Yak-15. Five days later, Captain O. R. Davis shot down a night-flying MiG-15.

Both of these kills were visuals that were identified by the exhaust pattern. On the night of 10 December, VMF(N)-513 recorded a 'first': a kill that did not involve any visual contact. Lieutenant Joseph

Corvi and his radar operator Sergeant Dan George picked up a bogie on the screen somewhere in the vicinity of Sinanju. The distance between the hunter and its quarry was too great to obtain a visual, so when Corvi fired

his 20-mm cannon it was at what he saw on the radar screen. Corvi later reported that, "we did not know we had made a kill until my R/O reported a wing and flaming debris flying past us."

It turned out that the enemy aircraft had been none other than a Po-2, which was one of the toughest aircraft to knock down. Some radars would not have picked up the mostly wooden aircraft at all.

4 October 1952
MiGS OVER THE YALU

The quality of the average MiG pilot was not getting any better, and it was becoming more and more obvious that the large formations met at altitude were training classes with very inexperienced pilots at the controls. Nonetheless, there were still some 'honchos' flying the MiGs who could mix it up with any F-86 pilot. Every time the two swept-wing fighters did meet over the Yalu, the primary tactic was to turn into the oncoming enemy. This created a closure speed of about Mach 2, and the reaction time was measured in

tenths of a second. A majority of these encounters were initially made at high altitudewhere bailing out could be fatal.The following incident clearly illustrates this fact.

Lieutenant Colonel R. E. Keyes, who was the Maintenance and Supply Group commander of the 4th Fighter Wing, recounts his MiG kill, made at point blank range. "I was flying missions with the 336th Squadron and this particular mission occurred on 4 October 1952. We were part of a fighter sweep over the Yalu River. Shortly after we had crossed the

bomb line, we were notified that there was very heavy MiG activity in the area where we were headed. We continued to climb to 40,000 ft, and about 40 miles south of the river we encountered two MiG-15s that were also heading north. They were moving extremely fast. Blue Lead tried to catch them but could not close the gap. As Blue-3, I observed a MiG at my three o'clock position. My wingman called and indicated that I should watch him, as he was turning into our formation. I turned slightly right, causing the enemy fighter to pass less than 60 ft in front of me: seeing that he would cross my nose, I opened fire, hitting him in the engine compartment. The MiG was a

Date	Pilot	Aircraft/Unit	Enemy	Date	Pilot	Aircraft/Unit	Enemy
9.9.52	F/L Ernest A. Glover, RCAF	F-86, 334th FIS	MiG-15	26.9.52	1st Lt Cecil G. Foster	F-86, 16th FIS	MiG-15
9.9.52	1st Lt Simon K. Anderson	F-86, 25th FIS	MiG-15	26.9.52	1st Lt Cecil G. Foster	F-86, 16th FIS	MiG-15
9.9.52	1st Lt Walter R. Copeland	F-86, 25th FIS	MiG-15	26.9.52	Lt Col Theon E. Markham	F-86, 39th FIS	MiG-15 ½
9.9.52	A1C Robert L. Davis	B-29, 343rd BS	prop. ½	28.9.52	1st Lt Charles G. Cleveland	F-86, 334th FIS	MiG-15
9.9.52	1st Lt Francis A. Humphreys	F-86, 39th FIS	MiG-15	28.9.52	Capt. Tom P. Garvin	F-86, 334th FIS	MiG-15
9.9.52	Lt Col Theon E. Markham	F-86, 39th FIS	MiG-15	28.9.52	Maj. Alex J. Gillis, USMC	F-86, 335th FIS	MiG-15
9.9.52	2nd Lt Thomas L. Moore	F-86, 25th FIS	MiG-15	28.9.52	Maj. Alex J. Gillis, USMC	F-86, 335th FIS	MiG-15
9.9.52	A1C Robert W. Smith	B29, 343rd BS	prop. ½	29.9.52	1st Lt Joseph R. Butler	F-86, 39th FIS	MiG-15
10.9.52	Capt. Jesse G. Folmar, USN	F4U-5, VMA-312	MiG-15	29.9.52	Lt Col Albert S. Kelly	F-86, 25th FIS	MiG-15
12.9.52	1st Lt Joe A. Caple	F-86, 39th FIS	MiG-15	2.10.52	1st Lt Francis A. Humphreys	F-86, 39th FIS	MiG-15
14.9.52	Capt. Norman L. Box	F-86, 25th FIS	MiG-15	3.10.52	Maj. Frederick C. Blesse	F-86, 334th FIS	MiG-15
14.9.52	Maj. John J. Hockery	F-86, 39th FIS	MiG-15	3.10.52	1st Lt Craig R. Canady	F-86, 25th FIS	MiG-15 ½
14.9.52	Capt. Leonard W. Lilley	F-86, 334th FIS	MiG-15	3.10.52	1st Lt Jesse L. Saunders	F-86, 39th FIS	MiG-15
15.9.52	Maj. Frederick C. Blesse	F-86, 334th FIS	MiG-15	3.10.52	1st Lt Asa S. Whitehead	F-86, 25th FIS	MiG-15 ½
15.9.52	1st Lt Charles G. Cleveland	F-86, 334th FIS	MiG-15	4.10.52	Capt. Manuel J. Fernandez Jr	F-86, 334th FIS	MiG-15
15.9.52	1st Lt Calvin G. Davey	F-86, 25th FIS	MiG-15	4.10.52	Lt Col Ralph E. Keyes	F-86, 336th FIS	MiG-15
15.9.52	Capt. Clifford D. Jolley	F-86, 335th FIS	MiG-15	9.10.52	Capt. Karl K. Dittmer	F-86, 335th FIS	MiG-15
15.9.52	Lt Col Carroll B. McElroy	F-86, 335th FIS	MiG-15	9.10.52	Capt. Karl K. Dittmer	F-86, 335th FIS	MiG-15
15.9.52	Capt. Robinson Risner	F-86, 336th FIS	MiG-15	11.10.52	Capt. Clyde A. Curtin	F-86, 335th FIS	MiG-15
15.9.52	Maj. Herman W. Visscher	F-86, 25th FIS	MiG-15	11.10.52	Maj. William B. Hoelscher	F-86, 335th FIS	MiG-15
15.9.52	Maj. Alex J. Gillis USMC	F-86, 335th FIS	MiG-15	11.10.52	Capt. Clifford D. Jolley	F-86, 335th FIS	MiG-15
16.9.52	Capt. Richard J. Condrick	F-86, 39th FIS	MiG-15 ½	11.10.52	1st Lt Robert W. McBride	F-86, 39th FIS	MiG-15
16.9.52	Capt. William L. Craig	F-86, 39th FIS	MiG-15	11.10.52	1st Lt Jesse L. Saunders	F-86, 39th FIS	MiG-15
16.9.52	Capt. Leonard W. Lilley	F-86, 334th FIS	MiG-15	11.10.52	S/L James D. Lindsay, RCAF	F-86, 39th FIS	MiG-15
16.9.52	Capt. Alphonso R. Pena	F-86, 335th FIS	MiG-15	12.10.52	1st Lt Charles A. Gabriel	F-86, 16th FIS	MiG-15
16.9.52	Capt. Walter G. Savage	F-86, 39th FIS	MiG-15 ½	12.10.52	1st Lt Paul A. Kauttu	F-86, 16th FIS	MiG-15
16.9.52	F/L Ernest A. Glover, RCAF	F-86, 334th FIS	MiG-15	12.10.52	Maj. Vernon J. Lyle	F-86, 25th FIS	MiG-15
17.9.52	Maj. Frederick C. Blesse	F-86, 334th FIS	MiG-15	18.10.52	1st Lt Paul A. Kauttu	F-86, 16th FIS	MiG-15
21.9.52	1st Lt Simon K. Anderson	F-86, 25th FIS	MiG-15	18.10.52	1st Lt Kirk Vandeventer	F-86, 39th FIS	MiG-15
21.9.52	1st Lt Joseph E. Fields Jr	F-86, 336th FIS	MiG-15	22.10.52	Maj. Robinson Risner	F-86, 336th FIS	MiG-15
21.9.52	Capt. Richard B. Moyle	F-86, 336th FIS	MiG-15	23.10.52	Capt. Houston N. Tuel	F-86, 336th FIS	MiG-15
21.9.52	Capt. Robinson Risner	F-86, 336th FIS	MiG-15	23.10.52	Capt. Murray A. Winslow	F-86, 335th FIS	MiG-15
21.9.52	Capt. Robinson Risner	F-86, 336th FIS	MiG-15	25.10.52	Col Royal N. Baker	F-86, 336th FIS	MiG-15
26.9.52	2nd Lt Glenn A. Carus	F-86, 39th FIS	MiG-15 ½	25.10.52	1st Lt Joseph E. Fields Jr	F-86, 336th FIS	MiG-15 ½
26.9.52	1st Lt Charles G. Cleveland	F-86, 334th FIS	MiG-15	25.10.52	Sqn Ldr Graham S. Hulse, RAF	F-86, 336th FIS	MiG-15 ½

blur as he flew past me.

"Glancing to the left, I saw an explosion. I turned hard left and came out behind him at his four o'clock position. Locking on once again, I fired a long burst, and as I closed on his six o'clock I saw the canopy fly off, followed by the seat. Both of these narrowly missed my canopy and then hit the side of my Sabre. The MiG pilot had already separated from the seat and passed about 10 ft under my right wing. He was clad in a bright flying suit and had red hair, no helmet, and his arms were flailing and his cheeks were puffed.

Since this ejection occurred at about Mach 1 and above 40,000 ft, this situation would normally have been fatal. As I passed over him, I looked back and noticed his chute deploying. I turned my F-86 back around and came by him again, for a picture with my gun camera. As I passed close by him, he appeared unconscious – head down on his chest and arms dangling at his side. The temperature outside my cockpit was about minus 40°. There was no sign of an oxygen mask. I assumed he died from the cold and lack of oxygen."

*Lt Ray Lewis was the pilot of **Rebel Girl**, an RF-51 of the 45th TRS, 67th TRW at Kimpo. The unit carried out the vast majority of FEAF's tactical reconnaissance work.*

November/December 1952

THE WAR GRINDS ON

The war on the ground was vicious and bloody, even though the MLR had been stable for some time. As 1952 came to a close, the war was fought one hill at a time, and the Chinese commanders were heedless of the slaughter of their troops, with human wave attacks still their primary offensive tactic. The firepower of the UN ground forces was impressive, even by World War II standards, and the intensity of the aerial close support far exceeded anything that had been seen by either side in the past. FEAF records show that 30 per cent of all United Nations offensive air strikes were done in support of friendly ground troops. In the European Theatre in World War II, close support from the air never exceeded 10 per cent.

In November, the Chinese field commanders threw everything they had in an attempt to capture Sniper Ridge and Triangle Hill. To help counter this, the 5th Air Force flew 2,374 close support sorties. The enemy body count was too high to tally and yet they continued to assault the two objectives, and finally were able to retake Triangle Hill with heavy casualties.

While the Chinese were close to retaking Triangle, Major Charles Loring, an F-80 pilot in the 80th Fighter Bomber Squadron, was leading a flight of four against gun positions shelling GIs who were

RF-80s, like this 15th Tactical Reconnaissance Squadron aircraft, were no match for MiGs and needed heavy escort when over the northernmost parts of North Korea.

holding on. On the first pass, Loring's aircraft was so severely damaged that he turned it over and dove straight into the gun emplacement. He was posthumously awarded the Medal of Honor.

There were 53 Sabres lost to enemy action in 1952. September proved to be the best month for MiG kills, with 63 recorded. But it was costly, in that nine F-86s were shot down and another three were lost to operational causes (more than likely, they ran out of fuel before reaching base). Stable front lines and a fight that took place from prepared emplacements were reminiscent of the trench warfare of World War I.

As far as aerial combat over North Korea goes, the most impressive year was yet to come. In less than seven months of combat before the war ended, 308 enemy aircraft would go down to the Sabres, as detailed in Part Four. **Warren Thompson**

Date	Pilot	Aircraft/Unit	Enemy	Date	Pilot	Aircraft/Unit	Enemy
26.10.52	1st Lt E. J. Hatzenbuehler Jr	F-86, 39th FIS	MiG-15 ½	26.11.52	S/L James D. Lindsay, RCAF	F-86, 39th FIS	MiG-15
26.10.52	Capt. John E. Taylor Jr	F-86, 335th FIS	MiG-15	30.11.52	Lt A. Joseph Corvi, USMC	F3D, VMF(N)-513	Po-2
26.10.52	1st Lt Edward H. Webster	F-86, 39th FIS	MiG-15 ½	2.12.52	1st Lt James F. Low	F-86, 335th FIS	MiG-15
1.11.52	Col Royal N. Baker	F-86, 335th FIS	MiG-15	3.12.52	1st Lt Clyde R. Gilbert	F-86, 39th FIS	MiG-15
1.11.52	Capt. Robert A. Windoffer	F-86, 336th FIS	MiG-15	3.12.52	2nd Lt Robert R. Hodge	F-86, 39th FIS	MiG-15 ½
2.11.52	1st Lt Thomas R. White	F-86, 16th FIS	MiG-15	3.12.52	1st Lt Edward H. Webster	F-86, 39th FIS	MiG-15 ½
3.11.52	Maj. William Stratton, USMC	F3D, VMF(N)-513	Yak-15	4.12.52	Maj. Robinson Risner	F-86, 336th FIS	MiG-15
6.11.52	Lt Col Albert S. Kelly	F-86, 25th FIS	MiG-15 ½	7.12.52	Col Royal N. Baker	F-86, 335th FIS	MiG-15 ½
6.11.52	1st Lt James W. Kumpf	F-86, 25th FIS	MiG-15 ½	7.12.52	Col Royal N. Baker	F-86, 335th FIS	MiG-15
6.11.52	1st Lt Kirk Vandeventer	F-86, 39th FIS	MiG-15	7.12.52	1st Lt Cecil G. Foster	F-86, 16th FIS	MiG-15
6.11.52	Capt. O. R. Davis, USMC	F3D, VMF(N)-513	MiG-15	7.12.52	Lt Col Louis A. Green	F-86, 336th FIS	MiG-15
15.11.52	1st Lt Calvin G. Davey	F-86, 25th FIS	MiG-15	7.12.52	1st Lt Edmund G. Hepner	F-86, 16th FIS	MiG-15
17.11.52	Col Royal N. Baker	F-86, 335th FIS	MiG-15	7.12.52	1st Lt John H. Ludwig	F-86, 335th FIS	MiG-15 ½
17.11.52	2nd Lt Stuart L. Brown Jr	F-86, 39th FIS	MiG-15	7.12.52	Capt. Houston N. Tuel	F-86, 336th FIS	MiG-15
17.11.52	Maj. William L. Cosby	F-86, 336th FIS	MiG-15	7.12.52	Flt Lt J. M. Nichols, RAF	F-86, 335th FIS	MiG-15
17.11.52	Maj. Edwin L. Heller	F-86, 16th FIS	MiG-15	???	Flt Lt J. M. Nichols, RAF	F-86, 335th FIS	MiG-15
17.11.52	Lt Col George I. Ruddell	F-86, 39th FIS	MiG-15	8.12.52	Maj. Edwin L. Heller	F-86, 16th FIS	MiG-15 ½
17.11.52	Lt Col Chester L. Van Etten	F-86, 335th FIS	MiG-15	8.12.52	1st Lt Gene H. Woodworth	F-86, 16th FIS	MiG-15 ½
18.11.52	Lt Col Albert S. Kelly	F-86, 25th FIS	MiG-15	9.12.52	Sqn Ldr Graham S. Hulse, RAF	F-86, 336th FIS	MiG-15
18.11.52	Capt. Leonard W. Lilley	F-86, 334th FIS	MiG-15	10.12.52	1st Lt James F. Low	F-86, 335th FIS	MiG-15
18.11.52	Lt(jg) John D. Middleton, USN	F9F-2, VF-781	MiG-15	16.12.52	Col Royal N. Baker	F-86, 335th FIS	MiG-15 ½
18.11.52	Lt Royce Williams, USN	F9F-2, VF-781	MiG-15	16.12.52	Capt. Clyde A. Curtin	F-86, 335th FIS	MiG-15
20.11.52	1st Lt Glenn A. Carus	F-86, 39th FIS	MiG-15	16.12.52	Capt. Manuel J. Fernandez Jr	F-86, 334th FIS	MiG-15
20.11.52	1st Lt David P. Copeland	F-86, 335th FIS	MiG-15	16.12.52	Capt. Leonard W. Lilley	F-86, 334th FIS	MiG-15
20.11.52	Capt. Manuel J. Fernandez Jr	F-86, 334th FIS	MiG-15	16.12.52	Capt. Jack E. Mass	F-86, 335th FIS	MiG-15 ½
20.11.52	Capt. Paul E. Jones	F-86, 39th FIS	MiG-15	16.12.52	1st Lt Ira M. Porter	F-86, 335th FIS	MiG-15
20.11.52	Capt. Paul E. Jones	F-86, 39th FIS	MiG-15	18.12.52	1st Lt James F. Low	F-86, 335th FIS	MiG-15
21.11.52	Maj. James P. Hagerstrom	F-86, 334th FIS	MiG-15	22.12.52	1st Lt Stuart L. Brown Jr	F-86, 39th FIS	MiG-15
21.11.52	Maj. Vernon J. Lyle	F-86, 25th FIS	MiG-15	22.12.52	1st Lt Harold E. Fischer	F-86, 39th FIS	MiG-15
21.11.52	1st Lt Richard B. Smith Jr	F-86, 39th FIS	MiG-15	22.12.52	Capt. Herbert Weber	F-86, 334th FIS	MiG-15
22.11.52	1st Lt Cecil G. Foster	F-86, 16th FIS	MiG-15	23.12.52	1st Lt John A. Inferrera	F-86, 39th FIS	MiG-15
22.11.52	Maj. Louis A. Green	F-86, 336th FIS	MiG-15	25.12.52	Capt. William S. Borders	F-86, 16th FIS	MiG-15
22.11.52	Capt. Howard P. Mann	F-86, 39th FIS	MiG-15	25.12.52	Maj. James P. Hagerstrom	F-86, 335th FIS	MiG-15
23.11.52	1st Lt William O. Johnson	F-86, 39th FIS	MiG-15	28.12.52	1st Lt Harold E. Fischer	F-86, 39th FIS	MiG-15
26.11.52	1st Lt Harold E. Fischer	F-86, 39th FIS	MiG-15	28.12.52	2nd Lt Biffle O. Pittman	F-86, 39th FIS	MiG-15

Focke-Wulf Fw 187 Falke

Even when converted from a single-seat fighter to a two-seat Zerstörer, the Fw 187 was extremely fast and manoeuvrable for a twin-engined aircraft. Fortunately for the Allies, the Luftwaffe stuck with the much less impressive Messerschmitt Bf 110.

Kurt Tank's Falcon

The German aircraft industry produced many advanced and innovative aircraft during World War II, most of which saw little or no service due to their appearance after the tide of war had turned. Less well known are aircraft developed in the early war years, such as the potentially unbeatable Focke-Wulf Fw 187, rejected for political rather than technical reasons.

In the mid-1930s, the idea of a twin-engined, single-seat fighter was considered novel. Indeed, the only such aircraft of pre-war origin to enjoy any success was the Lockheed P-38 Lightning. The benefits were obvious: by careful streamlining, the twin-engined aircraft could enjoy the same performance as a single-engined fighter, but could be much larger, allowing it to deliver a greater punch and carry much more fuel. With such potential rewards, Focke-Wulf's brilliant technical director, Dipl.-Ing. Kurt Tank, could hardly ignore the concept.

Kurt Tank began his studies into a twin-engined fighter in 1935, and by the following year had basic drawings available, which were touted to the Technische Amt. Despite impressive performance calculations, little interest was shown in the scheme, the reason being that it was believed bombers of sufficient speed were under development to render the need for fighter escorts unnecessary. Tank persisted, showing his drawings to the head of the TA's development section, Wolfram von Richthofen. Here, at last, his proposal was well received, and he was given authorisation for a three-prototype batch of an aircraft that was given the service designation Fw 187. Such an authorisation demanded an official requirement, and one was drawn around Tank's own proposal, with one major exception: the Daimler-Benz DB 600 engines which Tank favoured were to be replaced by Junkers Jumo 210s.

Tank set his most experienced designer, Oberingenieur R. Blaser, to work on the new

Despite being designed for the new Daimler-Benz DB 600 engines, the Fw 187 V1 emerged with Junkers Jumo 210Ds as fitted on early Bf 109s and Ju 87s. The two rows of dark spots at the rear of the port engine cowl are the externally-mounted engine instruments. Also noteworthy are the hinged radiator intakes.

In addition to Jumo 210G engines with fixed intakes, the Fw 187 V2 incorporated numerous minor improvements, including a narrower-chord rudder with a larger trim tab. At one time, the V2 also tested a twin mainwheel arrangement.

aircraft. Speed was the priority, and in order to achieve maximum performance the fuselage was made as small as humanly possible. 'Humanly' was the right description, for the fuselage at its widest could barely accommodate a pilot of average build. This left scant room for a dashboard, so certain engine instruments were located externally, on the inboard sides of the engine nacelles.

Otherwise, the Fw 187 was a conventional aircraft. The main structural component comprised the fuselage, the wing centre-section and the engine nacelles. Inboard, the wing was anhedralled, but the outer panels, fixed outboard of the engine nacelles, had dihedral, resulting in an inverted-gull layout. The wing was of high aspect ratio and featured long ailerons and small flaps. The undercarriage was hydraulically actuated, and all three units were fully retractable. Small glazed panels were installed in the lower part of the nose to improve the pilot's view for landing.

Work on the Fw 187 V1 first prototype was completed swiftly, and it was rolled out in the spring of 1937. No record has survived of its first flight date, but the pilot on the occasion was Dipl.-Ing. Flugkapitän Hans Sander. Under the power of two 680-hp (507-kW) Jumo 210Da engines driving Junkers-Hamilton three-bladed propellers, the Fw 187 V1 immediately displayed outstanding speed performance, notching up 326 mph (525 km/h), almost 50 mph (80 km/h) faster than the speed achieved by the much-vaunted Messerschmitt Bf 109B that was the talk of the Luftwaffe at the time. The Fw 187 was twice the weight of the Bf 109, too. Climb and dive speeds were impressive, and led to the name Falke (falcon) being bestowed on the type.

Further flight trials revealed no serious flaws, although there were several incidents. In one, the V1 suffered a starboard undercarriage collapse, with minor damage. In another, during diving tail flutter trials, the balance weight added to the rudder to neutralise flutter up to a

The extremely narrow fuselage and neatness of the armament installation can be seen in this view of one of the pre-production aircraft. Addition of a second seat eliminated any rear view (and the radio operator could see nothing in that direction) but the clear undernose panel provided a rare downwards view for a fighter.

certain speed actually incurred the fatal phenomenon. With his controls locked, Sander was preparing to bale out when the 'anti-flutter' weight broke off, ending the vibration and returning the aircraft to full control. During its trials career, the V1 was tested with a high-pressure twinwheel undercarriage, and the propellers were changed for VDM units. A pair of 0.31-in (7.9-mm) MG 17 machine-guns was added, one on each side of the fuselage.

In the summer, the V2 joined the flight trials programme. This aircraft had numerous minor improvements, including revised tail feathers with a narrow chord rudder and balanced elevators. The Jumo 210G was fitted, externally distinguished by stub exhausts and a fixed radiator bath in place of the semi-retractable unit of the Jumo 210Da. The tailwheel was made only semi-retractable.

Heavy fighter concept

Some months even before the V1 had taken to the air, the Fw 187 in its original form had been overtaken by events. The type's original sponsor, von Richthofen, had been replaced in the TA development section in June 1936 by Ernst Udet. Although this outstanding fighter pilot recognised the Fw 187's performance, he could not accept that it could fight effectively since its manoeuvrability (although good for an aircraft of its size) was considerably less than

In this view the slim fuselage and inverted-gull wing layout are shown to advantage. This aircraft was the third prototype, and the first aircraft with two seats.

that of a single-engined fighter. In the latter part of 1936 the Fw 187 programme was reviewed, and Tank's original proposal for a fast, long-legged interceptor was replaced by a requirement for a *Zerstörer*. This heavy fighter concept insisted on a two-place cockpit and heavy armament.

By the time the new demand came down from the TA, Focke-Wulf had completed too much of the V1 and V2 to change, and so it was the V3 third prototype which was the first to have two seats. Squeezing one man into the original Fw 187 had proved marginal, but the addition of a second necessitated much redesign. Blaser kept as close to the original as possible, and achieved his goal with only

Seen here after a fire in the starboard engine necessitated a forced landing, the Fw 187 V3 displays the new canopy needed to accommodate a second crewman, and (just visible) the trough for one of the additional pair of dummy 20-mm cannon. Another minor change is the revised layout of the engine instruments.

minimal alteration to overall dimensions. The radio operator was crammed in behind the pilot, facing aft. This pushed the fuselage fuel tank further aft, so, to compensate for the change in centre-of-gravity, the engines were moved forward. The rear of the engine nacelles, which on the V1 and V2 had projected beyond the trailing edge, now ended in line with the rear of the wing, and allowed the fitment of larger electrically-actuated flaps which offset the increase in landing weight.

A large 'greenhouse' canopy was fitted, arranged in two sections. The forward section hinged up from the front of the cockpit, while the aft hinged back from the rear. A simple flat-pane windshield was fitted. Mock 20-mm cannon were added in the lower corners of the fuselage to represent the *Zerstörer* weapon load. So equipped, the V3 flew on Jumo 210G power in the spring of 1938. In an early trial an engine fire caused a forced landing in which the aircraft lost both main undercarriage legs, although damage to the rest of the aircraft was minor. Soon after, on 14 May 1938, the V1 was lost in a needless aerobatic accident which cost test pilot Bauer his life. While the aircraft could not be faulted for either accident, the two crashes did not help the already tenuous cause of the Fw 187.

Nevertheless, sufficient support remained for the authorisation of a further three prototypes. The first two of these, the V4 and V5, were little changed from the V3, apart from featuring a blown windscreen which gave the pilot a much better forward view. However, the V6 was a much different aircraft. At last, Tank was

allowed to put his original engine choice into an Fw 187. With 1,000-hp (764-kW) available from the DB 600As at take-off, the V6 flew in early 1939 and provided a considerable leap in performance. The aircraft featured a surface cooling system, which led to innumerable problems, but, during accurately timed runs in October 1939, the V6 clocked 394.5 mph (635 km/h) in level flight, an outstanding achievement for what was a true service prototype.

By then three further Falkes were flying, the Fw 187A-0 pre-production batch. These aircraft were truly representative of the intended service machine, although they returned to Jumo power with a consequent drop in performance when compared to the V6. These aircraft introduced heavy armoured-glass windscreens, and an extra pair of MG 17s in the fuselage sides. The weight continued to rise, and without the extra power of the always-intended DB 600s, handling began to suffer. One weapon they clearly lacked was a rear-facing gun, which immediately ruled out the chance of a contract for the *Zerstörer* requirement. Even after successful official trials at Rechlin, the RLM remained steadfast in its support for the Messerschmitt Bf 110 in this role.

The end of the Falke

With the RLM decision there was no hope of getting the Fw 187 into production, yet the aircraft did play an active, if entirely insignificant, part in the conflict. The three Fw 187A-0s were retained by Focke-Wulf for various trials. In early 1940, as the RAF began to range into Germany on bombing forays, the aircraft manufacturers formed factory defence squadrons, known as *Industrie-Schutzstaffel*, manned by test pilots. At Bremen, Focke-Wulf flew the Fw 187A-0s in defence of the factory and, it is claimed, Dipl.-Ing. Mehlhorn used the

Owing to the spindly fuselage and wings, the Fw 187 appeared to have engines far too large for the design. In truth, the Jumo 210s fitted to the pre-production aircraft were not powerful enough to realise the type's true potential.

type to score several kills. There is little evidence to support or refute this claim.

What is certain is that the Propaganda Ministry issued several photographs of the three *Industrie-Schutzstaffel* aircraft claiming these to be the Luftwaffe's new *Zerstörer*. Bf 110 crews might have looked on and wished that it were so, especially after the mauling meted out by the RAF during the Battle of Britain. In the winter of 1940 all three aircraft were dispatched to Norway, where they were unofficially evaluated by service pilots, and in the summer of 1942 one appeared at Vaerlose in Denmark, attached to the Luftschiess-schule. The final record of the type is made in 1943, when it was being considered as a night-fighter. The fuselage proved so narrow that there was no practical way to fit in the necessary radar and equipment. By that time, Focke-Wulf were engaged on another twin-engined fighter programme: the Ta 154.

In retrospect, it is difficult to assess whether the intransigence of the TA and RLM cost the Luftwaffe a battle-winning weapon. Certainly

The V4 was fitted with a blown single-piece windscreen, but lacked the radio mast of the V3.

The V5 was similar to the V4. It also incorporated the modified windscreen, as did the V6.

The V6 was the only aircraft to fly with the DB 600A engines for which the type was designed.

in its original single-seat form the Fw 187 would have proved a formidable foe for any single-engined fighter. Even as a two-seat Zerstörer, the Fw 187 could surely have performed better in the escort fighter role than the Messerschmitt Bf 110 did during the fighting over England. However, had work on the Fw 187 progressed, it would no doubt have had a detrimental effect on the development of another Focke-Wulf design, one which would in mid-1941 give the Royal Air Force its most unpleasant surprise of the war: the Fw 190.

David Donald

Many propaganda pictures were produced to give the impression that the Fw 187 was in squadron service. The photographs only ever showed the three A-0 pre-production aircraft, of the Focke-Wulf Industrie-Schutzstaffel at Bremen, marked as '1', '4' and '7'. These aircraft did see service together during a brief sojourn with a fighter unit in Norway, and one was later used by a training unit.

Right: The Luftwaffe threw away a winner when it rejected the Fw 187. By the time the pre-production aircraft were complete, the RLM had lost interest. Had the type been developed from the outset with the intended DB 600 engine, its performance could surely not have been ignored.

Fw 187 production

Fw 187 V1	D-AANA	Jumo 210Da	semi-retractable radiator, fully retractable tailwheel
Fw 187 V2	–	Jumo 210G	revised fin, semi-retractable tailwheel, balanced elevators
Fw 187 V3	D-ORHP	Jumo 210G	two-seat cockpit, two mock-up 20-mm cannon, redesigned engine nacelles
Fw 187 V4	D-OSNP	Jumo 210G	fixed, blown windscreen
Fw 187 V5	D-OTGN	Jumo 210G	similar to V4
Fw 187 V6	CI+NY	DB 600A	surface cooling system
Fw 187A-01	–	Jumo 210Ga	all three pre-production aircraft with two MG FF cannon
Fw 187A-02	–	Jumo 210Ga	and four MG 17 machine-guns, flat-pane armoured
Fw 187A-03	–	Jumo 210Ga	windscreen

Specification
Fw 187A-0

Powerplant: two Junkers Jumo 210Ga 12-cylinder liquid-cooled engines, each rated at 700 hp (522 kW) for take-off and 730 hp (545 kW) at 3,280 ft (1000 m)

Performance: maximum speed 322 mph (518 km/h) at sea level, 329 mph (529 km/h) at 13,780 ft (4200 m); initial climb rate 3,445 ft (1050 m) per minute; climb to 6,560 ft (2000 m) in 1.9 minutes, to 19,685 ft (6000 m) in 5.8 minutes; service ceiling 32,810 ft (10000 m)

Weights: empty 8,157 lb (3700 kg); maximum take-off 11,023 lb (5000 kg)

Dimensions: wing span 50 ft 2⅕ in (15.30 m); length 36 ft 6 in (11.12 m); height 12 ft 7⅗ in (3.85 m); wing area 327.22 sq ft (30.4 m²)

Armament: two 20-mm MG FF cannon in lower fuselage and four 0.31-in (7.9-mm) MG 17 machine-guns in fuselage sides

This is another of the 'in-service' pictures issued during 1940. The factory code letters 'GA+WZ' are just visible under a new coat of 'operational' camouflage. The Allied aeronautical magazines of the day certainly believed the aircraft was serving in squadron strength.

North American B-25 Variant Briefing

The twin-finned warplane that achieved eminence on Jimmy Doolittle's 'Tokyo Raid' in World War II came from a company that had almost no experience making aircraft with more than one engine. Even so, it became the most versatile Allied medium bomber of the war.

The North American B-25 Mitchell struck back at Japan when the Allies were losing the war, fought in North Africa and the Mediterranean, became the first aircraft to carry a 75-mm cannon into combat, and in post-war years trained tens of thousands of pilots and navigators. Mitchells also fought with the US Marine Corps, the Royal Air Force, and a dozen other combat arms.

The Mitchell succeeded because the people who made it were giants. Few companies were better run than North American Aviation (NAA) with its president and general manager J. H. 'Dutch' Kindelberger, vice president Leland Atwood and vice president for engineering Ray Rice, as well as a small band of young, junior talent like aerodynamicist Edward Horkey and engineer/test pilot Alex Burton. Probably no other company could have embarked on not one major project but two – Mitchell and P-51 Mustang – with no established track record and little to offer but talent and hard work. Small wonder that by the post-war 1950s, when multi-engine pilots and radar observers were learning their craft in the Mitchell, NAA was able to boast with only a little exaggeration that it had manufactured "more airplanes than any other company." The company was a tribute to entrepreneurial spirit, a trademark of Americans in the middle of this century and a receding memory today.

Early development and flying of the NA-40 and B-25 (see entries) proceeded with few diffi-

Left: Probably the most famous of the Mitchell's many exploits was the Tokyo raid led by Lieutenant Colonel Jimmy Doolittle. On 18 April 1942, 16 B-25Bs took off from the USS Hornet east of Japan and raided Yokohama, Kobe and Osaka, in addition to Tokyo. In order to fool enemy fighters, the aircraft had 'broom handle' tail guns, as a manned position had been deleted with this model.

Left: B-25s of the United States' Twelfth Air Force fought across North Africa and through Sicily and Italy in the medium bomber role. The only combat zone where US Mitchells were not based was northwest Europe.

Right: In the Pacific, the B-25 came to be used for missions for which it was never intended. In the Pacific theatre it shone as a low-level strafer and skip-bomber. Hong Kong harbour was the target for this attack.

culties. The basic B-25 Mitchell, unchanged from start to finish, had a cantilever wing comprising a two-spar centre section which was permanently attached to the fuselage and contained integral fuel tanks and the engine mounts/nacelles, single-spar outer wing sections, and detachable wingtips. There was no XB-25 experimental prototype. From 1940, these medium bombers began to join US Army squadrons and the Mitchell became one of the most readily-recognised aircraft of the war.

Doolittle's raid

On 18 April 1942, 16 B-25B Mitchells each loaded with 2,000 lb (907 kg) of bombs took off from the deck of the aircraft-carrier USS *Hornet* (CV-8) – Admiral William F. 'Bull' Halsey commanded the operation, Captain Marc A. Mitscher the ship. The aircraft were led by Lieutenant Colonel James H. Doolittle on the 'Tokyo Raid', a daring low-level mission to bomb Japan for the first time.

Using aircraft from the 17th Bomb Group modified to carry 1,141 US gal (4319 litre) of fuel compared with the standard 694 US gal (2627 litres), Doolittle's B-25Bs had ventral turrets and Norden bombsights removed, and twin wooden rods installed in the tail to give the false impression of tail guns. Taken to within 800 miles (1290 km) of the Japanese mainland, Doolittle led his aircraft in low-level

attacks on targets in Tokyo, Kobe, Yokohama and Nagoya. All the raiders crashed or force-landed, the majority of the crews being repatriated by the Chinese and Russians. Doolittle was awarded the Medal of Honor for the mission. Doolittle's bombers launched at a gross weight of 31,000 lb (14062 kg), slightly higher than typical weight for a Mitchell. They were the heaviest aircraft ever to have been launched from the deck of a carrier at that time.

It cannot be true, as one historian asserted, that the raid "broke the morale of Japanese civilians in Tokyo who had been propagandised into believing that their defences were impregnable" – most Japanese never learned about the raid, then or later – but the bold attack did boost American morale, and hinted at what the industrial juggernaut of the American heartland would do to the Axis powers. Although US Army Air Forces (USAAF) had only 183 Mitchell bombers in inventory when the US

entered the war, once the nation was mobilised Americans were able to produce one modern warplane every five minutes, around the clock, 24 hours a day, 365 days a year. Typical of the manufacturing prowess brought to life by the Japanese attack on Pearl Harbor, and which in 1944 alone produced an incredible 96,318 warplanes (including 35,003 bombers), NAA's Kansas City factory turned out an average of 165 Mitchells per month (D and J models) during 40 months of production. Inglewood, where the Mitchell began, kept pushing B-25s out the front door long after it had committed

The North American Aviation Modification Center at Kansas City was but a short journey across the runway from the plant that built over 2,000 B-25Ds and over 4,000 B-25Js. Here aircraft were fitted to customer specifications and brought up to date with the latest technical orders. From front to back are: a B-25J for the USAAF, another for the USSR, an Inglewood-built B-25H and a PBJ-1J for the USMC.

much of its shop floor space to 10,000 California-built P-51 Mustangs.

When General George C. Kenney assumed command of the Southwest Pacific Air Force on 4 August 1942, he inherited only one unit of B-25 Mitchells, the 90th Bombardment Squadron of the 3rd Bomb Group. Lieutenant Colonel Paul 'Pappy' Gunn, an officer under Kenney in Australia, teamed up with NAA field service representative Jack Fox to install guns in the noses of their Mitchells. At the same time, Kenney's officers developed skip bombing techniques. The Mitchell as a big-gun platform has received plenty of attention; the Mitchell as a skip-bomber was more important, but the risk was high: skip bombing meant approaching at low altitude against intense, accurate defensive fire from heavily-armed Japanese land bases and seagoing vessels.

Gunn and Fox installed four 50-calibre (0.5-in/12.7-mm) machine-guns in the nose and a single gun in a blister pack on each side of the nose of a Mitchell, and loaded it up with parafrag bombs, each a 23-lb (10-kg) fragmentation bomb with a proximity fuse and a parachute. The parafrag bomb detonated a few feet

Above: The development of parachute-retarded bombs and the concentration of 14 forward-firing 0.50-in guns in the nose made the solid-nosed B-25 strafer one of the most formidable low-level ground-attack aircraft of the war. While the tail gunner duels with Japanese anti-aircraft positions, this Thirteenth Air Force B-25J strafer makes good its escape from a treetop-level attack on Victoria Harbour, North Borneo.

above the ground and inflicted widespread damage over a radius of 200 ft (61 m). The 3rd Bomb Group took the suggestions of Fox and Gunn and wreaked havoc on the Japanese.

The 3rd BG, commanded by Robert F. Strickland (who rose from first lieutenant to colonel in nine months in 1942), fought under hellish circumstances in New Guinea and the western Pacific, using a mix of B-25B, C and D aircraft with field-modified gun noses. By February 1943, Gunn, Fox and others at the Eagle Farm depot in Australia had produced 12 strafer bombers which were taken into action by 90th BS crews under Major Ed Larner.

Desert Mitchells

After B-25C and B-25D models began to appear in USAAF bomb squadrons during 1941, significant numbers of Mitchells began to appear in the Pacific, China and North Africa. In July 1942 Mitchells of the 12th Bomb Group joined Major General Lewis H. Brereton's Middle East Air Force (later Ninth Air Force) at Fayid, Egypt in time to participate in the battle of El Alamein that began on 23 October 1942. On 11 May 1944, Twelfth Air Force B-25s began Operation Strangle in central Italy, strafing and bombing supply routes along the Gustav Line, culminating in the liberation of Rome on 4 July 1944.

About the only place where the Mitchell did not play a big part was the European Theatre of Operations. A B-25C (42-53357) was flown to England in March 1943 to become the first air-

The US Navy purchased large numbers of B-25s which were used by the Marines under the Navy designation of PBJ-1. The Army (as the USAAF), the post-war independent USAF and even the Coast Guard operated Mitchells, making it one of the few fixed-wing aircraft to serve with all branches of the US military.

craft in a combat group; when the idea was dropped, the bomber was assigned to Eighth Air Force headquarters as a hack. Later, it flew 13 night photo missions over V-1 flying-bomb sites, but no B-25 Mitchell combat group ever flew from East Anglia, except in the post-war Hollywood film *Hanover Street*.

Even without Kenney, Gunn or Fox (or, for that matter, the Marine pioneer who came a little later, Jack Cram), the merits of the B-25 Mitchell as a gun platform had been obvious to NAA engineers almost from the beginning. Following the one-off XB-25E and XB-25F aircraft which tested de-icing systems, it was inevitable that NAA would produce a Mitchell bomber with a 75-mm cannon in the nose. The XB-25G, B-25G and B-25H (and corresponding Navy/Marine Corps PBJ-1H) were flying artillery pieces. Virtually all of these cannon-equipped Mitchells went to the Pacific and China. Unfortunately, the 75-mm cannon was not as effective as first supposed, in part because it required a crewman to manually reload it each time a round was fired. By the end of the war, many Gs and Hs had had their big guns removed and were performing effectively without them.

When the definitive B-25J model came along, it was produced in both glass- and solid-nosed variants, although the latter has been

One of the more unusual incidents of the war was when a Japanese lieutenant directed the bombing, by US Marine Mitchells, of his own former headquarters. On 10 August 1945, right at the very end of the war, Second Lieutenant Minoru Wada helped VMB-611 bomb and rocket the HQ of the 100th Army Division at Upian. The two Mitchells visible are a PBJ-1J (foreground) and a 'hose nose' radar-equipped PBJ-1D.

largely ignored in Mitchell literature. With eight 0.5-in (12.7-mm) machine-guns in the nose and more elsewhere, the solid-nose B-25J was in many respects the airborne arsenal that the cannon-equipped Mitchell was not.

The US Navy purchased Mitchells based on Army models. Except for a handful of ships used for developmental work, including one which operated aboard a carrier, the Navy's entire allocation of 706 Mitchells (a figure which includes 19 aircraft not actually delivered) was transferred to the Marine Corps under the designation PBJ-1.

Radar equipment

Marine Mitchells differed in several ways from their Army counterparts. Nearly all PBJs had a gun gas dispersion tube running along the lower fuselage from the bombardier's position back to a point in line with the cockpit windows. PBJ-1C and PBJ-1D aircraft had AN/APS-2 (later AN/APS-3) search radar installed in the lower belly, the location of a ventral, remotely-controlled turret in most Army bombers. In the air, the pilot extended the scanner of this set to achieve 360° sweep over a broad area of ocean. The pilot retracted the radome for ground clearance before landing. By the time they reached the South Pacific, PBJ-1Ds had both the belly radar kit and AN/APS-3 radar in a 'hose nose'. The nose-mounted radar apparently suited crews well, for when later PBJ-1Js arrived with the radar housed in a starboard wing pod the Marines routinely moved it up front.

Early PBJ Mitchells, like early B-25s, had relatively small windows in the waist position on both sides, from which flexible machine-guns were routinely deployed. Marine squadrons flew Mitchells with the larger 'picture windows' that became standard on the B-25H and J to give better visibility and field of fire for the gunners. At least one Marine squadron, VB-611, flew Mitchells with additional protection for the waist positions in the form of an armour plate fitted over the windows.

The Marine Corps had 16 Mitchell squadrons, nine of which saw combat in World War II. The first to reach combat, VMB-413, got as far as Hawaii aboard the escort carrier

USS *Kalinin Bay* (CVE-68), then flew to the New Hebrides. Coinciding with a tragedy when two planes with full crews were lost, Marine PBJs began combat operations with VMB-413 at Stirling Island on 14 March 1944.

VMB-612 drew the special mission as a 'low-altitude night striking force using radar' and, under Lieutenant Colonel Jack Cram, began operations at Saipan on 13 November 1944. The squadron suffered losses, moved on to Iwo Jima, became proficient with the 11.5-in (29.2-cm) Tiny Tim rocket, and even suffered the loss of one of its Mitchells at the hands of over-enthusiastic F4U Corsair pilots.

As the war progressed, the Mitchell cemented its reputation as one of the finest ground-attack warplanes of the conflict. With a reduction in the air and ground threat as the war went on, many B-25s and PBJs became more lightly armed than when they rolled out the factory door. Numerous B-25G and B-25H Mitchells had their 75-mm cannons removed, sometimes being replaced with field-installed machine-guns. PBJ-1Ds and Js of Marine squadron VMB-612 became the most lightly-armed Mitchells to fly actual combat missions,

The B-25 has proved a popular warbird in the United States and elsewhere. Around two dozen are believed to remain airworthy worldwide. On two occasions during the 50th anniversary commemorations of World War II, the US Navy allowed Mitchells to fly from its modern supercarriers. This is B-25J Pacific Princess lifting off from the USS Vinson in 1995 in emulation of the Doolittle raiders.

going into action with only a single tail gun

The Marines lost 26 Mitchells in combat and an additional 19 in non-combat mishaps while in the combat zone.

Post-war transports

Upon victory in World War II, numerous B-25s and PBJs were stripped to become transports. These hack Mitchells played a major role in the post-war occupation of Japan and in the Korean War. The B-25 Mitchell is also remembered as the aircraft that crashed into the 79th story of the Empire State Building in New York City in dense fog on 28 July 1945, killing its crew of six and 13 occupants of the building.

Except for two variants, all Mitchells were manufactured by the NAA plant in Inglewood, California and thus properly had a -NA suffix following their design, i.e. B-25C-NA. The exceptions are the B-25D and B-25J, all of which were built by NAA in Kansas City and thus properly had an -NC suffix, i.e. B-25J-NC. Total production was 9,889 aircraft including 920 which were offset to the Royal Air Force, although not all were delivered to the RAF.

Wartime users of the Mitchell included Australia, Brazil, China, Great Britain, the Netherlands East Indies Air Force, and the Soviet Union. Post-war users included Argentina, Bolivia, Chile, Colombia, Cuba, Dominican Republic, Mexico, Peru, Soviet Union, Uruguay, and Venezuela.

Robert F. Dorr

The all-American crew of a B-25C or D strafer of the 405th Bomb Squadron, 38th Bomb Group in New Guinea. The size of a B-25 crew and their roles differed depending on mark. The average crew was five, but B-25Hs were single-pilot and carried an extra gunner. All late aircraft had crew members with dual roles such as engineer/gunner, and field-modified strafers such as this dispensed with the bombardier.

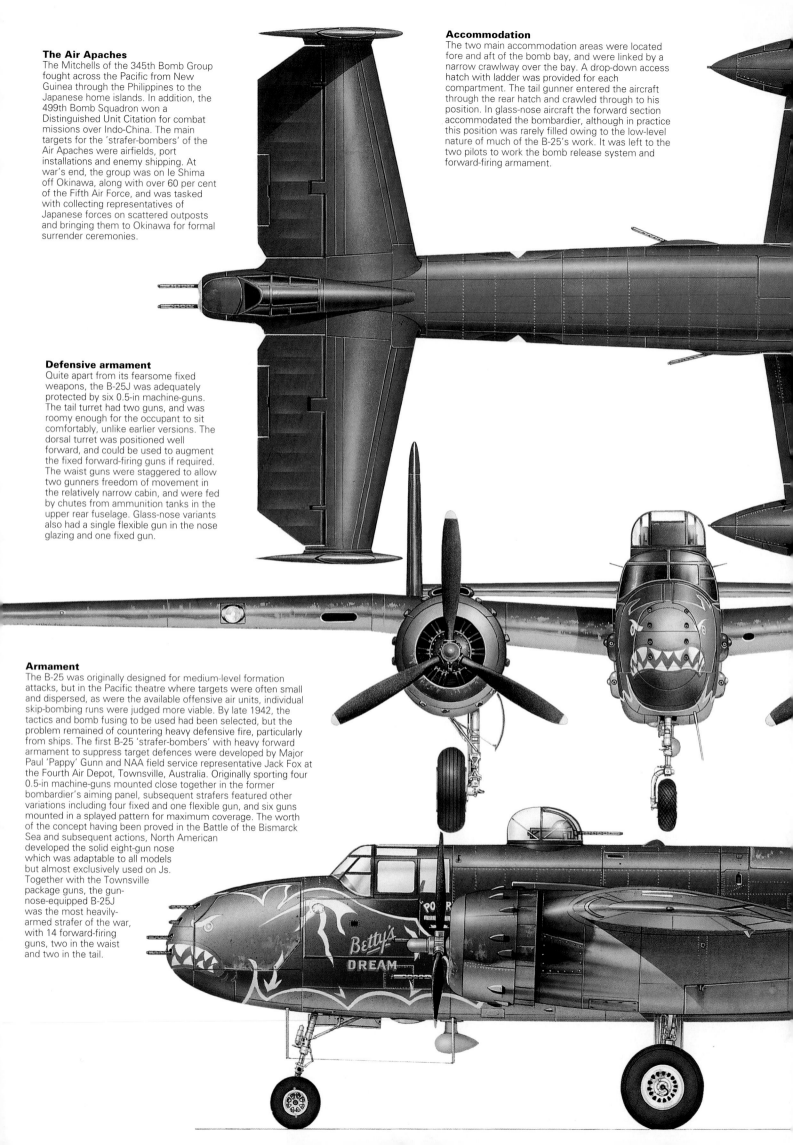

The Air Apaches
The Mitchells of the 345th Bomb Group fought across the Pacific from New Guinea through the Philippines to the Japanese home islands. In addition, the 499th Bomb Squadron won a Distinguished Unit Citation for combat missions over Indo-China. The main targets for the 'strafer-bombers' of the Air Apaches were airfields, port installations and enemy shipping. At war's end, the group was on Ie Shima off Okinawa, along with over 60 per cent of the Fifth Air Force, and was tasked with collecting representatives of Japanese forces on scattered outposts and bringing them to Okinawa for formal surrender ceremonies.

Accommodation
The two main accommodation areas were located fore and aft of the bomb bay, and were linked by a narrow crawlway over the bay. A drop-down access hatch with ladder was provided for each compartment. The tail gunner entered the aircraft through the rear hatch and crawled through to his position. In glass-nose aircraft the forward section accommodated the bombardier, although in practice this position was rarely filled owing to the low-level nature of much of the B-25's work. It was left to the two pilots to work the bomb release system and forward-firing armament.

Defensive armament
Quite apart from its fearsome fixed weapons, the B-25J was adequately protected by six 0.5-in machine-guns. The tail turret had two guns, and was roomy enough for the occupant to sit comfortably, unlike earlier versions. The dorsal turret was positioned well forward, and could be used to augment the fixed forward-firing guns if required. The waist guns were staggered to allow two gunners freedom of movement in the relatively narrow cabin, and were fed by chutes from ammunition tanks in the upper rear fuselage. Glass-nose variants also had a single flexible gun in the nose glazing and one fixed gun.

Armament
The B-25 was originally designed for medium-level formation attacks, but in the Pacific theatre where targets were often small and dispersed, as were the available offensive air units, individual skip-bombing runs were judged more viable. By late 1942, the tactics and bomb fusing to be used had been selected, but the problem remained of countering heavy defensive fire, particularly from ships. The first B-25 'strafer-bombers' with heavy forward armament to suppress target defences were developed by Major Paul 'Pappy' Gunn and NAA field service representative Jack Fox at the Fourth Air Depot, Townsville, Australia. Originally sporting four 0.5-in machine-guns mounted close together in the former bombardier's aiming panel, subsequent strafers featured other variations including four fixed and one flexible gun, and six guns mounted in a splayed pattern for maximum coverage. The worth of the concept having been proved in the Battle of the Bismarck Sea and subsequent actions, North American developed the solid eight-gun nose which was adaptable to all models but almost exclusively used on Js. Together with the Townsville package guns, the gun-nose-equipped B-25J was the most heavily-armed strafer of the war, with 14 forward-firing guns, two in the waist and two in the tail.

North American B-25J Mitchell
499th Bomb Squadron, 345th Bomb Group
Okinawa 1945

The solid-nose B-25J was the ultimate combat version of a bomber that was built in greater numbers than any of its main competitors. More than twice as many Mitchells rolled from the two North American plants at Inglewood and Kansas City than the total production of sleek Martin Marauders, and one-third more than of the faster-still Douglas Havoc. The aircraft is best-known for its service in the Pacific and Mediterranean theatres, although the RAF also flew it (as the Mitchell Mk III) in Europe. Many also served with the US Marine Corps as the PBJ-1J.

Flying the B-25
Once the the constant-dihedral wing of the first B-25s had been replaced, the Mitchell proved to be an extremely stable bombing and gunnery platform, and a better aircraft for training new bomber pilots than its contemporaries. The addition and removal of armour on the different versions and the relocation of gun armament affected the centre of gravity, most notably on the cannon-armed Mitchells, although none was as tricky to fly as the Marauder; correctly trimmed, the B-25 needed little attention from the pilot even in relatively rough air. The Mitchell was one of the few bombers that was used equally successfully at medium altitude and at mast-top height. Able to take a great deal of punishment and still return to base, and fitted with reliable engines and systems, the B-25 served long after the war in a variety of military and civilian roles. It still flies in respectable quantities today, unlike its contemporaries.

Markings
The four constituent squadrons of the 345th BG had some of the most colourful markings and nicknames of any USAAF combat unit in any theatre. Within a couple of months of entering combat in June 1943, the 498th BS 'Falcon Squadron' had painted its namesake in vivid green, yellow and red on the noses of its B-25 strafers. Not to be outdone, the 499th 'Bats out of Hell' applied the fearsome bat insignia shown here. The aircraft of the 501st BS 'Black Panthers' wore variations on a panther head theme, and the 500th BS 'Mustangs' sported a relatively subdued snorting mustang in a disc on the vertical tails. When the 345th adopted the 'Air Apaches' name in July 1944, following a ballot held among group personnel, all the group's aircraft were adorned with the Indian warrior tail insignia, which was eventually approved as the 345th's official badge.

B-25 Mitchell Variants

XB-21 Dragon

To compete in a February 1937 US Air Corps design competition, North American developed its NA-21 experimental medium bomber. NAA's first aircraft with more than one engine, the NA-21 was a large, twin-engined 'tail dragger' weighing about 40,000 lb (18143 kg). It was originally equipped with a nose wheel when on designers' drawing boards.

The NA-21 had a larger bomb capacity than the B-17 Flying Fortress, five 0.3-in (7.62-mm) machine-guns, and the first hydraulic power-driven turret on a US Army Air Corps (USAAC) aircraft, designed by Edgar Schmued. It was taken for its first flight at Los Angeles' Mines Field on 22

December 1936 by test pilot D. W. 'Tommy' Tomlinson. Tomlinson reputedly described the tests as a "nightmare" when the engines suffered several critical failures. The XB-21 was found to be severely underpowered with two 800-hp (660-kW) Pratt & Whitney R-1830 Twin Wasp engines.

The aircraft was entered into competition at the AAC's Materiel Division, Wright Field, Ohio, on 4 March 1937. The Air Corps chose the Douglas B-18A for a production contract instead, mostly because the latter aircraft was about half the price of the NA-21. However, the Army did purchase the NAA prototype and designated it XB-21. Sy Morehouse and Alex Burton apparently brought it back to Inglewood from Wright Field in mid-1937.

NAA rebuilt the NA-21, changed its designation to NA-39, and submitted the aircraft again to the Air Corps as the XB-21 Dragon (38-485). It was powered by two 910-hp (683-kW) Pratt & Whitney R-2180 Twin Hornet engines with a Westinghouse F-10 turbosupercharger unit that boosted horsepower at medium altitudes to 1,250 hp (938 kW). Tomlinson made the maiden flight of the rebuilt XB-21 at Mines Field on the second anniversary of the airframe, 22 December 1938.

NAA ferried the XB-21 eastward for its second stay at Wright Field in early 1939. NAA offered to build five service-test YB-21s and 50 production B-21As for $122,600 per aircraft, as compared with the $63,977 price of a B-18A. It was an offer Army leaders were able to resist, and the service stayed

The stocky NA.21 had a number of advanced features for its day, such as hydraulic turrets (mock-ups here), but was underpowered, unreliable and expensive. Despite two attempts to sell it to the Army, they remained unimpressed.

with the B-18A even though it was not a stellar performer. The lacklustre and oversized XB-21 remained at Wright Field where the Army used it as a flying laboratory. It appears the aircraft accumulated several hundred flying hours, although few photos of it have survived and none depict it in flight.

NA-40

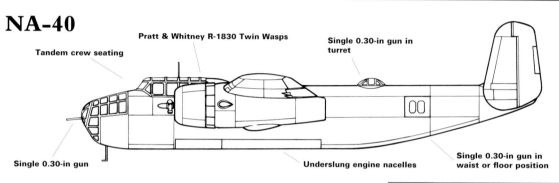

Tandem crew seating — Pratt & Whitney R-1830 Twin Wasps — Single 0.30-in gun in turret — Single 0.30-in gun — Underslung engine nacelles — Single 0.30-in gun in waist or floor position

The NA-40, North American's entry in the US Army Air Corps' twin-engined attack bomber competition of 1938, was made possible in part by the Inglewood, California manufacturer's work on its earlier NA-21 and NA-39 (XB-21) experimental bombers. Powered by two 1,100-hp (825-kW) Pratt & Whitney R-1830-56C3G radial engines driving 12-ft (3.7-m) three-bladed Curtiss Electric propellers, the NA-40 was a twin-engined, twin-tail, shoulder-wing bomber intended for a crew of five. The type was characterised by a 'greenhouse'-style canopy and (initially) a solid nose. NAA test pilot Paul Balfour and test engineer Lyons made the first flight of the

silvery NA-40 (civil registry X14221) at Los Angeles' Mines Field on 29 January 1939.

If the future of World War II's best-known medium bomber had depended on the NA-40, things would have been different. It was not merely "less than the perfect design," as NAA aerodynamicist Edward Horkey has acknowledged; it was almost a disaster. The tail shook. As tests proceeded, the empennage vibrated at different speeds, angles and altitudes – and with different cowl flap settings, differently-shaped engine exhaust stacks, even differently-shaped engine nacelles.

Maximum speed was a disappointing 265 mph (426 km/h). Jiggling with the nacelle

shape produced improvement in the shaking, but it was clear that the NA-40 needed major surgery. In its initial configuration, it accumulated just five hour and 20 minutes of flying time in 14 sorties. The solution seemed to be a new powerplant. On 28 February 1939, the NA-40 went back to the shop to receive a new powerplant and a letter suffix to its company designation.

The portly NA-40 was unstable, underpowered, and virtually unarmed. Here, the skin has yet to acquire its highly polished finish.

NA-40B

As the NA-40B, North American's bomber prototype was fitted with two 1,600-hp (1200-kW) Wright R-2600-A71-3 engines. The NA-40B had numerous minor changes to nacelle and fuselage shape, and had a glazed nose.

The NA-40B made its first flight at the hand of Balfour, Lyons and engineer Wheeler at Mines Field on 1 March 1939. The bomber was 20 mph (32 km) faster with the new engines. The vibration problem seemed to have been resolved. Balfour and others ferried the NA-40B to Wright Field where test flying was undertaken by Major Younger Pitts.

On 11 April 1939, with Pitts and two others on board, the NA-40B made a test flight and returned to Wright Field at 500 ft (155 m) with one engine shut down and feathered. The bomber turned away from

the field, descended, and struck the ground in the first turn of a flat spin. Miraculously, all three men were unharmed. The aircraft

did not initially burn, but after the crash it ignited and was swept by flames.

Much of the scheduled flight testing of

While not strictly the prototype for the B-25, the NA-40B, or NA-40-2 as it was sometimes called, introduced many of the features found on the Mitchell. With tandem pilot seating, the NA-40 had a very small frontal area.

the NA-40B had been completed by the time this attractive aircraft in its shiny natural metal finish went up in flames. NAA did not win a production award but its work on the NA-40/NA-40B, as with the earlier NA-21 and NA-39, was to prove invaluable when the company finally had an opportunity to manufacture a bomber in serious numbers.

Although the NA-40B was not, strictly, the prototype for the B-25 Mitchell, its features were to show up on the first B-25: cowling shape, twin tails, underslung nacelles, and constant dihedral wing.

B-25

The B-25 model (24 built) was bigger and faster than the NA-40/NA-40B and, at a gross weight of about 28,000 lb (12700 kg), was about 8,000 lb (3629 kg) heavier. The B-25 was powered by two 1,350-hp (1012-kW) Wright R-2600-9 Twin Cyclone engines driving three-bladed Hamilton Standard constant-speed propellers. The B-25 was to be manned by a crew of five, with pilot and co-pilot seated side-by-side. Bomb load was 3,000 lb (1361 kg). The bomber was lightly armed with three flexible 0.3-in (7.62-mm) guns in nose, waist and floor, plus one flexible 0.5-in (12.7-mm) gun in the tail. This model was known to its maker as the NA-62.

The B-25 began with an Air Corps proposal of 11 March 1939. Influenced by gathering war clouds in Europe, the service

revealed an ambitious requirement for a medium bomber with a bomb load of 3,000 lb (1361 kg), a range of 2,000 miles (3218 km), and maximum speed of 300 mph (482 km/h). A contract was inked on 10 September 1939 and an airframe was delivered to Wright Field on 4 July for static testing.

First flight of a B-25 (40-2165) was made on 19 August 1940 by Vance Breese. NAA retained this first aircraft for developmental work. The first B-25 was accepted by the

Many aircraft companies used Muroc Dry Lake (now Edwards AFB) to test their new designs. This is the first of 11,000 Mitchells, with one of four vertical fin designs trialled before the production configuration was fixed.

US Army in February 1941.

Meanwhile, early tests spelled trouble. The aircraft seemed to have only marginal directional stability. This was remedied by altering the outer wing panels to a horizontal cant. Beginning with the 10th production B-25 (40-2174), this not only resolved the problem but it also created the gull-winged

shape which was to characterise all future B-25s. The B-25 began life with vertical tails that were squared-off; these went through no fewer than five modifications before a rounded shape was chosen. The shape remained largely unchanged through the nearly 10,000 bombers that followed.

NAA modified two B-25s to become

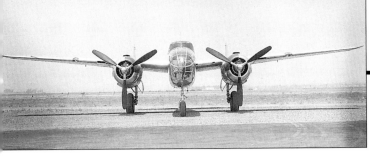

Above: In head-on view, the unbroken wing dihedral of the earliest B-25s is most evident. All the early B-25s were later retrofitted with the revised outer wing panels.

Right: The 'gull' wing effect was brought about by eliminating the dihedral in the wings outboard of the nacelles. The reduction in the aircraft's aesthetic appeal was countered by the increase in directional stability.

executive transports. The first operational B-25s went to the 17th Bombardment Group (Medium) commanded by Lieutenant Colonel Walter R. Peck, the component squadrons (34th, 37th, and 95th) of which were based at McChord AFB, Washington. Its first B-25, the fourth unbroken dihedral-ling aircraft (40-2168, later to be converted to a transport for General Arnold) arrived in February 1941. By the time of the Pearl Harbor attack, the group had moved to Lexington County Airport, South Carolina, but it soon shifted to the West Coast where it used B-25s on patrol duty.

B-25 serials: 40-2165/2188 (24).

B-25

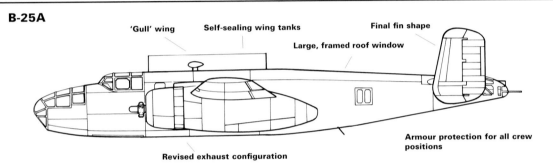

Wright R-2600-9 Cyclone 14 engines · Original exhaust configuration · Constant dihedral wing on first nine aircraft · Single 0.30-in calibre waist gun · Underfuselage 0.30-in calibre gun · One of several tail fin configurations · Low-profile tail turret with telescopic sight and single 0.50-in calibre gun · Retractable tail bumper

B-25A

The B-25A (40 built) retained R-2600-9 engines and introduced greater defensive firepower, reflecting combat experience in Europe, as well as self-sealing fuel tanks and pilot armour. These minor changes caused a reduction of fuel capacity by 246 US gal (931 litres) and slight reductions in range and maximum speed.

NAA test pilot Edward W. Virgin made the first flight of a B-25A (40-2189) on 25 February 1941. By this time, the Army had approved a suggestion by NAA's Lee Atwood that the bomber be named after Brigadier General William (Billy) Mitchell, the deceased advocate for air power who had shown two decades earlier that bombers could cripple and sink surface warships.

The 17th Bomb Group received early B-25As to bolster its B-25s; one of the former sank a Japanese submarine off the US West Coast on 24 December 1941.

B-25A serials: 40-2189/2228 (40).

The eighth and 13th B-25As await delivery in June of 1941. The single tail gun fired through a perspex tailcone which opened clamshell-fashion to allow the gun to elevate and traverse.

B-25A

'Gull' wing · Self-sealing wing tanks · Large, framed roof window · Final fin shape · Revised exhaust configuration · Armour protection for all crew positions

Above: Early Mitchells were used mainly for coastal patrols, and sank both Japanese and German submarines off the American coast.

B-25B (Mitchell Mk I)

The B-25B (120 built), dubbed Mitchell Mk I by the British, retained R-2600-9 engines but differed from preceding models in having top and bottom turrets added and the tail gun removed. The new guns were twin 0.5-in (12.7-mm) mounts and were in powered Bendix turrets. The change in armament made the B-25B slower than earlier Mitchells and reduced service ceiling from 27,000 ft (8359 m) to 23,500 ft (7275 m). On the B-25B, wing span was increased to 67 ft 7 in (20.91 m) from 67 ft 6 in (20.89 m) (this measurement was unchanged with all subsequent Mitchells) and fuselage

Above: The first B-25s for the RAF were a batch of 23 B-25Bs delivered in May-June 1942. Only three of these came to the UK, for test purposes; the rest served until the end of the war with No. 111 OTU in the Bahamas.

Left: The B-25B and some B-25As featured a square transparent hatch behind the cockpit. Also evident in this view is the asymmetric layout of the oil cooler vents above the wings.

length to 52 ft 11 in (16.39 m) from 52 ft 1 in (16.12 m).

In the Mitchell's best-known combat action, 16 B-25Bs under Lieutenant Colonel James H. Doolittle launched from USS *Hornet* (CV-8) on 18 April 1942 to attack targets in Japan, including Tokyo. It was the symbolic first offensive action by Americans reeling from the Pearl Harbor attack five months earlier.

About 40 B-25Bs were scheduled for delivery to the Dutch in the Netherlands East Indies but, as a result of the rapidly deteriorating situation facing the Americans in the South West Pacific, all were diverted to the 13th and 19th Bomb Squadrons of

B-25 Mitchell Variants

the 3rd Bomb Group. One aircraft in the B-25B contract (40-2243) crashed before delivery and was cancelled from the contract. The RAF received 23 B-25Bs as Mitchell Mk Is (FK161/FK183). Brazil took delivery of seven B-25Bs.

B-25B serials: 40-2229/2348 (120).

The ventral gun turret in its retracted position and the gunner's side windows can be seen on this aircraft, which is specially marked for the wargames held in November and December 1941.

B-25B

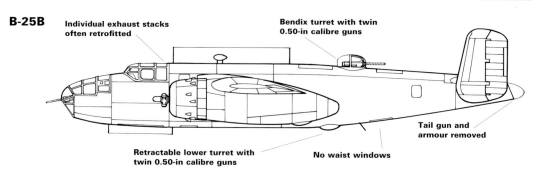

Individual exhaust stacks often retrofitted

Bendix turret with twin 0.50-in calibre guns

Tail gun and armour removed

Retractable lower turret with twin 0.50-in calibre guns

No waist windows

To capitalise on the propaganda value of the Doolittle raid, several B-25Bs of the 17th BG were painted in the markings of the raiders' aircraft and used to tour Stateside bases. All the aircraft on the actual raid were lost.

B-25C (PBJ-1C) (Mitchell Mk II)

The B-25C model (1,620 built) was the first Mitchell produced in the four-digit numbers which were to become *de rigeur* for the awakened American industrial machine. The C model had numerous changes, including a Holley carburettor replacing the Bendix Stromberg carburettor in earlier bombers. The B-25C had the 1,700-hp (1275-kW) R-2600-13 engines which were standard on all subsequent Mitchells except the F-10 photo ship and the B-25J. Beginning with the B-25C, length was reduced to 52 ft 1 in (16.12 m) from 52 ft 11 in (16.39 m). The B-25C and D introduced an autopilot, a feature which had been retrofitted on the Doolittle raid's B-25Bs. Other changes included the introduction of de-icer systems, a Stewart Warner cabin heater located in the left wing, revised bomb racks,

and strengthened wing structure.

Ed Virgin took the first B-25C (41-12434) aloft for its maiden flight on 9 November 1941. The first Mitchells to get overseas were 48 B-25Cs ferried to Australia in March 1942. These were assigned to the 3rd Bombardment Group which operated from New Guinea in 1942. The 22nd, 38th and 345th Bomb Groups in the Pacific also began operations with B-25Cs. The 11th

Right: Most RAF Mitchells served with the squadrons of No. 2 Group, such as this No. 98 Sqn aircraft. The Mitchell could lift over 4,000 lb (1814 kg) of ordnance, but for space reasons six 500-lb bombs was the usual maximum payload.

B-25C

Left: The periscope-sighted ventral turret was not widely liked. It often jammed in the down position, the sighting window was subject to mud spattering and stone damage while taxiing, and gunners became airsick attempting to aim it.

Dirty Dora of the 'Bats Outa Hell' boasted an impressive combat record. Many B-25Cs and Ds were converted to strafers by the simple expedient of removing the bombardier (redundant in ultra low level shipping attacks) and stuffing his compartment with 0.50s. A coat of paint over the nose glazing completed the effect.

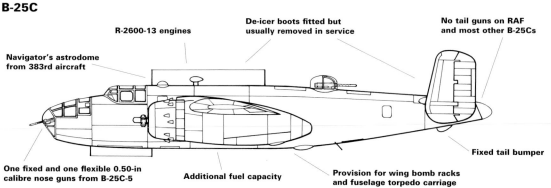

Navigator's astrodome from 383rd aircraft

R-2600-13 engines

De-icer boots fitted but usually removed in service

No tail guns on RAF and most other B-25Cs

One fixed and one flexible 0.50-in calibre nose guns from B-25C-5

Additional fuel capacity

Provision for wing bomb racks and fuselage torpedo carriage

Fixed tail bumper

and 22nd Bomb Squadrons, 7th Bomb Group, received a mix of B-25Bs, Cs and Ds in work-ups at Columbia Field, South Carolina, then proceeded to the China-Burma-India Theatre. These squadrons soon joined the 341st Bomb Group in China.

The Royal Air Force received 367 B-25Cs as the Mitchell Mk II (together with 212 B-25Ds and two B-25Gs also designated Mitchell Mk II). RAF serials were: FL164/FL218 (55), FL671/FL709 (39), FL851/FL874 (24), FR362/FR384 (23), FR393/FR397 (5), FR141/FR179 (39), FV940/FV999 (60), FW100/FW219 (120), MA956/MA957 (2). Total RAF aircraft, 367.

Below: Early B-25Cs and Ds are almost impossible to tell apart without using the serial number. This is a B-25C-1 of the 310th Bomb Group, operating from Berteaux, Morocco.

At least 41 of these aircraft were flown by No. 320 Sqn, Dutch navy, operating as a component of the RAF. At least 39 others went to the Dutch first and were later acquired by the British. Aircraft FL209 and FR268 crashed in transit prior to delivery.

One B-25C (42-32281) was converted to become the XB-25E. Another (serial

By 1940 NAA's Inglewood, Los Angeles plant was full to the brim with B-25s, P-51 Mustangs and T-6 Harvards for the Air Corps and for export, so a second factory was built at Dallas. Two of the company's most famous products are represented by the 1st Mustang I (P-51A) from the third RAF contract, and the number three B-25C, flying over southern California.

unknown) became the XB-25F. Yet another (41-13296) became the cannon-armed XB-25G. Sixty-three B-25Cs were converted to production B-25G standard. Of these, five aircraft (42-32384/32388) have ambiguous status: it is unclear whether the five were completed initially as B-25Cs or were 'new-built' from the start as B-25Gs. The five are not included on lists of B-25Cs manufactured in any surviving documents.

The B-25C was designated PBJ-1C in US naval service. Fifty were transferred to the US Navy as PBJ-1C aircraft (BuNos 34998/35047). The Mitchell was apparently the only aircraft in US naval aviation to have a letter suffix to its designation corresponding to its equivalent Army model. ('PB' for patrol bomber, an unwritten but understood '1' to indicate the first patrol bomber from this manufacturer, 'J' assigned to indicate North American, '-1' to indicate the first variant, and the non-standard 'C' corresponding to the Army's B-25C suffix. Normally, the letter suffix indicated a minor modification to a variant of a naval aircraft.)

Some B-25Cs were converted to become AT-24C trainers (later redesignated TB-25C), and 182 B-25Cs were supplied to the Soviet Union, although eight were lost at sea.

B-25C serials: 41-12434/13296 (863), 42-32233/32383 (151), 42-32389/32532 (144), 42-53332/53493 (162), 42-64502/64801 (300). Total B-25C, 1,620.

B-25D (PBJ-1D) (Mitchell Mk II)

Above: In the Pacific Theatre, low-level strafing and bombing attacks were found to be most effective against widely dispersed targets, and dedicated B-25s strafers such as B-25D-10 El Diablo IV were developed at the giant air depot at Townsville in Queensland, Australia.

Left: One of the original 'Townsville Strafers' undergoes an engine change in the field. Note the rather crudely packaged guns ahead of the wingroot. This concept would be refined by NAA and appear on the last two production models.

Below: Desert Vagabond Jr, an early B-25C, flies with others of the 12th Bomb Group's 434th Squadron, somewhere over Tunisia. Note the mix of desert-camouflaged and olive drab aircraft, and the pairs of 100-lb bombs on the underwing racks.

B-25 Mitchell Variants

Left: The USMC operated large numbers of Mitchells as PBJ-1s during the war. The vast majority of early examples were built at Kansas City as PBJ-1Ds. Many were equipped with ventral radomes for AN/APS-2 or -3 sea search radar.

The RAF operated a mix of B-25Cs and Ds as Mitchell IIs. Nulli Secundus, one of 212 RAF Ds, flew with No. 180 Squadron from Dunsfold, until it became a victim of flak and crash-landed near Hawkinge in January 1944.

PBJ-1D

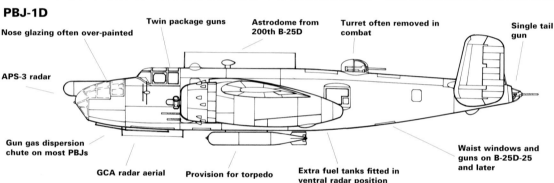

Nose glazing often over-painted

Twin package guns

Astrodome from 200th B-25D

Turret often removed in combat

Single tail gun

APS-3 radar

Gun gas dispersion chute on most PBJs

GCA radar aerial

Provision for torpedo

Extra fuel tanks fitted in ventral radar position

Waist windows and guns on B-25D-25 and later

The B-25D (2,090 built, in lots of 1,200 as NA-87 and 1,090 as NA-100) was a result of the decision made to assign much Mitchell production to NAA's Kansas City plant, where all the Ds were built. The aircraft itself was identical to the B-25C (except for

the location of its builder), albeit with minor modifications introduced in stages on the production line. The first B-25D (41-29648) went aloft for its initial flight on 3 January 1942 with Paul Balfour at the controls, the first Mitchell to fly at Kansas City.

The Royal Air Force received 212 B-25Ds (together with 367 B-25Cs and two B-25Gs) as the Mitchell Mk II. RAF serials are FR180/FR207 (38), FW220/FW280 (61), FV900/FV939 (40), HD302/HD345 (44), KL133/KL161 (29). Total RAF aircraft, 212.

Forty-five B-25D Mitchells (not 10, as widely reported) were converted to become F-10 photo aircraft. Others became AT-24A trainers (later redesignated TB-25D). A total of 152 B-25Ds was transferred to the US Navy as PBJ-1D bombers (BuNos 35048/35096, 35098/35193, 35196/35202). PBJ-1D and PBJ-1C aircraft were identical except for the location where they were

Stripped B-25s made good personnel and cargo haulers for units out of the front line. Jacquelyn Désirée sits peacefully 'somewhere in the Pacific', where she served as a 'hack' for the commander of the 27th Air Depot.

manufactured. They differed from Army aircraft in having AN/APS-2 or -3 search radar and a LORAN (long-range aid to navigation) system, four 0.5-in (12.7-mm) machine-guns in twin blister packs on the fuselage sides, up to three nose-mounted 0.5-in (12.7-mm) machine-guns, a modified bomb bay capable of handling mines, depth charges, or one high-explosive torpedo, and 10 underwing attachment points for 5-in (12.7-cm) HVARs (high-velocity aircraft rockets). Late production B-25Ds introduced a raised fairing above the tailplane to improve the comfort of the rear gunner, and this feature was common on PBJ-1Ds which normally had one tail gun. The internal bomb load of the PBJ-1D was the standard maximum of 2,000 lb (907 kg) in many combinations, plus up to 1,000 lb (454 kg) on standard wing racks fitted with B-7 bomb shackles.

The first PBJ squadron, VMB-413, was established at Cherry Point, North Carolina on 1 March 1943 and took on the job of training Marine Corps crews in a service which had previously operated only single-engined aircraft. Sixteen squadrons eventually served the Marine Corps, nine in combat. They were all formed at Cherry Point, the others being VMB-423, 433, 443, 611, 612, 613, 614, 621, 622, 623, 624, 453, 463, 473, and 483. PBJ-1Ds in the war zone had 'thimble' or 'hose nose' installations containing AN/APS-3 radar atop the nose bomb-aimer's station offering 145° of forward sweep. This configuration permitted retention of nose armament, although it was often removed to make the front end of the aircraft less crowded.

B-25D serials: 41-29648/30847 (1,200), 42-87113/87612 (500), 43-3280/3869 (590). Total B-25D, 2,290.

XB-25E

A converted B-25C (42-32281), the XB-25E was the first Mitchell to have an 'X' for 'experimental' prefix. It was one of three models (together with XB-25F and XB-25G) to be known by the company term NA-94. The XB-25E, nicknamed *Flamin' Maimie* (not *Mamie*, as widely reported), was intended to evaluate an improved engine exhaust gas-driven anti-icing system for Mitchells plus other medium and heavy bombers and transports which might operate in colder climates. NAA engineers developed exhaust gas-heated air exchangers capable of producing 10,000 BTU of heat per hour per pound of heat exchanger weight. These used exhaust heat from the two engines, pushed through a series of tubes and slots, so that all leading and trailing edges of the XB-25E were heated enough to prevent a build-up of ice.

The only visual difference of the XB-25E from standard Mitchells was the cowlings.

The sole XB-25E was distinguishable by the heat exchanger grilles on both sides of each cowl, and revised carburettor air intakes. Later the aircraft was fitted with paddle-bladed propellers and heated nose and tailcones as part of trials into propeller de-icing.

The carburettor air intake duct was faired internally in the top of the cowl and the anti-icing air intake duct similarly configured at the bottom. Each row of cylinders exhausted through a separate exchanger, one ported outboard and one inboard of each nacelle.

Joe Barton took the XB-25E skyward for its initial flight on 4 February 1944. The aircraft was later evaluated at the Ice Research Bureau at Wold-Chamberlain Field in Minneapolis and at Cooking Lake east of Edmonton, Alberta. Sporting modified propeller blades, the aircraft subsequently was tested by NACA (National Advisory

Committee for Aeronautics) at its Lewis Research Center, Cleveland, Ohio, from July 1944. By this time it was evident that the Mitchell was successful without improved de-icing capability (which was deemed unduly costly for the benefit it offered) and any thought of a production B-25E was shelved. The XB-25E was assigned the number NACA 123, although no evidence survives that the number was painted on

the aircraft.

The XB-25E was used at Lewis until February 1953, when it was returned to a now-independent US Air Force at Wright-Patterson AFB, Ohio. Most of the XB-25E was scrapped, but the forward fuselage section has been preserved by the Confederate Air Force in Midland, Texas.

XB-25E serial: 42-32281 (1).

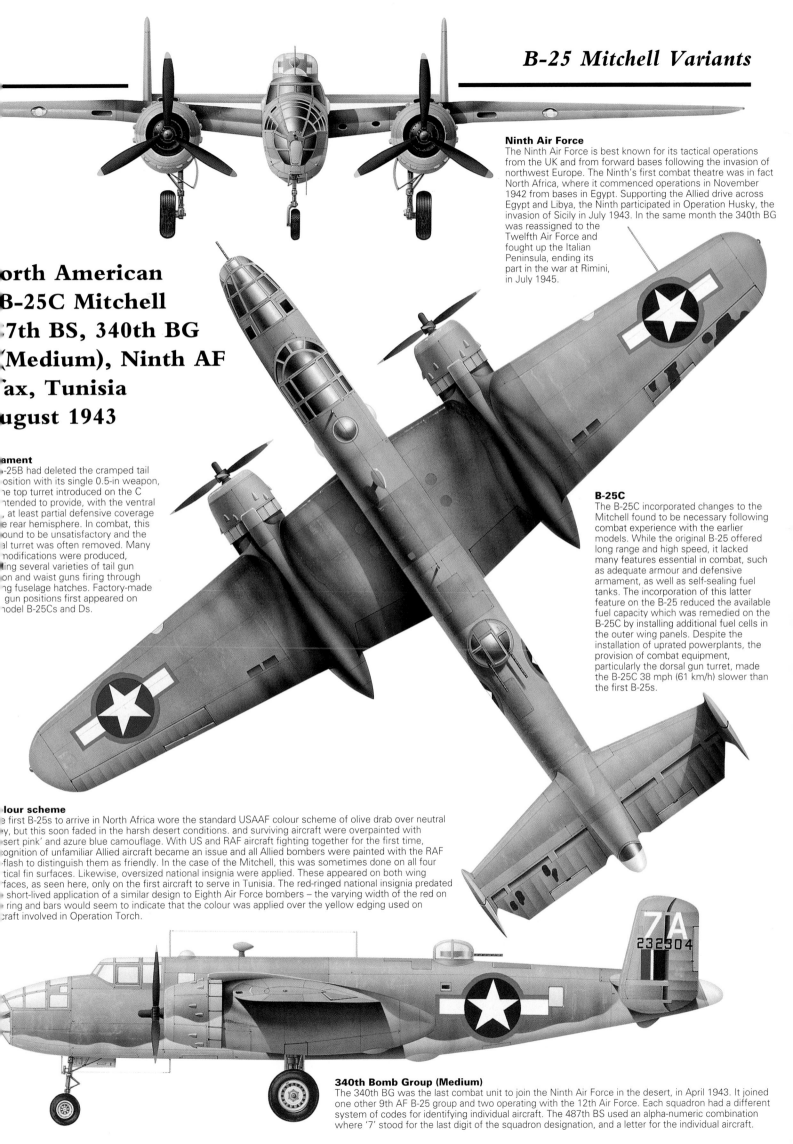

Ninth Air Force

The Ninth Air Force is best known for its tactical operations from the UK and from forward bases following the invasion of northwest Europe. The Ninth's first combat theatre was in fact North Africa, where it commenced operations in November 1942 from bases in Egypt. Supporting the Allied drive across Egypt and Libya, the Ninth participated in Operation Husky, the invasion of Sicily in July 1943. In the same month the 340th BG was reassigned to the Twelfth Air Force and fought up the Italian Peninsula, ending its part in the war at Rimini, in July 1945.

North American B-25C Mitchell 7th BS, 340th BG (Medium), Ninth AF ax, Tunisia ugust 1943

ament

-25B had deleted the cramped tail osition with its single 0.5-in weapon, he top turret introduced on the C ntended to provide, with the ventral , at least partial defensive coverage e rear hemisphere. In combat, this ound to be unsatisfactory and the al turret was often removed. Many modifications were produced, ing several varieties of tail gun on and waist guns firing through ng fuselage hatches. Factory-made gun positions first appeared on nodel B-25Cs and Ds.

B-25C

The B-25C incorporated changes to the Mitchell found to be necessary following combat experience with the earlier models. While the original B-25 offered long range and high speed, it lacked many features essential in combat, such as adequate armour and defensive armament, as well as self-sealing fuel tanks. The incorporation of this latter feature on the B-25 reduced the available fuel capacity which was remedied on the B-25C by installing additional fuel cells in the outer wing panels. Despite the installation of uprated powerplants, the provision of combat equipment, particularly the dorsal gun turret, made the B-25C 38 mph (61 km/h) slower than the first B-25s.

lour scheme

e first B-25s to arrive in North Africa wore the standard USAAF colour scheme of olive drab over neutral y, but this soon faded in the harsh desert conditions. and surviving aircraft were overpainted with sert pink' and azure blue camouflage. With US and RAF aircraft fighting together for the first time, cognition of unfamiliar Allied aircraft became an issue and all Allied bombers were painted with the RAF flash to distinguish them as friendly. In the case of the Mitchell, this was sometimes done on all four tical fin surfaces. Likewise, oversized national insignia were applied. These appeared on both wing faces, as seen here, only on the first aircraft to serve in Tunisia. The red-ringed national insignia predated short-lived application of a similar design to Eighth Air Force bombers – the varying width of the red on ring and bars would seem to indicate that the colour was applied over the yellow edging used on craft involved in Operation Torch.

340th Bomb Group (Medium)

The 340th BG was the last combat unit to join the Ninth Air Force in the desert, in April 1943. It joined one other 9th AF B-25 group and two operating with the 12th Air Force. Each squadron had a different system of codes for identifying individual aircraft. The 487th BS used an alpha-numeric combination where '7' stood for the last digit of the squadron designation, and a letter for the individual aircraft.

XB-25F

The XB-25F was a one-off experimental aircraft modified from B-25C standard. It was one of three models (together with XB-25E and XB-25G) known to the manufacturer as the NA-94. In most other respects, nothing is known about this aircraft. No record seems to have survived to indicate which B-25C was modified, hence no serial number. No 'first flight' information can be located. The dispositior of the aircraft is not known. It is known tha the XB-25F was intended to evaluate another type of de-icing system.

XB-25G

The XB-25G, identified by some sources as the manufacturer's NA-82 and by others as the NA-94, was the prototype for the first major version of the Mitchell to introduce 'flying artillery' in the form of a 75-mm cannon in the nose. The aircraft was a converted B-25C (41-13296). The XB-25G and production B-25G retained a second pilot, its crew consisting of pilot, co-pilot, navigator/cannoneer and two gunners. The XB-25G, B-25G and B-25H had wing span reduced from 52 ft (16.09 m) to 51 ft (15.78 m).

The concept of a 75-mm gun on a bomber had been tried on an experimental Douglas B-18 in the late 1930s and was further refined on the Beech XA-38 attack aircraft of 1942. For a cannon installation to be successful, the gun had to be lightweight and needed an automatic feed system. The M4 75-mm cannon developed by Captain Horace Dunn of the US Army Ordnance Department seemed to fill this requirement, although at an installation weight of 1,800 lb (816 kg) it proved too heavy for the XA-38. The M4 was also tried on the Douglas XA-26B Invader, although a cannon-armed A-26 was never ordered into production.

Positioned off-centre and firing from the lower left side of the nose, the M4 was essentially a French 75-mm tube with a vertically travelling breech block instead of the rotating block used by the French. For initial loading the breech was opened manually with a cocking lever. Loading was accomplished by forcing a round into the chamber with sufficient force to unlock the breech block, causing it to rise to the closed or locked position. The gun was then ready to fire. Located directly above the breech on the left side was a rack for 21 rounds of 15-lb (6.8-kg) ammunition. The M4 gun measured 9 ft 6 in (2.97 m) and weighed almost 900 lb (408 kg); it was mounted in a cradle to absorb recoil and extended under the co-pilot's seat. Altogether, the gun needed 14 ft (4.33 m) of space including recoil travel, a length which ruled out the forward fuselage sections of many combat aircraft, but not the relatively roomy B-25, which had a crawl tunnel that could easily be eliminated to make room for the gun. Contrary to myth, the installation of the cannon on the B-25 Mitchell did not result from field modifications in the Pacific by Captain Paul 'Pappy' Gunn, among others: NAA had the go-ahead for the XB-25G long before depot-modified strafers with a variety of nose armaments went into actic in the South Pacific.

Ed Virgin, with test engineer Paul Brewer, took the XB-25G up for its maiden flight (plus a second flight) on 22 October 1942. The next day, Virgin, Brewer and Quinn began inflight cannon firing tests w ordnance rounds that were initially 50 per cent to 75 per cent of normal weight and propellant. Firing the cannon produced a jc but no untoward vibration. The cannon sh was readily visible to the naked eye.

The XB-25G remained in service as a te ship. There were numerous problems witl the installation and operation of a 75-mm cannon in the Mitchell, and this prototype was used to evaluate the overall concept.

B-25G (PBJ-1G) (Mitchell Mk II)

Some B-25Gs were equipped with a camera port in the upper nose cowl. The pilot's windscreen of all production Gs and Hs was partly plated over, probably to protect the glazing (and the pilot) from the effects of flash and blast when the cannon was fired.

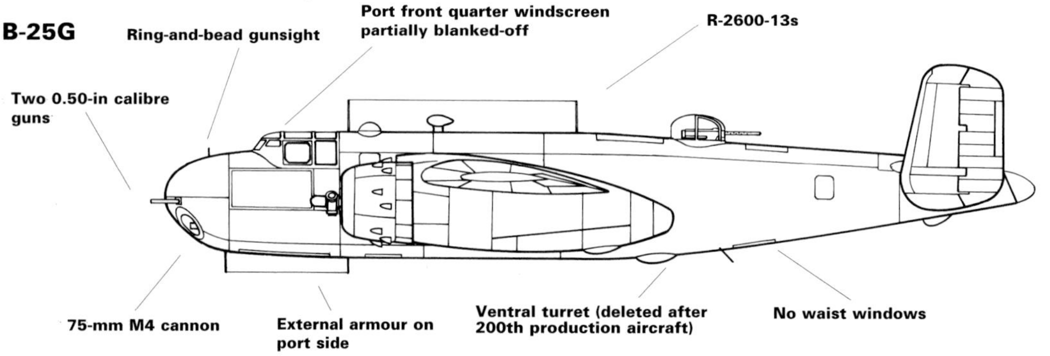
B-25G
Ring-and-bead gunsight
Port front quarter windscreen partially blanked-off
R-2600-13s
Two 0.50-in calibre guns
75-mm M4 cannon
External armour on port side
Ventral turret (deleted after 200th production aircraft)
No waist windows

The B-25G (400 built in Inglewood, plus 63 modified in Kansas City), alias the NA-96, introduced the M4 75-mm cannon as an operational weapon. Like the experimental prototype which preceded it, the B-25G had the Mitchell's greenhouse nose replaced by a shorter, solid nose which housed the cannon with 21 rounds, plus a pair of forward-firing 0.5-in (12.7-mm) machine-guns (400 rounds per gun). The G model introduced additional armour for protection of the pilot and top turret gunner. Some B-25Gs have been seen with twin side blister 0.5-in (12.7-mm) machine-guns, apparently retrofitted, which first appeared on the B-25H.

The B-25G had the same crew configuration as the XB-25G, including two pilots. The Army accepted its first B-25G in May 1943, its last in August 1943. G models from aircraft 42-65001 had the lower gun turret removed. With this heavy gun installation, the B-25G's maximum speed fell to 278 mph (447 km/h).

In addition to 400 B-25G Mitchells which came from the factory as new build aircraft, the NAA modification centre at Kansas City and Republic Aviation at Evansville, Indiana modified 63 B-25Cs to B-25G standard. These aircraft were 42-32384/32388, 42-64531, 42-64558, 42-64561, 42-64563, 42-64569, 42-64579/64582, 42-64584/64587, 42-64649, 42-64654, 42-64668, 42-64670/64675, 42-64692/64693, 42-64696/64707, 42-64753/64772, 42-64779/64780. As noted elsewhere, five aircraft (42-32384/32388) have an ambiguous status: it is unclear whether they were completed as B-25Cs or were new built as B-25Gs. The five are usually included on lists of B-25Gs manufactured, raising the total to 405.

What may at first appear to be a three-cannon Mitchell is in fact a standard B-25G with empty 75-mm shell cases being used as dust covers for the twi 0.50-in guns. ***Pride of the Yankees*** *of the 820th BS, 41st BG flew from Maki in the Gilbert Islands in the spring of 1944.*

The RAF received two B-25Gs (togethe with 367 B-25Cs and 212 B-25Ds) as the Mitchell Mk II (FR208/FR209).

Some B-25G bombers were converted AT-24B trainers (later redesignated TB-25(One G model Mitchell (42-65031) was transferred to the US Navy as a PBJ-1G (BuNo. 35097) although it is unclear what use, if any, the Navy or Marine Corps four for this solitary example.

B-25G serials: 42-64802/65201 (400). Total B-25G, 400.

This B-25G flew from Orlando on anti-submarine duty. Not all 'big-gun' Mitchells served in the Pacific They were used as medium-level bombers in Italy and on coastal patrol. The aircraft is in an army sea-search colour scheme.

*On a bulldozed coral strip on Tarawa, the crew of **Paper Doll** of the 820th BS, 41st BG board for another mission during January 1944. The G had a crew of five: pilot, co-pilot, two gunners and a navigator/cannoneer.*

Below: The RAF acquired 910 Mitchells but only two B-25Gs, which were evaluated at Boscombe Down before serving with a variety of trials units. They were given the same Mitchell Mk II designation as the B-25C and D.

B-25H (PBJ-1H)

The B-25H (1,000 built), known to the builder as the NA-98, was a refined version of the B-25G manufactured in Kansas City. A B-25C (43-32372) was modified to serve as the B-25H prototype. Nicknamed *Mortimer II* in remembrance of a field-modified strafer which had been dubbed *Mortimer*, the prototype was the only Mitchell to be powered by R-2600-20 engines. The production B-25H reverted to the R-2600-13. The B-25H dispensed with the co-pilot's position which had become familiar on all previous Mitchells. This bomber now had a crew consisting of pilot, navigator-radioman-cannoneer, dorsal gunner-flight engineer, camera operator-gunner, and tail gunner.

The B-25H was armed with a T13E1 75-mm cannon (in place of the M4 found on the B-25G). Also arrayed straight across the centre of the nose were four fixed, forward-firing 0.5-in (12.7-mm) machine-guns in the nose (in place of two on the B-25G). An important change to increase firepower, as well as an identifying feature, was the addition of two fixed 0.5-in (12.7-mm) machine-guns (200 rounds per gun) in 'twin pack' blisters on either side of the forward fuselage. The H model also had two 0.5-in (12.7-mm) machine-guns in an upper turret (moved from the aft fuselage to the forward fuselage), two flexible 0.5-in (12.7-mm) machine-guns for firing from waist gun windows in the aft fuselage, and two more 0.5-in (12.7-mm) machine-guns in the tail (600 rounds per gun). The lower turret found on previous Mitchells was

Below: As if the firepower of a Sherman tank was not enough, several arrangements were tested for firing 5-in (12.7-cm) rockets including, the one seen here on a B-25H, and another with reloadable tubes mounted in the bomb bay.

B-25H

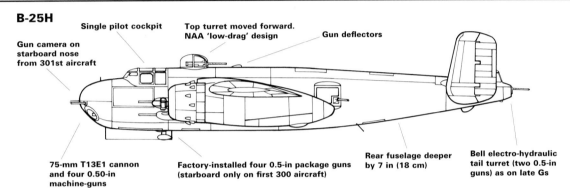

Gun camera on starboard nose from 301st aircraft

Single pilot cockpit

Top turret moved forward. NAA 'low-drag' design

Gun deflectors

75-mm T13E1 cannon and four 0.50-in machine-guns

Factory-installed four 0.5-in package guns (starboard only on first 300 aircraft)

Rear fuselage deeper by 7 in (18 cm)

Bell electro-hydraulic tail turret (two 0.5-in guns) as on late Gs

finally completely omitted since it had never been successful. The H model could carry a bomb load of 3,200 lb (1451 kg) or a 2,000-lb (907-kg) aerial torpedo, plus eight 5-in rockets under the wings.

The modified B-25C, now the first B-25H, was taken on its first flight by Ed Virgin on 15 May 1943. The first B-25H (43-

4105) flew on 31 July 1943 with Robert Chilton at the controls. The B-25H began to reach Army squadrons in the Southwest Pacific in February 1944 and the CBI Theatre soon afterward.

A total of 248 B-25H bombers was transferred to the US Navy for Marine Corps use as PBJ-1H (BuNos 35250/35297,

From this viewpoint, a number of differences from the B-25G are visible, including the four nose guns, staggered waist windows, and starboard package guns. The oil-cooler outlets are symmetrical as on Gs, Js and some Ds.

B-25 Mitchell Variants

North American PBJ-1H, USMC 1945

Crew
When the USMC acquired the Mitchell it was their first multi-engined aircraft and the first having separate stations for a co-pilot, bombardier and navigator. To train Marines to fly their own B-25 variants, a 'PBJ College' was set up at Cherry Point in November 1942. The PBJ-1H, however, was designed to be flown by one pilot, who also took over the bombardier's functions, dropping the bombs and firing the cannon with buttons on his control wheel. The navigator had a jump seat and chart board in the former co-pilot's position, but in combat doubled as the cannoneer, feeding the 21 shells one at a time into the breech of the 75-mm gun. Under a new concept of multiple operational skilling, all crew members except the tail gunner had such dual roles; the engineer and radio operator also acted as gunners.

Marine Mitchells
PBJs served with 15 Marine medium bomber (VMB) squadrons, although only seven of these saw service in the Pacific Theatre. They were: VMB-413, -423, -433, -443, -611, -612 and 613. Of these, only the last-named unit took the PBJ-1H into combat, in 1945, by which time there was a paucity of suitable targets upon which the Marines could use the cannon. Stateside, the 'big-gun' Mitchell was used for carrier suitability tests and for many trial weapons installations such as the 500-lb warhead 'Tiny Tim' rocket, which was used at the very end of the war by the PBJ-1Ds of VMB-612.

Cannon
The PBJ-1H had the same main armament as its Army counterpart the B-25H.The 75-mm T13E1 cannon looked a formidable weapon on paper, but in practice proved less than deadly as it was not allied with an effective gunsight and the low rate of fire prevented more than three or four shots being fired in a low-level attack run. The 5th Air Force developed a barrage technique for flak suppression with up to 12 cannon-armed Mitchells leading an attack in line abreast against targets such as airfields and beachheads, ahead of other attack aircraft such as A-20s or bomber B-25s.

Other armament
A tail gun position was reintroduced on late-model B-25Gs with room for the gunner to sit fully upright. To balance the weight of guns, gunner and armour, the dorsal turret was moved forwards to just behind the cockpit.

Radar
The PBJ carried a number of different radar configurations during its career. The original ventral position AN/APS-2 or -3 sea-search set was usually replaced with a nose-mounted scanner for the APS-3. PBJ-1H and J models left the factory with the pod fitted on the starboard wing tip, but some squadrons preferred the nose mounting and refitted the equipment there. AN/APQ-13 tail warning radar was fitted to many PBJs, while others sported yagi antenna under the wings or H-shaped GO aerials beneath the cockpit.

Fuselage
In order to accommodate an existing cannon design into the bombardier's crawlway of the B-25 in the shortest time, a new nose 26 in (66 cm) shorter than on previous models was built for the G, H and PBJ-1H. The aft fuselage on the H and J models was deepened by in (18 cm), to make more room for a tail turret with the gunner in a sitting position.

88872/89071). Some PBJ-1Hs were equipped with AN/APS-3 search radar in a 'thimble' protruding from the upper centre nose. VMB-613 was the only Marine squadron to operate the cannon-armed PBJ-1H in combat. One PBJ-1H with a tail hook (43-4700/BuNo. 35277) was tested on the aircraft-carrier USS *Shangri-La* (CV-38) on 15 November 1944. One report says this aircraft was equipped with swivelling main wheels for carrier operation.

Among the many Mitchells devoted to special weapons tests, one B-25H was modified to test 5-in Centre Jet air-to-ground rocket projectiles fired from bazooka-like tubes, two in the nose and one or more extending forward beneath the nose from the bomb bay.

B-25H serials: 43-4105/5104 (1,000). Total B-25H, 1,000.

Above: Basically a B-25H with naval equipment and a sea search radar, the PBJ-1H often served in mixed squadrons with PBJ-1Js.

Left: The forward-firing armament of the B-25H was impressive, but in service the cannon proved of limited worth. Many commanders preferred more machine-guns, and sometimes removed the big gun.

NA-98X Super Strafer

The NA-98X Super Strafer was a converted B-25H (43-4406) powered by twin Pratt & Whitney R-2800-51 Double Wasp engines, a powerplant which had not been recommended by NAA engineers when the Mitchell was first being developed, but which offered up to 2,000 hp (1500 kW). The NA-98X may have begun on the drawing board as a recommended configuration for the B-25H model even though the H model preceded it into the air. Certainly, it was NAA's answer to the fast, heavily-armed Douglas XA-26B Invader. From the beginning, it was primarily an NAA initiative, and was never of strong interest to the Army, although a flight in the aircraft by a British officer suggests there was RAF interest.

The NA-98X was readily identifiable by its bullet-nosed propeller spinners, P-51 Mustang-style squared-off wingtips, and high-speed induction cowlings. The NA-98X also introduced a computing gun sight for its eight fixed, nose-mounted 0.5-in (12.7-

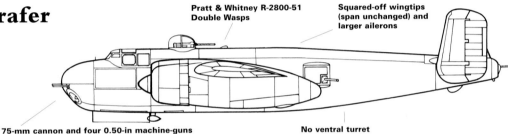

Pratt & Whitney R-2800-51 Double Wasps

Squared-off wingtips (span unchanged) and larger ailerons

75-mm cannon and four 0.50-in machine-guns

No ventral turret

mm) machine-guns, an NAA-designed low-drag canopy for the top gun turret, revised flight controls to reduce excessive stick forces, and a 1.4-sq ft (0.13-m²) area increase to the ailerons to compensate for the squared-off wingtips. It did not have the 'twin pack', blister-mounted quartet of fixed, forward-firing 0.5-in (12.7-mm) machine-guns found on most PBJs, some B-25Gs and all subsequent Mitchells

Joe Barton took the NA-98X aloft for its

first flight at Los Angeles Municipal Airport (Mines Field) on 31 March 1944. With its new engines, the NA-98X was an impressive performer and Barton eventually flew it to 350 mph (563 km/h), a dramatic contrast to the lukewarm 278 mph (447 km/h) of the B-25G. A number of others flew the NA-98X over the next three weeks.

This stellar performer was destined for tragedy. On 24 April 1944, with Major Perry Ritchie at the controls, the NA-98X finished

a test flight by making a high-speed run over NAA's Inglewood flight ramp. Ritchie had made this manoeuvre before and drawn a rebuke for it. At about 200 ft (62 m), both of the outer wing structures ripped off the engine nacelles, impacted the tail assembly, and tore it off. With no time for the crew to bail out of the wingless and tailless fuselage, the NA-98X crashed; Ritchie and First Lieutenant Winton Wey were killed. It was determined that Ritchie had knowingly exceeded briefed structural limitations and that the NA-98X design was not to blame for the fatal mishap. Still, the Army decided not to proceed with the better-performing, R-2800-powered Mitchell. Nor did the Army proceed with a version known on paper as the NA-108X. The B-25H and subsequent Mitchells stayed with the proven if less powerful R-2600.

The Super Strafer performed better than expected but, following its fatal crash, the Army lost interest in the project. At one time, a single-tail R-2800-powered aircraft was considered, as was a 'Strafer-Bomber' (NA-108X, a B-25J) with 18 guns and R-2800s. This proposal evolved into the solid-nosed B-25J.

B-25J (PBJ-1J) (Mitchell Mk III)

The B-25J (or company NA-108) was the final production version of the Mitchell. A total of 4,390 was built in Kansas City, counting 72 which flew and went into service but were not accepted contractually. The type was virtually identical to the B-25H except that the 75-mm cannon was deleted. There were two major configurations in which the B-25J appeared: a dedicated bomber with greenhouse nose and a strafer with a solid nose carrying eight fixed 0.5-in (12.7-mm) machine-guns. The B-25J reverted to a six-man crew, and used the more powerful 1,700-hp R-2600-29 engines also employed by the F-10 photo ship. The

B-25J restored a length of 52 ft 11 in (16.39 m).

Apart from the eight guns on the solid-nosed version, armament consisted of four

As delivered, PBJ-1Js were fitted with radar on the starboard wing tip, but crews preferred the nose mounting of the PBJ-1D and the unit was often relocated in combat.

B-25J Strafer Nose

Eight 0.50-in guns in solid nose

3,200 rounds of ammunition

B-25 Mitchell Variants

B-25J Glass nose

Additional armour plate, both sides — R-2600-13s — Deeper rear fuselage

One flexible and two fixed 0.50-in guns from B-25J-20 — Twin 0.50-in package guns — Provision for rockets, smoke tanks and depth charges

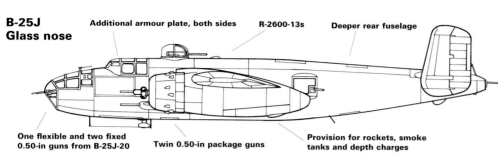

Below: The B-25J was the major production model and was exported to a total of 16 countries during and after the war. This Australian aircraft is on a test flight over Brisbane in July 1945.

Above: The B-25J was built with either the standard bomber nose or the eight-gun 'strafer' nose. The new nose could be field-fitted to all B-25 models, but was factory-supplied only on the B-25J.

Above: Both glass- and solid-nosed Mitchells often served within the same unit. These 47th BS, 41st BG aircraft on Okinawa are carrying Mk 13 glide torpedoes for an attack on Saseba, Japan, in late July 1945.

Some B-25Js were modified as the test platforms for the AN/APQ-7 Eagle Wing radar. Unlike most bombing radars which rotated 360°, the Eagle Wing swept a 60° arc ahead of the aircraft. It later proved very successful on B-29s over Japan.

Like other Army aircraft after 1944, B-25s were delivered unpainted. Crews often preferred camouflage to a few knots of extra speed, and hybrid schemes developed such as on this 340th BG B-25J.

'twin-pack', blister-mounted fixed 0.5-in (12.7-mm) machine-guns plus a fixed nose gun and a flexible nose gun for the bombardier in the glass-nosed variant. All B-25Js had two flexible 0.5-in (12.7-mm) machine-guns in an upper turret, two more on the sides of the aft fuselage, and two more in the tail for a total of 12 guns on the glass-nosed version and 18 on the solid-nosed ship.

Joe Barton flew the first B-25J (43-3870) on 14 December 1943 at Kansas City's Fairfax Field. The earliest B-25J was accepted by the Army in December 1943, the last in August 1945.

An unknown number of B-25Js flew with the airfoil-shaped AN/APQ-7 Eagle bombing radar, a vast improvement over existing aircraft radars sweeping from side to side in a 60° arc with frequency beam. This radar was flown operationally with B-29

Superfortresses in the Pacific but apparently not with Mitchells.

The RAF acquired 376 B-25Js as the Mitchell Mk III. RAF serials included HD346/HD400 (55), KJ561/KJ800 (240), KP308/KP328 (21). Total RAF aircraft, 376.

Some B-25Js were converted to become AT-24D trainers (later redesignated TB-25J). A total of 255 B-25J models was transferred to the US Navy as PBJ-1J Mitchells (BuNos 35194/35195, 35203/25249, 35798/35920, 38980/39012, 64943/64992). PBJ-1Js were manufactured with radar in a starboard wing pod but many were field-modified to the 'hose nose' configuration of earlier ships. Ten PBJ-1Js of VMB-612 were modified to carry two 11.5-in Tiny Tim air-to-ground rocket projectiles in parallel racks below the fuselage.

One B-25J (44-31357) was used by the US Coast Guard at Clark Field, Philippines with armament and top turret removed. It

Below: The Soviet Union operated thousands of US and British aircraft during World War II, but even today very little is known about how they were used or what their crews thought of them. Among such aircraft were 870 B-25s, like this J model seen in the United States prior to delivery.

was employed in liaison work in connection with establishing LORAN (long-range aid to navigation) stations in the western Pacific between April 1945 and August 1946, even though Army records say the aircraft was in storage at the time.

During World War II, NAA converted two B-25Js to become executive transports, and a third became the company's post-war executive transport. During the post-war era some became CB-25J and VB-25J transports. Six hundred became TB-25J advanced pilot trainers, and Hayes Aircraft converted 79 to TB-25L and 47 to TB-25N advanced pilot trainers. Hughes converted 117 to TB-25K radar trainers. Forty more J models became TB-25M radar trainers. A sole B-25J (44-30646) was modified by Hughes as a testbed for the company's E-3/4 fire control system for the F-86D/K Sabre interceptor.

Total B-25J production is quoted by most sources as 4,318 aircraft, but adding production batches produces a figure of 4,390. The disparity arises because 72 J models, while not fully finished, were airworthy and were included in the Army's termination inventory.

B-25J serials: 43-3870/4104 (235), 43-27473/28222 (750), 43-35946/36245 (300), 44-28711/31510 (2,800), 44-86692/86897 (206), 45-8801/8899 (99). Total B-25J, 4,390.

F-10

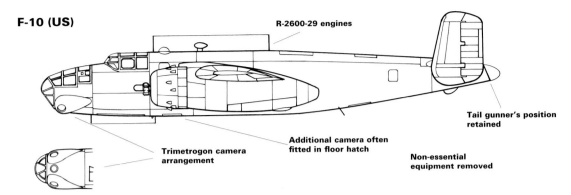

F-10 (US)

R-2600-29 engines

Tail gunner's position retained

Trimetrogon camera arrangement

Additional camera often fitted in floor hatch

Non-essential equipment removed

The F-10 Mitchell (45 converted from B-25D configuration, not 10 aircraft as is widely reported) was the photo-reconnaissance version of this medium bomber, used by the US Army and by the RCAF (Royal Canadian Air Force). Some F-10s were employed by USAAF Training Command to train aerial photographers. The type was meant not for combat reconnaissance but for photo-mapping and the compilation and refinement of topographic maps and aeronautical charts. Key to the F-10's role was the trimetrogon mapping system made up of three synchronised T-5 or K-17 6-in cameras. The F-10 used more powerful 1,700-hp (1275-kW) R-2600-29 engines. All F-10s had a distinctive chin fairing for camera ports on both sides of the nose and a camera port between these fairings at the bottom centre of the nose. The four ships used by the RCAF had a slightly differently shaped proboscis than their American equivalents. One F-10 (43-3374) was reconfigured to B-25B standard and placed on display at the USAF museum to represent one of the Doolittle raiders.

Some F-10s did serve in the combat zone. Singin' Sam was with the 18th Combat Mapping Squadron on Espirito Santo in mid-1943. Until about this time, the aircraft were designated simply as B-25Ds. Unlike most other F-10s, this one retains a dorsal turret.

The RCAF received four F-10s in 1944/45. The side camera ports for the trimetrogon camera system were considerably different from the USAAF arrangement. This aircraft, seen here in 1947, was from 13 (Photographic) Squadron, later renumbered 413 Squadron.

Serials of B-25Ds modified as F-10s: 41-29875/29881, 41-29883/29888, 41-29924, 41-29926/29927, 41-29929/29930, 41-29932, 41-29970, 41-29984, 41-29987/29991, 41-30132, 41-30181, 41-30195, 41-30426/30427, 41-30554, 41-30580, 43-3371/3372/3374, 43-3416, 43-3419, 43-3433/3434, 43-3437/3440, 43-3444, 43-3446.

AT-24

The AT-24 series were stripped-down Mitchells assigned to training duties during World War II, and should not be confused with the second generation of Mitchell trainers that evolved from the B-25J model in post-war years.

Designations in the AT-24 series were as follows: AT-24A – converted B-25Ds (redesignated TB-25D on 11 June 1948); AT-24B – converted B-25Gs (redesignated TB-25G); AT-24C – converted B-25Cs (redesignated TB-25C); AT-24D – converted B-25Js (redesignated TB-25J).

USAAF Training Command, headquartered at Fort Worth, Texas, undertook the largest effort in history to train pilots, bombardiers, navigators, radio operators, gunners and other aircrew. Until late in the war, advanced training of pilots suffered from the unavailability of aircraft with characteristics like those the pilots would encounter in operational duty. Dedicated twin-engined advanced trainers like the Curtiss AT-9 were found totally inadequate to prepare a pilot to step into an advanced combat aircraft such as the Mitchell. Flight training in the AT-24 Mitchell began at Brooks Field, Texas in July 1943, although significant numbers of Mitchells were not available for training purposes until a year later.

Successful as a pilot trainer, the B-25 apparently was never used for flexible gunnery training, a job assigned to B-17 Flying Fortresses, B-24 Liberators, and B-40 Flying Fortresses. Some B-25s and AT-24s were used as non-flying trainers for mechanics at Keesler Field, Mississippi. In 1946, the Army ended separate training for navigators, bombardiers and radio operators and combined the three functions in a training syllabus at Mather Field, California, using C-47 Skytrains and AT-24 Mitchells.

Left: With gun armament removed, these B-25Js became AT-24Ds with a stateside training unit and taught formation flying for pilots destined for Army bombers of all types.

In the Army's slightly confusing designation system, a B-25D stripped of armament for multi-engined pilot training became an AT-24A.

B-25 transports

With its carrying capacity, speed and range, the B-25 Mitchell was a natural choice for duty as a staff transport. In the post-war years, numerous Mitchells became transports through the simple expedient of redesignating them CB-25 or, in the case of some ships intended to carry dignitaries, VB-25 (separate entry). Long after the war, several civilian users created their own version of a business transport from surplus Mitchells. The process of converting the Mitchell to this kind of duty began, however, during and after the war with half a dozen ships modified by NAA at Inglewood.

NAA used the company terms RB-25(1) through RB-25(5) to refer to five Mitchells converted by the company into executive transports between November 1942 and February 1950. In Army parlance, an 'R' prefix on a fixed-wing aircraft prior to 11 June 1948 meant 'restricted' and applied to aircraft not intended for use on combat missions – appropriate to this situation – but NAA employees believed the prefix meant 'rebuilt'. NAA modified a sixth aircraft in 1949 as a prototype transport and trainer.

This CB-25J, nicknamed Coyote, was one of 80 Mitchells obtained by Brazil between 1941 and 1947. It was in service up to the late 1960s.

The designation CB-25 covered many variations, there being no set standard. This CB-25J flew with the Military Air Transport Service.

B-25 Mitchell Variants

RB-25 (1)

The first B-25 (40-2165) was modified as a transport with five seats behind the flight deck as well as a desk and intercom, plus two extra seats just forward of the bomb bay. The aft side windows on both sides of the cockpit and the top window escape panel above were skinned over and four new passenger windows were added at the rear fuselage. This aircraft was intended for company use and was dubbed *Whiskey Express* by employees. NAA used this

Mitchell transport extensively until 8 January 1945, when it was destroyed in an emergency belly landing while carrying pilot Ed Stewart, co-pilot Theron Morgan and crew chief Jack Maholm, all of whom were unharmed.

The first B-25 served NAA as a personnel transport for two years after its testing career was over. For most of its career, it wore a highly polished metal finish. The nose contained navigation gear.

RB-25 (2)

NAA modified a B-25 (40-2168) to become a personal transport for USAAF chief General

Henry H. 'Hap' Arnold. The aircraft was modified exactly as its predecessor and first flown by Bob Chilton in June or July 1944. No record seems to have survived of General Arnold's actual use of the aircraft,

which was retired in July 1945 with 300 hours' flying time. This aircraft joined the ranks of civilian Mitchells after the war, was used by briefly by Hughes Aircraft, and has had several civilian owners, most recently

Jeff Clyman of Tenafly, New York, who replaced its unique transport nose with a bombardier glass unit.

RB-25 (3)

The manufacturer modified a B-25J (43-4030) to serve as General Dwight D. Eisenhower's personal transport. A bunk was installed on the crawlway over the bomb bay. Insulation, a walnut cabinet, and

a coffee bar were among the ex-bomber's features. It had a solid nose and a distinctive tailcone which housed a jettisonable life raft. This aircraft was redesignated CB-25J in 1947, and VB-25J in 1948 (the 'C' prefix denoted a transport role, the 'V' for VIP transport). It reappears in the VB-25 entry.

Left: General Eisenhower's personal B-25 was delivered shortly before D-Day, the building and conversion of the aircraft taking less than three months from the official go-ahead. Here the aircraft is seen undergoing weight and balance checks shortly before being ferried to England. The smooth nose contours and cabin windows were features of most executive conversions.

Above: The Eisenhower aircraft – and the virtually identical RB-25(4) – were luxuriously appointed for the time. The interior was in dark blue and tan, and featured extensive soundproofing and padding. The bench table folded into the wall and a bed was provided above a lowered bomb bay roof.

RB-25 (4)

NAA also modified a B-25J (44-28945) as General Arnold's second personal transport, using the more luxurious interior

configuration of the Eisenhower aircraft. Ed Virgin flew this ship in tests beginning 24 November 1944. Arnold used the aircraft

until 1946 when it was returned to general military duty as a VB-25J. It re-appears in the VB-25 entry.

RB-25 (5)

NAA still needed a company transport after

its first Mitchell conversion was lost in a mishap. In January 1945, the company began converting a B-25J (44-30047) to a configuration similar to the previous two

transports. This aircraft first flew in its new configuration on 18 October 1945 with Ed Stewart as pilot. Just 32 flying hours later, it was aloft on 27 February 1946 off the

California coast when pilot Joe Barton reported a fire. The Mitchell was never see again; the experienced Barton and two others lost their lives.

The 'Executive Transport'

The most extensively modified B-25 transport conversion was NAA's own 'Executive Transport'. The aircraft used a windscreen and instrument panel from a Convair 240, and had a lengthened nose and repositioned flight deck

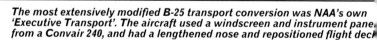

To wrap up the story of half a dozen Mitchell transports, in 1949 – when 1,000 Mitchells were in USAF inventory, most as trainers – NAA sought additional business with its design for a modified Mitchell for pilot training, radar training, and personnel transport, referred to in most documents as the 'executive transport'. The company acquired a PBJ-1J (44-30975/BuNo. 35848) and converted it to serve as a demonstrator for the hoped-for USAF production contract. The company also hoped to identify a civilian market for this aircraft. It acquired civil registry N5126N, and was different in appearance from any other Mitchell. The nose section forward of the propeller arc was redesigned, the flight deck moved forward 3 ft 4 in (1.03 m) and widened slightly. This permitted seating for six forward of the bomb bay and four more in the aft fuselage.

Ed Virgin and Miles Towner made the first flight of the 'executive transport' on 15 February 1950. On 25 March 1950 during a promotional tour, the aircraft crashed near Chandler, Arizona, killing seven NAA employees. NAA did not proceed further in its quest for new B-25 business.

VB-25 transports

The 'V' prefix came into use on 11 June 1948 to designate a transport intended for use by high-ranking officials. Some VB-25 Mitchells came into use when bombers were no longer needed for their original role. At least two were former NAA-modified staff transports.

VB-25Js 43-4030, 44-28945 and 44-30976 were assigned to the 1100th Special Air Missions Group at Bolling Field, Washington, DC in 1949. In the spring of 1953, they were transferred to the 1254th Air Transport Group (Special Missions) at Washington National Airport. 43-4030, the former RB-25(3) which had been Eisenhower's personal transport, ended up with the 1001st Air Base Wing at Andrews AFB, Maryland. 44-28945, the former RB-

Wearing the 'O' for 'obsolete' (more than 10 years old) prefix to its serial, this VB-25 served with the US Air Force Academy.

25(4), remained in service until 1959 when it was sold to civilian owners. Today property of the USAF Museum, it is on display at Ellsworth AFB, South Dakota.

Numerous B-25 Mitchells were employed as transports or station hacks throughout the USAF well into the 1950s, including some former TB-25N pilot trainers converted to VB-25N status. The last Mitchell in US military service was a transport (variant unknown) retired at Eglin AFB, Florida in July 1960.

Left: VB-25J-15 44-28945 was one of three transport Mitchells used by the 1100th Special Air Missions Group at Bolling Field near Washington DC as VIP transports. Like many post-war B-25s, the upper exhaust stacks have been replaced by a semi-collector ring and a conventional exhaust pipe.

Above: With the original individual flame-damping exhaust stacks, this VB-25J seen at Boston's Logan Field carries the insignia of a three-star general on a 'command plate' on a sliding tray below the cockpit. The VB-25s had their tail turret positions deleted completely, unlike most TB-25s which often retained the glazed position.

TB-25J/L/N pilot trainers

In 1948, USAF Air Training Command (ATC) discontinued the practice of having separate training for four-engined and twin-engined aircraft, and combined both into a twin-engined syllabus. This resulted in the retirement of the B-17 Flying Fortress from training duties; multi-engined pilot training was carried out by TB-25J/L/N Mitchells.

It is not widely known that the B-25 played a number of small roles in the Korean War. This TB-25J, wearing a scheme similar to pre-World War II Army aircraft, was a unit hack with the 452nd Bomb Group (a B-26 Invader outfit) at Taegu in 1951.

B-25 Mitchell Variants

TB-25J

Six hundred former AT-24Ds, plus additional B-25Js stripped of armament, trained pilots in the post-war era. Additional seating was installed for students so that a number of trainee pilots could get 'stick time' on a single training flight.

Above: Sporting the Capitol Building insignia of Air Force Headquarters Command, this highly polished TB-25J was at Bolling AFB in May 1954.

Below: The USAF Flight Test Center at Edwards operated this colourful TB-25J, seen here in January 1954. 'BD' was the post-war 'buzz number' assigned to all B-25 variants.

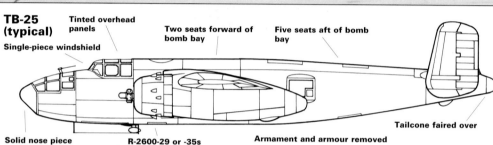

TB-25 (typical)

Single-piece windshield — Tinted overhead panels — Two seats forward of bomb bay — Five seats aft of bomb bay — Tailcone faired over — Solid nose piece — R-2600-29 or -35s — Armament and armour removed

Some of the most colourful B-25s were the TB-25Js of the USAF Instrument School at Moody AFB, Georgia in the mid-1950s. The striping, tailfins, engine cowls and nose panels were all insignia red, with black nacelles.

TB-25L

Hayes Aircraft of Birmingham, Alabama produced 79 TB-25L Mitchells by converting B-25Js. Hayes delivered the first TB-25L in April 1952, the last in December 1952. These aircraft had armament removed, and revised instrument panel, lighting system, oxygen and interphone. The pilot's three-piece windshield was replaced with one-piece safety glass. Two passenger seats were added forward of the bomb bay, five behind it. Thirty-five of these aircraft later became TB-25M navigator trainers.

This TB-25L is caught on the flight line of the 3500th Pilot Training Wing at Reese AFB, Texas in September 1958.

TB-25N

Hayes produced 47 TB-25N advanced pilot trainers, all converted B-25Js. These were modified to the same standard as the TB-25Ls.

In 1952, ATC reorganised pilot training into four phases: pre-flight, primary (T-6 Texan), basic (T-6, T-28), and crew training (T-33 Shooting Star, F-51 Mustang, F-80 Shooting Star, TB-25 Mitchell). In 1953, a further change led to the multi-engine crew syllabus using TB-25 Mitchells, TC-54 Skymasters and TB-50 Superfortresses.

In January 1960, ATC graduated its last class of pilots trained in the TB-25 Mitchell, ending specialised undergraduate pilot training and introducing generalised training for all pilots with the advanced phase in the T-33 Shooting Star. ATC figures show that no fewer than 30,000 multi-engine pilots earned their wings in the B-25 Mitchell during 2.5 million flight hours. ATC phased out its last TB-25 at James Connally AFB, Texas on 18 January 1960.

Left: TB-25Ns appeared in both glass- and solid-nosed versions. This highly-polished example was assigned to Strategic Air Command, and wears the organisation's 'Milky Way' sash.

This TB-25N was serving with Air Training Command Headquarters in 1955. A very small number of TB-25Ns were assigned to the ANG for weather reconnaissance and personnel transport.

TB-25K/M radar trainers

addition to instructing pilots, the B-25 as highly suitable for the training of navigators, especially radar operators. The se of former bombers for navigator training egan at Mather Field, California in 1946 but was not until later that specially-modified -25s were so employed.

he TB-25K trained the radar perators of F-94s and F-89s in the se of the E-1 fire control system. his example was with the 123rd IS at Portland, Oregon, seen here ith an example of the unit's perational equipment.

TB-25K

ughes modified 117 B-25Js to become B-25K trainers with the installation of the -1 fire control system from 1950. These rcraft had a prominent radome which otruded from the former greenhouse ose. An identifying feature was an nbroken astrodome atop the navigator's ompartment. The TB-25K carried strumentation in its modified bomb bay nd monitoring equipment for one structor and students in the rear fuselage.

Right: B-25s were used in combat in Korea in very small numbers. This B-25J was fitted with a receiver to monitor North Korean air defence adars. Together with B-26Bs of the 52nd Bomb Group, they flew unter-killer missions against nemy radar and gun sites. The Mitchell acted as the 'ferret', uiding the Invaders to the kill.

Below: When the RCAF acquired he CF-100 with the same E-1 fire ontrol system as the F-89, they lso modified a number of their Mitchells as radar operator trainers. 281 was given the Canadian esignation of Mitchell 3AI and erved with 2 Air Navigation School t Winnipeg in 1953.

TB-25M

Hughes modified 35 TB-25Ls to become TB-25M radar trainers, which differed from TB-25Ks in having the more advanced E-5 fire control system. This gave the radome on these aircraft a slightly different shape. Mitchells were supplanted by Convair T-29s for navigator and radar training.

Right: This B-25J was used in the development of the Hughes E-3/E-4 radar for the F-86D, the scanner for which can be clearly seen through the hemispherical Plexiglas nose dome. The aircraft is fitted with wing pylons and a rocket-shaped pod on the starboard side.

A number of aerospace contractors used B-25s in the development of radar and other avionic equipment, including this aircraft which Bendix owned and used to test its PB-20 Automatic Flight Control system. It is seen here at Teterboro, New York in October 1957.

B-25 camera ships

The B-25 Mitchell has been the star of the show in some of Hollywood's best and worst films, most notably:
– *Thirty Seconds Over Tokyo* (1944) about the Doolittle Tokyo raid, starring Spencer Tracy and Van Johnson and directed by Mervyn LeRoy.
– *God Is My Copilot* (1945), about Robert L. Scott's flying experiences in the CBI, starring Dennis Morgan and Raymond Massey, and directed by Robert Florey. Although the P-40 Tomahawk was supposed to be the principal aircraft in the film, no fewer than 18 B-25C/D/Gs from the 952nd B-25 Transition Group at Mather Field, California, appeared in the film.
– *Catch-22* (1970) based on the World War II tragi-comedy by Joseph Heller, starring Alan Arkin and Richard Benjamin and directed by Mike Nichols. The making of this film marked the last occasion when a formation of up to 16 B-25s was seen.
– *Hanover Street* (1979) a love story with Harrison Ford, Christopher Plummer and Lesley Anne Down and directed by Peter Hyams. Of this motion picture, aviation film critic James H. Farmer says, "Five B-25s were wasted in this dismal fiasco."

Apart from its own appearance in the movies, the B-25 Mitchell has consistently been the best-known and most reliable camera ship for aviation films featuring other aircraft, including *The Battle of Britain* and *Memphis Belle*. Few can forget the sight of a Mitchell with a much-modified nose introducing the short-lived miracle of Cinerama (a wide-screen projection method)

Below: This unidentified B-25 was one of the Tallmantz stable and received this crude-looking nose modification to film This is Cinerama *in the 1950s.*

in the 1950s, or Tallmantz's Mitchell carrying a camera protruding from more than 10 ft (3 m) below its underfuselage in order to photograph an aerial formation 360° around.

At least five B-25s were modified to serve as aerial camera platforms for cinema and advertising.

Probably the most famous Mitchell camera ship is B-25J N6578D, which gained the unforgettable appellation of The Psychedelic Monster *during its services as the photographic platform for* The Battle of Britain. *Originally a B-25J (44-31508), the aircraft was modified with a hemispherical nose piece, open tail position with air blast deflectors and a 360° camera mount on an extendible jointed arm. Filming could be directed from either of two astrodomes, and video equipment was linked to the cameras for instant playback. The aircraft wore a variety of colour schemes, most memorably this pattern of green, red and yellow with black and white wing stripes, purportedly to aid the film's fighter squadrons in formation keeping. It is currently airworthy in the US, named* Chapter XI.

Above: N9089Z was dubbed Moviemaker II *and was a camera platform on* The War Lover *and* 633 Squadron, *in which it also appeared briefly (as 'N908'). After filming, the aircraft was abandoned at Biggin Hill and, by way of the now-defunct Southend Museum, found its way to North Weald and aerial film-makers Aces High, where it is once again derelict. Apart from a faired-over tailcone, the aircraft, TB-25J 44-30861, remained mostly standard.*

Below: A similar fate befell 44-3117 which as N7614C came to the UK to film advertisements in 1970-71 with Flying W Productions of Medford, Oregon. The aircraft featured a similar nose to 'the Monster' and a rebuilt tail position. Stored and impounded at Dublin, Prestwick and Shoreham once filming was complete, the aircraft was eventually dismantled and trucked to Duxford, where it is undergoing restoration for the American Air Museum there.

The longest-serving of all B-25 camera ships is N1042B, which belonged to the Tallmantz organisation for 23 years before joining Aces High at North Weald in 1989. In 1972 it visited the UK for a Disney film with its unique 360° suspended camera housing (above). A veteran of Catch 22, *both as 'actor' and camera platform, the aircraft, by now known as* Dolly, *undertook the principal air-to-air photography on* Memphis Belle, *operating from Duxford and Binbrook (below). The aircraft is equipped with 180° camera ports in the nose and tail turret positions and an observation dome for the director. The aircraft, 44-30823, built as a B-25J and converted to a TB-25J and then a VB-25N before joining Frank Tallman's fleet, has since returned to the USA.*

Firebombers

the post-war USA, many surplus military craft were to be found fighting a new war – against the seasonal forest fire menace. The most popular aircraft types were those with high-capacity bomb bays such as B-17 Flying Fortresses and PBY Catalinas, and aircraft suited to the low-level environment like the A/B-26 Invader and TBM Avenger. The B-25 found some use as a firefighter (and as an insecticide sprayer) but a number of fatal structural failures led to the type being withdrawn from these roles in the early 1960s in the US, although small numbers have remained in use in Canada and Alaska into the 1990s.

Executive conversions

he B-25 never found the post-war success s a runaround for business executives that he A/B-26 Invader did, and there were fewer ommercially-produced conversions. The ain company to convert B-25s for civilian se was the Hayes Company, which, in ddition to TB-25s for the USAF, undertook any civil conversions.

Hayes B-25s and some other aircraft orted wingtip fuel tanks, often 230-US gal 71-litre) models from jet fighters, extending e Mitchell's range to around the 3,500-mile 630-km) mark.

The equipment fit and configuration of vilianised Mitchells varied greatly, but most orted some sort of solid nose piece, de-er boots and modern navigation and radio quipment. Few aircraft added additional vindows, in most cases adapting waist gun ositions and other hatches already present n bomber Mitchells.

Mitchells were also used as freighters and ankers supporting oil and mineral exploration vork, particularly in Canada, while others vere to be found (and often ended their ays) in the jungles of Latin America.

horn of military excrescences such s gun turrets, and with wingtip fuel anks, the B-25 made quite a sleek usinessman's runabout. N122B, nce a B-25D, served the Timken Roller Bearing Company, among thers. Today it is displayed on the SS Yorktown at Mt Pleasant, outh Carolina.

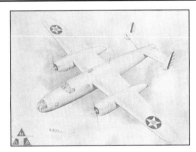

Above: Some B-25s have kept working since they left military service in the 1940s and 1950s. C-FDKU was sold by the USAF as a B-25J in 1948 and served the Bendix Corporation as an executive aircraft until 1972. When seen here in 1976 it was with Aurora Aviation in Alberta in this attractive colour scheme. In 1982 it became Tanker No. 1 with G+M Aircraft of St Albert, Alberta, where it was still serving in 1994.

XB-28

ust as the XB-21 was a prelude to the aga of the B-25 Mitchell, a very different AA bomber provided a postscript. If the XB-21 was plain and portly, the later XB-28 manufacturer's NA-63) was slim and leek, an aircraft which might have ecome a Mitchell replacement had ircumstances unfolded differently.

The XB-28 was conceived as a high-altitude, pressurised-cabin bomber with supercharged radial engines and remote un turrets. Powered by two 2,000-hp 1500-kW) Pratt & Whitney R-2800-11 win-row, 18-cylinder radial engines, this aircraft began on the design table as little more than an advanced Mitchell. As originally conceived, it would have had the same wing as the Mitchell and a similar, win-rudder tail. Early in the design stage, NAA realised it was working on a whole new aircraft and US Army Air Forces (as he Air Corps was renamed on 20 June 1941) agreed. The XB-28 evolved as a robust bombing machine, characterised by ricycle gear and single tail, able to carry 20 100-lb (45-kg) or eight 300-lb (136-kg) or four 1,000-lb (907-kg) bombs plus six 0.5-in 12.7-mm) machine-guns, two each in three remotely-operated turrets.

Above: As this NAA drawing shows, the original XB-28 design bore at least a passing resemblance to the B-25.

With Ed Virgin as pilot and Joe Barton as co-pilot, the XB-28 (40-3056) took to the air on 24 April 1942 from Los Angeles Municipal Airport, as Mines Field was called by then. A full, five-man crew carried out subsequent tests, the pilots being augmented by bombardier/navigator, primary gunner, and radio operator/gunner. The XB-28 turned out to be a "hot rod," as NAA's Jim Tuttle described it. Above

Below: The three gun turrets on the pressurised XB-28 were to be operated by two gunners situated in the forward fuselage, sighting with fisheye windows and periscopes.

24,000 ft (7430 m), the XB-28 could outrun the Lockheed P-38 Lightning. At a gross weight of 39,135 lb (17751 kg), it reached a maximum speed of 382 mph (614 km/h) at 25,000 ft (7740 m).

The Army had a strong interest in putting this promising bomber into production. Meanwhile, NAA produced a second airframe, the XB-28A (40-3058) or company NA-67, powered by improved R-2800-27 engines, with structural changes and a slight reduction in weight. Exactly a year after the first ship had flown, on 24 April 1943, test pilots Virgin and Barton went aloft from Los Angeles Municipal Airport in the XB-28A. Although it was only 1056 lb (478 kg) lighter than the first aircraft at a gross of 38,079 lb (17272 kg), it demonstrated even better performance. There was serious talk about a production B-28. Army officers especially liked the XB-28A as a prospect for the high-altitude photo-reconnaissance mission.

On 4 August 1943, the XB-28A was carrying out 'fixed-rudder, rate-of-roll' testing near Balboa, California. NAA's Bob Chilton was the pilot with Roy Ferrin as flight test engineer. Chilton was charged with rolling the bomber into a near 90° bank, holding the rudder fixed, and then applying a calibrated roll force. During one of these manoeuvres, Chilton found

himself in a roll to the left with the right engine at idle and full power on the left. He was able to level the wings but was losing altitude at an alarming rate.

Chilton decided they had to bail out. Ferrin went aft, levered open, and lashed the lower hatch. Both men bailed out and were rescued by boaters near Newport Beach (Chilton by a former RAF pilot who had been picked up in the English Channel during World War I and who now repaid the favour). The XB-28A went to the bottom of the Pacific with only a landing gear strut, supported by its floating tyre, to mark the bomber's grave.

A production B-28 remained an attractive notion to many, but in the end it was the very success of NAA's other medium bomber, the B-25 Mitchell, that spelled doom for the B-28. The Air Staff decided that production line continuity was more important than the improved capability a B-28 would provide (albeit, with a long delay before its introduction into service). Plans for a third prototype never materialised and the programme never progressed further. Although numerous Mitchells survive in today's world, neither of NAA's other two bombers – the XB-21 and XB-28 – was saved for posterity, and both exist today only as faded pictures of a departed era.

An unusual feature of the XB-28 was the routing of each exhaust system through superchargers to the rear of the nacelles, where the gasses added a small amount of extra thrust.

Royal Canadian Air Force 1950-1959: Part 2

The rapid technological advances of the 1950s, particularly the development of the ICBM, saw ever-increasing demands on national air defence systems around the world. Canada wanted interceptors, a ground-control system and long range surface-to-air missiles, but could not afford all three. The decisions made in this decade have affected Canadian defence and industry to the present day.

Above: The CL-44 Yukon was a stretched, pressurised derivative of the Argus (in turn a derivative of the Britannia). The RCAF operated 12 Yukons.

Right: Langar, Nottinghamshire was the base of 137 Transport Flight's small fleet of Bristol Freighters. They carried supplies between the Air Division bases in Europe.

Canadair's licence agreement with Bristol did not restrict it to just a maritime patrol variant of the Britannia. The company also developed three related designs, the CC-106 Yukon military transport, CL-44 civil freighter, and the stretched CL-44J passenger aircraft. They were closer to the original Britannia than was the Argus, but were longer (especially the CL-44J) and were all re-engineered to suit their roles. The RCAF's Yukons had cargo doors and self-contained loading equipment, while the CL-44s had a swing-tail to facilitate loading large items. They remain the largest aircraft ever built in Canada. The 'Iron Duke', as the Yukon was nicknamed, began to be delivered to the RCAF in late 1959. 412 (T) Squadron operated two VIP transports with the other 10 (and, later, all 12) assigned to 437 (T) Squadron. The type remained in service until it was struck off strength in September 1970, being replaced by five CC-137 Boeing 707s.

Air Transport Command operated a diverse fleet during the 1950s, including Dakota 3 and 4 (of an immense variety of sub-types), Expeditor 3 (also of numerous sub-types), C-119 Flying Boxcar, Canso (Canadian-built Catalina), Norseman, Goose, North Star, Cosmopolitan, Otter, Bristol Freighter, Comet and the sole Canadair C-5. The latter was a

derivative of the North Star programme, which was itself a version of the Douglas C-54 re-engined with Rolls-Royce Merlins, as described in the previous volume of *Wings of Fame*. The C-5 was the result of the insurance settlement covering the loss of a borrowed RCAF North Star in service with Trans-Canada Air Lines (CF-TEL/17519, but the aircraft never wore RCAF markings). The government authorised the construction of one more aircraft on the North Star production line.

The C-5 differed from all previous Canadair North Stars by having Pratt & Whitney R-2800 radials. It was also pressurised, unlike the RCAF's aircraft (but in common with the others built for TCA, Canadian Pacific Airlines, and BOAC). The aircraft was a hybrid, having an enlarged DC-4 fuselage, DC-6 landing gear, and the new engines. Considerably quieter than a North Star, it was also faster, and was intended from the start to serve as a VIP aircraft.

The C-5, serialled 17524, made its first flight

on 15 May 1950. It was reserialled 10000 (the previous VIP Dakota had been serialled 1000) on 17 February 1951. Taken on strength by the RCAF on 29 July 1950, it actually went to work a little sooner, flying Prime Minister Louis St Laurent from Ottawa to Calgary to open the annual Stampede. The aircraft remained in service until retired on 28 August 1966. It was sold to an American buyer (who later scrapped it) for $49,000 (Cdn). A bit of a scandal ensued when the Auditor General reported that three of the C-5's engines had been overhauled in 1965-66 at a cost of $40,000 and that, in early 1966, the Department of National Defence had refurbished the aircraft's interior and structure to gain an additional 1,500 hours of use at a cost of $343,000.

RCAF Chronology 1950–1959

1955

1955 Photo-surveys for the Mid-Canada Line completed except for northern islands.
RCAF ordered six Sikorsky H-34A helicopters, which were assigned the CTS (Chief of Technical Services) Control Number CH-126 and the Type Designator H-34
January No. 1 (F) Wing commenced its move from North Luffenham to Marville.
408 (P) Sqn received its first Dakota Mk IIIs and Mk IVs.

422 (F) Sqn received its first Sabre 5s
1 January No. 22 Wing (Auxiliary) formed to administer and control 406 'City of Saskatoon' (LB) Sqn (Aux)
February 423, 428, 433 and 440 AW(F) Sqns received their first CF-100 Canuck Mk 4Bs
3 February The majority of the surviving Silver Star 1s were struck off strength (two others had been s/o/s on 10 October 1953); under MAP, six went to Greece, four to Turkey, and the rest to the USAF and ANG
10 February 409 AW(F) Sqn received its first CF-100 Canuck Mk 4A, 18315
12-15 February Operation Big Sandy Lake, a joint RCAF/USAF extensive search for survivors from a

USAF B-47 that exploded in flight over northern Saskatchewan (en route from Thule to March AFB); two survivors were quickly found the first day and one more was found on the fourth day
March 439 (F) Sqn received its first Sabre 5s
1 March 1 (F) Wing relocated from North Luffenham to Marville in Operation Rhumba Queen; comprised 410, 439 and 441 (F) Squadrons
21 March Plans for the Distant Early Warning (DEW) Line announced. Construction of DEW Line began
22 March Fire destroyed an Avro Canada hangar plus two CF-100 Canucks, 18111 (Mk 3T) and 18348 (Mk 4B), a Sabre 5, 23024, and the Lancaster 100 Orenda testbed, FM209

24 March Three CF-100 Canuck Mk 4Bs (18320, '321, and '322) flown to Britain for evaluation by RAF Central Fighter Establishment; the trip, known as Random 12, was the first transatlantic flight by a Canadian-designed aircraft; after the evaluation, the three CF-100s were stored at RCAF Station Langar
30 March RCAF Station Greenwood received its first Neptune maritime reconnaissance aircraft, 24102 and 24103
31 March 404 and 405 (MR) Squadrons received their first Neptunes
April 400 'City of Toronto' (F) Sqn (Aux) received its first Silver Star 3.
416 and 444(F) Sqns received their first Sabre 6s.
432 AW(F) Sqn received its first CF-100

Above: The C-119 served in Canada and abroad throughout the decade, seen here dropping relief supplies over Quebec in January 1955.

Right: The Argus had Wright R-3370 engines for low-altitude performance. This is an Argus 2 of 404 Sqn exercising over the North Atlantic.

Only three Napier Eland-engined Cosmopolitan CL-540s were built. They flew with 412 Sqn.

408 Squadron's Canso Fs supported the unit's Lancaster 10Ps in the survey role, as did a number of other floatplane and amphibian types.

As the 1950s came to a close, the Yukon had begun to take on VIP duties as well, but the C-5 remained active until its retirement. The rest of the North Star fleet was retired by December 1965.

Six Bristol Freighters were based at Langar, in the British Midlands, and were used to support the operations of No. 1 Air Division, ferrying supplies and personnel to and from the continent and also transporting Sabres to Scottish Aviation in Prestwick for overhaul and repairs.

In the late 1950s, Canadair (then a wholly-owned subsidiary of General Dynamics) acquired the jigs and tooling for the Convair 440 Metropolitan, along with three unsold aircraft. The British engine maker Napier had already test flown a Convair 340 re-engined with its Eland turboprop and Canadair decided to produce new-build passenger aircraft with the Eland, develop a dual passenger/cargo version, and to re-engine its three CV-440s. The Canadair model numbers CL-66A, CL-66B and CL-66C were assigned, but the aircraft were marketed as the Model 540. The RCAF was in the market for a medium-range, turbo-prop-powered transport and its order for 10 CL-66Bs (as the CC-109 Cosmopolitan) proved to be the only one received by Canadair.

Two of the three re-engined CL-66Cs were loaned to the air force for crew training, pending the delivery of the new-build aircraft. In 1962 all three were acquired by the RCAF, in whose service they were known as Cosmopolitan CL-540s. When it was decided to replace the Elands with more reliable Allison 501s in the mid-1960s, the CL-540s were sold. One CC-109 was lost in a hangar fire and two were scrapped. The remaining seven were retired in 1994.

In October 1950, the RCAF evaluated a USAF C-119C Flying Boxcar at RCAF Station Rivers, Manitoba, and placed an order for 35 C-119Fs in 1952. Most served with 435 and 436 (Transport) Squadrons, with others employed by 4 (T) OTU, 104 Composite Unit, Electronic Warfare Unit, Central Experimental and Proving Establishment, and later with 408 (Transport Support and Area Reconnaissance) Squadron, as well as on United Nations duties, particularly following the Suez Crisis. The aircraft were later upgraded to C-119G standard and continued in service until 1965.

On 20 November 1956, 435 and 436 (Transport) Squadrons sent personnel and C-119s to Naples to form 114 Air Transport Unit (ATU) in support of Canadian peacekeeping efforts following the Suez Crisis. By 25 November, the first flights with supplies for the United Nations Emergency Force were en route to Egypt. That country imposed severe restrictions of the flights, limiting them to a narrow air corridor and daylight operations, and

---

Canuck Mk 4Bs

1 April CEPE began flight trials of the CF-100 Canuck Mk 5 using 18516. 439 (F) Sqn moved with 1 (F) Wing from North Luffenham to Marville, France. 441 (F) Sqn rejoined 1 (F) Wing after the latter had completed its move from North Luffenham to Marville; 441 had been temporarily attached to 3 (F) Wing at Zweibrucken since 21 December 1954

4 April 3 AW(F) OTU relocated from RCAF Station North Bay to RCAF Station Cold Lake, completing move on 22 May

6 April First award of Chadburn Trophy for 'air firing proficiency' in No. 1 Air Division was made to 4 (F) Wing at Baden-Soellingen.

30 April 409 AW(F) Sqn received its first CF-100 Canuck Mk 4Bs. 419 AW(F) Sqn exchanged its CF-100 Canuck Mk 4As for Mk 4Bs; 423 and 432 AW(F) Sqns retired their last Mk 4As

5 May Canada and the United States signed an agreement to build and operate a Distant Early Warning (DEW) Line as part of an integrated radar defence for North America

26 May First and only test of CF-100 Canuck's ejection seat using a person; pilot was Jan Zurakowski; 'ejectee' was Squadron Leader Pat Fifield of Martin-Baker, manufacturer of the model 2E seat; the test was successful

June The Minister of National Defence announced in Parliament that Auxiliary squadrons would not be equipped with the CF-100 Canuck all-weather fighter as previously planned. Release of drawings of CF-105 Arrow; only 28 months would elapse until the first aircraft was rolled out

1 June Operation Backlash III: H-19s of 108 Communications Flight began site surveys and site proving for Mid-Canada Line work

20-28 June NATO's largest air defence exercise, Carte Blanche, took place; it involved all 12 RCAF squadrons of 1 Air Division; 3,000 aircraft of NATO members took part with 2,500 sorties flown by RCAF aircraft

28 June First Silver Star 3 transferred from the RCAF to the Royal Canadian Navy arrived at HMCS Shearwater

July 414 (F) Sqn received its first

Sabre 6s

15 July Beginning of large-scale summer training exercise at Camp Gagetown, New Brunswick, involving both Regular and Auxiliary units of the RCAF; Mitchells, CC-119s, Lancasters and Mustangs participated

16 August Operation Backlash III: site clearing for Mid-Canada Line construction began

September Test, Development and Evaluation Flight formed within 404 (MR) Sqn at RCAF Station Greenwood; it would later become the Maritime Proving and Evaluation Unit. 404 (MR) Sqn retired its last Lancaster 10MRs. 413 (F), 422 (F) and 427 (F) Sqns exchanged their Sabre 5s for Sabre 6s

banning overnight stops. Before proceeding to the only airfield at which they were authorised to land, the C-119s had to overfly Rosetta in order for Egyptian controllers to verify its identity visually (leading to the painting of UNITED NATIONS in large letters on the aircraft's sides).

Despite these (and many other) restrictions, 21 flights were made between 25 and 30 November and the total reached 83 by the end of 1956. After making a flight into what was then French Somaliland to repatriate 90 Egyptian sailors captured by the French during the Suez Crisis, some of the restrictions began to be eased.

Later, 114 ATU was joined by 115 ATU, based at Abu Sueir and equipped with Dakotas and Otters. The Dakotas were used for communications duties (i.e. transport and utility roles), while the Otters patrolled the border and provided additional transport capabilities. After the RCAF gained access to the airfield at El Arish, 115 ATU moved there; it was also used by 114 ATU.

RCAF aircraft were involved in other United Nations operations, ranging from Africa to Southeast Asia. Over the years, the majority of the aircraft and personnel were from the transport component, with helicopters joining in later. Combat aircraft first took part during Operation Friction, Canada's part of the Gulf War of 1990/91.

The C-5's introduction, followed by that of the two de Havilland Comets in 1953, meant that the original two VIP North Stars could return to less glamourous duties. The Comets were ordered in November 1951. In February of that year, the Canadian government had ordered Avro Canada to stop all work on the C-102 Jetliner and to concentrate its activities on the CF-100 Canuck, this action no doubt related to the tensions of the Korean War. The first production CF-100 was handed over to the RCAF on 17 October. With its purchase of Comets, the RCAF became the world's first air force to operate jet-powered transport aircraft and, with the establishment of its transatlantic flights, became the world's first operator of jet transports on a scheduled service.

As a result of several crashes of civilian Comets and a painstaking investigation into their causes, the RCAF's two Comet 1As – 5301 and 5302 – were grounded in January 1954. After being modified, they returned to service in November 1957, remaining with 412 (T) Squadron until they were retired in 1963 and sold two years later.

Wearing large UN roundels and titles, this Dakota 4FP served with 115 ATU at El Arish in Egypt during the peacekeeping operation following Suez.

And so to the Arrow.

Can any other aircraft have generated such promise, mystique, and as many myths and legends as the CF-105 Arrow? Beyond question, it was the very best interceptor aircraft in the late 1950s and some of its attributes have never been exceeded. That it was so far ahead of its time is all the more remarkable considering the small population and economy of the country that created it. Unfortunately, those same factors ultimately contributed to the entire project's cancellation, an occurrence that simultaneously devastated the Canadian aviation industry, not to mention the lives of the tens of thousands of people working for Avro Canada and its suppliers. Not for nothing is 20 February 1959 known as 'Black Friday'.

The Arrow's story began in 1946 when the Royal Canadian Air Force determined that its front-line fighter squadrons should be equipped with a long-range, two-seat, twin-engined, all-weather/night interceptor. An RCAF evaluation team toured British and American aircraft manufacturers to see if anything they had in development would meet Canada's needs. None did, so the Canadian government took the enormous step of deciding to fund the design and development of the aircraft in Canada, resulting in the excellent CF-100 Canuck and its Orenda engines described earlier.

Aircraft designers are always looking far into the future. Although the prototype CF-100 Canuck Mk 1 first flew on 19 January 1950, Avro Canada proposed a swept-wing version, the CF-100S, in July 1948, and followed that in 1949 with a supersonic version, the CF-100D. During December 1950, the company was proposing a swept-wing, supersonic development to be known as the CF-103, and built a full-scale mock-up of it.

Due to various delays and doubts about the ability of the design to achieve supersonic flight, the CF-103 was cancelled in December 1951 and attention was turned to the company's Model C.104, although work continued on further developments of the CF-100. One of these called for a new wing that was thinner,

1 September No. 12 Air Defence Group retitled 5 Air Division; remained assigned to Air Defence Command at RCAF Stn Comox.
412 (T) Sqn moved from RCAF Station Rockcliffe to RCAF Station Uplands
3 September Two of the three CF-100 Canuck Mk 4Bs sent to Britain for evaluation, 18321 and 18322, arrived at the SBAC show at Farnborough
5 September First flying demonstration of CF-100 Canuck Mk 4B at Farnborough; pilot was Jan Zurakowski
12 September 435 (T) Sqn relocated from RCAF Station Edmonton to the nearby RCAF Station Namao
22 September Last (of 25)

Neptunes, 24125, received by RCAF
25-28 September CF-100 Canuck Mk 4B, 18321, flown to Grostenquin to begin a demonstration tour for 1 Air Division personnel
30 September C-5 North Star, 10000, of 412 (T) Sqn commenced round-the-world flight with the Minister of External Affairs Lester B. Pearson; stops included Moscow, North Africa and the Far East, returning on 15 November
October 411 'County of York' (F) Sqn (Aux) received its first Silver Star 3
1 October 418 'City of Edmonton' (LB) Squadron (Aux) relocated from RCAF Station Edmonton to nearby RCAF Station Namao

17 October 433 AW(F) Sqn relocated from RCAF Station Cold Lake to RCAF Station North Bay
Oct/Nov Sikorsky H-34 and Vertol H-21B helicopters entered RCAF service with 108 Communications Flight; they were employed in support of the construction of the Mid-Canada Line; previous RCAF helicopters had been used for SAR and training
November Operation Banana Belt began; required by US before it would underwrite its 75 per cent share of the cost of 53 CF-100 Mk 5s for Belgium; four Mk 4s, 18494/97, were delivered from Avro Canada to RCAF Station Cold Lake for operational suitability trials, including weapon systems trials; also

known as Operation Frozen Banana Belt, the Cold Lake trials ended 16 December, resuming at Eglin AFB in January 1956.
403 'City of Calgary' (F) Sqn (Aux) received its first Silver Star 3.
405 (MR) Sqn retired its last Lancaster 10MRs
1 November The Photographic Interpretation Section of 408 (P) Squadron became the RCAF Air Photographic Intelligence Centre at RCAF Station Rockcliffe
3 November RCAF received its first three Sikorsky H-34s (9630, '31, '32)
December Canadian government limited development of the CF-105 to 11 aircraft; subject to review after first flight
9 December RCAF's first CF-100

144

Above: Otter 3743 was one of four serving alongside the Dakotas of 115 ATU in 1959 as part of the RCAF commitment to the UN operation.

Below: Initial UN supply flights to Egypt were made by C-119s of 114 ATU based at Naples, later replaced by detatchments in Sicily.

The major RCAF UN involvement in the early part of the decade had been in Korea. North Stars shifted thousands of tons of freight and mail to the war zone.

slightly swept and of larger area. The goal of this redesign effort was to raise the limiting speed from Mach 0.85 to 0.95, in a dive.

Unfortunately for the design department, the flight test department, in the person of chief test pilot Jan Zurakowski, demonstrated that the straight-winged CF-100 could exceed Mach 1, albeit in a dive. In the Mk 4 prototype, 18112, an unofficial flight past Mach 1 (no calibration was available) was made at Malton (home of Avro Canada) on 4 December 1952. Another flight was made on 16 December in Ottawa, but the calibrated Sabre was unable to maintain position during the dive. Finally, on 18 December, Zurakowski attained a speed of Mach 1.06 during another attempt at Malton. Diving from 45,000 ft (13716 m), he broke the

sound barrier passing through 33,000 ft (10058 m), shaking the Malton area for the second time in two weeks.

Zurakowski later described himself as being 'public enemy number one' in the eyes of the Avro Canada design department, because his flights had caused an immediate cessation of official interest in the redesigned CF-100. On the other hand, the flights had also demonstrated that the production aircraft would not become uncontrollable if it exceeded the design speed of Mach 0.85 listed in the pilot's notes should it inadvertently be flown faster. (Avro Canada continued to propose new versions and developments of the CF-100, including several after the cancellation of the CF-105, but that is getting ahead of the story.)

The company's attention now focused on its C-104 proposal. In 1950, the company's advanced design group submitted several proposals to the government, one of which was the C-104. It was powered by two TR9 (later Orenda) engines, with provision for two crew and cannon armament. Avro Canada's proposal also included its Model C-105, propelled by a liquid-fuelled rocket. With a small wing area of just 600 sq ft (55 m²) and a weight at launch of 20,000 lb (907 kg), it can reasonably be described as radical. Perhaps hedging the bet somewhat, the proposal included a delta-winged version, too.

After studying these proposals during 1951, the RCAF decided that its 1950 requirements were becoming quickly outdated by the constantly-advancing state of the art. Consequently, in January 1952, they formed an 'All-Weather Interceptor Requirements Team' at Air Force Headquarters to take a fresh look at what it really wanted for its next fighter. In March 1952, the team issued its final report. In response, Avro Canada submitted two new designs, both described in great detail. The C-104/1 was a single-engined aircraft, while the twin-engined model was given the company designation C-104/2. Both aircraft featured delta wings. Although both met the RCAF's requirements, they did so in different ways. As it did many years later when choosing the F/A-18 over the F-16, the air force preferred the twin-engined design, probably for the same reason, i.e. the enhanced survivability over the vast expanse of Canadian territory. Accordingly, Avro Canada continued work on its C-104/2.

In April 1953, the Royal Canadian Air Force issued Specification AIR 7-3 'Design Studies of a Prototype Supersonic All-Weather Aircraft' to Avro Canada for an aircraft to meet the

---

Canuck Mk 5, 18513, was accepted and taken on strength
14 December Crash of an RCAF Bristol Freighter, 9696, at Marville

1956

1956 RCAF purchased four Vertol H-21B helicopters; they were assigned the CTS Control Number CH-125
January Operation Banana Belt moved to Eglin AFB; four USAF personnel also flew the aircraft; concluded after a big firepower demonstration on 2 May
9 January RCAF placed its second order for the CP-107 Argus, adding 12 Mk 2s to the initial order for one pre-production and 12 production Mk 1s

16 January A Silver Star 3 was flown from Vancouver to Shearwater with one 25-minute stop (at Fort William) in 6.17 hours; crew was Squadron Leader L. Hill and Flight Lieutenant A. Bowman; this was the first coast-to-coast jet crossing of Canada
February RCAF inspected the wooden mock-up of the CF-105 Arrow. CEPE assisted in cold weather trials of Sabre, Supermarine Swift, Hawker Hunter and Fairey Gannet
March 425 and 428 AW(F) Sqns received their first CF-100 Canuck Mk 5s
2 March Crash of four Sabres of 'Skylancers' aerobatic team near Strasbourg killed all four pilots
19 March Fire in hangar of 426 (T)

Sqn at Dorval, in which North Star 17513 (of CEPE, and recently demodified from its role as the 'Rockcliffe Ice Wagon') and CC-119 22124 were destroyed, along with much of 426's historical records; heroic efforts by personnel saved four North Stars and one CC-119; the headquarters building, which housed both 426 and 436 (T) Squadrons, was also destroyed, but most of the records and furniture were saved; the fire resulted in 436 moving to Trenton in July
20 March A 412 (T) Sqn North Star, began a tour of the Canadian Arctic with Governor-General Vincent Massey, flying over Geographic North Pole on 24 March and returning on 5 April
25 March Delivery of RCAF's last

Bristol Freighter, 9850
April 423 AW(F) Sqn operated CF-100 Canuck Mk 5s while its Mk 4Bs were overhauled at Malton by Avro Canada; the work, including the application of camouflage, was in preparation for the squadron's move to 2 (F) Wing at Grostenquin.
424 'City of Hamilton' (F) Sqn (Aux) received its first Expeditor 3 in preparation for conversion to the light transport and emergency rescue roles
June 421 (F) Sqn exchanged its Sabre 5s for Sabre 6s.
432 AW(F) Sqn received its first CF-100 Canuck Mk 5s
July 439 (F) Sqn exchanged its Sabre 5s for Sabre 6s.

Above: As with the later Cessna L-19s, Austers were used by army Air Observation Post Flights but maintained on the strength of the RCAF.

Left: The Argus Mk 1 was distinguishable from the Mk 2 by its slightly larger radome. This is the fourth of 12 Mk 1s produced.

RCAF's Operational Requirement OR 1/1-63 'Supersonic All-Weather Interceptor Aircraft'. The specifications were extraordinarily demanding by any standard, all the more so considering the Canadian budget and the virtual youth of the country's aviation industry. AIR 7-3 called for an aircraft capable of operating from a 6,000-ft (1830-m) runway, have a range of 600 nm (690 miles; 1110 km), top speed of Mach 1.5, crew of two, advanced missile armament coupled with an equally advanced fire control system suitable for operation in Canada's demanding environment, and the ability to manoeuvre at 2 *g* at 50,000 ft (15240 m).

Once again, the RCAF dispatched an evaluation team to see if any of Canada's allies had anything on the drawing board that could meet these requirement and, once again, none did. (Of interest is the fact that one of the designs considered by the team was the McDonnell F-101 Voodoo.) As was the case with the CF-100, the government decided to have the Canadian aviation industry design and produce an aircraft to meet its stringent requirements.

Avro Canada set to work developing its C-104/2 proposal, eventually assigning the company designation C-105 to the project. A variety of wing areas was studied, each offering its own combination of advantages and disadvantages. The designs were identified according to their wing area (i.e. the C-105/1000 had a wing area of 1,000 sq ft/93 m²) and the designers finally settled on the C-105/1200 (with an actual wing area of 1,225 sq ft/114 m²). This design became the company's C-105 proposal and it was submitted in May 1953. The RCAF quickly agreed that this design met its demand-

The CL-52 was a borrowed SAC B-47B which was fitted with an Orenda PS-13 Iroquois for the Arrow programme. The engine performed well, but the pod adversely affected flight characteristics.

ing specifications and, in July, a Ministerial Directive was issued by the Department of Defence Production that formally authorised the detailed design study for the aircraft to meet AIR 7-3, to be known as the CF-105.

As with the CF-100 before it, it was intended to work up to a definitive production aircraft in stages. Also like the CF-100, the aircraft's intended engines, the Orenda PS-13 Iroquois, would not be ready for the Mk 1 prototypes. Avro Canada adapted the design to use two of the new Rolls-Royce RB.106, which was then in an advanced stage of development in Britain.

Wind tunnel tests began in September 1953, only two months after receiving the government's authorisation to proceed. Low-speed testing was conducted in the National Research Council's Ottawa wind tunnel, with other tests carried out at several wind tunnels in

the United States. In addition, Avro Canada used free-flight models launched atop Nike rockets. The stainless steel models were instrumented to provide telemetry data of the aircraft at supersonic speeds and high altitude. Nine were launched from the Canadian Armament Research Defence Establishment at Point Petre, near Trenton, coming down in Lake Ontario. Two other launches were made from the NACA range near Langley, Virginia. (Of interest is that a group of enthusiasts began searching the waters of Lake Ontario off Point Petre in 1995 in an attempt to recover some of the models.)

During 1954, the Royal Canadian Air Force officially adopted the designation CF-105. Under the complicated system governing aircraft designations, this was actually the Chief of Technical Service (CTS) Control Number.

404, 405 and 407(MR) Sqns retitled as 404, 405 and 407 (MP) Sqns [Redesignation of Lancaster 10 MR as Lancaster 10 MP probably occurred at the same time]
July/Aug Exercise Morning Star: more than 25 RCAF aircraft took part in a large-scale Canadian army exercise held at Camp Gagetown, New Brunswick; jet aircraft were used in a tactical role as strike aircraft for the first time in a Canadian army training exercise.
August 402 'City of Winnipeg' (F) Sqn (Aux) retired its last Silver Star 3 and received its first Expeditor 3s.
403 'City of Calgary' (F) Sqn (Aux) also

received its first Expeditor 3s.
418 'City of Edmonton' (LB) Sqn (Aux) received its first Silver Star 3.
420 'City of London' (F) Sqn (Aux) retired its Mustang IVs, Harvard IIs, and Silver Star 3s in preparation for its disbandment.
428 AW(F) Sqn retired its last CF-100 Canuck Mk 4Bs, continuing to operate Mk 5s at RCAF Station Uplands.
441 (F) Sqn exchanged its Sabre 5s for Sabre 6s.
442 'City of Vancouver' (F) Sqn (Aux) and 443 'City of New Westminster' (F) Sqns (Aux) received their first Sabre 5s
24 August RCAF placed first order

for Canadair CC-106 Yukon: eight aircraft and 16 spare engines and propellers
26 August 1 Pilot Weapons School was redesignated as 4 AFS
30 August Four Sabres of 1 OFU flew from RCAF Station Sea Island (Vancouver, BC) to HMCS Shearwater (Dartmouth, NS); first section (Flight Lieutenant R. H. Annis and Flying Officer R. J. Childerhose) took 5.30 hours with a 10-minute stop at RCAF Station Gimli; second section (Flying Officers B. J. McComiskey and B. Merklinger) took 5.12 hours with stops at RCAF Stations Gimli (eight minutes) and St-Hubert (seven minutes)

September 406 'City of Saskatoon' (LB) Sqn (Aux) received its first Silver Star 3.
412 (T) Sqn received its first Mitchell IIIs for use as light transports for VIPs.
424 'City of Hamilton' (F) Sqn (Aux) retired its last Mustang IVs in preparation for conversion to the light transport and emergency rescue roles.
433 AW(F) Sqn received its first CF-100 Canuck Mk 5s
1 September 420 'City of London' (F) Sqn (Aux) disbanded
October 403 'City of Calgary' (F) Sqn (Aux) retired its last Mustang IVs and 424 'City of Hamilton' (F) Sqn (Aux)

The T-34A served for only a short time with the RCAF, being regarded as too docile for a trainer.

A Goose of 408 Squadron is seen at Golden Lake, Ontario in May 1953.

Prior to the arrival of the Otter, the Norseman was the principal utility transport, usually mounted on floats. This example served with 408 Squadron alongside a variety of other types.

It was not until 1976 that this system was drastically revamped and streamlined.)

Problems with the development of the RB.106 engines came to the fore later in 1954 and it became apparent that they would not be resolved in time to use the engines in the Mk 1 aircraft. Avro Canada then selected the Curtiss-Wright J67 but, in 1955, the US Air Force cancelled that programme. For its third choice, Avro Canada turned to the Pratt & Whitney J75, the same engine that powered the USAF's F-105 and F-106. Orenda's work on the PS-13 Iroquois was proceeding well, but it was felt that there was too much risk in beginning the test flight programme with both a new engine and a new airframe. Yet another redesign of the engine bay and intakes was, therefore, felt to be worth the effort.

In early 1957, 'Arrow' was officially adopted as the CF-105's name, and the two initial models became the Arrow 1 and Arrow 2.

The Arrow's capabilities posed extreme technical hurdles to be overcome, such as aerodynamic heating, sonic stresses caused by the engines and by aerodynamic forces, avionics cooling, the need for an extremely high-pressure hydraulic system (4000 psi compared with the then-typical 3000), and so on.

From the beginning, it had been decided to build the prototypes on the production tooling, rather than virtually hand-building them as had been done before. This concept was known as the Cook-Craigie plan in the United States, but even that country had not yet applied it to such

an advanced design as the CF-105 Arrow. Thorough testing of each system was, therefore, of the utmost importance, and a wide variety of test rigs was built to reduce to the absolute minimum the amount of risk associated with the production concept. The tests also reduced the amount of air testing required, shortening the flight test programme and speeding the service introduction of the Arrow.

The use of production tooling to produce the prototypes resulted in a very considerable cost saving. It took between 15 and 20 man-hours per pound to build the first Arrow, a figure that compared very favourably with the typical 25 to 40 man-hours per pound using earlier methods. Taking into account the 20-ton weight of the aircraft, the degree of improvement is even more impressive. A further advantage of using the production tooling to build the prototypes is demonstrated by the fact that the first Arrow differed in weight by a mere 68 lb (30 kg) from that predicted by its designers, and that its centre of gravity was within 0.25 per cent of the estimated location.

A key feature of the Arrow was its interchangeable weapons bay, which allowed fast rearming and simplified conversion to other roles. The bay was 18 ft (5.5 m) long, 8 ft (2.4 m) wide, and 3 ft (0.9 m) deep, larger than that of a B-29 bomber. An armament pack could be raised into position, attaching at four points. The pack's contents could be varied to suit the mission. Perhaps more important was that it allowed the weapons and/or extra fuel tanks to

be carried internally, thus reducing drag and improving speed and range. An Avro Canada drawing shows one configuration of the pack as being three Sparrow missiles, each on an extendible launch rail, not at all unlike that later used by the Lockheed F-117A.

As remarkable as the aircraft itself was the speed with which it was designed and built. The drawings were released to the production department in June 1955 and the first Arrow, 25201 (coded RL-201, which was not a serial as some authors apparently believe), was rolled out on 4 October 1957. A crowd of 12,000 was in attendance at ceremonies presided over by the Minister of National Defence, George R. Pearkes, VC. Unfortunately, the debut was overshadowed by the other aerospace achievement that day: the launch of the world's first artificial satellite, Sputnik 1, by the Soviet Union. The two events would prove to be closely tied by more than just by this date.

Five Arrow 1s were completed and took part in the flight test programme. 25201 made the first flight on 25 March 1958. This had followed a gradual process beginning with ground-running one engine on 4 December 1957, both engines then running together for the first time on 18 December. This was followed by low-speed taxiing tests, which began on 3 January 1958. The only snags reported by Jan Zurakowski were the failure of two microswitches. The 'snag sheet' from the first flight was duly framed by the engineering department. 'Zura's' only complaint was the

retired its last Silver Star 3s in preparation for conversion to the light transport and emergency rescue roles. 442 'City of Vancouver' (F) Sqn (Aux) retired its Mustang IVs and Vampire IIIs. 443 'City of New Westminster' (F) Sqn (Aux) retired its last Mustang IVs
1 October 410 (F) Sqn deactivated as a Sabre-equipped day fighter squadron in 1 (F) Wing at Marville in preparation for its reformation in Canada with CF-100s
8 October Primary Flying Training School (PFTS) formed at RCAF Station Centralia; equipped with DHC Chipmunks for *ab initio* training instead

of Harvards; students would then progress to a Flying Training School (FTS) equipped with the Harvard and then to an Advanced Flying School (AFS) for further training on the Silver Star
22 October 401 'City of Westmount' (F) Sqn (Aux) received its first Sabre 5s, the first Auxiliary squadron to do so. Officer exchange programme between RCAF and RAAF inaugurated; similar programmes with the RAF and USAF were already in place
23 October 411 'County of York' (F) Sqn (Aux) received its first Sabre 5s
28 October 400 'City of Toronto' (F) Sqn (Aux) and 438 'City of Montreal' (F)

Sqn (Aux) received their first Sabre 5s
November Mustang IVs and Vampire IIIs were withdrawn from service in the RCAF.
410 AW(F) Sqn received its first CF-100 Canuck Mk 5s
1-4 November Nimble Bat 1: 445 AW(F) Sqn flew its CF-100s from Uplands to Marville, becoming the first CF-100 squadron assigned to NATO; it replaced 410 (F) Sqn with Sabres
1 November 410 AW (F) Sqn reformed at RCAF Stn Uplands with CF-100 Canuck Mk 5s; assigned to Air Defence Command.
RCAF personnel from Debert, Moncton,

Chatham, Greenwood and Summerside joined the rescue operation at the Springhill, Nova Scotia, coal mine disaster
20 November 435 (T) and 436 (T) Sqns sent personnel and aircraft to help form 114 Air Transport Unit (ATU), based at Naples in support of United Nations Emergency Force (UNEF)
December Germany ordered 225 Sabre 6s, to which were added 75 more from 1 Air Division squadrons converting to the Sabre 6; the Sabre 5s were overhauled by Scottish Aviation.
423 AW(F) Sqn exchanged its borrowed CF-100 Canuck Mk 5s for its own Mk

The first Arrow is seen on the day it was rolled out at Malton. With an average take-off weight greater than a fully-loaded Lancaster and a length of 77 ft (23.5 m), the CF-105 was one of the largest interceptors ever built.

lack of a clock in the cockpit.

25202's first flight was on 1 August 1958, followed by 25203's on 22 September, 25204's on 27 October, and 25205's on 11 January 1959. Two landing accidents occurred during the course of the test flying programme, both caused by the collapse of one of the main landing gears. (The first accident involved the left main gear, the second involved the right main gear.) Only once did an Arrow ever have to divert to another field, and that was through no fault of its own. A TCA airliner was blocking the main runway at Malton (now Toronto's Lester B. Pearson IAP), so 25204 landed at RCAF Station Trenton before returning to Malton.

During its third flight (3 April 1958), 25201 exceeded Mach 1 while climbing. On 18 April, 25201 made two flights, its sixth and seventh, attaining Mach 1.25 and 1.52, respectively. The RCAF later announced that the Arrow had achieved the 'equivalent of 1000 mph' in level flight that day. During the course of 66 test flights involving all five Arrow 1s, Mach 1 was surpassed 28 times, with the highest speed being Mach 1.96 on 11 November 1958 in 25202. The longest flight was 1.45 hours in 25201 on 7 June 1958.

Two flights were made on what would be the final day any Arrow ever flew, 19 February 1959: one each by 25203 and 25201, the latter closing the flying as well as having begun it less than 11 months earlier. 25203's last flight was noteworthy in that it was the only time an Arrow's rear cockpit was occupied during a test flight, all others having been flown solo. The final summary of CF-105 Arrow 1 test flights is

Jan Zurakowski was Avro Canada's chief test pilot and took the first three Arrows on their maiden flights. He also did much of the development flying on the CF-100 series.

as follows: 25201 – 25 flights, 25.40 hours; 25202 – 25 flights, 25.40 hours; 25203 – 12 flights, 13.30 hours; 25204 – six flights, 7.00 hours; and 25205 – one flight, 0.40 hours. Totals: 66 flights, 70.30 hours.

Three Avro Canada pilots and one RCAF pilot flew the Arrow as follows: Jan 'Zura' Zurakowski – 21 flights (including the first flights of 25201, 25202, and 25203), 23.45 hours; Wladyslaw 'Spud' Potocki – 33 flights (including the first flights of 25204 and 25205), 34.35 hours; Peter Cope – five flights, 5.25 hours; and Flight Lieutenant Jack Woodman – six flights, 6.45 hours.

The first Arrow 2, 25206, was 98 per cent complete and was scheduled for completion on 'Black Friday'. It was due for RCAF acceptance within weeks of the cancellation. There were 29 Arrow 2s on order, 15 in what was known as Batch 87 and 14 in Batch 88.

The RCAF reserved a block of serials from 25201 to 25700 for the Arrow and some sources talk about long-term production runs of 300, even 500, aircraft. Obviously, not all would have been in service at the same time, but new models would have replaced older ones as had happened with the Sabre and CF-100.

In parallel with the development of the Arrow was that of the Orenda PS-13 (Project Study 13) Iroquois. In September 1953, the Gas Turbine Division (as it was then still known) was authorised by the Hawker Siddeley Group design council to proceed, as a private venture, with the design of an engine to power the CF-100's eventual successor. A major design requirement was for the aircraft to be able to be airborne in a maximum of 60 seconds, beginning with the pilot in the cockpit but not

---

4Bs in preparation for its relocation to 2 (F) Wing at Grostenquin
19 December Canada announced that it would train 360 West German pilots for the recently formed Luftwaffe, commencing in 1957
21 December The first Canadair CP-107 Argus Mk 1, 20710, was rolled out by Canadair at its Cartierville facility

1957
1957 The Canadian flag (Red Ensign) replaced the RAF-style fin flash; this had appeared earlier on the CF-100 Canuck Mk 4s painted in camouflage for the 1 Air Division squadrons; it had also

appeared on Sabres and other aircraft of 1 Air Division as early as 1955. Instrument Check Pilots School (ICPS) formed at RCAF Station Saskatoon
January 416 (F) Sqn retired its last Sabre 6s in preparation for its deactivation and return to Canada.
434 (F) Sqn exchanged its Sabre 5s for Sabre 6s
22 January 435 (T) Sqn completed its involvement with 114 ATU in support of the UNEF in the Middle East, followed by 436 (T) Sqn on 31 January
25 January 402 'City of Winnipeg' (F) Sqn (Aux) retitled as 402 'City of Winnipeg' (T) Sqn (Aux) and assigned to

Training Command; although designated as a transport unit, it was employed on navigation training.
403 'City of Calgary' (F) Sqn (Aux) retitled as 403 'City of Calgary' (T) Sqn (Aux) and assigned to Training Command in the light transport and emergency rescue roles
31 January 416 (F) Sqn deactivated as a day fighter squadron equipped with Sabres in preparation for returning to Canada and reforming with CF-100s at RCAF Station St-Hubert; it was replaced in 2 (F) Wing by 423 AW(F) Sqn
February 409 AW(F) Sqn received its first CF-100 Canuck Mk 5s

1 February 416 AW(F) Sqn reformed at RCAF Station St-Hubert, with CF-100 Canuck Mk 5s; assigned to Air Defence Command
12-15 February Nimble Bat 2: 423 AW(F) Sqn moved from RCAF Station St-Hubert to 2 (F) Wing at Grostenquin to replace 416 (F) Sqn
1 March Disbandment of No. 2 Group (Auxiliary), which had controlled No. 14 (Operational) Wing (Auxiliary) and No. 15 (Technical Training) Wing (Auxiliary). Activation of RCAF's Air Weapons Unit (AWU) at Sardinia as a replacement for the range at Rabat, Morocco

Above: The developed Arrow would have been the best interceptor of the 1960s. 25205 flew barely a month before the programme's demise.

Below: Apart from one aircraft that diverted to Trenton, all Arrows flew from Malton, now the site of Toronto's Pearson airport.

(9 m) long and 6 ft (1.8 m) in diameter. This arrangement meant that the engine's thrust was not in line with the aircraft's centreline, and it was also toed out slightly, resulting in asymmetrical thrust at higher power levels. Instrumentation racks were installed in the bomb bay to monitor the Iroquois in flight.

The aircraft was not officially taken on strength by the RCAF, but it wore full RCAF markings with X059 on the tail. The first flight of the CL-52 was its departure from Canadair's Cartierville facility, a one-chance-only deal as the short runway precluded an aborted take-off. That went well, but the huge pod affected the aircraft's flying characteristics and the first few landings were fraught with dangers.

Following a demonstration run at 19,000 lb (84.52 kN) of thrust (without afterburner) in the test cell on 1 November 1957 for Canadian government representatives, an Iroquois was installed in the CL-52's pod and run at altitude for the first time on 13 November. On 17 December 1958, the first pre-production Iroquois was delivered by Orenda to Avro Canada (across the road) and the second followed four days later. By mid-February, both were being prepared for the first Arrow 2, 25206. However, the 20 February 1959 cancellation included the Iroquois as well as the Arrow.

That the Arrow was cancelled, the Iroquois along with it, is historical fact. The reasons for the cancellation continue to be the subject of speculation and misunderstanding, all of which have contributed to the rise of myths and legends surrounding the aircraft.

John Diefenbaker and his Progressive Conservative Party had defeated the Liberal Party of Louis St Laurent, forming a minority government in Parliament in June 1957. (American readers should note that the parties' names should not be taken as literally as they would be as political terms south of the border.) Another election was soon called and, on 31 March 1958, Diefenbaker was re-elected in a landslide of a magnitude never before seen in Canada, winning a solid majority in Parliament. Although Diefenbaker had been in favour of the Arrow programme when leading a minority government, Avro Canada was concerned that his support might not last now that his government's decisions could be easily passed by its majority, rather than tempered by the necessity of securing support from other Members of Parliament.

The formation of NORAD meant that the United States' and Canada's air defences were integrated and that their defence policies were becoming more closely aligned. While

with the engines running.

Detailed design was completed on 1 May 1954 and an Iroquois was first run on 15 December. A year later, the engine was producing more than 19,000 lb (84.52 kN) of thrust during sustained runs and, on 24 June 1956, the Iroquois successfully completed its first 50-hour pre-flight rating test. The first operation of the afterburner followed on 3 July and 1,000 hours of running time was reached on 19 September.

To flight-test the earlier Orenda engines, two had been installed in the outer nacelles of a Lancaster (designated 10.O), but that would not be possible for the heavier and much more powerful Iroquois. The US Air Force loaned one of its B-47B Stratojets to Canada for the test programme.

The aircraft, 50-2059, was flown to Canadair for modifications, and the company assigned its model number CL-52 to the project. The Iroquois could not be mounted under the wing in place of one of the B-47's six engines (two pods of two plus two singles), so it was mounted on the right side of the rear fuselage under the horizontal tail. The nacelle was about 30 ft

---

6 March 1 FTS disbanded at RCAF Station Centralia; it had been reactivated there on 1 September 1947
1 April No. 22 Wing (Auxiliary) disbanded
7 April 413 (F) Sqn deactivated as a day fighter unit in 3 (F) Wing in preparation for its return to Canada to reform as an All-Weather (Fighter) Squadron with CF-100s; replaced at Zweibrucken by 440 AW (F) Sqn
18 April Canada announced expansion of NATO aircrew training programme with inclusion of 70 students from Norway, 55 from Denmark, and 30 from the Netherlands

annually, commencing in July
19 April A team from No. 1 Air Division won the Fourth Allied Tactical Air Force commander's gunnery trophy, competing against teams of French F-84s and USAFE F-100s at Cazaux, France
23 April First CP-107 Argus, 20710, taken on strength by RCAF, but returned to company to conduct flight test programme; it later rejoined the RCAF and served as a fully operational aircraft, unlike most prototypes
1 May 413 AW(F) Sqn reformed at RCAF Station Bagotville with CF-100 Canuck Mk 5s; assigned to Air Defence

Command
11 May Nimble Bat 3: 440 AW(F) Sqn moved from RCAF Station Bagotville to 3 (F) Wing at Zweibrucken to replace 413 (F) Sqn
15 May CEPE relocated from RCAF Station Rockcliffe to RCAF Station Uplands (both in Ottawa)
28 May 408 (P) Sqn completed its last SHORAN 'line'
June 430 (F) Sqn received its first Sabre 6s
5 June First two of seven Cessna L-19Es delivered
24 June Random 30, the final operation of 1 OFU, completed the

delivery of 24 Sabres and six Silver Stars to Europe; a total of more than 800 aircraft was delivered; two Reverse Randoms had returned Sabre 5s to Canada for the Auxiliary
30 June 408 (P) Sqn completed the aerial surveying of Canada, concluding with the Arctic islands; the project had begun in 1924
July 414 (F) Sqn retired its last Sabre 6s in preparation for its deactivation and return to Canada
4 July Final intake of NATO aircrew to be trained under terms of the original agreement; over 4,600 personnel from 10 nations (Belgium, Denmark, France,

149

Below: In rare sunshine, a Sabre 6 of 441 Squadron, 1 Air Division, cavorts near Marville, February 1957.

Above: The air defence of Europe was a deadly serious business at the height of the Cold War. This is a 422 Sqn dispersal at Baden-Soellingen.

Below: In 1955 No. 2 (Fighter) Wing formed the 'Skylancers' aerobatic team with Sabre 5s drawn from 430 Sqn ('BH' codes) and 421 Sqn ('AX').

NORAD was described as a partnership, there was never much doubt that the Americans were the dominant partner. Had Canada chosen not to join a continental air defence, it is certain that if the Soviet Union launched an attack, the Americans would have sent their aircraft into Canadian air space to defend the United States. If nothing else, partnership in NORAD ensured Canada a 'seat at the table' and the ability to have a say in how, and where, USAF interceptors would operate.

The first formal recognition of joint responsibility for the defence of North America had come in August 1940 with the signing of the Ogdensburg Agreement. (At the time of the agreement, Canada was at war but the United States was not.) Simply put, both Canada and the United States were to come to the aid of the other in the event of an attack by a third party. To co-ordinate this, a Permanent Joint Defence Board was established and it oversaw many projects through the war years and into

the 1950s. However, each country operated independently in their co-operation. In other words, sovereignty of territory and control of national defences remained with their respective governments.

On 12 May 1958, this arrangement took a major step in a different direction. On that date, the two countries signed an agreement in Washington, DC, to form a joint military organisation to be known as the North American Air Defence Command ('Defense' south of the border), or NORAD. (In 1981, it was renamed North American Aerospace Defence Command.)

The previous policy of co-operation and co-ordination of the RCAF's and USAF's Air Defence Commands was replaced by one of complete integration. The first Commander-in-Chief (CINC) of NORAD was USAF General Earle Partridge and the Deputy CINCNORAD was Air Marshal Roy Slemon. Until taking up his appointment, Slemon had been Chief of the

Air Staff and it is a measure of the importance attached to NORAD that his new job was not considered to be either a demotion or a lateral move.

The Air Officer Commanding the RCAF's Air Defence Command, Air Vice-Marshal W. R. McBrien, became the Regional Commander for the Canadian region of NORAD, with a USAF officer as his deputy. This pattern has continued ever since, with the Commander coming from one country and his Deputy from the other.

The new arrangement put Canada and the RCAF at the top of the decision-making for joint operations with a major ally for the first time. (During World War II, the RCAF had operated independently through the Home War Establishment for the defence of Canada, but its overseas forces constituted an element of the Royal Air Force).

The 12 May 1958 agreement was back-dated to August 1957. At that time, a skeleton staff

Greece, Italy, the Netherlands, Norway, Portugal, Turkey and the United Kingdom) had been trained since August 1950; training for students from Denmark, the Netherlands, Norway and West Germany would continue under another agreement
14 July 414 (F) Sqn deactivated as a day fighter unit in 4 (F) Wing in preparation for its return to Canada to reform as an All-Weather (Fighter) Squadron with CF-100s; replaced at

Baden-Soellingen by 419 AW (F) Sqn
15 July 407 (MP) Squadron and 408 (P) Squadron (retitled 408 (R) Sqn on 18 July) commenced Arctic ice patrols to assist ships involved in support of construction of the DEW Line
30 July CF-100 Canuck Mk 4B, 18439, flew non-stop from RCAF Station Comox to RCAF Station St-Hubert in 4.30 hours; believed to be the longest distance covered by a 'Clunk'
31 July 1 Overseas Ferry Unit

disbanded.
DEW Line became fully operational
August 108 Communications Flight concluded its support operations for construction of the Mid-Canada Line; only one of its aircraft, an H-21, was lost during this time and that was on a training flight
5 August 414 AW(F) Sqn reformed at RCAF Station North Bay with CF-100 Canuck Mk 5s; assigned to Air Defence Command.

Nimble Bat 4: 419 AW (F) Sqn moved from RCAF Station North Bay to 4 (F) Wing at Baden-Soellingen to replace 414 (F) Sqn
7 August Canada and the United States announced the signing of an interim agreement to integrate Canadian and US air defences into a single command, named NORAD (North American Air Defence Command; 'Defense' south of the border); renamed North American Aerospace Defence

The CF-100s of the Air Division gained camouflage in 1956. Plans to replace them with CF-105s as they had in turn replaced the Sabre were scrapped with the Arrow's cancellation.

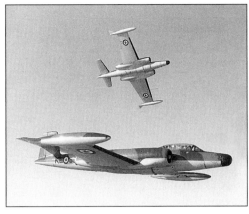

Above: A pair of freshly-painted CF-100 Mk 4Bs of 440 Squadron fly near Bagotville prior to their transfer to Zweibrucken in April 1957.

was assigned to what would become NORAD's headquarters at Colorado Springs. Discussion and negotiations leading up to the agreement had taken place over a lengthy period. The Royal Canadian Air Force held strong beliefs about how best to accomplish the air defence of Canada in particular and the North American continent in general, the cornerstone of which was that this defence would be most effective if the two countries' air defences and radar networks were integrated. At the same time, the RCAF wanted to ensure the identity of the service was maintained and was of the opinion that the best way to do this was through a joint organisation.

Parliament debated the NORAD agreement in June 1958. Some questions were asked about whether or not Canadian sovereignty was being reduced, or even surrendered, but, for the most part, Canadians recognised that the country could not defend itself unaided against the Soviet Union. The launch of Sputnik 1 (on the same day that the Arrow was rolled out) had raised the spectre of atomic warheads delivered by intercontinental ballistic missiles, and this realisation no doubt increased the acceptance of the need for NORAD.

When the RCAF's Air Defence Command was integrated into NORAD, it consisted of nine operational squadrons of Avro Canada CF-100 Canucks stretched between RCAF Station Comox, British Columbia, and RCAF Station Chatham, New Brunswick. The Auxiliary's Sabre squadrons had by then converted to the light transport role. Their range had been far too short to be able to deal adequately with bombers carrying atomic weapons, which would have been able to get too close to their targets before being intercepted. The CF-100s, while having longer range and an all-

weather capability, were subsonic, and this was felt to be insufficient. (During the early 1950s, the plans called for the Auxiliary squadrons to be equipped with CF-100s, giving a total of 20 all-weather interceptor squadrons.)

The Canadian contribution to NORAD, therefore, had to consist of more than just the nine CF-100 squadrons, and so took on a share of the three radar chains: the Distant Early Warning (DEW) Line, Mid-Canada Line, and the Pinetree Line. Canadian personnel were posted to NORAD Headquarters and Canadian territory was used to provide bases for interceptor aircraft and missiles. Canada's contribution was, in fact, on the order of about 10 per cent of the total. While that did not reflect the proportion of the area of Canada compared with that of the United States, it did approximate the relative proportions of the two populations.

Ranging in size from small outposts with 'gap-filler' radars to sprawling air bases, NORAD encompassed about 700 locations, with radar chains stretching from Midway Island in the Pacific across Alaska, the Canadian North, Greenland, and down to the Azores. Approximately 70 fighter interceptor squadrons were among its assets.

USAF units stationed on Canadian territory in Newfoundland and Labrador came under the control of the RCAF officer commanding the Canadian NORAD Region. American units in Greenland and Alaska were under USAF control. The NORAD agreement allowed for each partner to fly military aircraft in the air space of the other. The organisation's regions and sectors were based on operational considerations, not on borders.

At least until ICBMs of sufficient range became a bigger concern than bombers, NORAD's main tasks were to monitor North American air space and its approaches and to control the interception of unidentified and hostile aircraft. As an unidentified object

appeared on a DEW Line radar station's screen, its track was plotted and the information relayed to Colorado Springs and to RCAF Station St-Hubert, which at that time was the headquarters of the Canadian NORAD Region (it later moved to North Bay). If the object continued south, it would be passed on to the Mid-Canada Line for tracking and, if still unidentified, an interceptor would be launched to investigate. Throughout the flight, the crew was in contact with a ground controller, who was also linked with the radar lines. NORAD's purpose could perhaps be best described as being North America's guardian, and that role did not include calling out the USAF's Strategic Air Command. That organisation was quite separate and not part of NORAD. Later, SAC would be more closely linked with NORAD, but would always remain a separate entity.

The NORAD Commander-in-Chief was as responsible to Canada as was his deputy to the United States. Canada's policy was that partnership in NORAD reduced the risk of becoming involved in a war without its consent. It lost no more sovereignty or independence to the United States than the latter did to Canada, and certainly far less than it had surrendered during World War II.

Primarily to defend SAC bases, but also the cities and other assets near them, the United States established BOMARC missile bases across its northern tier. These missiles (originally designated F-99, then IM-99, and eventually IM-10) had a nuclear warhead and a relatively short range, although that was improved in the second model.

The Canada/US border is often referred to as the '49th parallel' but, in fact, that ignores the heavily-populated industrial heartland of southern Ontario, which extends well below that latitude. The span across the Great Lakes also meant that any US BOMARC missiles in that area would be well to the south of those

Command in 1981
8 August First Belgian air force crews arrived at 3 AW(F) OTU for CF-100 training, initially with Mitchell and simulator
1 September Air Marshal C. R. Slemon was succeeded by Air Marshal H. L. Campbell as Chief of the Air Staff; Slemon then became Deputy Commander-in-Chief of NORAD, the number two position at each NORAD centre being reserved for an officer of

the other country.
424 'City of Hamilton' (F) Sqn (Aux) retitled as 424 'City of Hamilton' (T) Sqn (Aux) and adopted the light transport and emergency rescue roles
9 September WS 10 (Waffenschule 10) of the Luftwaffe received its first ex-RCAF Sabre 5s; RCAF personnel, belonging to the Canadian Advisory Group, were assigned to assist with the training of German pilots
12 September RCAF's Air Defence

Command, and all of the All-Weather (Fighter) squadrons and Fighter squadrons assigned to it, reassigned to NORAD
24 September Belgian AF crews at 3 AW (F) OTU begin flying training on CF-100 Canuck Mk 3D, moving to Mk 4A on 11 October and completing course with familiarisation flying on Mk 5 at Avro in mid-November
29 September Last two of seven Cessna L-19s delivered

1 October 407 (MP) Squadron and 408 (P) Squadron finished their Arctic ice patrols in support of DEW Line construction
4 October Avro Canada CF-105 Arrow Mk 1 prototype, 25201, rolled out at Malton
7 October 53 CF-100 Canuck Mk 5s for the Belgian air force were first taken on strength by the RCAF on this date and then struck off strength for delivery to Belgium; 25 per cent of the cost was

151

The completion of the DEW line and related radar chains allowed the accurate direction of fighters in the vast Canadian airspace.

NORAD co-operation could not be better exemplified than with this pairing of a 410 Sqn CF-100 Mk 5 and an Air Defense Command F-102A.

SAC was a completely separate entity to NORAD, but often exercised in Canadian skies.

further east and west. Whether or not one construes it as a threat, the Americans made it clear that those bases would be established unless Canada set up two further to the north.

The Americans also wanted the SAGE (Semi-Automatic Ground Environment) system extended across Canada. SAGE allowed interceptors to operate under ground control.

The Cabinet Defence Committee and the Minister of National Defence appear to have been badly misinformed (or else they thoroughly misunderstood what they were told by their advisers) about the BOMARC, SAGE and Arrow programmes. Canada could not afford all three and the government's assessments of the Arrow's cost appear to have been badly flawed or misrepresented. As has been seen more recently with the B-2, unit costs will rise dramatically as the number of aircraft produced declines because the same amount of research and development must be done whether one or 200 are built.

The Canadian government came to believe, as did others at the time, that ICBMs would soon supplant manned bombers, rendering manned interceptor aircraft obsolete. It also came to believe, somehow, that the BOMARC

would counter the ICBM threat, although it was clearly designed solely to destroy bomber streams. The Arrow did not need SAGE, the Americans did. The Cabinet Defence Committee appears to have accepted that SAGE and the BOMARCs were a given, rather than just a recommendation.

The cost of SAGE and the BOMARCs contributed to a reduction in the number of Arrows planned for the RCAF. Originally, those plans called for a one-to-one replacement of the CF-100, even equipping Auxiliary squadrons with the type. The latter idea was dropped when it was decided not to give the Auxiliaries CF-100s.

During a meeting with the Secretary of the Air Force and senior USAF personnel on 29 January 1958, the Canadian Ambassador to Washington was told that, in the Secretary's personal opinion, the USAF could buy Arrows in 'squadron strength' to be based in Canada where they would be operated and maintained by RCAF personnel. The Ambassador's response was that this form of 'charity' would

cause political problems in Canada and that the country wanted to contribute to defence, not benefit from it.

During 1958, the government debated the continuation of the Arrow and Avro Canada learned on 3 September that the programme was in serious trouble. Official cost estimates comparing the CF-105 to the F-106 failed to take into account the Arrow's more expensive Sparrow missiles and Astra fire control system. Avro Canada had already proposed replacing these with the Hughes MA-1 fire control system and Falcon missiles, which would have brought the cost down by about $3.5 million per aircraft. While the company was strongly in favour of the substitutions, neither the RCAF nor the Minister of National Defence shared that view.

At a cabinet meeting on 7 September 1958, the cancellation of the Arrow was discussed. For some reason, the Minister of Finance asserted that the "military authorities had now decided that the aircraft was not necessary." Although both the Minister of National Defence (a retired army major general) and the Chairman of the Chiefs of Staff (an army general) supported cancelling the Arrow in favour of the BOMARC, the previous cabinet meeting had not reached a decision. At no time do the possibilities for reducing costs appear to have been discussed and almost nothing was said about the technical success of the Arrow. The government's biggest concern was the effect on the economy (and its own political

paid by Canada, with the US covering the other 75 per cent under MAP
November   RCAF's two Comet 1As, 5301 and 5302, returned to service as Comet 1XBs after modifications; the aircraft were grounded in January 1954 after several civilian Comets crashed; both withdrawn from service 16 September 1963
8 November   No. 14 (Operational) Wing (Auxiliary) retitled as No. 14 Wing (Auxiliary)
23 November   445 AW (F) Sqn became first CF-100 unit from 1 Air Division to deploy to AWU at Sardinia

5 December   Jump Moat 1: 15 CF-100 Canuck Mk 5s departed RCAF Station Bagotville for delivery to Marville
20 December   Formal acceptance by Belgium of the 53 CF-100 Canuck Mk 5s transferred from Canada; RCAF crews had flown them to Marville, from where they were ferried by BAF crews to Beauvechain, home of 1 All-Weather Wing, the parent formation of 11, 349 and 350 Squadrons BAF

1958

Early 1958   Two-letter unit codes replaced by 'RCAF'; individual aircraft letter code replaced earlier by last three digits of serial number
1958   Wing Commander J. G. Showler was awarded the McKee Trans-Canada Trophy for 1957 in recognition of the work of 408 (P) Squadron (commanded then by Wing Commander Showler); between 1954 and 1957, the squadron had photographed approximately 3.5 million sq miles (9.06 million km²) of the Canadian north.

RCAF purchased three Vertol H-44A helicopters (a civilianised variant of the H-21); they were assigned the CTS Control Number CH-127 and the Type Designator H-44B
1 June   5 (H) OTU formed at RCAF Station Rockcliffe from No. 108 Communications Flight's Training Section; equipped with Sikorsky H-34s
17 June   A Dakota IV, KN666, of 115 ATU was forced to land at Abu Sueir by MiG-15s of the United Arab Republic
25 June   Jump Moat 4: 11 CF-100 Canuck Mk 5s departed RCAF Station Bagotville for delivery to Belgium

The **BOMARC** missile which 'brought down' the Arrow saw only a brief period of RCAF service, and with nuclear warheads even less time.

Above: On two occasions during the Arrow test programme, exactly six months apart, an undercarriage failure on landing led to an excursion from the runway. This is the second incident (the first was to 201), 11 November 1958.

fortunes) that would result from the massive unemployment that would follow a cancellation.

On 17 September, the president of Avro Canada, Crawford Gordon, visited the Prime Minister. Gordon reminded him of the company's recommendation to replace the Sparrow/Astra combination with the Falcon/MA-l, and that he had been told by the Americans that they were willing to supply the weapons at a reduced cost.

Gordon's visit was reported to Cabinet on 21 September, at which time the Prime Minister proposed "carrying on the development programme until March but not beginning the production programme on the Arrow or the Iroquois at this time." This took into account the view that the economy could handle the cancellation better after the winter. At the same meeting, the cabinet approved the two BOMARC squadrons as well as two 'heavy' radars and some 'gap-fillers' for the Pinetree Line (actually more of a system than a 'long thin line' of radar stations).

Cabinet also decided not to place any production orders for the Arrow or the Iroquois engine and to conduct a comprehensive review of the programme's requirements before 31 March 1959. In addition, the Chiefs of Staff were instructed to report if they considered that more BOMARCs or any interceptor aircraft were required.

On 23 September 1958, Diefenbaker announced that the Sparrow/Astra combination would be cancelled and replaced by the Falcon and MA-l, thus reducing the cost of an Arrow from $12.5 million to $9 million. A secret brief to the cabinet in July had said that adding the Arrow, SAGE and BOMARC (with their related support) would increase Canada's defence budget by 25 to 30 per cent. (In 1955, fully 55 per cent of the Canadian defence budget was for the design development, and production of CF-100s for the RCAF; 35 per cent of this went to 'non-Avro sources', of which 50 per cent went to sub-contractors, 40 per cent for finished parts, and 10 per cent for raw materials. Across Canada, 40,000 people were involved in CF-100 production, 10,000 of them at Avro Canada.) A series of attacks on the Arrow's 'obsolescence' began to appear in the press but Air Marshal Slemon was quoted as stating that interceptors would still be needed for some time to come.

Those remarks were discussed in a cabinet meeting on 22 December. The Prime Minister was less than pleased that Slemon had spoken out and stated his intention to adhere to his September decision, adding the programme's future would have to be discussed before Parliament opened. Oddly, the Minister of

National Defence's response was that it was still his understanding that development was to be terminated by 31 March.

A recent meeting with the American Secretary of State, John Foster Dulles, had revealed that the United States was no longer interested in obtaining the Arrow for the US Air Force. It was still proceeding with the F-108 and Dulles described the US aircraft industry as 'slack'. Under these circumstances, buying foreign aircraft was out of the question.

There had been French interest in the Iroquois for their Mirage IV but, by 31 October, France reportedly concluded that the programme would be terminated. How they came to form such an opinion is unknown.

On 29 December 1958, the RCAF agreed to the replacement of the armament and fire control system and also agreed to accept the 21st Arrow, 25221, as the production standard. The design of the Arrow 2 was to be frozen with 25206.

At the 13 January cabinet meeting, the Minister of National Defence read a statement from Air Marshal Campbell that summarised the success of the Arrow programme so far. The Minister then stated that the US Air Force had 800 interceptors with funding available for another 650, that the F-106C and D had been cancelled in favour of the F-108, which was not dependent on the SAGE system (neither was the Arrow) and, oddly, added that the F-108 was now on the NORAD inventory. It most certainly was not.

Several meetings of the cabinet and its defence committee ensued and all, despite statements from the Chief of the Air Staff that 100 to 115 interceptors were required, agreed that the Arrow should be cancelled. The need to re-equip the Air Division's squadrons with new aircraft to replace their obsolete Sabres was also

---

15 July 408 (P) Squadron commenced Arctic ice patrols to assist the ships involved in DEW Line construction and support
16 July First flights of CF-100 Canuck Mk 5Ms, 18638 and 18639, in support of CEPE's 'Ultra West' Detachment at Point Mugu
August 405 (MP) Sqn received its first CP-107 Argus Mk 1s and retired its last Neptunes.
443 'City of New Westminster' (F) Sqn (Aux) retired its last Sabre 5s and received its first Expeditor 3s
1 August First flight of second

CF-105 Arrow Mk 1, 25202; pilot was Jan Zurakowski
25 August 3 FTS disbanded due to reduced requirements of NATO and RCAF training
30 August 1 Air Division won the Gusnemer Trophy (for aerial gunnery supremacy in Allied Air Forces Central Europe); Canada won it again in 1959 and 1960.
401 'City of Westmount' (F) Sqn (Aux) retired its last Harvard IIs and received its first Expeditor 3s, as did 411 'County of York' (F) Sqn which also retired its Sabre 5s

1 September 442 'City of Vancouver' (F) Sqn (Aux) retitled 442 'City of Vancouver' Sqn (Aux) and 443 'City of New Westminster' (F) Sqn (Aux) retitled as 443 'City of New Westminster' Sqn (Aux); retired last Harvard IIs, both units converting to the light transport and emergency rescue role
3 September First launch of a Sparrow 2 from a CF-100 Canuck Mk 5M, 18638; crew was Wing Commander W. A. Speck and Flying Officer B. P. Hope; target was a Del Mar Radop towed by another aircraft
22 September First flight of third

CF-105 Arrow Mk 1, 25203; pilot was Jan Zurakowski;
23 September Government announced that the RCAF would be equipped with two squadrons of BOMARC missiles, that limited development of the CF-105 Arrow would continue, that a decision on whether to put the aircraft into production would be deferred until March 1959, and that it would be modified to accept the Hughes MX-1179 fire control system and Falcon missile instead of the Astra and Sparrow, both of which were cancelled; this was the beginning of the end for the Avro

Above: These substantial temporary structures were built at McChord AFB, Washington to provide better conditions for personnel servicing North Stars involved in the Korean airlift.

The **Rockliffe Ice Wagon** *was a CL-2 North Star Mk 1 modified to study aircraft icing. Atop the fuselage is an aerofoil with de-icer boots on the leading edge.*

Above: The famous 'Golden Hawks' were formed at the end of 1959 and flew Sabre 5s for five seasons.

discussed. When the question was raised regarding the perception that Canada would be spending money to defend its allies at the same time it was cancelling the Arrow, it was stated that the Air Division's role would be changed to the strike/attack role. This begs the question of whether the role was changed in order to allow the government to claim that the Arrow was not suitable for use by the Air Division.

On 14 February, the cabinet agreed to cancel the Arrow and Iroquois programmes, but a formal vote was not to be held until other ministers, especially the Minister of Defence Production, were in attendance. That vote took place on 17 February and the resolution covered four points:

1. that development of the Arrow and Iroquois be cancelled when the announcement was made;

2. that an announcement about the cancellation, a production-sharing agreement with the United States, and the acquisition of atomic warheads be made in Parliament;

3. that the contractors be notified of the cancellation at the same time as parliament; and

4. that an agreement be reached with the United States for the implementation of agreed arrangements for the cost-sharing of the BOMARC and SAGE installations in Canada and the associated extension of radar coverage in Canada.

At about 11:00 am, 20 February 1959, the Prime Minister began his announcement to the House of Commons that the Arrow and Iroquois programmes were to be terminated immediately. He implied that cost was a major factor in the cancellation, but did not state this outright. He said that ICBMs were replacing bombers and that the Arrow could not defend Canada against the new weapons, omitting the fact that the BOMARC was an anti-bomber, and not an anti-missile, defence. He also did not mention that the BOMARCs were virtually forced on Canada in order to avoid having them based south of the Great Lakes. The Prime Minister also quoted inaccurate figures for the unit cost of the Arrow, giving a figure of $7.8 million, despite the fact that Avro Canada had offered to build 100 at a cost of $3.75 million each.

Later that day, 'Black Friday', approximately 14,000 employees of Avro Canada and its Orenda subsidiary were laid off. Still more at the many suppliers were also quickly affected. The Canadian aviation industry was dealt a crippling blow in a single stroke.

Although a few attempts were made to push the idea of completing some of the nearly-ready Arrow 2s and using them with the Arrow 1s in a research programme, nothing came of it, with the cost again being put forward as the reason. Some people pointed out that the cancellation charges could instead be applied to completing the aircraft then under construction, giving the RCAF as many as 37 Arrows, but this, too, fell on deaf ears.

Boeing factory technicians arrived in Malton in the spring of 1959 to help remove the Iroquois and its nacelle from the CL-52 so the aircraft could be returned to the United States. It was then flown to Davis-Monthan AFB where some parts were removed, and it was then scrapped, presumably due to the stress endured by the airframe from the Iroquois' 19,000 lb (84.5 kN) of thrust.

In March, it was decided to relinquish the Department of National Defence's interest in the airframes, engines and associated materiel to the Department of Defence Production for disposal as scrap. While this worked its way through the bureaucracies of the RCAF, DND and DDP, one last attempt was made to gain permission to complete the first Arrow 2 and use it to attempt a speed record. To do so would have raised difficult questions about the

Canada CF-105 Arrow

October 401 'City of Westmount' (F) Sqn (Aux) retired its last Silver Star 3 and Sabre 5s.
442 'City of Vancouver' Sqn (Aux) received its first Expeditor 3s
1 October 400 'City of Toronto' (F) Sqn (Aux) retitled as 400 'City of Toronto' Sqn (Aux) and received its first Expeditor 3s.
411 'County of York' (F) Sqn (Aux) retired its last Silver Star 3 and was retitled 411 'County of York' Sqn (Aux). Together with 406 'City of Saskatoon' Sqn (Aux), they transferred from Air Defence Command to Air Transport Command and converted to the light transport and

emergency rescue roles
9 October 1,815th and last Canadair Sabre (a Mk 6), c/n 1815, rolled off the assembly line; delivered to the Luftwaffe, it later went to Pakistan as 815
27 October First flight of the fourth CF-105 Arrow Mk 1, 25204; pilot was W. 'Spud' Potocki: also RCAF acceptance date
28 October 412 (T) Sqn's C-5 North Star, 10000, began a round-the-world flight with Prime Minister John Diefenbaker, visiting Allied and Commonwealth countries, returning on 20 December
1 November 408 (P) Squadron's

Arctic ice patrols ended.
401 'City of Westmount' (F) Sqn (Aux) retitled 401 'City of Westmount' Sqn (Aux) and converted to the light transport and emergency rescue roles.
438 'City of Montreal' (F) Sqn (Aux) retitled 438 'City of Montreal' Sqn (Aux); retired its last Sabre 5s; received its first Expeditor 3s and converted to the light transport and emergency rescue roles
11 November Highest speed reached by a CF-105 Arrow, Mach 1.96, set in 25202; pilot was W. 'Spud' Potocki
December 424 'City of Hamilton' Sqn (Aux) retired its last Harvard IIs
4 December The 692nd and last CF-100, 18792 (a Mk 5), was rolled out

at Malton, past the CF-105 Arrow prototype, 25201, which had made 46 test flights to date

1959

1 January Tactical Air Command disbanded; its Regular Force units were transferred to Air Transport Command. and its Auxiliary units were transferred to Training Command.
418 'City of Edmonton' Sqn (Aux) reassigned to Training Command.
105 Communications and Rescue (C&R) Flight absorbed by 435 (T) Sqn
7-12 January 416 AW(F) Sqn deployed to RCAF Station Cold Lake for Exercise Dirty Dart

During the decade, the helicopter evolved from a novelty to a useful workhorse, such as this H-19A of 108 Communications Flight at Bagotville.

Above: The Vampire was only ever regarded as transitional equipment between piston-engined fighters and more capable jets. In November 1956 the last examples were phased out.

cancellation and the idea was rejected. The Arrows were to be scrapped.

Work began on 22 April and was completed by mid-July. The winning bid for the job, including the completed aircraft, those still on the production line, components, jigs and fixtures, was just $300,000. The press was barred from the plant. Employees could watch, but not take photos. A reporter for the *Star Weekly*, a newspaper supplement, rented an aircraft and his photos are the only ones in existence of the scrapping.

Rumours persist to this day that one Arrow was saved. Incomplete records about the one that diverted to Trenton fuelled some of these, but that Arrow, 25204, returned to Malton the next day and was on the ramp when the scrapping was photographed from the air. (Neither the pilot who flew 25204 to Trenton nor the one who returned it to Malton had an entry for the return flight in their logbooks, but company records showed who the pilots were.) The forward fuselage of 25206 was cut off and was used by the Institute for Aviation

Medicine, finally ending up in the National Aviation Museum, along with an Iroquois, a main landing gear, and some other components.

Some believe that one or more Arrows went to Mountain View, near Trenton, and were hidden away. The runway is too short and the facility can only be approached on the ground by crossing bridges. The BCATP hangars were inspected by the author a couple of years ago and the floors appeared quite solid. Some claim that there is a mysteriously-guarded building at CFB Petawawa that 'could' contain an Arrow. On the other hand, maybe it's full of little green men in space suits.

In fact, one of the Arrows, 25202, was inside the plant having its landing gear repaired after an accident at the time the cancellation was announced and was not, therefore, visible in the aerial photographs showing the others being scrapped. This is the origin of the 'missing Arrow' myth.

Without question, the Arrow and the Iroquois were superb technical accomplishments, as even the Prime Minister admitted on 24 February 1959. He nonetheless claimed the aircraft had been "overtaken by events" and "would have been obsolete by the time it was ready for squadron use."

How good the Arrow was and how good it could ultimately have become had development of new variants gone ahead will never be known. Not only were the airframes, engines, jigs, tooling and fixtures destroyed, so were all of the drawings, documents and other reports. Many blame Diefenbaker, but it appears that he knew nothing about the extent of the destruction of this material. The most plausible

explanation to have been advanced for the eradication of everything connected with the programme is that of security. So many aspects of the programme had been on the cutting edge of technology that only by destroying the material could it be ensured that none ever fell into enemy hands. However, the source for the 'security concerns' explanation also refers to official correspondence from the Department of Defence Production that, in addition to retaining the cockpit for the Institute of Aviation Medicine, also ordered that one complete set of drawings, technical reports and related production material be kept.

In July 1959, the government announced that it would acquire a version of the Lockheed F-104 Starfighter to replace the Sabres of 1 Air Division. The F-104 was selected from a field that included the Fiat G91, Dassault Mirage III, Republic F-105 Thunderchief, Blackburn Buccaneer, and Grumman F11F-1F Super Tiger.

The Air Division's CF-100 squadrons were to be withdrawn and not replaced. This was in line with the change in role from interceptor to strike/attack, to which reconnaissance was added for some of the CF-104 squadrons.

For its NORAD-dedicated CF-100 squadrons, Canada attempted to work a deal in which the RCAF would receive F-101 Voodoos and the USAF would acquire up to 232 (one source says just 35) Canadair CC-106 Yukons. The American aircraft industry was not at all pleased with that idea, so the acquisition of CF-101 Voodoos for the RCAF was tied to licence-production of the CF-104 and realigned responsibilities for NORAD radar sites. In late 1961, the first of 56 CF-101Bs and 10 CF-101Fs began to arrive in Canada to equip five squadrons.

The cancellation of the Arrow was a severe blow to the Canadian psyche and is well-known to many people to this day. Everyone seems to know someone whose father worked for Avro Canada or Orenda. Both NASA and the American aerospace industry became major beneficiaries of the cancellation as they hired former Avro Canada and Orenda engineers, more than a few of whom rose to very senior positions.

The cancellation came just three days before the 50th anniversary of the first powered flight in Canada and 39 days before the 35th anniversary of the formation of the Royal Canadian Air Force. Although the RCAF continued to serve in NORAD and NATO, with the UN and at home, the 'Golden Years' ended on 'Black Friday'. **Jeff Rankin-Lowe**

---

11 January First flight of the fifth CF-105 Arrow Mk 1, 25205; the last of the type to reach flying status, this was its only flight; pilot was W. 'Spud' Potocki; also RCAF acceptance date
February 408 (R) Sqn retired its last Consolidated Canso As
1 February Canada took over management of the DEW Line
19 February CF-105 Arrow Mk 1, 25203, made the type's only flight with an observer (D. E. Darrah); this was the last-ever flight of a CF-105
20 February On 'Black Friday', the government announced immediate cancellation of CF-105 Arrow programme and of its Orenda Iroquois engine; this

resulted in the immediate layoff of 14,000 employees of Avro Canada and of another 15,000 employed by approximately 2,500 subcontractors; the five Arrows had completed 70.30 flying hours in 66 flights; 25206, the first Mk 2, was 98 per cent complete, 25206 85 per cent, 25207 80 per cent, 25209 57 per cent, and 25210 46 per cent.
First RCAF Neptune to be retrofitted with J34 auxiliary jet pods, 24103, made its first post-modification flight; all Neptunes would be upgraded in 1959/60
28 February Air Force Headquarters authorised the expenditure of $13.4 million (Cdn) for the purchase of 10 Grumman SA-16B Albatross aircraft

(designated CSR-110 by the RCAF)
2 March Personnel reported to 'Golden Hawks', the RCAF's new aerobatic team, co-located at Chatham with 1 (F) OTU
24 March Last Canadair-built T-33AN Silver Star 3, 21656, received by RCAF
April 404 (MP) Sqn received its first CP-107 Argus Mk 1s
1 April Electronic Warfare Unit (EWU) formed at RCAF Station St-Hubert with CF-100s Mk 5Cs and C-119s
8 April 1 FIS relocated from RCAF Station Trenton to RCAF Station Moose Jaw with a Detachment at RCAF Station Portage
17 April 405 (MP) Sqn flew non-stop

from RCAF Station Greenwood to Gibraltar in 13 hours; first transatlantic Argus flight
22 April All completed CF-105 Arrows were cut up for scrap, along with those nearing completion; jigs and fixtures were scrapped; blueprints and other material connected with the programme were destroyed; only the forward fuselage of 25206 (the first Mk 2), and some components were saved; similarly, the Iroquois programme's cancellation resulted in the destruction of all but one of the 14 completed engines
May All three DHC Chipmunk Mk 1s were withdrawn from use
1 May Maritime Proving and

A Decade of Air Power

The Royal Canadian Air Force Order of Battle 1959

Air Force Headquarters: Ottawa, Ontario, Canada
Air Defence Command HQ: RCAF Station St-Hubert, Montreal, Quebec, Canada
Air Transport Command HQ: RCAF Station Trenton (moved from RCAF Station Lachine 1 September 1959)
Maritime Air Command HQ: Halifax, Nova Scotia
Air Materiel Command HQ: RCAF Station Rockcliffe, Ottawa, Ontario
Training Command HQ: RCAF Station Winnipeg, Manitoba
1 Air Division HQ: Metz, France
5 Air Division HQ (ADC): RCAF Station Comox, British Columbia

FIGHTER AND MP BASES

RCAF Station Bagotville, Quebec
413 All-Weather (Fighter) Squadron: CF-100 Mk 3 (dual) (2), CF-100 Mk 5 (18)
432 All-Weather (Fighter) Squadron: CF-100 Mk 3 (dual) (2), CF-Mk 5 (18)
Electronic Warfare Unit: CF-100 Canuck Mk 4A (1) and Mk 5 (2)
Station Flight: Silver Star 3PT (1), Expeditor 3TM (1), Expeditor 3NM (1)

RCAF Station Cold Lake, Alberta
3 All-Weather (Fighter) OTU: CF-100 Canuck Mk 3 (duals) (17), CF-100 Mk 4A (40), Silver Star 3PT (2), Expeditor 3N or 4NM (2)
Weapons Practice Unit (WPU): CF-100 Canuck Mk 5 (3), Silver Star 3AT (8)
CEPE Aircraft and Armament Evaluation Detachment (AAED): H-34A (1), Silver Star 3AT (1), Mitchell TT (1), Lancaster 10DC (2), Sabre 6 (3), CF-10C Canuck Mk 4A (1), CF-100 Canuck Mk 5 (3), CF-100 Canuck Mk 5M (6)
Station Flight: Expeditor 3N or 4NM (1), Sikorsky H-5 (1), Otter (1)

RCAF Station Comox, British Columbia
407 (Maritime Patrol) Squadron: Neptune (12), Expeditor 3TM (2)
409 All-Weather (Fighter) Squadron: CF-100 Mk 3 (dual) (2), CF-100 Mk 5 (18)
Station Flight: Silver Star 3PT (1), Expeditor 3NM (2)

RCAF Station Greenwood, Nova Scotia
404 (Maritime Patrol) Squadron: Neptune (2), CP-107 Argus (10), Expeditor 3TM (2) (transitioning from Neptune to Argus)
405 (Maritime Patrol) Squadron: CP-107 Argus (10), Expeditor 3TM (2)
2 (Maritime) OTU: (Argus Conversion Unit) CP-107 Argus (4)

9 Field Technical Training Unit: (FTTU) (for Neptune and CP-107 Argus)
103 Rescue Unit (RU): Canso 2SR (2), H-34A (2), Otter (3), Dakota 3SR (1)

RCAF Station North Bay, Ontario
414 All-Weather (Fighter) Squadron: CF-100 Mk 3 (dual) (2), CF-100 Mk 5 (18)
433 All-Weather (Fighter) Squadron: CF-100 Mk 3 (dual) (2), CF-100 Mk 5 (18)
3 Field Technical Training Unit: (for CF-100 Canuck)
Station Flight: Silver Star 3PT (1), Expeditor 3NM (2)
To form with BOMARC:
1 (SAM) Squadron: (later redesignated 446 (SAM) Squadron, North Bay)
2 (SAM) Squadron: (later redesignated 447 (SAM) Squadron, La Macaza)

RCAF Station St-Hubert, Montreal, Quebec
401 'City of Westmount' Squadron (Auxiliary): Expeditor 3 (6; to reduce to four and add four Otters)
416 All-Weather (Fighter) Squadron: CF-100 Mk 3 (dual) (2), CF-100 Mk 5 (18)
425 All-Weather (Fighter) Squadron: CF-100 Mk 3 (dual) (2), CF-100 Mk 5 (18)
438 'City of Montreal' Squadron (Auxiliary): Expeditor 3 (6; to reduce to four and add four Otters)
104 Composite Unit: Silver Star 3PT (5), Harvard Mk II or Harvard 4 (2), Dakota FP (1), Dakota SC (1), Expeditor 3N and 3NM (5), Expeditor 3T and 3TM (6)
Electronic Warfare Unit (Det): C-119 Flying Boxcar (3)
Station Flight: Silver Star 3

RCAF Station Summerside, Prince Edward Island
2 (Maritime) OTU: Neptune (10), Dakota 3N or 4NM (1)
Maritime Proving and Evaluation Unit: CP-107 Argus , Neptune

RCAF Station Uplands, Ottawa, Ontario
410 All-Weather (Fighter) Squadron: CF-100 Mk 3 (dual) (2), CF-100 Mk 5 (18)
412 (Transport) Squadron: Dakota SC (1; at NORAD HQ), Dakota 4ST (4), Dakota 4 (1), Dakota FP (8), Mitchell 3 (2), North Star IMST (2), C-5 (1), Comet 1XB (2)
428 All-Weather (Fighter) Squadron: CF-10C Mk 3 (dual) (2), CF-100 Mk 5 (18)
Central Experimental & Proving Establishment (CEPE): Harvard (1), Sabre 5 (1), Sabre 6 (4), C-119 (2), Dakota 4D (1), Dakota 3N (1), Dakota 4 (1), Expeditor 3TM (1), Expeditor 3NM (1), Silver Star 3AT (1), Silver Star 3PT (2), CF-100 Canuck Mk 4A (2), CF-100 Canuck Mk 5 (1)
Operational Proving Unit: CF-100 Mk 5 (3), Sabre 6 (2), Silver Star 3PT (1)
AFHQ Jet Training Flight: CT-133 Silver Star 3PT (10)
Station Flight: Silver Star 3PT (1), Expeditor 3NM (2)

TRANSPORT, TRAINING AND SUPPORT BASES

RCAF Station Aylmer, Ontario
Station Flight: Expeditor 3NM (1)

RCAF Station Borden, Ontario
Station Flight: Expeditor 3T (4), Expeditor 3NM

RCAF Station Centralia, Ontario
Primary Flying Training School (PFTS): Chipmunk (24), Harvard II and 4 (3), Expeditor 3T (4), Expeditor 3NM (2)

RCAF Station Chatham, New Brunswick
1 (Fighter) OTU: Sabre (56), Silver Star 3AT (6), Silver Star 3PT (12)
'Golden Hawks': Sabre 5 , Silver Star 3PT
Station Flight: Expeditor 3TM (1), Expeditor 3NM (1), Sikorsky H-5 (1)

RCAF Station Dartmouth, Nova Scotia
101 Composite Unit (KU): Dakota 4SC (1), Dakota FP (1), Expeditor 3N and 3NM (4)

RCAF Station Downsview, Toronto, Ontario
400 'City of Toronto' Squadron (Auxiliary): Expeditor 3 (6; to reduced to four and add four Otters)
411 'County of York' Squadron (Auxiliary): Expeditor 3 (6; to reduced to four and add four Otters)
436 (Transport) Squadron: C-119 Flying Boxcar (10)
Station Flight: Silver Star 3PT (2), Expeditor 3NM (4), Harvard II or 4 (1)

Gander, Newfoundland
103 Rescue Unit: Canso A, H-5, Dakota 4MSR

RCAF Station Gimli, Manitoba
3 Advanced Flying School (AFS): Silver Star 3PT (73), Expeditor 3T (2)
7 Field Technical Training Unit (FTTU): (for Silver Star 3)
Station Flight: Expeditor 3NM, Harvard 4, Silver Star 3

RCAF Station Goose Bay, Labrador, Newfoundland
Station Flight: Otter (1), Dakota 3SR (1)

RCAF Station Lachine, Dorval, Montreal, Quebec
Note: Air Transport Command HQ, 426 (T) Sqn and most of 4 (T) OTU moved from Lachine to Trenton during 1959
4 (Transport) OTU Detachment: Cosmopolitan (2)

RCAF Station Lincoln Park, Calgary, Alberta
403 'City of Calgary' Squadron (Auxiliary): Expeditor 3TM (6), Expeditor 3NM (2) (to reduce to 4 Expeditors and add 4 helicopters)

North Luffenham in Rutland was the headquarters of 1 (Fighter) Wing until 1955.

In 1959, the RCAF had 22 C-119 Flying Boxcars in service, some with detachments in Sicily.

The Comet was introduced in 1953, and again in 1957 after modification to Comet 1XB standard.

Evaluation Unit (MP&EU) formed at RCAF Station Greenwood; previously the Test, Development and Evaluation Flight within 404 (MP) Squadron; equipped with one Argus and two Neptunes
12 May Canadian government authorised the transfer of 19 Expeditors to France and six to Portugal, all under MAP
13 May Last Lancaster 10MP, FM219, retired by 407 (MP) Sqn and departed RCAF Station Comox for storage
16 May First public performance of 'Golden Hawks' at Torbay, Newfoundland's Air Force Day
28 May RCAF accepted its last CF-100 Canuck, a Mk 5, 18792. Operation Beachflight began as 25

Expeditors departed for delivery to France and Portugal under MAP
31 May RCAF Station MacDonald closed
8 June FIS (Advanced) activated at RCAF Station Portage
15 June 419 AW (F) Sqn temporarily assigned to 3 (F) Wing at Zweibrucken while Baden-Soellingen's runways were resurfaced, returning on 9 October
July 412 (T) Sqn received its first Cosmopolitan CL-540, on loan from Canadair for crew training; deliveries of the 10 CC-109 Cosmopolitans would begin in 1960; both of the loaned 540s, along with the third Canadair conversion, would all be purchased in 1962 and serve until 1966; the seven surviving CC-109s lasted until 1994.

MP&EU moved to RCAF Station Summerside from RCAF Station Greenwood; equipped with Argus and Neptunes
1 July Queen Elizabeth II unveiled the Commonwealth Air Force Memorial in Ottawa, commemorating the 798 men and women who lost their lives in Canada and its adjacent waters and who have no known graves.
Joint RCAF/RCN Maritime Commands were established on the East and West Coasts
2 July Minister of National Defence announced in Parliament that the RCAF would acquire a version of the Lockheed F-104 Starfighter to replace the Canadair Sabres in 1 Air Division in the autumn of 1962; they would be employed in the

low-level strike and reconnaissance roles; beside the F-104, other types considered included the Fiat G91, Dassault Mirage III, Republic F-105, Blackburn Buccaneer, and Grumman Super Tiger
31 July Excavation work commenced on the Semi-Automatic Ground Environment (SAGE) site at RCAF Station North Bay; the site became the control centre for the air defences of Canada as part of NORAD
August MP&EU relocated from RCAF Station Greenwood to RCAF Station Summerside
14 August Announcement that Canadair would build the Starfighter as the CF-104 under licence from Lockheed, which would be responsible

129 Acceptance and Ferry Flight Detachment: Silver Star 3PT (1; based at Lethbridge, Alberta), Harvard II or 4 (1), Dakota 3 or 4M (2), Expeditor 3NM (1), Expeditor 3TM (1)
Station Flight: Harvard II, Harvard 4, Silver Star 3

RCAF Station Macdonald, Manitoba
No. 1 Pilot Weapons School: Harvard 2, Harvard IV, Dakota
4 Advanced Flying School: Silver Star 3, Expeditor 3NM, Expeditor 3T

RCAF Station Moose Jaw, Saskatchewan
1 Flying Instructor School (Basic): Silver Star 3PT (14), Harvard II and 4 (23), Expeditor 3 (3)
2 Flying Training School (FTS): Harvard II and 4 (53), Expeditor 3 (5)
2 Advanced Flying School (AFS): Silver Star 3PT (79; six used by 2 AOS)
Station Flight: Harvard 4

RCAF Station Namao, Edmonton, Alberta
418 'City of Edmonton' Squadron (Auxiliary): Expeditor 3NM (2), Expeditor 3TM (6; to reduce to four Expeditors and add either four helicopters or four Otters)
435 (Transport) Squadron: Dakota FP (2), C-119 Flying Boxcar (6)
CEPE Climatic Detachment Namao: Dakota 3M (1), Silver Star 3AT (1), Silver Star 3PT (1), Expeditor 3N or 3NM (1)

Camp Petawawa, Ontario
No. 1 Air Observation Post Flight: L-19

RCAF Station Rivers, Manitoba
Canadian Joint Air Training Centre (CJATC): C-119 (4), Dakota 3C or 4MS (1), Expeditor 3T (1), H-13 (5; of which two were Army-owned and Air Force-maintained), L-19A (10), Silver Star 3AT (6)
2 Air Observation Post (AOP) Flight: Camp Shilo, Manitoba L-19A (5; maintained by CJATC)

RCAF Station Penhold, Alberta
4 Flying Training School (FTS): Harvard II and 4 (53), Expeditor 3 (5)

RCAF Station Portage, Portage la Prairie, Manitoba
1 Flying Instructor School (Advanced): Silver Star 3
1 Advanced Flying School (AFS): Silver Star 3PT (18), Expeditor 3T (20)
2 Field Technical Training Unit (FTTU): (for Silver Star 3)
Station Flight: Harvard 4, Silver Star 3

RCAF Station Rockcliffe, Ottawa, Ontario
408 (Reconnaissance) Squadron: Lancaster 10P (5), Lancaster 10AR (3)
AFHQ Piston Training Flight: Expeditor 3NM (10), Expeditor 3TM (4), Dakota SC (1), Dakota 3N or 3NM (2)
1 Air Observation Post (AOP) Flight: Camp Petawawa, Ontario L-19A (5) (maintained by AFHQ Piston Training Flight)

RCAF Station Saskatoon, Saskatchewan
Central Flying School (CFS): Silver Star 3PT (7), Harvard II or 4 (2), Chipmunk (2), Dakota 3N (1), Dakota 3 or 4M (1), Expeditor 3T (1), Sabre 5 (3), Mitchell PT (2)
406 'City of Saskatoon' Squadron (Auxiliary): Expeditor 3TM (6), Expeditor 3NM (2; to reduce to four Expeditors and add four helicopters)

RCAF Station Sea Island, Vancouver, British Columbia
442 'City of Vancouver' Squadron (Auxiliary): Expeditor 3 (6; to reduce to four and add four Otters)
443 'City of New Westminster' Squadron (Auxiliary): Expeditor 3 (6; to reduce to four and add four Otters)
121 Composite Unit (KU): Silver Star 3 PT (2), Dakota SR (2), Dakota SC (1), Dakota FP (1), Expeditor 3N or 3NM (1), H-21A (2), Canso 2F (1), Canso 2SR (2), Otter (2)
Station Flight: Silver Star 3, Expeditor 3NM

Camp Shilo, Manitoba
No. 2 Air Observation Post Flight: L-19

RCAF Station St John's (St Jean), Quebec
Station Flight: Expeditor 3NM (2)

Torbay, Newfoundland
107 Rescue Unit (RU): Lancaster 10MB (3)

RCAF Station Trenton, Ontario
426 (Transport) Squadron: North Star 1 (12)
102 Composite Unit (KU): Canso 2SR (2), Dakota FP (1), Dakota 3 and 4SR (3), Dakota 3 or 4SC (1), Expeditor 3NM (5), Otter (4), Silver Star 3PT (2)
4 (Transport) OTU: North Star (2), C-119 (3), Dakota 3 and 4 (3), H-34A (2), H-21 (1), Expeditor 3T (1)
4 Field Technical Training Unit (FTTU): (for North Star, Cosmopolitan, C-119 and CC-106 Yukon)
6 Field Technical Training Unit (FTTU): (for Silver Star 3)
6 Repair Depot: (various)
129 Test and Ferry Flight: Mitchell PT (1), Dakota 3 or 4M (2), Harvard II or 4 (1), Expeditor 3NM (2), Expeditor 3TM (1), Silver Star 3PT (1)

RCAF Station Winnipeg, Manitoba
402 'City of Winnipeg' Squadron (Auxiliary): Expeditor 3TM (6). Expeditor 3NM (2) (to reduce to four Expeditors and add four Otters)
2 Air Observer School (AOS): Mitchell PT (14), Mitchell AI (APS-33) (9), Mitchell AI (APS-40) (8), Dakota 3N and 4NM (18), Dakota 3R and 4MR (7), Expeditor 3NM (19)
111 Composite Unit (KU): Dakota 3SC (1), Dakota 3SR (2), Dakota FP (1), Otter SR (2), H-34A (2), Harvard II or 4 (2), Lancaster 10AR (2), Silver Star 3PT (2)
Station Flight: Expeditor 3N, Silver Star 3

OVERSEAS BASES

El Arish, Egypt (UN duties)
115 Air Transport Unit (ATU): Dakota (3), Otter (4) (supported by Dets of C-119s in Sicily)

Capodichino (Naples), Italy
115 Air Transport Unit: C-119s on detachment from 435 and 436 Transport Squadrons

1 AIR DIVISION

1 (Fighter) Wing: Marville, France (Rocroi, France)
439 (Fighter) Squadron: Sabre 6 (25)
441 (Fighter) Squadron: Sabre 6 (25)
445 All-Weather (Fighter) Squadron: CF-100 Canuck Mk 4B (18)
1 (F) Wing HQ Flight: Expeditor 3TM (1); Silver Star 3PT (2)

2 (Fighter) Wing: Grostenquin, France (St-Hubert, Belgium)
421 (Fighter) Squadron: Sabre 6 (25)
423 All-Weather (Fighter) Squadron: CF-100 Canuck Mk 4B (18)
430 (Fighter) Squadron: Sabre 6 (25)
2 (F) Wing HQ Flight: Expeditor 3TM (1), Silver Star 3PT (2)
109 Communications Flight: Dakota 3 and 4 (9), Dakota SC (1)

3 (Fighter) Wing: Zweibrucken, West Germany (Sandweiller, Luxembourg)
427 (Fighter) Squadron: Sabre 6 (25)
434 (Fighter) Squadron: Sabre 6 (25)
440 All-Weather (Fighter) Squadron: CF-100 Canuck Mk 4B (18)
3 (F) Wing HQ Flight: Expeditor 3TM (1), Silver Star 3PT (2)
5 Field Technical Training Unit (FTTU): (for Sabre and CF-100)

4 (Fighter) Wing: Baden-Soellingen, West Germany (Bertrix, Belgium)
419 All-Weather (Fighter) Squadron: CF-100 Canuck Mk 4B (18)
422 (Fighter) Squadron: Sabre 6 (25)
444 (Fighter) Squadron: Sabre 6 (25)
4 (F) Wing HQ Flight: Expeditor 3TM (1), Silver Star 3PT (2)

Air Weapons Unit: Decimomannu, Sardinia
Silver Star 3AT (2; and deployed squadrons)

30 Air Materiel Base: RAF Langar, UK
137 Transport Flight: Bristol Freighter (5)

RCAF Advisory Group: Oldensburg, West Germany

Aircraft storage sites
Dunnville, Ontario; Mountain View, Ontario; Saskatoon, Saskatchewan; Calgary, Alberta; Lethbridge, Alberta

At one time it was planned to replace the CF-100s one-for-one with Arrows, including those of 1 Air Division and the Auxiliary units with up to 500 being acquired.

The Mitchell 3PT was used into the 1960s in the pilot training role.

for producing the dual-control CF-104Ds; it was also announced that Orenda would build the J79 jet engines under licence from General Electric
26 August Operation Western Way: 10 Silver Star 3s transferred to Turkey under MAP
28 August FIS (Basic) activated at RCAF Station Moose Jaw
September RCAF Station MacDonald closed.
Two CP-107 Argus Mk 2s, 20725 and 20731, flew to Australia and New Zealand on a goodwill tour
1 September Air Transport Command Headquarters relocated from RCAF Station Lachine (Dorval, Montreal) to RCAF Station Trenton, as was 426 (T) Sqn; 4 (T) OTU at RCAF Station Trenton

absorbed 5 (H) OTU.
Operation Western Way: 12 Canadair Silver Star 3s ferried to Turkey under MAP; 10 more joined the flight at Baden-Soellingen
9 September Operation Western Way: 12 Silver Star 3s transferred to Turkey (from 1 Air Division) under MAP
11 September Training Command relocated from RCAF Station Trenton to RCAF Station Winnipeg and absorbed No. 14 (Training) Group there
22 September Operation Western Wear: five Silver Star 3s transferred to Greece, five to Portugal and five to France under MAP. Six Silver Star 3s transferred to 1 Air Division and six to storage in Canada as 1 Air Division attrition replacements; the 12 replaced

those transferred from 1 Air Division to Turkey
1 October Operation Western Wear: 12 Silver Star 3s transferred to France under MAP, 11 more on 2 October and one more on 4 October
1 November Electronic Warfare Unit (EWU) relocated its CF-100 Canuck Mk 4A and Mk 5 aircraft to RCAF Station Bagotville, leaving its CC-119s to operate from St-Hubert
4 November The first large electronic computer to be installed by a Canadian military organisation, an IBM 705 Mk II, was put into service at Air Materiel Command Headquarters, Rockcliffe
15 November First flight of first Canadair CC-106 Yukon, initially serialled 15501; original order for eight later

increased to 12; the Yukon was the largest aircraft built in Canada to that time and would only be exceeded by its derivative, the stretched CL-44J
24 November First CC-106 Yukon received by the RCAF, but returned to Canadair for flight trials; delivered 1 May 1962 (the last of the 12 aircraft to be delivered); operational use of the Yukon began in 1961
18 December The final group of pilots and navigators to be trained under the original NATO training scheme graduated and were presented with their wings by Air Marshal C. R. Slemon; 40 RCAF, seven RNLAF, and three RNoAF pilots and navigators received their wings after training at Gimli, Portage and Winnipeg.

INDEX

INDEX

Picture acknowledgments

Front cover: Ministry of Defence (MoD). **4:** USAF, Robert F. Dorr (RFD). **5:** Larry Davis Collection, USAF. **6:** USAF (two). **7:** Jim Rotramel via RFD, Robert F. Dorr. **8:** USAF (three), Larry Davis Collection. **9:** Larry Davis Collection. **10:** USAF (two), Dave Ostrowski via RFD. **11:** Dave Ostrowski via RFD, Larry Davis Collection. **12:** Carley via RFD, USAF. **13:** via RFD, Larry Davis Collection, Robert F. Dorr. **14:** David W. Menard, Larry Davis Collection, Robert F. Dorr, USAF (two), David W.Menard/Larry Davis Collection. **15:** USAF via RFD, David W.Menard/Larry Davis Collection, Larry Davis Collection (two). **16:** via RFD, Dave Ostrowski via RFD, Ron Picciani/Larry Davis Collection, USAF, Colonel L.J. Doub via RFD. **17:** Robert F. Dorr, USAF via RFD, M. Berent via RFD, Dave Ostrowski via RFD, Larry Davis Collection. **18:** Larry Davis Collection (all). **19:** Colonel T. Barnes via RFD, Norm Taylor via RFD (two). **20:** W. Dunlap via RFD, Norm Taylor, Larry Davis Collection, Dave Ostrowski via RFD, via RFD. **21:** Larry Davis Collection, via RFD (three). **22:** Norm Taylor (three), Larry Davis Collection (two), Major B. Gordon via RFD. **23:** Norm Taylor, Jim Rotramel via RFD, USAF via RFD, Thad Crooks via Warren Thompson, Larry Davis Collection (two). **24:** Larry Davis Collection, R. Lock via RFD, USAF via T. Panopalis, Donald L. Jay via RFD, Robert F. Dorr. **25:** via RFD, USAF via RFD, Tom Brown via Warren Thompson, Larry Davis Collection. **26:** Republic, Cradle of Aviation Museum. **27:** Republic (two). **28:** Republic (two), Cradle of Aviation Museum (two). **29:** Republic (two), Cradle of Aviation Museum. **30:** Robert F. Dorr, Cradle of Aviation Museum. **31:** Cradle of Aviation Museum (five). **32:** Republic, Republic via Robert F. Dorr. **33:** Hughes Aircraft (three). **34-35:** BAe via Michael Stroud. **36:** MoD (two). **37:** Mike Rondot, Robbie Shaw, BAe, Avro. **38:** Avro (four), Shell, Lincolnshire Echo. **39:** Avro (two), MoD. **40:** Avro, Ministry of Supply, MoD. **41:** Hawker Siddeley, Aerospace, Avro (two). **42:** via Michael Stroud, Avro (two). **43:** MoD (two), Flight Refuelling Ltd. **44:** BAe, Avro (two), MoD. **45:** MoD, Bristol Siddeley, Bristol Siddeley via Michael Stroud (two), via Peter R. March. **46:** Avro, MoD (two), BAe. **47:** MoD (two), Avro, COI, BAe. **48:** MoD (two), via Austin J. Brown/APL (two). **49:** MoD (two). **50:** Avro via Michael Stroud, Avro (two), MoD. **51:** Peter R. March, via Michael Stroud, MoD. **52:** MoD (two), BAe. **54:** MoD, Jeremy Flack/API, BAe via Michael Stroud. **55:** MoD (three), Peter R. March. **56:** BAe, MoD (two). **57:** Lincolnshire Echo, MoD (three), USAF. **58:** MoD (three), MoD via Peter R. March. **59:** MoD (five), Aerospace. **60:** via Peter R. March, BAe, Avro (two). **62:** MoD (three). **63:** MoD (two), BAe. **64:** MoD (three), NZ Wings, RNZAF via Austin J. Brown/APL, Peter R. March. **65:** MoD (three), Peter R. March (two), Michael Stroud. **66:** BAe via Michael Stroud, RAF Museum, MoD (two). **67:** Mike Rondot (two), via Austin J. Brown/APL, MoD (two), B. Redfern. **68:** Terry Senior, BAe, Phil Spencer. **69:** Terry Senior, Alfred Alderson via Alan Todd. **70:** Austin J. Brown/APL, Peter R. March. **75:** Paul Jackson (two), Tim Senior (three). **76:** Tim Senior (two), Bristol Siddeley via Michael Stroud. **77:** Paul Jackson, Jim Winchester, RAF Museum, Tim Senior (four). **78:** Mel James (four), Aerospace (two), Paul Jackson, MoD. **79:** Mel James, RAF Museum (two), Peter R. March, Mike Jenvey, Andrew March. **80:** BAe, Paul Jackson, T. Malcolm English, BAe via Peter R. March, RAF Museum. **81:** BAe via Peter R. March, Bob Downey via Austin J. Brown/APL, Austin J. Brown/APL, Graham Robson, MAP via Tim Senior, Peter R. March. **82:** Peter R. March (two), Andrew March, Graham Robson, Paul Jackson. **83:** Graham Robson (three), Peter R. Ma█ Andrew March (two), David Donald (three), Tim Senior (three). **84:** Avro (five), Avro via Michael Stroud, P█ R. March, Michael Stroud. **85:** Avro, Bristol Siddeley (two), Aerospace, MoD. **86:** Austin J. Brown/APL (t█ MoD, RNZAF via NZ Wings, BAe. **87:** Avro (two), MoD, Peter R. March (two), BAe, Australian News, BA█ via Michael Stroud. **88:** BAe, Avro, Peter R. March, MAP via Tim Senior. **89:** Peter R. March (two), Robb█ Shaw, Austin J. Brown/APL, Jeremy Flack/API, Terry Senior (two). **90:** BAe, Terry Senior (three). **91:** Terry Senior (two), Michael Stroud, MoD. **92:** Terry Senior (two), Aerospace, Phi█ via Peter R. March. Spencer. **93:** Aerospace, Terry Senior (four), Peter R. March, BAe via Peter R. March. **94:** Terry Senior (t█ BAe via Peter R. March, via Terry Senior, MAP via Tim Senior. **95:** Lincolnshire Echo, MAP via Tim Senio█ Terry Senior (three), RCAF, Peter R. March. **96:** Richard Oakley via Warren Thompson (WT), Charles Hig█ via WT. **97:** Ed Haller via WT, James Hardin via WT, Robert Jones via WT. **98:** Guy Brown via WT, Robe█ Fortney via WT, Pat Marcella via WT. **99:** Hans Peterman via WT, Harold Saabye via WT. **100:** Ben Sow█ via WT, Peter B. Mersky (two), James Bathrick via WT, Gene Bezore via WT. **101:** Frank Ross via WT, Harold Beasley via WT. **102:** Milton Riggs via WT, Don Baker via WT, T.R. White via WT, Gobel James v█ WT. **104:** Jeff Dibrell via WT, John Ferebee via WT, USAF via WT, T.R. White via WT. **105:** Richard Alb█ via WT, Leroy Bain via WT. **106:** Robert Howard via WT (three). **107:** Ernie Banks via WT, Ken Lamorea█ via WT, Al Gamblin via WT. **108:** Robert Bowlin via WT, Bill Smart via WT. **109:** John Jonhson via WT, William Thomas via WT. **110:** Russ Rogers via WT, Don Brown via WT. **111:** Don Brown via WT, Archi█ Gratch via WT. **113:** George McKay via WT, Robert Biscoe via WT. **114-117:** Aerospace. **118:** USAF (t█ **119:** USAF, NAA via Jerry Scutts. **120:** USAF, USMC, via Peter B. Mersky. **121:** Jim Dunn, via René J. Francillon. **124:** NAA (two), via Jerry Scutts, NAA via Robert F. Dorr. **125:** NAA via Jerry Scutts, Aerospa█ (three), NAA, RAF. **126:** Aerospace, Larry Davis Collection (two), IWM, MAP. **127:** USAF (three), NAA vi█ Jerry Scutts, Larry Davis Collection. **128:** via Jerry Scutts, Aerospace, Larry Davis Collection, via Robert █ Dorr. **130:** Aerospace, Larry Davis Collection, USAF. **131:** USAF, A&AEE, Aerospace (two). **133:** Aerospace, US Navy, via Jerry Scutts, via Peter B. Mersky. **134:** USAF (two), via Jerry Scutts (two), RAA█ Jim Sullivan via Robert F. Dorr. **135:** USAF (four), Aerospace (two). **136:** via Jerry Scutts (two), NAA via Aerospace. **137:** C.A. Johnson, David W. Menard via Norm Taylor, Larry Davis Collectic█ **138:** Larry Davis Collection (two), via René J. Francillon, Peter Bowers via Norm Taylor, Norm Tay█ Collection. **139:** Aerospace (two), Larry Davis Collection. **140:** Aerospace (three), Larry Davis Collection, Gary Brown Collection via Michael Stroud, Jim Winchester, Tony Harmsworth. **141:** Mike Hooks, Jerry Scutts, NAA (two), USAF. **142:** Canadair, DND. **143-145:** DND via Jeff Rankin-Lowe. **146█ DND via Jeff Rankin-Lowe, DND via Jeff Rankin-Lowe (three). **148:** DND via Jeff Rankin-Lowe, Avro Canada. **149-150:** DND via Jeff Rankin-Lowe. **151:** Aerospace, DND via Jeff Rankin-Lowe. **152:** Aerospace, DND via Jeff Rankin-Lowe (two). **153:** DND, Aerospace. **154-155:** DND via Jeff Rank█ Lowe. **156:** DND, DND via Jeff Rankin-Lowe (two). **157:** Avro Canada, DND via Jeff Rankin-Lowe.